A Field Guide
to the
Natural Communities
of Michigan

A FIELD GUIDE
TO THE Natural

Communities of Michigan

OSHUA G. COHEN | MICHAEL A. KOST | BRADFORD S. SLAUGHTER | DENNIS A. ALBERT

MICHIGAN STATE UNIVERSITY PRESS | EAST LANSING

Copyright © 2015 by Michigan Natural Features Inventory

Publication of this book was supported by an award from the MSU Foundation.

⊖ The paper used in this publication meets the minimum requirements
of ANSI/NISO Z39.48-1992 (R 1997) (Permanence of Paper).

MICHIGAN STATE UNIVERSITY PRESS
East Lansing, Michigan 48823-5245

Printed and bound in China.

21 20 19 18 17 16 15   1 2 3 4 5 6 7 8 9 10

LIBRARY OF CONGRESS CONTROL NUMBER: 2014931995
ISBN: 978-1-61186-134-1 (pbk.)
ISBN: 978-1-60917-419-4 (ebook: PDF)

Book design and composition by Charlie Sharp, Sharp Des!gns, Lansing, MI
Cover design by Shaun Allshouse, www.shaunallshouse.com

COVER PHOTO: Northern bald occurring along a volcanic escarpment overlooking the
Carp River, which is immediately flanked by northern wet meadow and northern shrub
thicket and backed by extensive old-growth mesic northern forest, Porcupine Mountains
Wilderness State Park, Gogebic and Ontonagon Counties. Photo by Joshua G. Cohen.

PAGE i: Rich conifer swamp, Luce County, Bradford S. Slaughter.
PAGES ii–iii: Muskeg, Luce County, Joshua G. Cohen.

Michigan State University Press is a member of the Green Press Initiative and is
committed to developing and encouraging ecologically responsible publishing practices.
For more information about the Green Press Initiative and the use of recycled paper
in book publishing, please *visit www.greenpressinitiative.org.*

Visit Michigan State University Press at *www.msupress.org*

To our parents,
who introduced us to the intrinsic beauty
and complexity of the natural world,
and to our children,
who inspire us to conserve it.

Contents

Acknowledgments

The first version of this field guide (Kost et al. 2010) was funded by the Michigan Department of Environmental Quality (DEQ) and the U.S. Environmental Protection Agency Region 5 Wetland Grant Program. The authors thank Amy Lounds, Peg Bostwick, and Matt Smar of the Michigan DEQ for their support of natural community classification, sampling, and inventory. We are also indebted to the Michigan Department of Natural Resources Wildlife Division (WLD), Parks and Recreation Division (PRD), and Forest Resources Division (FRD) for providing funding to survey, classify, and describe the natural communities of Michigan. Over the years, the support, guidance, and friendship of Michael Donovan (WLD), Mark MacKay (WLD), Ray Rustem (WLD), Patrick Lederle (WLD), Steven Beyer (WLD), Glenn Palmgren (PRD), Ray Fahlsing (PRD), Amy Clark Eagle (FRD), Kim Herman (FRD), Cara Boucher (FRD), and David Price (FRD) have been invaluable. In addition, we are extremely grateful to Glenn Palmgren and Doug Pearsall of The Nature Conservancy for reviewing the initial manuscript and providing insightful comments that have helped improve this field guide.

This work would not be possible without the dedication of many present and past Michigan Natural Features Inventory (MNFI) field scientists and collaborators who contributed data allowing us to classify and describe the natural communities of Michigan. We would like to acknowledge especially the contributions of Adrienne Bozic, Larry Brewer, William Brodowicz, Kim Chapman, Patrick Comer, Richard Corner, Jacqueline Courteau, David Cuthrell, John Fody, Phyllis Higman, Jeffrey Lee, Jesse Lincoln, Aaron Kortenhoven, William MacKinnon, Glenn Palmgren, Michael Penskar, Gary Reese, Rebecca Schillo, Jodi Spieles, Alan Tepley, Steve Thomas, and Christopher Weber. In particular, Mike Penskar has provided botanical and ecological mentoring and kept us laughing with his wit.

The natural community classification builds upon the foundation created by many others who have strived to identify, describe, and classify natural landscapes. In particular, we acknowledge the strong influence of John T. Curtis of Wisconsin and Burton V. Barnes of Michigan in shaping this classification. Because this field guide summarizes and builds upon information contained in our earlier publication "Natural Communities of Michigan: Classification and Description," we express our thanks to our former coauthors, Rebecca Schillo, Christopher Weber, and Kim Chapman.

A critical component of this field guide is the distribution maps that accompany each of the natural community descriptions. We are indebted to Helen Enander for producing these maps. We also recognize Rebecca Rogers for maintaining our Biotics database, and Kraig Korroch for developing computer applications to generate plant species lists.

In addition to photos by the authors, we thank the following individuals for generously providing photographs: Adrienne Bozic, Suzan Campbell, Robert Clancy, Ted Cline, Tim Deady, Michael Penskar, Gary Reese, and Steve Thomas.

Much appreciated administrative support was provided by Sue Ridge, Nancy Toben, Yu Man Lee, Ed Schools, and Brian Klatt. We also thank Pat Rickley and Chester B. McMannis for keeping us inspired, and Martha Gove for providing helpful editorial comments. Finally, this project would not have been possible without the help of the staff at Michigan State University Press. We are especially grateful to Julie Loehr, Annette Tanner, and Elise Jajuga.

Patterned fen, Chippewa County

JOSHUA G. COHEN

Introduction

Recently burned boreal forest,
Keweenaw County
JOSHUA G. COHEN

This field guide provides a system for dividing the complex natural landscape of Michigan into easily understood and describable components called natural communities. A natural community is defined as an assemblage of interacting plants, animals, and other organisms that repeatedly occurs under similar environmental conditions across the landscape and is predominantly structured by natural processes rather than modern anthropogenic disturbances. Unlike land-cover classification systems, which include significantly modified lands such as agricultural fields and tree plantations, this natural community classification describes the diversity of native ecosystem types that have been relatively unaltered by modern human intervention. Because of its emphasis on native ecosystems, this field guide is a useful resource for identifying, conserving, and restoring important places that represent a broad range of ecological conditions.

This book is meant to serve as a tool for those seeking to understand, describe, document, and restore the diversity of natural communities native to Michigan. It builds upon our earlier and substantially more detailed publication, "Natural Communities of Michigan: Classification and Description" (Kost et al. 2007), which is available for viewing and downloading at the Michigan Natural Features Inventory (MNFI) website. It also draws from our earlier and more condensed version of this book (Kost et al. 2010). The first version of the natural community classification for Michigan was produced by Kim A. Chapman (1986) and supplied the overall framework and basis for these later efforts.

ORGANIZATION AND METHODS

The classification is organized hierarchically by ecological class, group, and type. Five broad ecological classes are subdivided into eighteen ecological groups, which are further refined into the 77 natural community types that are the focus of this field guide (table 1). The five ecological classes are Palustrine, Terrestrial, Palustrine/Terrestrial, Primary, and Subterranean/Sink. These broad classes are distinguished based on differences in substrate, hydrology, and landscape setting.

The Palustrine class is comprised of wetlands, ecosystems that are saturated or inundated with water for varying periods during the growing season and characterized by hydrophytic vegetation and soils that have developed under these conditions. The Palustrine class includes 32 wetland natural community types, which are organized into six ecological groups based on community structure (i.e., physiognomy), species composition, soil characteristics, and hydrology. The Palustrine groups are Marsh, Wet Prairie, Fen, Bog, Shrub Wetland, and Forested Wetland. Important factors in further classifying Palustrine natural community types within these ecological groups include soil chemistry, the presence of mineral versus organic soil, hydrology, species composition, community structure, geographic distribution, and landscape setting.

The Terrestrial class includes upland ecosystems that have xeric to mesic soils with plants adapted to these growing conditions. The Terrestrial class includes 18 upland natural community types, which

are organized into the three ecological groups of Prairie, Savanna, and Forest based on community structure. Further classification to natural community type is based on species composition, soil characteristics, natural processes, geographic distribution, and landscape setting.

The Palustrine/Terrestrial class is a unique class that includes the ecological group of Wooded Dune and Swale, and the wooded dune and swale complex natural community type. Wooded dune and swale complex has characteristics of both wetlands and uplands. The community occurs on a repeated pattern of alternating dunes and swales adjacent to the Great Lakes, and supports a mixture of upland and wetland communities.

The Primary class includes natural communities that occur on bedrock, cobble, and exposed mineral soils and are characterized by little to no soil development. The Primary class includes 24 natural community types, which are organized into seven ecological groups based on substrate composition, substrate orientation, landscape setting, and community structure. The Primary ecological groups are Dunes, Sand/Cobble Shore, Bedrock Lakeshore, Bedrock Grassland, Bedrock Glade, Lakeshore Cliff/Bluff, and Inland Cliff. Further classification to natural community type within each ecological group is based on substrate type, community structure, landscape setting, and species composition.

The Subterranean/Sink class includes natural communities that occur in karst landscapes below the general land surface. These karst features form from the

TABLE 1. NATURAL COMMUNITY TYPES BY ECOLOGICAL CLASS AND GROUP

PALUSTRINE

MARSH
- Submergent Marsh
- Emergent Marsh
- Great Lakes Marsh
- Inland Salt Marsh
- Coastal Plain Marsh
- Intermittent Wetland
- Northern Wet Meadow
- Southern Wet Meadow
- Interdunal Wetland

WET PRAIRIE
- Wet Prairie
- Wet-mesic Prairie
- Wet-mesic Sand Prairie
- Lakeplain Wet Prairie
- Lakeplain Wet-mesic Prairie

FEN
- Poor Fen
- Patterned Fen
- Northern Fen
- Prairie Fen
- Coastal Fen

BOG
- Bog
- Muskeg

SHRUB WETLAND
- Inundated Shrub Swamp
- Northern Shrub Thicket
- Southern Shrub-Carr

FORESTED WETLAND
- Poor Conifer Swamp
- Rich Conifer Swamp
- Rich Tamarack Swamp
- Hardwood-Conifer Swamp
- Floodplain Forest
- Northern Hardwood Swamp
- Southern Hardwood Swamp
- Wet-mesic Flatwoods

TERRESTRIAL

PRAIRIE
- Hillside Prairie
- Dry Sand Prairie
- Dry-mesic Prairie
- Mesic Prairie
- Mesic Sand Prairie

SAVANNA
- Pine Barrens
- Oak-Pine Barrens
- Oak Barrens
- Oak Openings
- Lakeplain Oak Openings
- Bur Oak Plains

FOREST
- Dry Northern Forest
- Dry-mesic Northern Forest
- Mesic Northern Forest
- Boreal Forest
- Dry Southern Forest
- Dry-mesic Southern Forest
- Mesic Southern Forest

PALUSTRINE/TERRESTRIAL

WOODED DUNE & SWALE
- Wooded Dune & Swale Complex

PRIMARY

DUNES
- Open Dunes
- Great Lakes Barrens

SAND/COBBLE SHORE
- Sand & Gravel Beach
- Limestone Cobble Shore
- Sandstone Cobble Shore
- Volcanic Cobble Shore

BEDROCK LAKESHORE
- Limestone Bedrock Lakeshore
- Sandstone Bedrock Lakeshore
- Granite Bedrock Lakeshore
- Volcanic Bedrock Lakeshore

BEDROCK GRASSLAND
- Alvar

BEDROCK GLADE
- Limestone Bedrock Glade
- Granite Bedrock Glade
- Volcanic Bedrock Glade
- Northern Bald

LAKESHORE CLIFF/BLUFF
- Clay Bluff
- Limestone Lakeshore Cliff
- Sandstone Lakeshore Cliff
- Granite Lakeshore Cliff
- Volcanic Lakeshore Cliff

INLAND CLIFF
- Limestone Cliff
- Sandstone Cliff
- Granite Cliff
- Volcanic Cliff

SUBTERRANEAN/SINK

KARST
- Cave
- Sinkhole

underground dissolution of limestone, dolomite, or gypsum. The Subterranean/ Sink class includes one ecological group, Karst. This ecological group includes two natural community types, cave and sinkhole, which are distinguished based on their distinct landscape settings. A cave is a cavity that has formed beneath the earth's surface, and a sinkhole is a subsidence or depression in the earth's surface caused by the dissolution of the surficial bedrock.

The sections and chapters of this book correspond with this organizational framework. The five main sections of the book match the ecological classes, which are broken into chapters by ecological group. A brief discussion of each ecological group is provided at the beginning of each chapter, including information about the factors influencing the further classification to natural community type.

This classification of natural community types is based on a combination of data derived from statewide and regional surveys, ecological sampling and data analysis, literature review, and expert assessment. Within this book are lists of the 77 recognized natural communities, dichotomous keys to help users identify natural community types, and a glossary of key terms. The natural community types are listed alphabetically with their state ranks as well as by ecological group (see tables 1 and 2). State ranks refer to the conservation rankings assigned to each natural community type. These rankings correspond to the status or rarity of the natural community types in Michigan (table 2). For each natural community type, we provide photographs, the state conservation rank, a short description, an ecoregional distribution map, a list of characteristic plants organized by plant life form (physiognomy), and suggestions of where to visit the natural community type.

NATURAL COMMUNITY TYPE DESCRIPTIONS

The natural community descriptions provide information on physiography (landscape context), hydrology, soils, natural processes, and vegetation (see table 3 for soil pH ranges and descriptions). Much

of this information was compiled from field data collected in each of the natural communities, and extensive literature review. In addition, important resources for understanding and describing the natural community types included the following resources: "Regional Landscape Ecosystems of Michigan, Minnesota, and Wisconsin" (Albert 1995); "Vegetation of Michigan circa 1800" (Comer and Albert 1998); "Quaternary Geology of Michigan" (Farrand and Bell 1982); *Vegetation of Wisconsin* (Curtis 1959); NatureServe Explorer (NatureServe 2013); "Plant Communities of the Midwest" (Faber-Langendoen 2001); and *Terrestrial Vegetation of the United States* (Grossman et al. 1998). Lastly, we also drew from our previous written work of 55 natural community abstracts and our natural community classification, all of which are available at the MNFI website. The abstracts provide detailed descriptions of the natural community types, and thorough references from the scientific literature. MNFI's most detailed bibliography on Michigan's natural communities can be found in our publication "Distribution Maps of Michigan's Natural Communities" (Albert et al. 2008), which is also available for viewing and downloading at the MNFI website.

DISTRIBUTION MAPS

The ecoregional distribution maps used in this book are modified versions of maps first collated in "Distribution Maps of Michigan's Natural Communities" (Albert et al. 2008), which contains both ecoregional and county distribution maps for each natural community type. These distribution maps were derived from a combination of sources from statewide

TABLE 2. NATURAL COMMUNITY STATE RANKS

COMMUNITY NAME	STATE RANK	COMMUNITY NAME	STATE RANK	COMMUNITY NAME	STATE RANK
Alvar	S1	Intermittent Wetland	S3	Poor Conifer Swamp	S4
Bog	S4	Inundated Shrub Swamp	S3	Poor Fen	S3
Boreal Forest	S3	Lakeplain Oak Openings	S1	Prairie Fen	S3
Bur Oak Plains	SX	Lakeplain Wet Prairie	S1	Rich Conifer Swamp	S3
Cave	S1	Lakeplain Wet-mesic Prairie	S1	Rich Tamarack Swamp	S3
Clay Bluff	S2	Limestone Bedrock Glade	S2	Sand & Gravel Beach	S3
Coastal Fen	S2	Limestone Bedrock Lakeshore	S2	Sandstone Bedrock Lakeshore	S3
Coastal Plain Marsh	S2	Limestone Cliff	S2	Sandstone Cliff	S2
Dry Northern Forest	S3	Limestone Cobble Shore	S3	Sandstone Cobble Shore	S2
Dry Sand Prairie	S2	Limestone Lakeshore Cliff	S1	Sandstone Lakeshore Cliff	S2
Dry Southern Forest	S3	Mesic Northern Forest	S3	Sinkhole	S2
Dry-mesic Northern Forest	S3	Mesic Prairie	S1	Southern Hardwood Swamp	S3
Dry-mesic Prairie	S1	Mesic Sand Prairie	S1	Southern Shrub-Carr	S5
Dry-mesic Southern Forest	S3	Mesic Southern Forest	S3	Southern Wet Meadow	S3
Emergent Marsh	S4	Muskeg	S3	Submergent Marsh	S4
Floodplain Forest	S3	Northern Bald	S1	Volcanic Bedrock Glade	S2
Granite Bedrock Glade	S2	Northern Fen	S3	Volcanic Bedrock Lakeshore	S3
Granite Bedrock Lakeshore	S2	Northern Hardwood Swamp	S3	Volcanic Cliff	S2
Granite Cliff	S2	Northern Shrub Thicket	S5	Volcanic Cobble Shore	S3
Granite Lakeshore Cliff	S1	Northern Wet Meadow	S4	Volcanic Lakeshore Cliff	S1
Great Lakes Barrens	S2	Oak Barrens	S1	Wet Prairie	S2
Great Lakes Marsh	S3	Oak Openings	S1	Wet-mesic Flatwoods	S2
Hardwood-Conifer Swamp	S3	Oak-Pine Barrens	S2	Wet-mesic Prairie	S2
Hillside Prairie	S1	Open Dunes	S3	Wet-mesic Sand Prairie	S2
Inland Salt Marsh	S1	Patterned Fen	S2	Wooded Dune & Swale Complex	S3
Interdunal Wetland	S2	Pine Barrens	S2		

STATE RANKS

S1 Critically imperiled in the state because of extreme rarity (often five or fewer occurrences) or because of some factor(s) such as very steep declines making it especially vulnerable to extirpation from the state

S2 Imperiled in the state because of rarity due to very restricted range, very few occurrences (often 20 or fewer), steep declines, or other factors making it very vulnerable to extirpation from the state

S3 Vulnerable in the state due to a restricted range, relatively few occurrences (often 80 or fewer), recent and widespread declines, or other factors making it vulnerable to extirpation

S4 Uncommon but not rare; some cause for long-term concern due to declines or other factors

S5 Common and widespread in the state

SX Community is presumed to be extirpated from the state; not located despite intensive searches of historical sites and other appropriate habitat, and virtually no likelihood that it will be rediscovered

S? Incomplete data

and regional surveys, literature review, and expert assessment. Specific sources critical to the production of these maps included the "Vegetation of Michigan circa 1800" (Comer and Albert 1998), "Regional Landscape Ecosystems of Michigan, Minnesota, and Wisconsin" (Albert 1995), *Geology of Michigan* (Dorr and Eschman 1970), "Quaternary Geology of Michigan" (Farrand and Bell 1982),

"Bedrock Geology of Northern Michigan" (Reed and Daniels 1987), the three-volume collection *Michigan Flora* (Voss 1972, 1985, 1996), *Field Manual of Michigan Flora* (Voss and Reznicek 2012), and MNFI's Biotics database (MNFI 2014). The circa 1800 vegetation map provides a hypothesis of the historical distribution of native vegetation across Michigan and was helpful in developing distribution maps for communities that today have limited distributions within Michigan, such as many of the prairie and savanna types. Maps of current distribution of natural community types were developed from the following: interpretation of the ecological factors that influence natural community distributions in Michigan, including climate, bedrock geology, landforms, soils, and natural disturbances; the collective field experience of the authors; and data from documented natural community occurrences. Spatial records documenting the locations (occurrences) of high-quality natural communities are maintained within MNFI's Biotics database (MNFI 2014). This database is especially useful for determining the distribution of natural communities that are rare to critically imperiled, since survey efforts have focused on this subset of Michigan's natural community types. For those natural community types for which specific plant species are strong indicators, plant distribution maps (Reznicek et al. 2011; Voss and Reznicek 2012; USDA 2013) were reviewed to corroborate natural community type distribution maps. Occurrences of rare species that are known to be characteristic of specific natural community types were also utilized.

For the maps in this field guide, the distribution of each natural community

TABLE 3. SOIL pH RANGES

pH LEVEL	DESCRIPTION
Below 4.5	Extremely acidic
4.5–5.0	Very strongly acidic
5.1–5.5	Strongly acidic
5.6–6.0	Medium acidic
6.1–6.5	Slightly acidic
6.6–7.3	Circumneutral
7.4–7.8	Mildly alkaline
7.9–8.4	Moderately alkaline
8.5–9.0	Strongly alkaline
Above 9.0	Very strongly alkaline

was assigned to one of three categories of abundance for each ecoregion or subsection of Michigan (see Albert 1995 and the introductory map): prevalent or likely prevalent, infrequent or likely infrequent, and absent or likely absent. For most communities, the assigned categories apply to both current and historical distributions. However, for those communities that have been significantly reduced or eliminated from the landscape due to anthropogenic disturbance (e.g., prairies and savannas), these categories apply to historic distributions, and this caveat is noted on the individual distribution maps.[1] Because the distribution maps are essentially hypotheses of the current or historic distributions of the natural community types, it is important to interpret the categories of abundance as follows: the category of "prevalent or likely prevalent" indicates that a community is likely common or was likely common within an ecoregion; the category of "infrequent or likely infrequent" indicates that a community is likely uncommon or was likely uncommon within an ecoregion; and the category of "absent

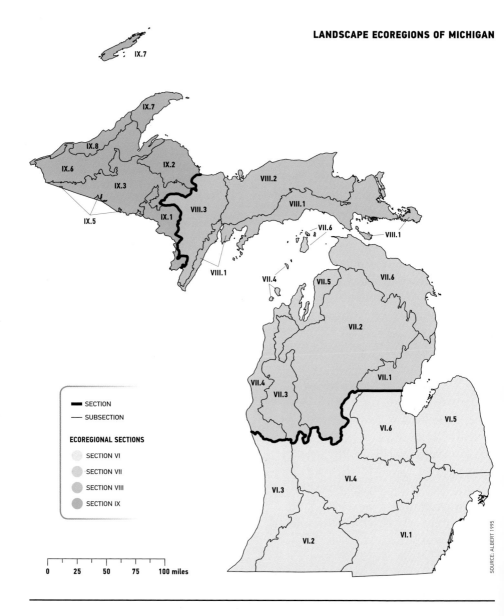

SOURCE: ALBERT 1995

or likely absent" is used to indicate that a community is unlikely to occur or was unlikely to occur within an ecoregion. We encourage readers to provide us with information to improve these maps, which we continually update as our inventory efforts progress.

PLANT LISTS

Like the community descriptions, the lists of characteristic plants were primarily compiled from field data collected on each of the natural communities, but were also informed by literature review. Especially helpful resources for compiling the plant lists were *Field Manual of Michigan Flora* (Voss and Reznicek, 2012), and *Michigan Flora Online* (Reznicek et al. 2011), which include specific habitat information for most plants; the "Floristic Quality Assessment for Michigan" (Herman et al. 2001); and the USDA Plants Database, Natural Resources Conservation Service (USDA 2013), which is available on the Web. The scientific nomenclature used in this book follows the *Field Manual of Michigan Flora*, and plants were organized by life form or physiognomy following the designations of the *Michigan Flora Online*. Plant species were selected for inclusion in the lists of characteristic species if they frequently occur in a particular natural community type, and especially if they are found in few other community types. As such, plants that occur in a very broad range of community types were sometimes excluded from the lists in favor of species that may be better indicators of particular natural community types because of their narrow niche requirements. Rare plants included in the lists are indicated with an asterisk. The current state and, in some cases, federal listing of these species can be viewed at the MNFI website. Bryophytes (namely, mosses) and lichens are included in these lists where we have survey data or supporting literature. However, the relationship of prevalent bryophytes and lichens and natural community types needs further study.

PLACES TO VISIT

For each natural community type, we include a list of places where interested readers can visit the natural community. We have found that learning about natural communities and being able to identify them is facilitated by visiting benchmark examples across the range of variability of the natural community types throughout their distribution. We have tried to include sites that are easily accessible, either on public lands or on lands accessible to the public (e.g., land trust preserves). We remind readers that many natural communities are fragile. Readers interested in visiting sites listed in this field guide are advised to contact listed land conservancies about access to their preserves, directions, and maps. Finding some of the listed areas may also require some ecological sleuthing, including the use of topographic maps, aerial photographs, and a compass. For three of the natural community types, we do not include any suggestions of places to visit because the community type is extirpated (bur oak plains) or nearly extirpated and no remaining sites occur on lands accessible to the public (mesic prairie and oak openings). However, readers may be able to find remnants of these natural community types along railroad tracks and adjacent to cemeteries in southwestern Michigan.

KEYS

In addition to a simple dichotomous key separating the five ecological classes, we have provided dichotomous keys for each ecological class that include characteristics to progressively separate the ecological groups and natural community types. Each key includes a series of paired statements or couplets representing mutually exclusive choices. By progressively following these couplets, readers will arrive at a natural community type. The keys were developed as tools to help readers identify natural communities in the field, but are also useful for learning about the critical factors that distinguish the ecological groups and natural community types. Before using the keys in the field, first take time to study the site you would like to classify and walk as much of the area of interest as possible. Think about where you are in the landscape (e.g., upland vs. wetland, outwash plain vs. lakeplain, etc.) and determine the dominant vegetation structure and composition as well as the soils and critical natural processes that influence the area. When utilizing the keys in the field, avoid ecotones or transition zones, and be mindful that natural communities are constantly changing in space and time. Sites that are shifting from one type to another through succession, or following a natural disturbance such as windthrow, beaver flooding, or fire can be especially difficult to classify. It is also critical to remember that the scale of consideration can influence how a site is classified. Natural community types are typically less than 100 acres, but several matrix-forming natural community types can be hundreds to thousands of acres and can occur as landscape complexes (e.g., wooded dune and swale complex, floodplain forest, patterned fen, muskeg, and mesic northern forest). These landscape complexes often contain diverse ecological zones that can also be interpreted as inclusions of natural community types.

The keys are intended as an aid in pointing the reader in the right direction, but are not meant to be used alone to definitively classify natural community types. Once you have worked your way through the key, we encourage you to examine the accompanying description and plant list for the possible natural community type to help confirm your identification. Additional helpful resources for identifying and understanding Michigan's natural communities include our natural community abstracts and natural community classification, both of which are available online along with photos and comprehensive descriptions.

GLOSSARY

Understanding and identifying Michigan's natural communities is facilitated by a broad range of natural-history knowledge. Users will find that the value of this book will be enriched by the study of Michigan's climatic influences, surficial geology, hydrology, ecosystem processes, soils, and flora. We provide a glossary of key terms and concepts that we think are critical for field ecologists and natural community identification. Readers should note that this glossary provides definitions for terminology used in this book that are consistent with their usage in the text and appropriate to their application in Michigan.

DISCUSSION

The landscape of Michigan is extremely varied, and as such, identifying natural communities is not always a simple task.

The line between two natural community types can be quite clear where vegetation changes abruptly and where environmental gradients are sharp. However, where gradual changes occur in soils, hydrology, and other factors, natural communities can subtly grade into one another, making it difficult to determine where to draw the line between natural community types. In addition, the climatic tension zone and areas along the Great Lakes shoreline with lake-moderated climate often support species with both northern and southern affinities, and therefore often pose challenges for natural community classification. Readers should also remember that every place in the landscape is unique: no two examples of a natural community type are identical in their physical environment and species composition. The detailed information presented in the keys and the natural community descriptions gives a range of variability for each natural community type, and there will be no exact matches in the field. It is our hope that the accompanying keys, photographs, descriptions, range maps, and plant lists will allow users to more easily and confidently identify Michigan's natural communities and recognize repeating patterns across the landscape.

LIMITATIONS

This field guide is based on a classification system that has numerous limitations. Readers should recognize that the division of the natural world into discrete categories is inherently an artificial process and a matter of human convenience, and subject to human bias. We acknowledge that the natural community classification used in this field guide is designed to aid the conservation of biodiversity in Michigan. Classifying natural

communities can inform conservation planning and biodiversity stewardship by allowing resource managers, landowners, land-use planners, and scientists to communicate effectively and share a common language about an area's biodiversity and ecological context. In addition, the classification of complex systems is limited by human capacity to perceive subtle differences. Our understanding of patterns of variations in the natural world is constantly changing and improving. For the classification system presented in this book, the level of information used to describe the different natural community types is uneven. We have copious information for those natural communities that have been systematically inventoried and intensively sampled, while for others, we have only cursory data, or only a few benchmark sites remain to be studied due to anthropogenic disturbances such as fire suppression. We view this classification as a perpetually evolving tool that we will continually improve as our knowledge of ecological processes and natural communities progresses through continued inventory, sampling, and monitoring. We welcome information about Michigan's natural communities and high-quality examples of natural communities from interested readers. Finally, this classification system deals with vegetated communities in a relatively natural condition. It does not include aquatic communities (e.g., deepwater habitat of streams, rivers, ponds, and lakes) or anthropogenic systems, communities initiated and maintained by human activities (e.g., agricultural fields, tree plantations, wetland mitigations, and "native grassland" plantings).

OTHER CLASSIFICATION EFFORTS

Michigan's natural community classification is part of a broader effort to classify plant communities within an ecological context throughout North America and globally. MNFI is part of a national network of state heritage programs, coordinated through NatureServe, engaged in this classification effort. Several recent publications address state-level natural community classification systems, including *Wetland, Woodland, Wildland: A Guide to the Natural Communities of Vermont* (Thompson and Sorenson 2005), *Wisconsin's Natural Communities: How to Recognize Them, Where to Find Them* (Hoffman 2002), *Natural Landscapes of Maine: A Guide to Natural Communities and Ecosystems* (Gawler and Cutko 2010), *The Terrestrial Natural Communities of Missouri* (Nelson 2010), *Wild North Carolina: Discovering the Wonders of Our State's Natural Communities* (Blevins and Schafale 2011), *The Nature of New Hampshire: Natural Communities of the Granite State* (Sperduto and Kimball 2011), and *The Natural Communities of Georgia* (Edwards et al. 2013).

In addition to these state-level efforts, NatureServe has developed two classification systems at the national and international levels. The International Vegetation Classification (IVC) (Faber-Langendoen et al. 2012) is a hierarchical vegetation classification system with association as the basic unit, reflecting patterns of plant species occurrence and frequency. Associations are defined by "diagnostic species, usually from multiple growth forms or layers, and more narrowly [by] similar composition that reflect topo-edaphic climate, substrates, hydrology, and disturbance regimes" (NatureServe 2013). Michigan's natural communities tend to be comparable or crosswalk to one or more IVC associations, which each have a global conservation ranking. The state ranks developed for Michigan's natural community types are independent of the global ranks assigned to associations. The International Terrestrial Ecological Systems Classification (Comer et al. 2003) defines groups of plant communities that tend to co-occur within landscapes with similar ecological processes, substrates, and/or environmental gradients. The basic unit of this classification is the ecological system, which corresponds to one or more Michigan natural community types. The Michigan natural community types are defined at a scale that we feel ensures the identification, mappability, conservation, and management of Michigan's important ecosystems and ecological functions. Readers interested in framing Michigan's natural community classification in a broader context are encouraged to study the classification systems developed by other states and by NatureServe.

CONSERVATION APPLICATION

This classification is meant to guide the identification of natural habitats that represent the range of native ecosystems known to occur in Michigan, both historically and today. Protecting, managing, and restoring representative natural communities is critical to biodiversity conservation, since native organisms are best adapted to environmental and biotic forces with which they have survived and evolved over the millennia. MNFI maintains a database of occurrences of exemplary natural communities, rare plants, and rare animals found in Michigan. These occurrences provide critical information for assessing the conservation status of each natural community and rare species. The natural community classification and database make it possible for exemplary occurrences of each community to be identified, documented, and described. Together, the classification and associated database of exemplary natural community occurrences serve as a powerful tool for setting conservation goals aimed at protecting, monitoring, and managing a network of lands that represent the broad range of native ecosystems known to occur in Michigan. This "coarse filter" approach to the conservation of biodiversity provides a strategy for identifying the critical lands necessary for conserving the diversity of native plants and animals that represent Michigan's natural heritage.

Open dunes, North Manitou Island, Sleeping Bear
Dunes National Lakeshore, Leelanau County

JOSHUA G. COHEN

Key to the Natural Community Types of Michigan

CLASS KEY

IA. Palustrine (wetland) or terrestrial (upland) community or a relatively equal mixture of both. Characterized by soil development. (GO TO IIA OR IIB)

IIA. Palustrine (wetland) or terrestrial (upland) community. (GO TO IIIA OR IIIB)

IIIA. Wetland soils and vegetation prevalent. Uplands absent or limited in extent to occasional islands and peninsulas. [PALUSTRINE CLASS, 2]

IIIB. Upland soils and vegetation prevalent. Wetlands absent or limited in extent to occasional pockets and vernal pools. [TERRESTRIAL CLASS, 136]

IIB. Relatively equal mixture of upland and terrestrial communities occurring as a landscape complex. [PALUSTRINE/TERRESTRIAL CLASS, 216]

IB. Primary substrate prevalent. Characterized by little to no soil development. (GO TO IVA OR IVB)

IVA. Surface feature that occurs on bedrock, cobble, or exposed mineral soil. [PRIMARY CLASS, 224]

IVB. Subterranean or sink feature located in areas of karst topography. [SUBTERRANEAN/SINK CLASS, 332]

PALUSTRINE CLASS KEY

1A. Open (non-forested) wetland. Mature trees absent or contributing 25% or less overall canopy cover and/or tall shrubs (> 1.5 m [5 ft]) absent or contributing 50% or less canopy cover. (GO TO 2A OR 2B)

2A. Dominated by submergent vegetation and/or emergent graminoid vegetation with inundated to saturated organic or mineral soils or dominated by grasses, with sedges important but generally not dominant or locally dominant and seasonally inundated to saturated mineral soils with variable organic content. (GO TO 3A OR 3B)

3A. Dominated by submergent vegetation and/or emergent graminoid vegetation with inundated to saturated soils. (GO TO 4A OR 4B) [MARSH GROUP, 4]

4A. Standing water greater than 15 cm (6 in) deep usually present throughout the growing season. (GO TO 5A OR 5B)

5A. Occurrence not limited to shorelines of the Great Lakes and areas strongly influenced by Great Lakes water-level fluctuation and features such as connecting channels and river mouths. (GO TO 6A OR 6B)

6A. Vegetation primarily submergent with leaves submerged or with leaves primarily submergent or floating on water surface during growing season. Occurring within shallow to occasionally deep waters of lakes, ponds, rivers, and streams. Common submergent and floating-leaved plants include common waterweed (*Elodea* canadensis), water star-grass (*Heteranthera dubia*), water-milfoils (*Myriophyllum* spp.), naiads (*Najas* spp.), pondweeds (*Potamogeton* spp.), water-celery (*Vallisneria americana*), muskgrasses (*Chara* spp.), stoneworts (*Nitella* spp.), coontail (*Ceratophyllum demersum*), bladderworts (*Utricularia* spp.), sweet-scented waterlily (*Nymphaea odorata*), yellow pond-lilies (*Nuphar* spp.), and water shield (*Brasenia schreberi*). [SUBMERGENT MARSH, 6]

6B. Vegetation primarily emergent with leaves protruding above the water (when present) during growing season. Occurring along the shores of lakes and streams or in depressions where standing water occurs throughout the year. Common emergent plants include bulrushes (*Schoenoplectus* spp.), sedges (*Carex* spp.), bur-reed (*Sparganium* spp.), water-plantain (*Alisma* spp.), spike-rushes (*Eleocharis* spp.), and broad leaved cat-tail (*Typha latifolia*). [EMERGENT MARSH, 10]

5B. Occurrence limited to shorelines of the Great Lakes and areas strongly influenced by Great Lakes water-level fluctuation including connecting channels and river mouths. [GREAT LAKES MARSH, 14]

4B. Standing water absent or intermittently present seasonally and/or from year to year and typically less than 15 cm (6 in) deep during mid-summer and early fall, but soil usually remaining saturated throughout the year. (GO TO 7A OR 7B)

7A. Soil saturated to inundated by sodium- and chloride-laden groundwater from natural brine aquifers. Indicator plants include Olney's bulrush

(*Schoenoplectus americanus*) and dwarf spike-rush (*Eleocharis parvula*). [INLAND SALT MARSH, 18]

7B. Soil saturated to inundated but not by sodium- and chloride-laden groundwater from natural brine aquifers. (GO TO 8A OR 8B)

8A. Occurrence not limited to shorelines of the Great Lakes and areas strongly influenced by Great Lakes water-level fluctuation and features such as dune fields. (GO TO 9A OR 9B)

9A. Characterized by large water-table fluctuations (both seasonally and from year to year) with mineral soils and organics ranging from inundated to saturated. (GO TO 10A OR 10B)

10A. Occupies perimeters or entire basins of softwater seepage lakes and other isolated depressions characterized by large water-table fluctuations (both seasonally and from year to year). Soils mineral or occasionally shallow muck (< 1 m [39 in]) over sand or loamy sand with underlying clay lenses occasionally present. Atlantic and Gulf coastal plain disjunct plants common to locally dominant. Prevalent coastal plain disjuncts include black-fruited spike-rush (*Eleocharis melanocarpa*), round-headed rush (*Juncus scirpoides*), Eaton's panic grass (*Dichanthelium spretum*), bald-rush (*Rhynchospora scirpoides*), bog yellow-eyed-grass (*Xyris difformis*), and meadow beauty (*Rhexia virginica*). [COASTAL PLAIN MARSH, 20]

10B. Occupies perimeters or entire basins of softwater seepage lakes and other isolated depressions characterized by large water-table fluctuations (both seasonally and from year to year). Soils mineral or occasionally shallow muck (< 1 m [39 in]) over sand or loamy sand with underlying clay lenses occasionally present. Atlantic and Gulf coastal plain disjunct plants absent, rare, or limited in number. [INTERMITTENT WETLAND, 24]

9B. Characterized by relatively stable water table during the growing season with mineral soils and organics ranging from inundated in the spring to predominantly saturated throughout the growing season. (GO TO 11A OR 11B)

11A. Located north of the climatic tension zone in northern Lower Michigan and also in the Upper Peninsula. Vegetation dominated by sedges (*Carex stricta, C. lacustris, C. lasiocarpa, C. utriculata*, and/or *C. vesicaria*). Other important species include blue-joint (*Calamagrostis canadensis*), fringed brome (*Bromus ciliatus*), rattlesnake grass (*Glyceria canadensis*), marsh wild-timothy (*Muhlenbergia glomerata*), and green bulrush (*Scirpus atrovirens*). Soils are typically strongly acidic to neutral, shallow to deep peat, but can include saturated mineral soil. Frequently invaded by tag alder (*Alnus incana*) and occurring in association with northern shrub thicket. [NORTHERN WET MEADOW, 28]

11B. Located south of the climatic tension zone in southern Lower Michigan. Vegetation dominated by tussock sedge (*Carex stricta*) and sometimes by wiregrass sedge (*C. lasiocarpa*) and lake sedge (*C. lacustris*). Other important species include

blue-joint (*Calamagrostis canadensis*), sedges (*Carex aquatilis, C. comosa, C. prairea, C. utriculata*), fringed brome (*Bromus ciliatus*), marsh wild-timothy (*Muhlenbergia glomerata*), joe-pye-weed (*Eutrochium maculatum*), and common boneset (*Eupatorium perfoliatum*). Soils are typically neutral to mildly alkaline peats. Frequently invaded by dogwoods (*Cornus* spp.), willows (*Salix* spp.), and meadowsweet (*Spiraea alba*) and occurring in association with southern shrub-carr. [SOUTHERN WET MEADOW, 32]

8B. Occurrence limited to shorelines of the Great Lakes and areas strongly influenced by Great Lakes water-level fluctuation and features such as dune fields. [INTERDUNAL WETLAND, 36]

3B. Dominated by grasses, with sedges important to locally dominant, and seasonally inundated to saturated soils. (GO TO 12A OR 12B) [WET PRAIRIE GROUP, 40]

12A. Occurring inland on outwash plains, old glacial lakebeds, abandoned stream channels, and river terraces. Distribution not limited to glacial lakeplain in southeastern or southwestern Lower Michigan. (GO TO 13A OR 13B)

13A. Soils loam to silt loam often with high organic content. Occurring in southern Lower Michigan. (GO TO 14A OR 14B)

14A. Seasonally inundated soils. Dominant grasses include blue-joint (*Calamagrostis canadensis*) and cordgrass (*Spartina pectinata*), with tussock sedge (*Carex stricta*) locally dominant. [WET PRAIRIE, 42]

14B. Occasionally inundated soils. Dominant grasses include big bluestem (*Andropogon gerardii*) and Indian grass (*Sorghastrum nutans*), with blue-joint (*Calamagrostis canadensis*), cordgrass (*Spartina pectinata*), and tussock sedge (*Carex stricta*) locally common. [WET-MESIC PRAIRIE, 44]

13B. Soils sand to sandy loam often with high organic content. Occurring in both northern and southern Lower Michigan. Dominant grasses may include big bluestem (*Andropogon gerardii*), little bluestem (*Schizachyrium scoparium*), Indian grass (*Sorghastrum nutans*), blue-joint (*Calamagrostis canadensis*), cordgrass (*Spartina pectinata*), and prairie dropseed (*Sporobolus heterolepis*). Tussock sedge (*Carex stricta*) may be locally dominant. [WET-MESIC SAND PRAIRIE, 46]

12B. Occurring on lakeplains both along Great Lakes shoreline and inland. Distribution limited to glacial lakeplain in southeastern or southwestern Lower Michigan. (GO TO 15A OR 15B)

15A. Vegetation dominated by bluejoint grass (*Calamagrostis canadensis*) and cordgrass (*Spartina pectinata*). Common species typically include sedges (*Carex aquatilis, C. buxbaumii, C. pellita, C. prairea, C. stricta*), Baltic rush (*Juncus balticus*), twig-rush (*Cladium mariscoides*), and swamp milkweed (*Asclepias incarnata*). [LAKEPLAIN WET PRAIRIE, 50]

15B. Vegetation dominated by big bluestem (*Andropogon gerardii*), switch grass (*Panicum virgatum*), little bluestem (*Schizachyrium scoparium*), and/or Indian grass (*Sorghastrum nutans*). Common species typically include sedges (*Carex* spp.), Ohio goldenrod (*Solidago ohioensis*), Riddell's goldenrod (*Solidago riddellii*), common mountain mint (*Pycnanthemum virginianum*), swamp-betony (*Pedicularis lanceolata*), marsh blazing-star (*Liatris spicata*), colic root (*Aletris farinosa*), tall coreopsis (*Coreopsis tripteris*), and ironweed (*Vernonia* spp.). [LAKEPLAIN WET-MESIC PRAIRIE, 52]

2B. Dominated by graminoids and forbs with low shrubs, stunted conifers, and brown mosses or sphagnum mosses often prevalent. Characterized almost exclusively by saturated organic soils (peat or marl). (GO TO 16A OR 16B)

16A. Minerotrophic or mineral-rich peatland with slightly acidic to alkaline saturated peats or marl or slightly minerotrophic peatland with strongly acidic to slightly acidic saturated peats. Sphagnum mosses are absent or locally common to dominant. (GO TO 17A OR 17B) [FEN GROUP, 56]

17A. Slightly minerotrophic peatland with strongly acidic to slightly acidic saturated peats. (GO TO 18A OR 18B)

18A. Community structure lacks repeating pattern of low peat rises (strings) and alternating hollows (flarks). Vegetation dominated by few-seed sedge (*Carex oligosperma*) and/or wiregrass sedge (*C. lasiocarpa*), often with sphagnum either throughout ground layer or dominating widely scattered, low peat mounds, along with ericaceous shrubs and stunted conifers. [POOR FEN, 58]

18B. Community structure characterized by a repeated, alternating pattern of low peat rises (strings) and hollows (flarks). Strings may support scattered and stunted black spruce (*Picea mariana*) and tamarack (*Larix laricina*), low shrubs including bog birch (*Betula pumila*), shrubby cinquefoil (*Dasiphora fruticosa*), bog rosemary (*Andromeda glaucophylla*), leatherleaf (*Chamaedaphne calyculata*), sedges (*Carex oligosperma, C. sterilis,* and *C. lasiocarpa*), and tufted bulrush (*Trichophorum cespitosum*). The alternating flarks are seasonally inundated and may support open lawns of mosses, sedges (*Carex lasiocarpa, C. limosa, C. livida, C. oligosperma,* and *C. exilis*), common bog arrow-grass (*Triglochin maritima*), bog buckbean (*Menyanthes trifoliata*), and arrow-grass (*Scheuchzeria palustris*). [PATTERNED FEN, 62]

17B. Minerotrophic or mineral-rich peatland with slightly acidic to alkaline saturated peats or marl. (GO TO 19A OR 19B)

19A. Community structure characterized by a repeated, alternating pattern of low peat rises (strings) and hollows (flarks). Strings may support scattered and stunted northern white-cedar (*Thuja occidentalis*), tamarack (*Larix laricina*), and black spruce (*Picea mariana*); low shrubs including bog birch (*Betula pumila*), shrubby cinquefoil (*Dasiphora fruticosa*), bog rosemary (*Andromeda glaucophylla*), and leatherleaf (*Chamaedaphne calyculata*); tufted bulrush (*Trichophorum cespitosum*); and sedges (*Carex lasiocarpa, C. sterilis,* and *C. oligosperma*). The alternating flarks are seasonally inundated and may support open lawns of mosses, sedges (*Carex*

lasiocarpa, C. limosa, C. livida,* and *C. exilis*), common bog arrow-grass (*Triglochin maritima*), bog buckbean (*Menyanthes trifoliata*), and arrow-grass (*Scheuchzeria palustris*). [PATTERNED FEN, 62]

19B. Community structure lacks repeating pattern of low peat rises (strings) and alternating hollows (flarks). (GO TO 20A OR 20B)

20A. Occurrence not limited to shorelines of the Great Lakes and areas strongly influenced by Great Lakes water-level fluctuation and processes. Dominance shared by sedges, grasses, rushes, bulrushes, and forbs. Scattered conifers and shrubs common. Soils neutral to moderately alkaline deep peat or marl. Vegetation sparse where marl covers the surface. Vegetation zonation well developed and strongly influenced by surface and subsurface groundwater seepage. Calciphiles well represented, including Kalm's lobelia (*Lobelia kalmii*), Ohio goldenrod (*Solidago ohioensis*), bog goldenrod (*S. uliginosa*), false asphodel (*Triantha glutinosa*), grass-of-Parnassus (*Parnassia glauca*), beak-rush (*Rhynchospora capillacea*), common bog arrow-grass (*Triglochin maritima*), twig-rush (*Cladium mariscoides*), rush (*Juncus brachycephalus*), golden-seeded spike-rush (*Eleocharis elliptica*), beaked spike-rush (*Eleocharis rostellata*), white camas (*Anticlea elegans*), shrubby cinquefoil (*Dasiphora fruticosa*), and alder-leaved buckthorn (*Rhamnus alnifolia*). (GO TO 21A OR 21B)

21A. Located north of the climatic tension zone in northern Lower Michigan and the Upper Peninsula. Additional common species include sedges (*Carex lasiocarpa, C. chordorrhiza, C. leptalea, C. limosa, C. livida,* and *C. sterilis*), tufted bulrush (*Trichophorum cespitosum*), bog birch (*Betula pumila*), northern white-cedar (*Thuja occidentalis*), and tamarack (*Larix laricina*). [NORTHERN FEN, 66]

21B. Located south of the climatic tension zone in southern Lower Michigan, primarily in interlobate regions. Additional common species include sedges (*Carex stricta, C. sterilis, C. lasiocarpa, C. buxbaumii, C. prairea, C. leptalea, C. interior,* and *C. tetanica*), big bluestem (*Andropogon gerardii*), little bluestem (*Schizachyrium scoparium*), Indian grass (*Sorghastrum nutans*), flat-topped white aster (*Doellingeria umbellata*), whorled loosestrife (*Lysimachia quadriflora*), common mountain mint (*Pycnanthemum virginianum*), Riddell's goldenrod (*Solidago riddellii*), sage willow (*Salix candida*), poison sumac (*Toxicodendron vernix*), and tamarack (*Larix laricina*). [PRAIRIE FEN, 70]

20B. Occurrence limited to shorelines of the Great Lakes and areas strongly influenced by Great Lakes water-level fluctuation and processes. Located in protected bays and abandoned coastal embayments along the shorelines of northern Lake Huron and Lake Michigan. Soils grade from calcareous sand or clay along shoreline to alkaline marl and organic deposits farther inland. Vegetation comprised of sedges, rushes, and calciphiles including spike-rushes (*Eleocharis elliptica* and *E. rostellata*), false asphodel (*Triantha glutinosa*), limestone calamint (*Clinopodium arkansanum*), Kalm's lobelia (*Lobelia kalmii*), grass-of-Parnassus (*Parnassia glauca*), Indian paintbrush (*Castilleja coccinea*), bird's-eye primrose (*Primula mistassinica*), small fringed gentian (*Gentianopsis virgata*), white camas (*Anticlea elegans*), and shrubby cinquefoil (*Dasiphora fruticosa*). [COASTAL FEN, 74]

16B. Ombrotophic or nutrient-poor peatland with extremely acidic to strongly acidic saturated peats. Ground layer dominated by continuous carpet of sphagnum mosses. (GO TO 22A OR 22B) [BOG GROUP, 78]

22A. Trees absent or occurring in localized areas of peatland with overall canopy cover typically less than 10%. Occurring statewide but uncommon in southern Lower Michigan. [BOG, 80]

22B. Tree canopy cover typically 10 to 25%, consisting of scattered and stunted black spruce (*Picea mariana*) and tamarack (*Larix laricina*) with pines (*Pinus* spp.) locally common. Occurring north of the climatic tension zone, predominantly in the Upper Peninsula and less frequently in northern Lower Michigan. [MUSKEG, 84]

1B. Forested or tall shrub-dominated wetland. Mature trees contributing greater than 25% overall canopy cover and/or tall shrubs (> 1.5 m [5 ft]) contributing more than 50% canopy cover. (GO TO 23A OR 23B)

23A. Mature trees contributing 25% or less overall canopy cover. Tall shrubs (> 1.5 m [5 ft]) dominant, contributing greater than 50% overall canopy cover. (GO TO 24A OR 24B) [SHRUB WETLAND GROUP, 88]

24A. Dominated by buttonbush (*Cephalanthus occidentalis*). Typically occurring in small, isolated depressions south of the climatic tension zone in southern Lower Michigan. Standing water often present throughout growing season. [INUNDATED SHRUB SWAMP, 90]

24B. Dominated by shrub species other than buttonbush (*Cephalanthus occidentalis*). (GO TO 25A OR 25B)

25A. Shrub canopy dominated by tag alder (*Alnus incana*). Occurring predominantly north of the climatic tension zone in northern Lower Michigan and the Upper Peninsula along streams and lake edges, on outwash channels, outwash plains, and lakeplains. [NORTHERN SHRUB THICKET, 94]

25B. Shrub canopy dominated by dogwoods (*Cornus sericea, C. amomum,* and *C. foemina*) and willows (*Salix bebbiana, S. discolor, S. exigua,* and *S. petiolaris*). Occurring predominantly south of the climatic tension zone in southern Lower Michigan on outwash channels, outwash plains, and lakeplains. [SOUTHERN SHRUB-CARR, 98]

23B. Mature trees contributing greater than 25% overall canopy cover. (GO TO 26A OR 26B) [FORESTED WETLAND GROUP, 102]

26A. Conifers important, common to dominant in canopy layer. (GO TO 27A OR 27B)

27A. Conifers overwhelmingly dominant. (GO TO 28A OR 28B)

28A. Ombrotophic or nutrient-poor peatland. Canopy strongly dominated by black spruce (*Picea mariana*), frequently with tamarack (*Larix laricina*), and occasionally with jack pine (*Pinus banksiana*) as codominants. Substrate extremely acidic to very strongly acidic, deep fibric peat. Sphagnum mosses dominant in ground layer. Ericaceous shrubs including leatherleaf (*Chamaedaphne calyculata*), Labrador-tea (*Rhododendron groenlandicum*), bog laurel (*Kalmia polifolia*), and, in southern Lower Michigan, highbush blueberry (*Vaccinium corymbosum*) locally abundant to dominant. Hydrology strongly influenced by precipitation due to peat accumulation above groundwater table. Occurring mostly north of the climatic tension zone in depressions of glacial outwash, glacial lakeplains, ground moraine, and kettles in coarse-textured moraines and ice-contact topography. [POOR CONIFER SWAMP, 104]

28B. Minerotrophic or mineral-rich peatland. Canopy strongly dominated by northern white-cedar (*Thuja occidentalis*) or tamarack (*Larix laricina*). (GO TO 29A OR 29B)

29A. Occurring primarily north of the climatic tension zone in northern Lower Michigan and the Upper Peninsula and rarely in southern Lower Michigan. Canopy strongly dominated by northern white-cedar (*Thuja occidentalis*). Tall shrub layer typically sparse but can be well-developed with tag alder (*Alnus incana*). Substrate very strongly acidic to moderately alkaline, with subsurface peat typically circumneutral to moderately alkaline. Hydrology strongly influenced by groundwater movement. [RICH CONIFER SWAMP, 108]

29B. Occurring primarily south of the climatic tension zone in southern Lower Michigan and occasionally in northern Lower Michigan and the Upper Peninsula. Canopy strongly dominated by tamarack (*Larix laricina*). Tall shrub layer typically well developed, with winterberry (*Ilex verticillata*) and/or poison sumac (*Toxicodendron vernix*) common to abundant. Substrate neutral to moderately alkaline, deep peat (> 1 m [39 in]). Hydrology strongly influenced by groundwater movement. [RICH TAMARACK SWAMP, 112]

27B. Conifers codominant or subdominant to hardwoods. (GO TO 30A OR 30B)

30A. Occurring along headwater streams (1st and 2nd orders), and on poorly drained glacial outwash, lakeplain, and moraines. (GO TO 31A OR 31B)

31A. Tamarack (*Larix laricina*) dominant. Canopy associates include white pine (*Pinus strobus*), black ash (*Fraxinus nigra*), yellow birch (*Betula alleghaniensis*), red maple (*Acer rubrum*), swamp white oak (*Quercus bicolor*), and American elm (*Ulmus americana*). Substrate neutral to moderately alkaline, deep peat (> 1 m [39 in]). Tall shrub layer typically well developed with winterberry (*Ilex verticillata*) and/or poison sumac (*Toxicodendron vernix*) common to abundant. Hydrology strongly influenced by groundwater movement. Occurring primarily south of the climatic tension zone in southern Lower Michigan and occasionally in northern Lower Michigan and the Upper Peninsula. In interlobate regions, is often associated with prairie fen. [RICH TAMARACK SWAMP, 112]

31B. Tamarack (*Larix laricina*) occasional to absent. Overall canopy comprised of a mixture of hardwood and conifer species, but either group may be locally dominant. Common trees include yellow birch (*Betula alleghaniensis*), black ash (*Fraxinus nigra*), red maple (*Acer rubrum*), American elm (*Ulmus americana*), hemlock (*Tsuga canadensis*), northern white-cedar (*Thuja occidentalis*), white pine (*Pinus strobus*), and tamarack. Substrate neutral to strongly acidic, deep to shallow peat or poorly drained mineral soils. Tall shrub layer poorly developed. Hydrology influenced by groundwater movement. Occurring statewide. [HARDWOOD-CONIFER SWAMP, 116]

30B. Occurring in floodplains of 3rd order or greater streams and rivers and characterized by fluvial landforms, such as natural levee, first bottom, backswamp, oxbow, and terrace. Typically dominated by hardwoods such as silver maple (*Acer saccharinum*) and green ash (*Fraxinus pennsylvanica*). Where organic soils accumulate in areas of groundwater seepage, backswamps, and meander scars, conifers [tamarack (*Larix laricina*), hemlock (*Tsuga canadensis*), northern white-cedar (*Thuja occidentalis*), and white pine (*Pinus strobus*)] can be important, especially north of the climatic tension zone. [FLOODPLAIN FOREST, 120]

26B. Conifers absent or rare in canopy layer. Hardwoods dominant throughout. (GO TO 32A OR 32B)

32A. Occurring in floodplains of 3rd order or greater streams and rivers and characterized by fluvial landforms, such as natural levee, first bottom, back-swamp, oxbow, and terrace. Dominant overstory species include silver maple (*Acer saccharinum*), green ash (*Fraxinus pennsylvanica*), cottonwood (*Populus deltoides*), swamp white oak (*Quercus bicolor*), bur oak (*Quercus macrocarpa*), bitternut hickory (*Carya cordiformis*), sycamore (*Platanus occidentalis*), and hackberry (*Celtis occidentalis*). Where organic soil accumulates in areas such as groundwater seepages, backswamps, and meander scars, tree species may include black ash (*Fraxinus nigra*), yellow birch (*Betula alleghaniensis*), and red maple (*Acer rubrum*). [FLOODPLAIN FOREST, 120]

32B. Occurring along headwater streams (1st and 2nd orders), and on poorly drained glacial outwash, lakeplain, and/or depressions in moraines or ice-contact topography. (GO TO 33A OR 33B)

33A. Distributed north of the climatic tension zone in northern Lower Michigan and the Upper Peninsula. Canopy dominated by black ash (*Fraxinus nigra*) with lesser importance of red maple (*Acer rubrum*), American elm (*Ulmus americana*), yellow birch (*Betula alleghaniensis*), green ash (*Fraxinus pennsylvanica*), balsam fir (*Abies balsamea*), and northern white-cedar (*Thuja occidentalis*). Soils are slightly acidic to neutral, hydric mineral soils and shallow muck over mineral soils. Occurring on poorly drained lakeplains,

outwash plains, and fine- to medium-textured glacial till. [NORTHERN HARDWOOD SWAMP, 124]

33B. Distributed south of the climatic tension zone in southern Lower Michigan. (GO TO 34A OR 34B)

34A. Located in depressions on glacial outwash, moraines, and lakeplain throughout southern Lower Michigan. Dominant tree species comprised of lowland hardwoods including silver maple (*Acer saccharinum*), red maple (*A. rubrum*), green ash (*Fraxinus pennsylvanica*), black ash (*F. nigra*), swamp white oak (*Quercus bicolor*), bur oak (*Q. macrocarpa*), and occasionally pin oak (*Q. palustris*). Mineral and organic soils are typically circumneutral. [SOUTHERN HARDWOOD SWAMP, 128]

34B. Located almost exclusively on level lakeplain in southeastern Lower Michigan. Dominant tree species comprised of highly diverse mixture of lowland and upland hardwoods including oaks (*Quercus* spp.), hickories (*Carya* spp.), maples (*Acer* spp.), and ashes (*Fraxinus* spp.). Soils typically slightly to medium acidic sandy loam or loam over mildly alkaline sandy clay loam, clay loam, or clay. An underlying impermeable clay lens is often present, which allows for prolonged pooling of water. Can occur as a mosaic of poorly drained areas and upland islands. [WET-MESIC FLATWOODS, 132]

TERRESTRIAL CLASS KEY

1A. Mature trees absent or canopy cover less than 5% with generally less than one tree per acre. (GO TO 2A OR 2B) [PRAIRIE GROUP, 138]

2A. Native grass, sedge, and forb community occurring along steep slopes of outwash channels and moraines with south- to west-facing slopes associated with river valleys, streams, or kettle lakes and surrounded by oak forest or oak savanna. [HILLSIDE PRAIRIE, 140]

2B. Native grass, sedge, and forb community occurring on rolling moraines, level to undulating outwash plains, and flat lakeplains. (GO TO 3A OR 3B)

3A. Late summer vegetation generally short (< 1.0 m [39 in]) and patchy. Dominant plants include little bluestem (*Schizachyrium scoparium*), Pennsylvania sedge (*Carex pensylvanica*), and scattered patches of big bluestem (*Andropogon gerardii*). Occurring on loamy sands on well-drained to excessively well-drained, sandy glacial outwash plains and lakebeds primarily north of the climatic tension zone in the north-central and western Lower Peninsula and occasionally in southern Lower Michigan. Often associated with oak barrens, oak-pine barrens, or pine barrens. [DRY SAND PRAIRIE, 144]

3B. Late summer vegetation generally tall (> 1.0 m [39 in]) and dense. Dominant plants include big bluestem (*Andropogon gerardii*), little bluestem (*Schizachyrium scoparium*), and Indian grass (*Sorghastrum nutans*). (GO TO 4A OR 4B)

4A. Comprised of upland prairie species. Restricted to southern Lower Michigan. Upper layer of soils do not show evidence of a fluctuating water table. (GO TO 5A OR 5B)

5A. Soils loamy sand, sand, or occasionally sandy loams, dark brown to tan in color. Characteristic species include Pennsylvania sedge (*Carex pensylvanica*), bastard-toadflax (*Comandra umbellata*), leadplant (*Amorpha canescens*), thimbleweed (*Anemone cylindrica*), black-eyed Susan (*Rudbeckia hirta*), round-headed bush-clover (*Lespedeza capitata*), butterfly-weed (*Asclepias tuberosa*), and smooth aster (*Symphyotrichum laeve*). Occurring on both outwash and moraines within range of former oak openings in southern Lower Michigan but most prevalent in southwestern Lower Michigan. [DRY-MESIC PRAIRIE, 148]

5B. Soils loam or occasionally sandy loam, black to dark brown in color. Cordgrass (*Spartina pectinata*) occasionally subdominant. Other characteristic herbs include porcupine grass (*Hesperostipa spartea*), prairie dropseed (*Sporobolus heterolepis*), switch grass (*Panicum virgatum*), rattlesnake-master (*Eryngium yuccifolium*), golden alexanders (*Zizia aurea*), and prairie violet (*Viola pedatifida*). Occurring on level to slightly undulating glacial outwash in southwestern Lower Michigan. [MESIC PRAIRIE, 152]

4B. Comprised predominantly of upland prairie species, but also includes species more commonly associated with wetlands, including blue-joint (*Calamagrostis canadensis*), rushes (*Juncus* spp.), flat-topped white aster (*Doellingeria umbellata*), balsam ragwort (*Packera paupercula*), and common mountain mint (*Pycnanthemum virginianum*). Occurring on lakeplains (especially on old beach ridges elevated above poorly drained lakeplains), outwash, old glacial lakebeds, abandoned stream channels, and river terraces throughout the Lower Peninsula. Soils sandy loam to loamy sand, occasionally showing evidence of a fluctuating water table such as iron mottling. [MESIC SAND PRAIRIE, 156]

1B. Mature trees present at densities greater than one tree per acre and canopy cover ranging from 5 to 100%. (GO TO 6A OR 6B)

6A. Tree canopy cover less than 60% with ground flora primarily native grasses, sedges, forbs, and low shrubs associated with open- or partial-canopy conditions. (GO TO 7A OR 7B) [SAVANNA GROUP, 160]

7A. Mature trees pines (*Pinus* spp.) or mixture of pine and oak (*Quercus* spp.) species. (GO TO 8A OR 8B)

8A. Scattered jack pine (*Pinus banksiana*) or jack pine thickets among native graminoids. Ground layer dominated by Pennsylvania sedge (*Carex pensylvanica*), or Pennsylvania sedge, little bluestem (*Schizachyrium scoparium*), big bluestem (*Andropogon gerardii*), forbs, and low shrubs. Occurring in northern Michigan on excessively drained, sandy outwash plains and lakeplains. [PINE BARRENS, 162]

8B. Scattered and clumped oak and pine species with ground flora of native grassland species. Mature tree species may include white oak (*Quercus alba*), northern pin oak (*Q. ellipsoidalis*), black oak (*Q. velutina*), white pine (*Pinus strobus*), red pine (*P. resinosa*), and jack pine (*P. banksiana*). Ground layer dominated by

little bluestem (*Schizachyrium scoparium*), Pennsylvania sedge (*Carex pensylvanica*), big bluestem (*Andropogon gerardii*), forbs, and low shrubs. Occurring both north and south of the climatic tension zone on sandy outwash plains, lakeplains, and occasionally coarse-textured end moraines. [OAK-PINE BARRENS, 166]

7B. Mature trees oaks (*Quercus* spp.) with little to no pine (*Pinus* spp.). Located south of the climatic tension zone in southern Lower Michigan. (GO TO 9A OR 9B)

9A. Scattered white oak (*Quercus alba*) or mixed oak species among tall and short prairie grasses. (GO TO 10A OR 10B)

10A. Savanna community occurring on moraines and outwash areas primarily within southern Lower Michigan. (GO TO 11A OR 11B)

11A. Scattered black oak (*Quercus velutina*), white oak (*Q. alba*), and occasionally northern pin oak (*Q. ellipsoidalis*) among prairie grasses occurring on infertile, droughty soils on glacial outwash and south- to west-facing, steep, coarse-textured moraines. Characteristic shrubs and forbs include American hazelnut (*Corylus americana*), New Jersey tea (*Ceanothus americanus*), serviceberries (*Amelanchier* spp.), bearberry (*Arctostaphylos uva-ursi*), sweetfern (*Comptonia peregrina*), blue toadflax (*Nuttallanthus canadensis*), prickly-pear (*Opuntia humifusa*), jointweed (*Polygonella articulata*), wild lupine (*Lupinus perennis*), dwarf dandelion (*Krigia virginica*), hairy puccoon (*Lithospermum caroliniense*), and birdfoot violet (*Viola pedata*). [OAK BARRENS, 170]

11B. Scattered white oak (*Quercus alba*), bur oak (*Q. macrocarpa*), and chinquapin oak (*Q. muehlenbergii*), with occasional pignut hickory (*Carya glabra*), shagbark hickory (*C. ovata*), red oak (*Q. rubra*), and black oak (*Q. velutina*) among prairie grasses and a mix of prairie and forest ground flora. Prevalent fire-tolerant shrubs include American hazelnut (*Corylus americana*), New Jersey tea (*Ceanothus americanus*), and leadplant (*Amorpha canescens*), and characteristic forbs include milkweeds (*Asclepias* spp.), prairie coreopsis (*Coreopsis palmata*), yellow coneflower (*Ratibida pinnata*), Culver's root (*Veronicastrum virginicum*), and tick-trefoils (*Desmodium* spp.). Nearly completely extirpated from Michigan but once prevalent in the southern Lower Peninsula on moderately fertile sandy loams and loamy sands of outwash and coarse-textured moraines. [OAK OPENINGS, 174]

10B. Savanna community occurring on sand ridges, level sandplains, and depressions within lakeplains of southeastern Lower Michigan and Saginaw Bay. Soils are very fine-textured sandy loams, loamy sands, or sands. Dominant tree species include white oak (*Quercus alba*) and black oak (*Q. velutina*) on well-drained soils, and bur oak (*Q. macrocarpa*), pin oak (*Q. palustris*), and swamp white oak (*Q. bicolor*) in poorly drained depressions. [LAKEPLAIN OAK OPENINGS, 178]

9B. Scattered bur oak (*Quercus macrocarpa*) among tall prairie grasses occurring historically in the southwestern Lower Peninsula on outwash plains and river terraces but now believed extirpated from Michigan. Soils fertile, fine-textured loam, sandy loam, or silt loam. [BUR OAK PLAINS, 182]

6B. Tree canopy cover 60% or more with ground flora primarily native forbs, sedges, and grasses associated with closed-canopy conditions. (GO TO 12A OR 12B) [FOREST GROUP, 186]

12A. Forested community primarily occurring north of the climatic tension zone in northern Lower Michigan and the Upper Peninsula. (GO TO 13A OR 13B)

13A. Overstory dominated by pines (*Pinus* spp.) and/or sugar maple (*Acer saccharum*), American beech (*Fagus grandifolia*), basswood (*Tilia americana*), hemlock (*Tsuga canadensis*), and yellow birch (*Betula alleghaniensis*). (GO TO 14A OR 14B)

14A. Overstory dominated by pines (*Pinus* spp.) and/or mixture of pine and oak. (GO TO 15A OR 15B)

15A. Overstory dominated by jack pine (*Pinus banksiana*) or red pine (*P. resinosa*), or jack pine and northern pin oak (*Quercus ellipsoidalis*). Soils droughty, low-nutrient, extremely acidic to very strongly acidic sands. Occurring on sandy glacial outwash, sandy glacial lakeplains, and sand ridges within peatlands. [DRY NORTHERN FOREST, 188]

15B. Overstory dominated or codominated by white pine (*Pinus strobus*), often with red pine (*P. resinosa*), white oak (*Quercus alba*), black oak (*Q. velutina*), red oak (*Q. rubra*), and/or hemlock (*Tsuga canadensis*). Soils extremely acidic to very strongly acidic sand or loamy sand.

Occurring on sandy glacial outwash, sandy glacial lakeplains, and less often on thin glacial drift over bedrock, inland dune ridges, and coarse-textured moraines. [DRY-MESIC NORTHERN FOREST, 192]

14B. Overstory dominated by sugar maple (*Acer saccharum*), hemlock (*Tsuga canadensis*), American beech (*Fagus grandifolia*), basswood (*Tilia americana*), white pine (*Pinus strobus*), and/or yellow birch (*Betula alleghaniensis*). [MESIC NORTHERN FOREST, 196]

13B. Overstory dominated by northern white-cedar (*Thuja occidentalis*), white spruce (*Picea glauca*), and balsam fir (*Abies balsamea*). Occurring primarily along northern shorelines of the Great Lakes, on Great Lakes islands, and locally inland. [BOREAL FOREST, 200]

12B. Forested community primarily occurring south of the climatic tension zone in southern Lower Michigan. (GO TO 16A OR 16B)

16A. Overstory dominated by oaks. (GO TO 17A OR 17B)

17A. Soils droughty, infertile, strongly to medium acidic sand, loamy sand, or sandy loam. Occurring principally on glacial outwash, and less frequently on sand dunes, sandy glacial lakeplains, and coarse-textured moraines. Overstory dominated by black oak (*Quercus velutina*) and/or white oak (*Q. alba*) with canopy associates including pignut hickory (*Carya glabra*), sassafras (*Sassafras albidum*), black cherry (*Prunus serotina*), and/or northern pin oak (*Q. ellipsoidalis*). [DRY SOUTHERN FOREST, 204]

17B. Soils dry-mesic, moderately fertile, slightly acidic to neutral sandy loam or loam. Occurring on glacial outwash, coarse-textured moraines, sandy glacial lakeplains, and occasionally kettle-kame topography and sand dunes. Overstory dominated by white oak (*Quercus alba*), black oak (*Q. velutina*), and/or red oak (*Q. rubra*), often with abundant pignut hickory (*Carya glabra*), shagbark hickory (*C. ovata*), bitternut hickory (*C. cordiformis*), red maple (*Acer rubrum*), white ash (*Fraxinus americana*), black cherry (*Prunus serotina*), northern pin oak (*Q. ellipsoidalis*), basswood (*Tilia americana*), and/or sassafras (*Sassafras albidum*). [DRY-MESIC SOUTHERN FOREST, 208]

16B. Overstory dominated by sugar maple (*Acer saccharum*) and American beech (*Fagus grandifolia*), with abundant red oak (*Quercus rubra*), white ash (*Fraxinus americana*), and/or basswood (*Tilia americana*). [MESIC SOUTHERN FOREST, 212]

PALUSTRINE/TERRESTRIAL CLASS KEY

1. Relatively equal mixture of upland and terrestrial communities or zones occurring as a landscape complex. (GO TO 2A OR 2B)

2A. Restricted to the Great Lakes shoreline. Occurring north of the climatic tension zone in northern Lower Michigan and the Upper Peninsula. Characterized by repeated pattern of alternating dunes and swales and supporting a mixture of upland and wetland communities. [WOODED DUNE & SWALE GROUP, 218; WOODED DUNE & SWALE COMPLEX, 220]

2B. Not restricted to the Great Lakes shoreline. Occurring throughout Michigan or restricted to lakeplains of southeastern Lower Michigan. Supporting a mixture of upland and wetland zones. (GO TO 3A OR 3B)

3A. Occurring in floodplains of 3rd order

or greater streams and rivers throughout Michigan. Characterized by fluvial landforms, such as natural levee, first bottom, backswamp, oxbow, and terrace, that support a diversity of upland and wetland zones. [FLOODPLAIN FOREST, 120]

3B. Not occurring in floodplains of streams and rivers. Restricted to lakeplains of southeastern Lower Michigan. Characterized by sand ridges and depressions that support upland and wetland zones. [LAKEPLAIN OAK OPENINGS, 178]

PRIMARY CLASS KEY

1A. Substrate primarily dune sands. Occurring in areas of extensive dune development. (GO TO 2A OR 2B) [DUNES GROUP, 226]

2A. Vegetation primarily grasses and low shrubs with scattered trees. Characteristic vegetation includes marram grass (*Ammophila breviligulata*), sand reed grass (*Calamovilfa longifolia*), little bluestem (*Schizachyrium scoparium*), bearberry (*Arctostaphylos uva-ursi*), creeping juniper (*Juniperus horizontalis*), sand cherry (*Prunus pumila*), willows (*Salix cordata* and *S. myricoides*), and common juniper (*Juniperus communis*). [OPEN DUNES, 228]

2B. Vegetation primarily evergreen trees and shrubs with scattered or clumped pines (*Pinus* spp.), white spruce (*Picea glauca*), and northern white-cedar (*Thuja occidentalis*) over dense, low shrub cover dominated by common juniper (*Juniperus communis*), creeping juniper (*J. horizontalis*), bearberry (*Arctostaphylos uva-ursi*),

and sand cherry (*Prunus pumila*), and patches of grasses, especially sand reed grass (*Calamovilfa longifolia*) and little bluestem (*Schizachyrium scoparium*). Occurring in dune fields and in depressions among dune ridges. [GREAT LAKES BARRENS, 232]

1B. Substrate primarily sand and gravel, cobble, bedrock, or clay. (GO TO 3A OR 3B)

3A. Substrate primarily sand and gravel or cobble. Located along Great Lakes shoreline. (GO TO 4A OR 4B) [SAND/COBBLE SHORE GROUP, 236]

4A. Substrate sand and gravel. Very sparsely vegetated with forbs and grasses such as sea rocket (*Cakile edentula*), Baltic rush (*Juncus balticus*), silverweed (*Potentilla anserina*), and beach pea (*Lathyrus japonicus*). [SAND & GRAVEL BEACH, 238]

4B. Substrate cobble. Very sparsely vegetated. (GO TO 5A OR 5B)

5A. Located along northern Lakes Michigan and Huron. Cobble comprised chiefly of limestone and/or dolomite. [LIMESTONE COBBLE SHORE, 242]

5B. Located primarily along Lake Superior. Comprised chiefly of sandstone or volcanic cobble. (GO TO 6A OR 6B)

6A. Cobble comprised chiefly of sandstone. [SANDSTONE COBBLE SHORE, 246]

6B. Cobble comprised chiefly of volcanic rocks including basalt and volcanic conglomerates. [VOLCANIC COBBLE SHORE, 250]

3B. Substrate primarily bedrock or steeply sloping bluffs of clay. Located along Great Lakes shoreline or inland. (GO TO 7A OR 7B)

7A. Substrate level to gently sloping (slightly tilted) bedrock with trees absent to rare. (GO TO 8A OR 8B)

8A. Located along Great Lakes shoreline. (GO TO 9A OR 9B) [BEDROCK LAKESHORE GROUP, 254]

9A. Located along northern Lakes Michigan and Huron on the Niagaran Cuesta in the eastern Upper Peninsula and locally in the northern Lower Peninsula. Sparse cover of native vegetation on limestone and/or dolomite bedrock. [LIMESTONE BEDROCK LAKESHORE, 256]

9B. Located along Lake Superior. Sparse cover of native vegetation on sandstone, granitic, volcanic, or metamorphic bedrock. (GO TO 10A OR 10B)

10A. Substrate primarily sandstone

bedrock. [SANDSTONE BEDROCK LAKESHORE, 260]

10B. Substrate primarily volcanic or granitic bedrock. (GO TO 11A OR 11B)

11A. Substrate primarily granitic bedrock, which may include granite, quartzite, schist, gabbro, gneiss, and a diversity of other resistant igneous and metamorphic rock types. [GRANITE BEDROCK LAKESHORE, 264]

11B. Substrate primarily volcanic in origin including basalt and volcanic conglomerate bedrocks. [VOLCANIC BEDROCK LAKESHORE, 268]

8B. Located inland from the Great Lakes shoreline and dominated by graminoids, including grasses, sedges, and spikerushes. [BEDROCK GRASSLAND GROUP 272; ALVAR, 274]

7B. Substrate level to steeply sloping bedrock with scattered canopy or sparsely vegetated community with vertical to near-vertical exposures of bedrock or steeply sloping bluffs of clay. (GO TO 12A OR 12B)

12A. Substrate level to steeply sloping bedrock. Characterized by savanna community structure with scattered native trees and shrubs. (GO TO 13A OR 13B) [BEDROCK GLADE GROUP, 278]

13A. Located primarily along the Niagaran Cuesta in the eastern Upper Peninsula and northeastern Lower Peninsula. Substrate primarily level to gently sloping, slightly tilted, or occasionally stair-stepped with thin soils over limestone and/or dolomite bedrock. [LIMESTONE BEDROCK GLADE, 280]

13B. Located primarily in the western Upper Peninsula. Substrate level to steep or stair-stepped with thin soils and areas of exposed granitic or volcanic bedrock. (GO TO 14A OR 14B)

14A. Substrate granitic bedrock, which may include granite, schist, gabbro, gneiss, slate, and a diversity of other resistant igneous and metamorphic rock types. Distributed primarily in northern Marquette County. [GRANITE BEDROCK GLADE, 284]

14B. Substrate volcanic in origin including basalt and volcanic conglomerate bedrock. Distributed primarily in the Keweenaw Peninsula, Ontonagon County, and Gogebic County. (GO TO 15A OR 15B)

15A. Substrate level to steep or stair-stepped. Not positioned on the tops of high bedrock escarpments. [VOLCANIC BEDROCK GLADE, 288]

15B. Substrate level to steeply sloping. Positioned on the tops of high bedrock escarpments. Low shrubs, flagged trees, and dwarfed, misshapen trees distorted into a krummholz growth form are common. [NORTHERN BALD, 292]

12B. Sparsely vegetated community with vertical to near-vertical exposures of bedrock or steeply sloping bluffs of clay. (GO TO 16A OR 16B)

16A. Located along the Great Lakes shoreline or along rivers draining into the

Great Lakes. (GO TO 17A OR 17B) [LAKESHORE CLIFF/BLUFF GROUP, 296]

17A. Steep to near-vertical clay slopes along the shorelines of Lake Michigan and Lake Superior or along rivers draining into the Great Lakes. [CLAY BLUFF, 298]

17B. Vertical or near-vertical exposure of bedrock along lakeshore. (GO TO 18A OR 18B)

18A. Located primarily along northern Lakes Michigan and Huron on the Niagaran Escarpment in the eastern Upper Peninsula. Substrate limestone and/or dolomite bedrock. [LIMESTONE LAKESHORE CLIFF, 302]

18B. Located primarily along Lake Superior. Substrate sandstone, granitic, or volcanic bedrock. (GO TO 19A OR 19B)

19A. Located primarily along Lake Superior with rare occurrences along Lake Huron. Substrate primarily sandstone bedrock. [SANDSTONE LAKESHORE CLIFF, 306]

19B. Restricted to Lake Superior shoreline. Substrate granitic or volcanic bedrock. (GO TO 20A OR 20B)

20A. Composed of granitic bedrock, which may include granite, quartzite, schist, gabbro, gneiss, and a diversity of other resistant igneous and metamorphic rock types. Restricted to shoreline in Marquette County. [GRANITE LAKESHORE CLIFF, 310]

20B. Composed of volcanic bedrock including basalt and volcanic conglomerate. Virtually restricted to shoreline along

Keweenaw Peninsula and Isle Royale. [VOLCANIC LAKESHORE CLIFF, 312]

16B. Located inland from the Great Lakes shoreline. (GO TO 21A OR 21B) [INLAND CLIFF GROUP, 314]

21A. Occurring primarily on the Niagaran Escarpment in the eastern and south-central Upper Peninsula and rarely in the western Upper Peninsula and northeastern Lower Michigan. Substrate limestone and/or dolomite bedrock including Kona dolomite in Marquette County. [LIMESTONE CLIFF, 316]

21B. Occurring primarily in the western and north-central Upper Peninsula. Substrate sandstone, granitic, or volcanic bedrock. (GO TO 22A OR 22B)

22A. Occurring primarily in the Upper Peninsula and very rarely in the southern Lower Peninsula. Substrate sandstone bedrock. [SANDSTONE CLIFF, 320]

22B. Restricted to the Upper Peninsula. Substrate granitic or volcanic bedrock. (GO TO 23A OR 23B)

23A. Cliff primarily composed of granitic bedrock, which may include granite, quartzite, schist, gabbro, gneiss, and a diversity of other resistant igneous and metamorphic rock types. [GRANITE CLIFF, 324]

23B. Cliff primarily composed of volcanic bedrock including basalt and volcanic conglomerate. [VOLCANIC CLIFF, 328]

SUBTERRANEAN/SINK CLASS KEY

1. Subterranean or sink feature located in areas of karst topography primarily along the Niagaran Cuesta in the eastern Upper Peninsula and northeastern Lower Peninsula. (GO TO 2A OR 2B) [KARST GROUP, 334]

2A. Occurring as cavities beneath the earth's surface, often with an opening to the surface, characterized by little or no light, no primary producers, and biotic communities of one or two trophic levels that import energy from outside the system. [CAVE, 336]

2B. Occurring as large depressions caused by the dissolution and collapse of sub-surface limestone, dolomite, or gypsum. Bottoms of depressions sometimes filled with water. Exposed limestone vertical walls and large boulders sometimes present. Vegetative composition and structure generally reflect that of surrounding landscape. [SINKHOLE, 338]

A Field Guide
to the
Natural Communities
of Michigan

Northern bald overlooking the Carp River,
Porcupine Mountains Wilderness State Park,
Ontonagon County
JOSHUA G. COHEN

Bog, Loon Lake, Atlanta State Forest
Management Unit, Presque Isle County
JOSHUA G. COHEN

Palustrine Class

MARSH GROUP

Marshes are herbaceous wetland communities found throughout Michigan. Marshes typically occur in association with aquatic features including the Great Lakes, inland lakes, abandoned lakebeds, ponds, rivers, streams, seeps, and beaver floodings. The soils range from inundated to saturated and are predominantly organics but can also include mineral soils. Water levels and soil saturation in Marshes can vary seasonally and from year to year. Natural processes that influence species composition and community structure of Marshes can include fluctuating water levels, seasonal flooding, storm waves, groundwater seepage, flooding by beaver, and fire.

Nine natural community types fall within the Marsh group, including submergent marsh, emergent marsh, Great Lakes marsh, inland salt marsh, coastal plain marsh, intermittent wetland, northern wet meadow, southern wet meadow, and interdunal wetland. Classification of these Marsh types is based on species composition, community structure, soil chemistry and composition, hydrology, geographic distribution, and landscape setting.

Emergent marsh, Thompson's Harbor State Park, Presque Isle County
JOSHUA G. COHEN

S4 SUBMERGENT MARSH

Submergent marsh is an herbaceous plant community that occurs in deep to sometimes shallow water in lakes and streams throughout Michigan. Soils are characterized by loosely consolidated, acidic to alkaline organic deposits of variable depth that accumulate over all types of mineral soil and bedrock.

Natural processes that influence species composition and community structure include fluctuating water levels, storm waves, currents, and flooding

LANDSCAPE ECOSYSTEMS
— SECTION
— SUBSECTION

COMMUNITY RANGE
○ ABSENT OR LIKELY ABSENT
◔ INFREQUENT OR LIKELY INFREQUENT
● PREVALENT OR LIKELY PREVALENT

JOSHUA G. COHEN

by beaver. Vegetation is comprised of both rooted and non-rooted plants that occur completely beneath the water surface (i.e., submergent plants), rooted floating-leaved plants, and non-rooted floating plants. Characteristic plants include sweet-scented waterlily (*Nymphaea odorata*), yellow pond-lilies (*Nuphar variegata* and *N. advena*), bladderworts (*Utricularia* spp.), pondweeds (*Potamogeton* spp.), water-shield (*Brasenia schreberi*), duckweeds (*Lemna* spp.), and water meal (*Wolffia* spp.).

CHARACTERISTIC PLANTS

SUBMERGENT PLANTS
- coontail (*Ceratophyllum demersum*)
- muskgrasses (*Chara* spp.)
- common waterweed (*Elodea canadensis*)
- pipewort (*Eriocaulon aquaticum*)
- water star-grass (*Heteranthera dubia*)
- water-milfoils (*Myriophyllum* spp.)
- naiads (*Najas flexilis* and others)
- stoneworts (*Nitella* spp.)

7

Submergent marsh dominated by sweet-scented waterlily (*Nymphaea odorata*)

- pondweeds (*Potamogeton friesii, P. praelongus, P. strictifolius, P. zosteriformis, Stuckenia* spp., and others)
- submergent bulrush (*Schoenoplectus subterminalis*)
- bladderworts (*Utricularia* spp.)
- water-celery (*Vallisneria americana*)

ROOTED FLOATING–LEAVED PLANTS
- water-shield (*Brasenia schreberi*)
- yellow pond-lilies (*Nuphar advena* and *N. variegata*)
- sweet-scented waterlily (*Nymphaea odorata*)
- pondweeds (*Potamogeton amplifolius, P. illinoensis*, and others)

NON-ROOTED FLOATING PLANTS
- small duckweed (*Lemna minor*)
- star duckweed (*Lemna trisulca*)
- red duckweed (*Lemna turionifera*)
- great duckweed (*Spirodela polyrhiza*)
- water meals (*Wolffia* spp.)

PLACES TO VISIT

- BARRY: Otis Lake Marsh, Barry State Game Area
- CASS: Forked Lake Marsh, Crane Pond State Game Area
- ONTONAGON: Lake of the Clouds, Porcupine Mountains Wilderness State Park

Submergent marsh occurring in a beaver flooding

Submergent marsh, Keweenaw County

S4 EMERGENT MARSH

Emergent marsh is a shallow-water wetland that occurs along the shores of lakes and streams throughout Michigan. Water depth of 15 cm (6 in) or more is usually present throughout the growing season. The community develops on all types of mineral soil and bedrock, sometimes covered by

loosely consolidated, acidic to alkaline organic deposits of variable depth. Natural processes that influence species composition and community

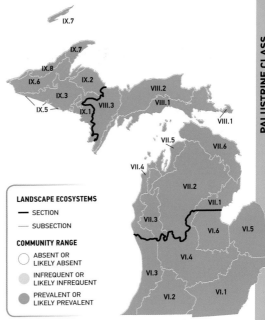

structure include fluctuating water levels, seasonal flooding, and flooding by beaver. Vegetation is comprised of narrow- and broad-leaved graminoids (i.e., grass-like plants) and herbs that extend above the water surface (i.e., emergent plants), as well as floating-leaved plants. Characteristic plants include bulrushes (*Schoenoplectus* spp.), spike-rushes (*Eleocharis* spp.), sedges (*Carex* spp.), pickerel-weed (*Pontederia cordata*), arrowheads (*Sagittaria* spp.), broad-leaved cat-tail (*Typha latifolia*), and yellow pond-lilies (*Nuphar variegata* and *N. advena*).

CHARACTERISTIC PLANTS

SUBMERGENT PLANTS
- coontail (*Ceratophyllum demersum*)
- muskgrasses (*Chara* spp.)
- common waterweed (*Elodea canadensis*)
- water star-grass (*Heteranthera dubia*)
- milfoils (*Myriophyllum* spp.)
- naiads (*Najas flexilis* and others)
- stoneworts (*Nitella* spp.)

JOSHUA G. COHEN

11

Emergent marsh dominated by wiregrass sedge (*Carex lasiocarpa*)

- pondweeds (*Potamogeton* spp.)
- submergent bulrush (*Schoenoplectus subterminalis*)
- bladderworts (*Utricularia gibba, U. intermedia*, and *U. vulgaris*)
- water-celery (*Vallisneria americana*)

ROOTED FLOATING-LEAVED PLANTS
- water-shield (*Brasenia schreberi*)
- yellow pond-lilies (*Nuphar advena* and *N. variegata*)
- sweet-scented waterlily (*Nymphaea odorata*)
- large-leaved pondweed (*Potamogeton amplifolius*)
- Illinois pondweed (*Potamogeton illinoensis*)

NON-ROOTED FLOATING PLANTS
- small duckweed (*Lemna minor*)
- star duckweed (*Lemna trisulca*)
- red duckweed (*Lemna turionifera*)
- great duckweed (*Spirodela polyrhiza*)
- water meals (*Wolffia* spp.)

EMERGENT PLANTS
GRAMINOIDS
- sedges (*Carex aquatilis, C. comosa, C. lacustris, C. lasiocarpa, C. oligosperma, C. stricta*, and others)
- three-way sedge (*Dulichium arundinaceum*)
- spike-rushes (*Eleocharis acicularis, E. elliptica, E. equisetoides, E. obtusa,*

E. palustris, E. quinqueflora, and others)
- manna grasses (*Glyceria borealis, G. canadensis,* and *G. striata*)
- cut grass (*Leersia oryzoides*)
- common reed (*Phragmites australis* subsp. *americanus*)
- hardstem bulrush (*Schoenoplectus acutus*)
- threesquare (*Schoenoplectus pungens*)
- softstem bulrush (*Schoenoplectus tabernaemontani*)
- wild rice (*Zizania aquatica*)*[2]
- northern wild rice (*Zizania palustris*)

FORBS
- water-plantain (*Alisma subcordatum* and *A. triviale*)
- pipewort (*Eriocaulon aquaticum*)
- smartweeds (*Persicaria amphibia, P. hydropiper, P. lapathifolia,* and others)

- pickerel-weed (*Pontederia cordata*)
- arrowheads (*Sagittaria graminea, S. latifolia,* and *S. rigida*)
- bur-reeds (*Sparganium americanum, S. angustifolium, S. emersum, S. eurycarpum, S. fluctuans,* and *S. natans*)
- broad-leaved cat-tail (*Typha latifolia*)

FERNS
- marsh fern (*Thelypteris palustris*)

PLACES TO VISIT
- JACKSON: South Portage Marsh, Waterloo State Recreation Area
- OAKLAND: Moss Lake, Proud Lake State Recreation Area
- ONTONAGON: Lake of the Clouds, Porcupine Mountains Wilderness State Park

Emergent marsh, Alpena County

GREAT LAKES MARSH

Great Lakes marsh is an herbaceous wetland community occurring statewide along shorelines of the Great Lakes and their major connecting rivers. Great Lakes marsh can be found in association with open, protected, and sand-spit embayments; within dune and swale complexes, tombolos, and barrier-beach lagoons; in buried river mouths and river deltas; and in bays and channels within the connecting rivers. The community develops on all types of mineral soil and occasionally on bedrock, sometimes covered by loosely consolidated, acidic to alkaline organic deposits of variable depth. Vegetation patterns and diversity are strongly influenced by water-level fluctuations and the local configurations of shoreline. Vegetation zones generally include a deep marsh with floating-leaved and submergent plants; an emergent marsh of mostly narrow-leaved species such as bulrushes; and a sedge-dominated wet meadow that can be inundated by storms. Characteristic plants include bulrushes (*Schoenoplectus* spp. and *Scirpus* spp.), spike-rushes (*Eleocharis* spp.), rushes (*Juncus* spp.), broad-leaved cat-tail (*Typha latifolia*), blue-joint (*Calamagrostis canadensis*), sedges (*Carex* spp.), sweet-scented waterlily (*Nymphaea odorata*), yellow pond-lilies (*Nuphar variegata* and *N. advena*), duckweeds (*Lemna* spp.), coontail (*Ceratophyllum demersum*), and pondweeds (*Potamogeton* spp.).

BRADFORD S. SLAUGHTER

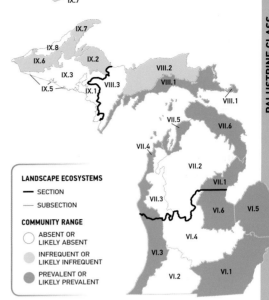

CHARACTERISTIC PLANTS

SUBMERGENT PLANTS

- coontail (*Ceratophyllum demersum*)
- common waterweed (*Elodea canadensis*)
- slender naiad (*Najas flexilis*)
- pondweeds (*Potamogeton obtusifolius, P. pectinatus, P. richardsonii, P. robbinsii, P. zosteriformis, Stuckenia pectinata*, and others)
- bladderworts (*Utricularia intermedia, U. vulgaris*, and others)
- water-celery (*Vallisneria americana*)

ROOTED FLOATING-LEAVED PLANTS

- water-shield (*Brasenia schreberi*)
- variegated yellow pond-lilies (*Nuphar advena* and *N. variegata*)
- sweet-scented waterlily (*Nymphaea odorata*)
- pondweeds (*Potamogeton gramineus, P. illinoensis, P. natans*, and others)

NON-ROOTED FLOATING PLANTS

- small duckweed (*Lemna minor*)
- star duckweed (*Lemna trisulca*)
- red duckweed (*Lemna turionifera*)
- great duckweed (*Spirodela polyrhiza*)
- water meal (*Wolffia* spp.)

EMERGENT PLANTS

GRAMINOIDS

- ticklegrasses (*Agrostis hyemalis* and *A. scabra*)
- blue-joint (*Calamagrostis canadensis*)
- narrow-leaved reedgrass (*Calamagrostis stricta*)
- sedges (*Carex aquatilis, C. bebbii, C. comosa, C. hystericina, C. lacustris, C. lasiocarpa, C. stricta, C. viridula*, and others)
- twig-rush (*Cladium mariscoides*)
- tufted hair grass (*Deschampsia cespitosa*)
- Lindheimer's panic grass (*Dichanthelium lindheimeri*)

- spike-rushes (*Eleocharis acicularis, E. elliptica, E. palustris, E. quinqueflora*, and others)
- rushes (*Juncus balticus, J. brevicaudatus, J. canadensis*, and others)
- cut grass (*Leersia oryzoides*)
- common reed (*Phragmites australis* subsp. *americanus*)
- beak-rush (*Rhynchospora capillacea*)
- hardstem bulrush (*Schoenoplectus acutus*)
- threesquare (*Schoenoplectus pungens*)
- softstem bulrush (*Schoenoplectus tabernaemontani*)
- bulrushes (*Scirpus atrovirens* and *S. cyperinus*)

FORBS

- Canada anemone (*Anemone canadensis*)
- swamp milkweed (*Asclepias incarnata*)
- hedge bindweed (*Calystegia sepium*)
- marsh bellflower (*Campanula aparinoides*)
- water hemlock (*Cicuta bulbifera*)
- limestone calamint (*Clinopodium arkansanum*)
- marsh cinquefoil (*Comarum palustre*)
- common boneset (*Eupatorium perfoliatum*)

15

An aerial photograph of Great Lakes marsh from Mismer Bay

- grass-leaved goldenrod (*Euthamia graminifolia*)
- joe-pye-weed (*Eutrochium maculatum*)
- small bedstraw (*Galium trifidum*)
- small fringed gentian (*Gentianopsis virgata*)
- swamp mallow (*Hibiscus moscheutos*)
- jewelweed (*Impatiens capensis*)
- wild blue flag (*Iris versicolor*)
- marsh pea (*Lathyrus palustris*)
- Kalm's lobelia (*Lobelia kalmii*)
- common water horehound (*Lycopus americanus*)
- balsam ragwort (*Packera paupercula*)
- grass-of-Parnassus (*Parnassia glauca*)
- water smartweed (*Persicaria amphibia*)
- pickerel-weed (*Pontederia cordata*)
- silverweed (*Potentilla anserina*)
- bird's-eye primrose (*Primula mistassinica*)
- common arrowhead (*Sagittaria latifolia*)
- common skullcap (*Scutellaria galericulata*)
- Ohio goldenrod (*Solidago ohioensis*)

- bur-reeds (*Sparganium* spp.)
- nodding ladies'-tresses (*Spiranthes cernua*)
- panicled aster (*Symphyotrichum lanceolatum*)
- bog arrow-grasses (*Triglochin maritima* and *T. palustris*)
- broad-leaved cat-tail (*Typha latifolia*)
- horned bladderwort (*Utricularia cornuta*)
- blue vervain (*Verbena hastata*)

FERNS
- marsh fern (*Thelypteris palustris*)

FERN ALLIES
- common horsetail (*Equisetum arvense*)
- water horsetail (*Equisetum fluviatile*)

SHRUBS
- tag alder (*Alnus incana*)
- silky dogwood (*Cornus amomum*)
- red-osier dogwood (*Cornus sericea*)

- shrubby cinquefoil (*Dasiphora fruticosa*)
- Kalm's St. John's-wort (*Hypericum kalmianum*)
- sweet gale (*Myrica gale*)
- willows (*Salix candida, S. exigua, S. petiolaris*, and others)
- meadowsweet (*Spiraea alba*)

TREES
- paper birch (*Betula papyrifera*)
- green ash (*Fraxinus pennsylvanica*)
- balsam poplar (*Populus balsamifera*)
- quaking aspen (*Populus tremuloides*)

PLACES TO VISIT
- ALPENA: El Cajon Bay and Misery Bay, Atlanta State Forest Management Unit
- BAY: Pinconning, Pinconning County Park
- CHEBOYGAN: Duncan Bay, Cheboygan State Park
- CHIPPEWA: Munuscong River Mouth, Sault Sainte Marie State Forest Management Unit
- EMMET: Waugoshance Point, Wilderness State Park
- HURON: Wildfowl Bay Islands, Wildfowl Bay Wildlife Area
- MACKINAC: Pointe Aux Chenes, Hiawatha National Forest
- MACKINAC: St. Martin Bay, Hiawatha National Forest
- OTTAWA: Pottawattomie Bayou, Grand Haven Township Park

Great Lakes marsh, Duncan Bay, Cheboygan State Park, Cheboygan County

S1 INLAND SALT MARSH

Inland salt marsh is an herbaceous wetland occurring on mineral soil saturated by sodium- and chloride-laden groundwater from natural brine aquifers. In Michigan, salt marshes and seeps are concentrated in areas where Silurian or Devonian halites (rock salt deposits) occur near the surface. Species composition and open conditions are maintained by the saline conditions, fluctuating water levels, and, historically, by occasional fires. Characteristic species include Olney's bulrush (*Schoenoplectus americanus*),

threesquare (*S. pungens*), and dwarf spike-rush (*Eleocharis parvula*). Today, inland salt marsh is nearly extirpated from Michigan and is restricted to a few sites along the Maple River in northern Clinton County.

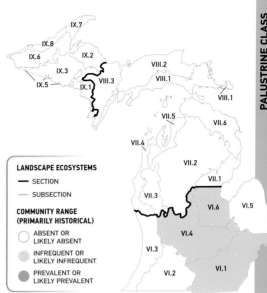

LANDSCAPE ECOSYSTEMS
— SECTION
— SUBSECTION

**COMMUNITY RANGE
(PRIMARILY HISTORICAL)**
○ ABSENT OR
LIKELY ABSENT
◐ INFREQUENT OR
LIKELY INFREQUENT
● PREVALENT OR
LIKELY PREVALENT

MICHAEL R. PENSKAR

CHARACTERISTIC PLANTS

GRAMINOIDS
- bald spike-rush (*Eleocharis erythropoda*)
- dwarf spike-rush (*Eleocharis parvula*)*
- reed (*Phragmites australis* subsp. *americanus*)
- Olney's bulrush (*Schoenoplectus americanus*)*
- threesquare (*Schoenoplectus pungens*)

FORBS
- water plantain (*Alisma subcordatum*)
- spearscale (*Atriplex patula*)
- purslane (*Portulaca oleracea*)
- water-pimpernel (*Samolus parviflorus*)
- water parsnip (*Sium suave*)
- broad-leaved cat-tail (*Typha latifolia*)

PLACES TO VISIT

- CLINTON: Maple River, Maple River State Game Area

19

S2 COASTAL PLAIN MARSH

Coastal plain marsh is a graminoid-, shrub-, and herb-dominated wetland that contains numerous plant species disjunct from their primary ranges in the Atlantic and Gulf coastal plains. The community occurs primarily in the western Lower Peninsula along the shorelines of inland lakes and in depressions in sandy pitted outwash plains, outwash channels, and lakeplains. Coastal plain marsh is characterized by fluctuating water levels that can vary significantly both seasonally and interannually. The sandy

soils underlying coastal plain marshes are strongly to very strongly acidic and nutrient-poor and are sometimes covered by a layer of peat or sandy peat. Fluctuating water levels and occasional fires maintain species composition and open conditions. Characteristic species

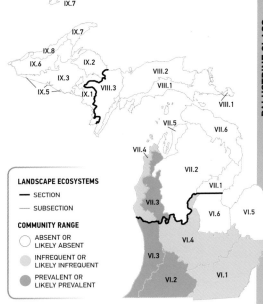

LANDSCAPE ECOSYSTEMS

— SECTION

— SUBSECTION

COMMUNITY RANGE

○ ABSENT OR LIKELY ABSENT

◐ INFREQUENT OR LIKELY INFREQUENT

● PREVALENT OR LIKELY PREVALENT

BRADFORD S. SLAUGHTER

include submergent species, such as water-shield (*Brasenia schreberi*), sweet-scented waterlily (*Nymphaea odorata*), pondweeds (*Potamogeton* spp.), and bladderworts (*Utricularia* spp.), and graminoids, including tall beak-rush (*Rhynchospora macrostachya*), brownish beak-rush (*Rhynchospora capitellata*), autumn sedge (*Fimbristylis autumnalis*), blue-joint (*Calamagrostis canadensis*), and twig-rush (*Cladium mariscoides*). Prevalent coastal plain disjuncts can include black-fruited spike-rush (*Eleocharis melanocarpa*), round-headed rush (*Juncus scirpoides*), Eaton's panic grass (*Dichanthelium spretum*), bald-rush (*Rhynchospora scirpoides*), bog yellow-eyed-grass (*Xyris difformis*), and meadow beauty (*Rhexia virginica*).

CHARACTERISTIC PLANTS

GRAMINOIDS

- sedge (*Bulbostylis capillaris*)
- blue-joint (*Calamagrostis canadensis*)

21

- sedges (*Carex lasiocarpa, C. oligosperma, C. pellita, C. scoparia,* and others)
- twig-rush (*Cladium mariscoides*)
- umbrella sedge (*Cyperus bipartitus*)
- Eaton's panic grass (*Dichanthelium spretum*)
- purple spike-rush (*Eleocharis atropurpurea*)*
- Engelmann's spike-rush (*Eleocharis engelmannii*)*
- bright green spike-rush (*Eleocharis flavescens*)
- black-fruited spike-rush (*Eleocharis melanocarpa*)*
- Robbin's spike-rush (*Eleocharis robbinsii*)
- three-ribbed spike-rush (*Eleocharis tricostata*)*
- autumn sedge (*Fimbristylis autumnalis*)
- two-flowered rush (*Juncus biflorus*)
- brown-fruited rush (*Juncus pelocarpus*)
- round-headed rush (*Juncus scirpoides*)*
- dwarf bulrush (*Lipocarpha micrantha*)*
- brownish beak-rush (*Rhynchospora capitellata*)
- tall beak-rush (*Rhynchospora macrostachya*)*
- bald-rush (*Rhynchospora scirpoides*)*
- Pursh's tufted bulrush (*Schoenoplectus purshianus*)
- Smith's bulrush (*Schoenoplectus smithii*)
- Torrey's bulrush (*Schoenoplectus torreyi*)*
- tall nut-rush (*Scleria triglomerata*)*

FORBS
- screw-stem (*Bartonia virginica*)
- water-shield (*Brasenia schreberi*)
- spatulate-leaved sundew (*Drosera intermedia*)
- pipewort (*Eriocaulon aquaticum*)
- slender goldentop (*Euthamia caroliniana*)
- northern St. John's-wort (*Hypericum boreale*)
- Canadian St. John's-wort (*Hypericum canadense*)

Coastal plain marsh during a high-water year

- seedbox (*Ludwigia alternifolia*)
- yellow pond-lilies (*Nuphar advena* and *N. variegata*)
- sweet-scented waterlily (*Nymphaea odorata*)
- smartweeds (*Persicaria* spp.)
- cross-leaved milkwort (*Polygala cruciata*)*
- field milkwort (*Polygala sanguinea*)
- pondweeds (*Potamogeton* spp.)
- meadow beauty (*Rhexia virginica*)*
- tooth-cup (*Rotala ramosior*)
- little ladies'-tresses (*Spiranthes tuberosa*)
- hyssop hedge nettle (*Stachys hyssopifolia*)
- bushy aster (*Symphyotrichum dumosum*)
- Virginia marsh St. John's-wort (*Triadenum virginicum*)
- horned bladderwort (*Utricularia cornuta*)
- humped bladderwort (*Utricularia gibba*)
- purple bladderwort (*Utricularia purpurea*)
- small purple bladderwort (*Utricularia resupinata*)
- lance-leaved violet (*Viola lanceolata*)
- bog yellow-eyed-grass (*Xyris difformis*)
- slender yellow-eyed-grass (*Xyris torta*)

FERNS
- Virginia chain-fern (*Woodwardia virginica*)

FERN ALLIES
- bog clubmoss (*Lycopodiella inundata*)

MOSSES
- sphagnum mosses (*Sphagnum* spp.)

SHRUBS
- black chokeberry (*Aronia prunifolia*)
- buttonbush (*Cephalanthus occidentalis*)
- leatherleaf (*Chamaedaphne calyculata*)
- dogwoods (*Cornus* spp.)
- whorled loosestrife (*Decodon verticillatus*)
- shrubby St. John's-wort (*Hypericum prolificum*)
- swamp dewberry (*Rubus hispidus*)

- steeplebush (*Spiraea tomentosa*)
- highbush blueberry (*Vaccinium corymbosum*)

TREES
- red maple (*Acer rubrum*)
- black gum (*Nyssa sylvatica*)
- pin oak (*Quercus palustris*)

PLACES TO VISIT

- ALLEGAN: 116th Avenue Pond, Goose Lake, 36th Ave, Allegan State Game Area
- MUSKEGON: Pine Island Marsh Candidate Research Natural Area, Manistee National Forest
- NEWAYGO: Little Robinson Lake Marshes, Manistee National Forest
- VAN BUREN: Hamilton Township Coastal Plain Marsh Nature Sanctuary, Michigan Nature Association
- VAN BUREN: Ross Coastal Plain Marsh Preserve, The Nature Conservancy

BRADFORD S. SLAUGHTER

Coastal plain disjuncts such as meadow beauty (*Rhexia virginica*) are characteristic of coastal plain marsh

S3 INTERMITTENT WETLAND

Intermittent wetland is a graminoid-, shrub-, and herb-dominated wetland that occurs statewide. Intermittent wetland is found along lakeshores and in depressions characterized by seasonally and interannually fluctuating water levels. The community occurs on acidic sands or shallow sandy peats. Fluctuating water levels and occasional fires maintain species composition and

open conditions. Intermittent wetland exhibits traits of both peatlands and marshes, with characteristic vegetation including sedges (*Carex* spp.), rushes (*Juncus* spp.), spike-rushes (*Eleocharis*

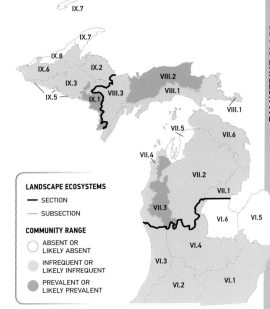

LANDSCAPE ECOSYSTEMS
— SECTION
— SUBSECTION

COMMUNITY RANGE
○ ABSENT OR LIKELY ABSENT
◔ INFREQUENT OR LIKELY INFREQUENT
● PREVALENT OR LIKELY PREVALENT

JOSHUA G. COHEN

spp.), bulrushes (*Schoenoplectus* spp. and *Scirpus* spp.), ticklegrass (*Agrostis hyemalis* and *A. scabra*), blue-joint (*Calamagrostis canadensis*), twig-rush (*Cladium mariscoides*), panic grasses (*Dichanthelium* spp.), three-way sedge (*Dulichium arundinaceum*), pipewort (*Eriocaulon aquaticum*), slender goldentop (*Euthamia caroliniana*), grass-leaved goldenrod (*Euthamia graminifolia*), lance-leaved violet (*Viola lanceolata*), mosses, and ericaceous shrubs such as leatherleaf (*Chamaedaphne calyculata*).

CHARACTERISTIC PLANTS

GRAMINOIDS
- ticklegrasses (*Agrostis hyemalis* and *A. scabra*)
- blue-joint (*Calamagrostis canadensis*)
- wiregrass sedge (*Carex lasiocarpa*)
- few-seed sedge (*Carex oligosperma*)
- twig-rush (*Cladium mariscoides*)
- Eaton's panic grass (*Dichanthelium spretum*)
- three-way sedge (*Dulichium arundinaceum*)

25

Intermittent wetland inundated during the early growing season

- bright green spike-rush (*Eleocharis flavescens*)
- Robbin's spike-rush (*Eleocharis robbinsii*)
- autumn sedge (*Fimbristylis autumnalis*)
- northern manna grass (*Glyceria borealis*)
- Canadian rush (*Juncus canadensis*)
- brown-fruited rush (*Juncus pelocarpus*)
- beak-rushes (*Rhynchospora capitellata* and *R. fusca*)
- Pursh's tufted bulrush (*Schoenoplectus purshianus*)
- Smith's bulrush (*Schoenoplectus smithii*)
- Torrey's bulrush (*Schoenoplectus torreyi*)*

FORBS
- water-shield (*Brasenia schreberi*)
- spatulate-leaved sundew (*Drosera intermedia*)
- pipewort (*Eriocaulon aquaticum*)
- slender goldentop (*Euthamia caroliniana*)
- grass-leaved goldenrod (*Euthamia graminifolia*)
- northern St. John's wort (*Hypericum boreale*)
- wild blue flag (*Iris versicolor*)
- swamp candles (*Lysimachia terrestris*)
- variegated yellow pond-lily (*Nuphar variegata*)
- sweet-scented waterlily (*Nymphaea odorata*)
- smartweeds (*Persicaria* spp.)
- pondweeds (*Potamogeton* spp.)
- hyssop hedge nettle (*Stachys hyssopifolia*)
- bushy aster (*Symphyotrichum dumosum*)
- horned bladderwort (*Utricularia cornuta*)
- humped bladderwort (*Utricularia gibba*)
- purple bladderwort (*Utricularia purpurea*)
- small purple bladderwort (*Utricularia resupinata*)
- lance-leaved violet (*Viola lanceolata*)

MOSSES
- sphagnum mosses (*Sphagnum* spp.)

SHRUBS
- leatherleaf (*Chamaedaphne calyculata*)
- meadowsweet (*Spiraea alba*)
- steeplebush (*Spiraea tomentosa*)

TREES
- tamarack (*Larix laricina*)
- black spruce (*Picea mariana*)
- jack pine (*Pinus banksiana*)
- red pine (*Pinus resinosa*)
- white pine (*Pinus strobus*)

PLACES TO VISIT
- BARAGA: Baraga Plains, Baraga Plains State Waterfowl Management Area
- BARRY: Dagget Lake Wetlands and Norris Road Wetland, Barry State Game Area
- CHEBOYGAN: Duck Lake, Atlanta State Forest Management Unit
- CRAWFORD: Frog Lakes, Grayling State Forest Management Unit
- LUCE: Swamp Lakes, Newberry State Forest Management Unit and The Nature Conservancy (Swamp Lakes Preserve)
- SCHOOLCRAFT: Michaud Lake, Shingleton State Forest Management Unit

Intermittent wetland in late summer when the water levels have drawn down

S4 NORTHERN WET MEADOW

Northern wet meadow is a groundwater-influenced, sedge- and grass-dominated wetland that occurs in the Upper Peninsula and northern Lower Peninsula. Northern wet meadow typically borders streams but is also found on pond and lake margins and above beaver dams. The community typically develops on strongly acidic to circumneutral sapric peat but can

also occur on saturated mineral soils. Natural processes that influence species composition and community structure include seasonal flooding, flooding by beaver, and fire. Sedges in the genus

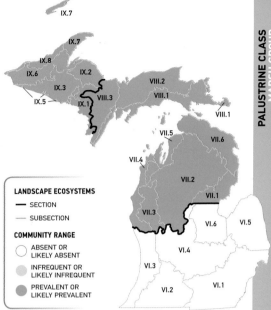

LANDSCAPE ECOSYSTEMS
— SECTION
— SUBSECTION

COMMUNITY RANGE
○ ABSENT OR LIKELY ABSENT
◔ INFREQUENT OR LIKELY INFREQUENT
● PREVALENT OR LIKELY PREVALENT

Carex, in particular tussock sedge (*C. stricta*) and lake sedge (*C. lacustris*), dominate the community along with blue-joint (*Calamagrostis canadensis*).

CHARACTERISTIC PLANTS

GRAMINOIDS
- fringed brome (*Bromus ciliatus*)
- blue-joint (*Calamagrostis canadensis*)
- sedges (*Carex lacustris, C. lasiocarpa, C. stricta, C. utriculata, C. vesicaria,* and others)
- twig-rush (*Cladium mariscoides*)
- spike-rush (*Eleocharis erythropoda* and *E. palustris*)
- rattlesnake grass (*Glyceria canadensis*)
- marsh wild-timothy (*Muhlenbergia glomerata*)
- fowl meadow grass (*Poa palustris*)
- green bulrush (*Scirpus atrovirens*)

FORBS
- swamp milkweed (*Asclepias incarnata*)
- marsh bellflower (*Campanula aparinoides*)
- water hemlocks (*Cicuta bulbifera* and *C. maculata*)

JOSHUA G. COHEN

Northern wet meadow and northern shrub thicket often occur along slow-moving streams

- swamp thistle (*Cirsium muticum*)
- marsh cinquefoil (*Comarum palustre*)
- flat-topped white aster (*Doellingeria umbellata*)
- downy willow-herb (*Epilobium strictum*)
- common boneset (*Eupatorium perfoliatum*)
- grass-leaved goldenrod (*Euthamia graminifolia*)
- joe-pye-weed (*Eutrochium maculatum*)
- rough bedstraw (*Galium asprellum*)
- bog bedstraw (*Galium labradoricum*)
- small bedstraw (*Galium trifidum*)
- jewelweed (*Impatiens capensis*)
- wild blue flag (*Iris versicolor*)
- marsh pea (*Lathyrus palustris*)
- cardinal flower (*Lobelia cardinalis*)
- great blue lobelia (*Lobelia siphilitica*)
- common water horehound (*Lycopus americanus*)
- northern bugle weed (*Lycopus uniflorus*)
- swamp candles (*Lysimachia terrestris*)

- tufted loosestrife (*Lysimachia thyrsiflora*)
- wild mint (*Mentha canadensis*)
- water smartweed (*Persicaria amphibia*)
- great water dock (*Rumex orbiculatus*)
- common arrowhead (*Sagittaria latifolia*)
- common skullcap (*Scutellaria galericulata*)
- tall goldenrod (*Solidago altissima*)
- Canada goldenrod (*Solidago canadensis*)
- late goldenrod (*Solidago gigantea*)
- swamp goldenrod (*Solidago patula*)
- rough goldenrod (*Solidago rugosa*)
- panicled aster (*Symphyotrichum lanceolatum*)
- side-flowering aster (*Symphyotrichum lateriflorum*)
- swamp aster (*Symphyotrichum puniceum*)
- purple meadow-rue (*Thalictrum dasycarpum*)
- marsh St. John's-wort (*Triadenum fraseri*)
- broad-leaved cat-tail (*Typha latifolia*)
- blue vervain (*Verbena hastata*)
- marsh violet (*Viola cucullata*)

FERNS

- sensitive fern (*Onoclea sensibilis*)
- marsh fern (*Thelypteris palustris*)

SHRUBS

- tag alder (*Alnus incana*)
- bog birch (*Betula pumila*)
- red-osier dogwood (*Cornus sericea*)
- shrubby cinquefoil (*Dasiphora fruticosa*)
- sweet gale (*Myrica gale*)
- willows (*Salix* spp.)
- meadowsweet (*Spiraea alba*)
- steeplebush (*Spiraea tomentosa*)

TREES

- red maple (*Acer rubrum*)
- tamarack (*Larix laricina*)
- white pine (*Pinus strobus*)
- balsam poplar (*Populus balsamifera*)

- quaking aspen (*Populus tremuloides*)
- northern white-cedar (*Thuja occidentalis*)

PLACES TO VISIT

- DICKINSON: Lost Lake, Crystal Falls State Management Unit
- KALKASKA: Cannon Creek, Grayling State Forest Management Unit
- MARQUETTE: Kipple Creek, Van Riper State Park
- ONTONAGON: Carp River and Lake of the Clouds, Porcupine Mountains Wilderness State Park
- ROSCOMMON: Hudson Creek, Roscommon State Forest Management Unit
- SCHOOLCRAFT: Creighton Marsh, Shingleton State Forest Management Unit

Northern wet meadow along Cannon Creek, Kalkaska County

S3 SOUTHERN WET MEADOW

Southern wet meadow is a groundwater-influenced, sedge-dominated wetland that occurs in the central and southern Lower Peninsula. Southern wet meadow occurs along lakes and streams and occupies abandoned glacial lakebeds. Natural processes that influence species composition and community structure include seasonal flooding, flooding

by beaver, and fire. The community typically develops on circumneutral sapric peat. Sedges in the genus *Carex*, in particular tussock sedge (*C. stricta*) and lake sedge (*C. lacustris*), dominate

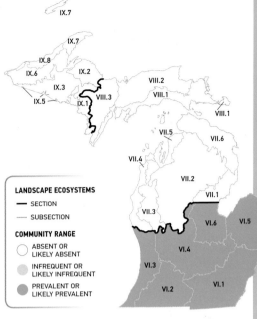

LANDSCAPE ECOSYSTEMS
— SECTION
---- SUBSECTION

COMMUNITY RANGE
○ ABSENT OR LIKELY ABSENT
◔ INFREQUENT OR LIKELY INFREQUENT
● PREVALENT OR LIKELY PREVALENT

the community. Common associates include blue-joint (*Calamagrostis canadensis*), marsh bellflower (*Campanula aparinoides*), common boneset (*Eupatorium perfoliatum*), joe-pye-weed (*Eutrochium maculatum*), northern bugle weed (*Lycopus uniflorus*), goldenrods (*Solidago* spp.), and asters (*Symphyotrichum* spp.).

BRADFORD S. SLAUGHTER

CHARACTERISTIC PLANTS

GRAMINOIDS

- fringed brome (*Bromus ciliatus*)
- blue-joint (*Calamagrostis canadensis*)
- sedges (*Carex aquatilis, C. bebbii, C. comosa, C. hystericina, C. lacustris, C. lasiocarpa, C. pellita, C. prairea, C. sartwellii, C. stipata, C. stricta, C. utriculata, C. vulpinoidea*, and others)
- bald spike-rush (*Eleocharis erythropoda*)
- marsh wild-timothy (*Muhlenbergia glomerata*)
- leafy satin grass (*Muhlenbergia mexicana*)
- fowl meadow grass (*Poa palustris*)

33

JOSHUA G. COHEN

Swamp milkweed (*Asclepias incarnata*) is a
prevalent species of southern wet meadow

FORBS

- swamp agrimony (*Agrimonia parviflora*)
- Canada anemone (*Anemone canadensis*)
- thimbleweed (*Anemone virginiana*)
- angelica (*Angelica atropurpurea*)
- swamp milkweed (*Asclepias incarnata*)
- hedge bindweed (*Calystegia sepium*)
- marsh bellflower (*Campanula aparinoides*)
- water hemlock (*Cicuta bulbifera*)
- swamp thistle (*Cirsium muticum*)
- flat-topped white aster (*Doellingeria umbellata*)
- common boneset (*Eupatorium perfoliatum*)
- joe-pye-weed (*Eutrochium maculatum*)

- rough bedstraw (*Galium asprellum*)
- bog bedstraw (*Galium labradoricum*)
- small bedstraw (*Galium trifidum*)
- jewelweed (*Impatiens capensis*)
- wild blue flag (*Iris versicolor*)
- marsh pea (*Lathyrus palustris*)
- Michigan lily (*Lilium michiganense*)
- great blue lobelia (*Lobelia siphilitica*)
- northern bugle weed (*Lycopus uniflorus*)
- tufted loosestrife (*Lysimachia thyrsiflora*)
- water smartweed (*Persicaria amphibia*)
- clearweed (*Pilea pumila*)
- common mountain mint (*Pycnanthemum virginianum*)
- great water dock (*Rumex orbiculatus*)
- common arrowhead (*Sagittaria latifolia*)
- common skullcap (*Scutellaria galericulata*)
- Canada goldenrod (*Solidago canadensis*)
- late goldenrod (*Solidago gigantea*)
- swamp goldenrod (*Solidago patula*)
- rough goldenrod (*Solidago rugosa*)
- smooth swamp aster (*Symphyotrichum firmum*)
- panicled aster (*Symphyotrichum lanceolatum*)
- side-flowering aster (*Symphyotrichum lateriflorum*)
- swamp aster (*Symphyotrichum puniceum*)
- purple meadow-rue (*Thalictrum dasycarpum*)
- marsh St. John's-wort (*Triadenum fraseri*)
- broad-leaved cat-tail (*Typha latifolia*)
- blue vervain (*Verbena hastata*)
- Missouri ironweed (*Vernonia missurica*)

FERNS

- sensitive fern (*Onoclea sensibilis*)
- marsh fern (*Thelypteris palustris*)

SHRUBS

- silky dogwood (*Cornus amomum*)
- gray dogwood (*Cornus foemina*)

- red-osier dogwood (*Cornus sericea*)
- ninebark (*Physocarpus opulifolius*)
- swamp gooseberry (*Ribes hirtellum*)
- swamp rose (*Rosa palustris*)
- willows (*Salix* spp.)
- meadowsweet (*Spiraea alba*)
- poison sumac (*Toxicodendron vernix*)
- nannyberry (*Viburnum lentago*)

TREES
- red maple (*Acer rubrum*)
- black ash (*Fraxinus nigra*)
- green ash (*Fraxinus pennsylvanica*)
- tamarack (*Larix laricina*)
- American elm (*Ulmus americana*)

PLACES TO VISIT

- BARRY: Havens Road Meadow and Bassett Lake Meadow, Barry State Game Area
- JACKSON: Riethmiller Road Wet Meadow, Waterloo State Recreation Area
- OAKLAND: Graham Lakes, Bald Mountain State Recreation Area
- OAKLAND: Indian Springs Wet Meadow, Indian Springs Metropark
- OAKLAND: Moss Lake, Proud Lake State Recreation Area
- ST. JOSEPH: Mill Creek Wet Meadow, Three Rivers State Game Area

Southern wet meadow, Barry State Game Area, Barry County

S2 INTERDUNAL WETLAND

Interdunal wetland is a rush-, sedge-, and shrub-dominated wetland situated in depressions within open dunes or between beach ridges along the shorelines of the Great Lakes. The community occurs on circumneutral to moderately alkaline sands that are occasionally covered by a thin layer of

muck or marl. Water levels fluctuate both seasonally and from year to year in synchrony with changes in Great Lakes water levels and strongly influence

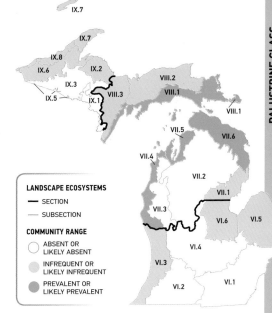

LANDSCAPE ECOSYSTEMS
— SECTION
— SUBSECTION

COMMUNITY RANGE
○ ABSENT OR LIKELY ABSENT
◐ INFREQUENT OR LIKELY INFREQUENT
● PREVALENT OR LIKELY PREVALENT

species composition and community structure. Additional natural processes that impact interdunal wetland include desiccation, especially during the late growing season, and burial by shifting sands. Dominant plants are Baltic rush (*Juncus balticus*), twig-rush (*Cladium mariscoides*), and horned bladderwort (*Utricularia cornuta*), and characteristic shrubs include shrubby cinquefoil (*Dasiphora fruticosa*) and Kalm's St. John's-wort (*Hypericum kalmianum*).

CHARACTERISTIC PLANTS

GRAMINOIDS

- ticklegrass (*Agrostis hyemalis*)
- blue-joint (*Calamagrostis canadensis*)
- sedges (*Carex aquatilis, C. garberi, C. lasiocarpa, C. stricta, C. viridula,* and others)
- twig-rush (*Cladium mariscoides*)
- tufted hair grass (*Deschampsia cespitosa*)
- Lindheimer panic grass (*Dichanthelium lindheimeri*)
- golden-seeded spike-rush (*Eleocharis elliptica*)

JOSHUA G. COHEN

37

Interdunal wetlands are often dominated by twig-rush (*Cladium mariscoides*) with scattered jack pine (*Pinus banksiana*) occurring along the margins

- spike-rush (*Eleocharis quinqueflora*)
- Baltic rush (*Juncus balticus*)
- beak-rush (*Rhynchospora capillacea*)
- hardstem bulrush (*Schoenoplectus acutus*)
- threesquare (*Schoenoplectus pungens*)
- false asphodel (*Triantha glutinosa*)
- common bog arrow-grass (*Triglochin maritima*)
- slender bog arrow-grass (*Triglochin palustris*)

FORBS
- purple false foxglove (*Agalinis purpurea*)
- marsh bellflower (*Campanula aparinoides*)
- Indian paintbrush (*Castilleja coccinea*)

- limestone calamint (*Clinopodium arkansanum*)
- marsh cinquefoil (*Comarum palustre*)
- common boneset (*Eupatorium perfoliatum*)
- grass-leaved goldenrod (*Euthamia graminifolia*)
- small fringed gentian (*Gentianopsis virgata*)
- geocaulon (*Geocaulon lividum*)
- Kalm's lobelia (*Lobelia kalmii*)
- swamp candles (*Lysimachia terrestris*)
- balsam ragwort (*Packera paupercula*)
- grass-of-Parnassus (*Parnassia glauca*)
- silverweed (*Potentilla anserina*)
- bird's-eye primrose (*Primula mistassinica*)
- Houghton's goldenrod (*Solidago houghtonii*)*

- Ohio goldenrod (*Solidago ohioensis*)
- horned bladderwort (*Utricularia cornuta*)

FERN ALLIES
- smooth scouring rush (*Equisetum laevigatum*)
- variegated scouring rush (*Equisetum variegatum*)

SHRUBS
- shrubby cinquefoil (*Dasiphora fruticosa*)
- Kalm's St. John's-wort (*Hypericum kalmianum*)
- sweet gale (*Myrica gale*)
- sand dune willow (*Salix cordata*)
- blue-leaf willow (*Salix myricoides*)

TREES
- tamarack (*Larix laricina*)
- jack pine (*Pinus banksiana*)
- northern white-cedar (*Thuja occidentalis*)

PLACES TO VISIT
- BERRIEN: Warren Dunes, Warren Dunes State Park
- EMMET: Sturgeon Bay, Wilderness State Park
- MACKINAC: Big Knob Campground, Sault Sainte Marie State Forest Management Unit
- MASON: Nordhouse Dunes, Ludington State Park and Manistee National Forest
- MUSKEGON: Muskegon Dunes, Muskegon State Park

Interdunal wetland, Ludington Dunes State Park, Mason County

WET PRAIRIE GROUP

Wet Prairies, diverse open wetlands that are dominated by grasses, sedges, and forbs, are infrequently occurring natural communities found primarily in southern Lower Michigan. Wet Prairies occur on outwash plains, outwash channels near moraines, and lakeplains on saturated to seasonally inundated mineral soils with variable organic content. Natural processes that influence species composition and community structure of Wet Prairies can include fire, fluctuating water levels, and flooding by beaver.

Five natural community types fall within the Wet Prairie group, including wet prairie, wet-mesic prairie, wet-mesic sand prairie, lakeplain wet prairie, and lakeplain wet-mesic prairie. Classification of these Wet Prairie types is based on species composition; differences (often subtle) in soil chemistry, moisture, and composition; hydrology; geographic distribution; and landscape setting.

Lakeplain wet prairie, Bay City State Recreation Area, Bay County

JOSHUA G. COHEN

S1 WET PRAIRIE

Wet prairie is a native lowland grassland occurring on level, saturated and/or seasonally inundated stream and river floodplains, lake margins, and isolated depressions in the southern Lower Peninsula. The community is typically found on outwash plains and outwash channels near moraines, and usually occurs on circumneutral loams or silt loams with high organic content. Natural processes that influence species composition and community structure include fluctuating water levels, flooding by beaver, and fire. Dominant plant species include blue-joint (*Calamagrostis canadensis*) and cordgrass (*Spartina pectinata*), with sedges (*Carex* spp.)

often important subdominants. Today, wet prairie is nearly extirpated from Michigan due to changes in land use and colonization by shrubs and trees.

CHARACTERISTIC PLANTS

GRAMINOIDS
- big bluestem (*Andropogon gerardii*)
- fringed brome (*Bromus ciliatus*)
- blue-joint (*Calamagrostis canadensis*)
- sedges (*Carex buxbaumii*, *C. pellita*, *C. stricta*, and others)
- fowl manna grass (*Glyceria striata*)
- leafy satin grass (*Muhlenbergia mexicana*)
- Indian grass (*Sorghastrum nutans*)
- cordgrass (*Spartina pectinata*)

FORBS

- swamp agrimony (*Agrimonia parviflora*)
- hog-peanut (*Amphicarpaea bracteata*)
- angelica (*Angelica atropurpurea*)
- groundnut (*Apios americana*)
- marsh-marigold (*Caltha palustris*)
- hedge bindweed (*Calystegia sepium*)
- marsh bellflower (*Campanula aparinoides*)
- common boneset (*Eupatorium perfoliatum*)
- joe-pye-weed (*Eutrochium maculatum*)
- tall sunflower (*Helianthus giganteus*)
- star-grass (*Hypoxis hirsuta*)
- marsh pea (*Lathyrus palustris*)
- Michigan lily (*Lilium michiganense*)
- fringed loosestrife (*Lysimachia ciliata*)
- starry false Solomon-seal (*Maianthemum stellatum*)
- swamp saxifrage (*Micranthes pensylvanica*)
- cowbane (*Oxypolis rigidior*)
- swamp-betony (*Pedicularis lanceolata*)
- common mountain mint (*Pycnanthemum virginianum*)
- black-eyed Susan (*Rudbeckia hirta*)
- tall goldenrod (*Solidago altissima*)
- Canada goldenrod (*Solidago canadensis*)
- late goldenrod (*Solidago gigantea*)
- Riddell's goldenrod (*Solidago riddellii*)
- New England aster (*Symphyotrichum novae-angliae*)
- purple meadow-rue (*Thalictrum dasycarpum*)
- broad-leaved cat-tail (*Typha latifolia*)
- golden alexanders (*Zizia aurea*)

FERNS

- sensitive fern (*Onoclea sensibilis*)
- marsh fern (*Thelypteris palustris*)

SHRUBS

- dogwoods (*Cornus* spp.)
- shrubby cinquefoil (*Dasiphora fruticosa*)
- ninebark (*Physocarpus opulifolius*)

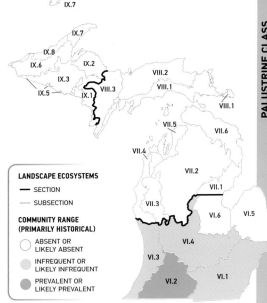

LANDSCAPE ECOSYSTEMS

— SECTION
--- SUBSECTION

COMMUNITY RANGE
(PRIMARILY HISTORICAL)

○ ABSENT OR LIKELY ABSENT
◐ INFREQUENT OR LIKELY INFREQUENT
● PREVALENT OR LIKELY PREVALENT

- willows (*Salix* spp.)
- meadowsweet (*Spiraea alba*)

PLACES TO VISIT

- BARRY: Turner Creek Wet Prairie, Barry State Game Area
- JACKSON: Waterloo Wet Prairie, Waterloo State Recreation Area

MICHAEL A. KOST

Wet prairie associated with Turner Creek, Barry State Game Area, Barry County

S1 WET-MESIC PRAIRIE

Wet-mesic prairie is a native lowland grassland occurring on moist, occasionally inundated stream and river floodplains, lake margins, and isolated depressions in the southern Lower Peninsula. The community is typically found on glacial outwash plains and outwash channels near moraines. Wet-mesic prairie occurs primarily on circumneutral loams or silt loams with variable organic content, but soils can also include sand, sandy clay loam, sandy loam, and shallow muck overlying mineral soil. Natural processes that influence species composition and community structure include fluctuating water levels, fire, and flooding by beaver. Dominant or subdominant plant species include big bluestem (*Andropogon gerardii*), Indian grass (*Sorghastrum nutans*), blue-joint (*Calamagrostis canadensis*), cordgrass (*Spartina pectinata*), and sedges (*Carex* spp.). Today, wet-mesic prairie is nearly extirpated from Michigan due to changes in land use and colonization by shrubs and trees.

CHARACTERISTIC PLANTS

GRAMINOIDS
- big bluestem (*Andropogon gerardii*)
- fringed brome (*Bromus ciliatus*)
- blue-joint (*Calamagrostis canadensis*)
- sedges (*Carex bebbii*, *C. buxbaumii*, *C. pellita*, *C. stricta*, and others)
- golden-seeded spike-rush (*Eleocharis elliptica*)
- little bluestem (*Schizachyrium scoparium*)
- Indian grass (*Sorghastrum nutans*)
- cordgrass (*Spartina pectinata*)

FORBS

- purple false foxglove (*Agalinis purpurea*)
- swamp agrimony (*Agrimonia parviflora*)
- thimbleweed (*Anemone virginiana*)
- white camas (*Anticlea elegans*)
- hedge bindweed (*Calystegia sepium*)
- swamp thistle (*Cirsium muticum*)
- rattlesnake-master (*Eryngium yuccifolium*)*
- grass-leaved goldenrod (*Euthamia graminifolia*)
- wild strawberry (*Fragaria virginiana*)
- northern bedstraw (*Galium boreale*)
- bottle gentian (*Gentiana andrewsii*)
- fringed gentian (*Gentianopsis crinita*)
- marsh blazing-star (*Liatris spicata*)
- Kalm's lobelia (*Lobelia kalmii*)
- wild bergamot (*Monarda fistulosa*)
- grass-of-Parnassus (*Parnassia glauca*)
- common mountain mint (*Pycnanthemum virginianum*)
- yellow coneflower (*Ratibida pinnata*)
- black-eyed Susan (*Rudbeckia hirta*)
- prairie dock (*Silphium terebinthinaceum*)
- goldenrods (*Solidago gigantea, S. ohioensis, S. riddellii*, and others)
- smooth aster (*Symphyotrichum laeve*)
- New England aster (*Symphyotrichum novae-angliae*)
- purple meadow-rue (*Thalictrum dasycarpum*)
- Culver's root (*Veronicastrum virginicum*)
- golden alexanders (*Zizia aurea*)

FERN ALLIES

- common horsetail (*Equisetum arvense*)

SHRUBS

- dogwoods (*Cornus* spp.)
- shrubby cinquefoil (*Dasiphora fruticosa*)
- common juniper (*Juniperus communis*)
- ninebark (*Physocarpus opulifolius*)
- willows (*Salix* spp.)

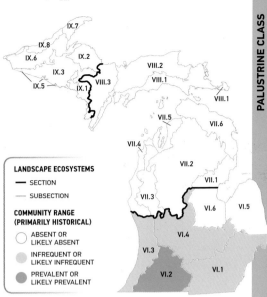

LANDSCAPE ECOSYSTEMS
— SECTION
-- SUBSECTION

COMMUNITY RANGE (PRIMARILY HISTORICAL)
- ○ ABSENT OR LIKELY ABSENT
- INFREQUENT OR LIKELY INFREQUENT
- PREVALENT OR LIKELY PREVALENT

PLACES TO VISIT

- LIVINGSTON: Williamsville Lake Prairie, Unadilla Wildlife Area
- OAKLAND: Indian Springs Wet-mesic Prairie, Indian Springs Metropark
- WASHTENAW: Hudson Mills Wet-mesic Prairie, Hudson Mills Metropark
- WASHTENAW: Pinckney Prairie, Pinckney State Recreation Area

JOSHUA G. COHEN

Wet-mesic prairie, Pinckney State Recreation Area, Washtenaw County

45

S2 WET-MESIC SAND PRAIRIE

Wet-mesic sand prairie is a native lowland grassland that is found within abandoned lakebeds, stream channels, and shallow depressions on sandy outwash plains and lakeplains in both southern and northern Lower Michigan. The community occurs on loamy sands or fine sands, usually with

high organic content, and sometimes covered by a thin layer of muck. Wet-mesic sand prairie is characterized by a seasonally and interannually

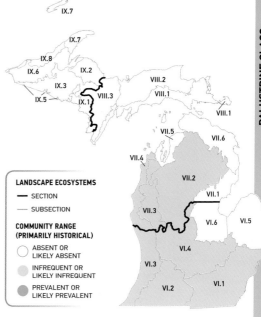

LANDSCAPE ECOSYSTEMS

— SECTION

— SUBSECTION

COMMUNITY RANGE (PRIMARILY HISTORICAL)

○ ABSENT OR LIKELY ABSENT

◐ INFREQUENT OR LIKELY INFREQUENT

● PREVALENT OR LIKELY PREVALENT

BRADFORD S. SLAUGHTER

fluctuating water table that allows both wetland and upland plants to occur. Natural processes that influence species composition and community structure include fluctuating water levels, flooding by beaver, and fire. The community is dominated by grasses and sedges including big bluestem (*Andropogon gerardii*), blue-joint (*Calamagrostis canadensis*), tussock sedge (*Carex stricta*), little bluestem (*Schizachyrium scoparium*), cordgrass (*Spartina pectinata*), switch grass (*Panicum virgatum*), and Indian grass (*Sorghastrum nutans*).

CHARACTERISTIC PLANTS

GRAMINOIDS

- ticklegrasses (*Agrostis hyemalis* and *A. scabra*)
- big bluestem (*Andropogon gerardii*)
- blue-joint (*Calamagrostis canadensis*)
- sedges (*Carex buxbaumii*, *C. flava*, *C. leptalea*, *C. pellita*, *C. pensylvanica*, *C. stricta*, and others)

47

- panic grasses (*Dichanthelium* spp.)
- golden-seeded spike-rush (*Eleocharis elliptica*)
- fowl manna grass (*Glyceria striata*)
- blue flags (*Iris versicolor* and *I. virginica*)
- rushes (*Juncus balticus, J. brachycarpus,* *J. effusus, J. greenei, J. scirpoides,* *J. vaseyi,* and others)
- switch grass (*Panicum virgatum*)
- brownish beak-rush (*Rhynchospora capitellata*)
- little bluestem (*Schizachyrium scoparium*)
- wool-grass (*Scirpus cyperinus*)
- tall nut-rush (*Scleria triglomerata*)*
- Indian grass (*Sorghastrum nutans*)
- cordgrass (*Spartina pectinata*)
- prairie dropseed (*Sporobolus heterolepis*)*

FORBS

- colic root (*Aletris farinosa*)
- white camas (*Anticlea elegans*)
- tall green milkweed (*Asclepias hirtella*)*
- harebell (*Campanula rotundifolia*)
- swamp thistle (*Cirsium muticum*)
- bastard-toadflax (*Comandra umbellata*)
- tall coreopsis (*Coreopsis tripteris*)
- slender goldentop (*Euthamia caroliniana*)
- grass-leaved goldenrod (*Euthamia graminifolia*)
- wild strawberry (*Fragaria virginiana*)

Wet-mesic sand prairie, Muskegon State Game Area, Newaygo County

- marsh blazing-star (*Liatris spicata*)
- cardinal flower (*Lobelia cardinalis*)
- pale spiked lobelia (*Lobelia spicata*)
- common water horehound (*Lycopus americanus*)
- lance-leaved loosestrife (*Lysimachia lanceolata*)
- wild bergamot (*Monarda fistulosa*)
- small sundrops (*Oenothera perennis*)
- balsam ragwort (*Packera paupercula*)
- water smartweed (*Persicaria amphibia*)
- common mountain mint (*Pycnanthemum virginianum*)
- common skullcap (*Scutellaria galericulata*)
- common blue-eyed-grass (*Sisyrinchium albidum*)
- goldenrods (*Solidago gigantea, S. ohioensis, S. riddellii, S. rugosa*, and others)
- hyssop hedge nettle (*Stachys hyssopifolia*)
- bushy aster (*Symphyotrichum dumosum*)
- long-leaved aster (*Symphyotrichum robynsianum*)
- purple meadow-rue (*Thalictrum dasycarpum*)
- marsh St. John's-wort (*Triadenum fraseri*)
- Culver's root (*Veronicastrum virginicum*)
- lance-leaved violet (*Viola lanceolata*)
- arrow-leaved violet (*Viola sagittata*)

FERNS
- marsh fern (*Thelypteris palustris*)

SHRUBS
- tag alder (*Alnus incana*)
- black chokeberry (*Aronia prunifolia*)
- leatherleaf (*Chamaedaphne calyculata*)
- dogwoods (*Cornus* spp.)
- shrubby cinquefoil (*Dasiphora fruticosa*)
- Kalm's St. John's-wort (*Hypericum kalmianum*)
- shrubby St. John's-wort (*Hypericum prolificum*)
- pasture rose (*Rosa carolina*)
- dewberries (*Rubus* spp.)
- willows (*Salix* spp.)
- meadowsweet (*Spiraea alba*)
- steeplebush (*Spiraea tomentosa*)

PLACES TO VISIT

- CRAWFORD & KALKASKA: Portage Creek Complex, Grayling State Forest Management Unit, and Traverse City State Forest Management Unit
- LAKE: Tussing Prairie, Manistee National Forest
- NEWAYGO: Muskegon Wet-mesic Sand Prairie, Muskegon State Game Area
- OCEANA: Lidkey Swamp Prairie, Manistee National Forest

S1 LAKEPLAIN WET PRAIRIE

Lakeplain wet prairie is a native lowland grassland that occurs on level, seasonally inundated glacial lakeplains in the southern Lower Peninsula. Lakeplain wet prairie is found along and near the shoreline of Lake Huron in Saginaw Bay, within the St. Clair River Delta, and near Lake Erie. The community develops on slightly acidic to moderately alkaline sands, sandy loams, or silty clays. Natural processes that influence species composition and community structure include seasonal flooding, cyclic changes in Great Lakes water levels, flooding by beaver, and fire. Lakeplain wet prairie is dominated by grasses, sedges, rushes, and a diversity of forbs. Dominant grasses, sedges, and rushes typically include blue-joint (*Calamagrostis canadensis*), cordgrass (*Spartina pectinata*), sedges (*Carex aquatilis, C. pellita, C. stricta, C. prairea, C. buxbaumii,* and *C. tetanica*), Baltic rush (*Juncus balticus*), twig-rush (*Cladium mariscoides*), and switch grass (*Panicum virgatum*). Today, lakeplain wet prairie is nearly extirpated from Michigan due to changes in land use, colonization by shrubs and trees, and competition from invasive plants.

CHARACTERISTIC PLANTS

GRAMINOIDS
- big bluestem (*Andropogon gerardii*)
- blue-joint (*Calamagrostis canadensis*)
- sedges (*Carex aquatilis, C. aurea, C. buxbaumii, C. diandra, C. pellita, C. prairea, C. stricta,* and others)
- twig-rush (*Cladium mariscoides*)
- fowl manna grass (*Glyceria striata*)

- rushes (*Juncus balticus, J. canadensis, J. dudleyi, J. tenuis, J. torreyi*, and others)
- switch grass (*Panicum virgatum*)
- common reed (*Phragmites australis* subsp. *americanus*)
- threesquare (*Schoenoplectus pungens*)
- Indian grass (*Sorghastrum nutans*)
- cordgrass (*Spartina pectinata*)

FORBS

- purple false foxglove (*Agalinis purpurea*)
- swamp agrimony (*Agrimonia parviflora*)
- Canada anemone (*Anemone canadensis*)
- swamp milkweed (*Asclepias incarnata*)
- hedge bindweed (*Calystegia sepium*)
- water hemlock (*Cicuta bulbifera*)
- swamp thistle (*Cirsium muticum*)
- common boneset (*Eupatorium perfoliatum*)
- grass-leaved goldenrod (*Euthamia graminifolia*)
- joe-pye-weed (*Eutrochium maculatum*)
- sneezeweed (*Helenium autumnale*)
- southern blue flag (*Iris virginica*)
- marsh blazing-star (*Liatris spicata*)
- pale spiked lobelia (*Lobelia spicata*)
- whorled loosestrife (*Lysimachia quadriflora*)
- winged loosestrife (*Lythrum alatum*)
- common mountain mint (*Pycnanthemum virginianum*)
- common skullcap (*Scutellaria galericulata*)
- goldenrods (*Solidago gigantea, S. ohioensis, S. riddellii*, and others)
- nodding ladies'-tresses (*Spiranthes cernua*)
- asters (*Symphyotrichum lanceolatum* and others)
- purple meadow-rue (*Thalictrum dasycarpum*)
- Culver's root (*Veronicastrum virginicum*)
- golden alexanders (*Zizia aurea*)

SHRUBS

- dogwoods (*Cornus* spp.)
- shrubby cinquefoil (*Dasiphora fruticosa*)

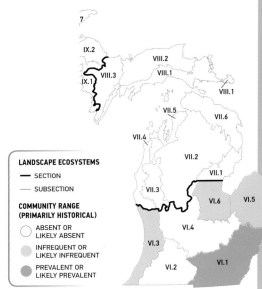

LANDSCAPE ECOSYSTEMS
— SECTION
— SUBSECTION

COMMUNITY RANGE
(PRIMARILY HISTORICAL)
○ ABSENT OR LIKELY ABSENT
◐ INFREQUENT OR LIKELY INFREQUENT
● PREVALENT OR LIKELY PREVALENT

- Kalm's St. John's-wort (*Hypericum kalmianum*)
- willows (*Salix* spp.)

PLACES TO VISIT

- BAY: Killarney Beach, Bay City State Recreation Area
- TUSCOLA: Sebewaing Bay, Fish Point State Game Area

JOSHUA G. COHEN

Cordgrass (*Spartina pectinata*) is often a dominant component of lakeplain wet prairies

51

S1 LAKEPLAIN WET-MESIC PRAIRIE

Lakeplain wet-mesic prairie is a native lowland grassland that occurs on moist, level, seasonally inundated glacial lakeplains in the southern Lower Peninsula. The community develops on slightly acidic to moderately alkaline sands, sandy loams, or silty clays. Natural processes that influence species composition and community structure include seasonal flooding, cyclic changes in Great Lakes water levels, flooding by beaver, and fire. Prairie grasses, sedges,

and a diversity of forbs dominate the community. Dominant species typically include big bluestem (*Andropogon gerardii*), cordgrass (*Spartina pectinata*), switch grass (*Panicum virgatum*), little bluestem (*Schizachyrium*

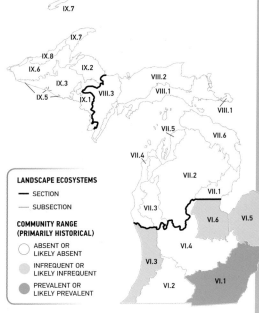

LANDSCAPE ECOSYSTEMS
— SECTION
-- SUBSECTION

**COMMUNITY RANGE
(PRIMARILY HISTORICAL)**
○ ABSENT OR LIKELY ABSENT
◐ INFREQUENT OR LIKELY INFREQUENT
● PREVALENT OR LIKELY PREVALENT

scoparium), Indian grass (*Sorghastrum nutans*), common mountain mint (*Pycnanthemum virginianum*), tall coreopsis (*Coreopsis tripteris*), and marsh blazing star (*Liatris spicata*). Today, lakeplain wet-mesic prairie is nearly extirpated from Michigan due to changes in land use, colonization by shrubs and trees, and competition from invasive plants.

CHARACTERISTIC PLANTS

GRAMINOIDS
- big bluestem (*Andropogon gerardii*)
- blue-joint (*Calamagrostis canadensis*)
- sedges (*Carex aurea, C. buxbaumii, C. crawei, C. prairea, C. stricta, C. tetanica,* and others)
- twig-rush (*Cladium mariscoides*)
- western panic grass (*Dichanthelium implicatum*)
- slender wheat grass (*Elymus trachycaulus*)
- rushes (*Juncus brachycephalus, Juncus greenei, Juncus torreyi,* and others)
- switch grass (*Panicum virgatum*)

ROBERT E. CLANCY

53

Big bluestem (*Andropogon gerardii*) is a common dominant of lakeplain wet-mesic prairie and other prairie types

- common reed (*Phragmites australis* subsp. *americanus*)
- little bluestem (*Schizachyrium scoparium*)
- bulrush (*Scirpus pendulus*)
- nut-rush (*Scleria verticillata*)
- Indian grass (*Sorghastrum nutans*)
- cordgrass (*Spartina pectinata*)

FORBS
- purple false foxglove (*Agalinis purpurea*)
- common false foxglove (*Agalinis tenuifolia*)
- swamp agrimony (*Agrimonia parviflora*)
- colic root (*Aletris farinosa*)
- Canada anemone (*Anemone canadensis*)
- tuberous Indian plantain (*Arnoglossum plantagineum*)*
- tall green milkweed (*Asclepias hirtella*)*

- swamp milkweed (*Asclepias incarnata*)
- purple milkweed (*Asclepias purpurascens*)*
- Sullivant's milkweed (*Asclepias sullivantii*)*
- butterfly-weed (*Asclepias tuberosa*)
- hedge bindweed (*Calystegia sepium*)
- tall coreopsis (*Coreopsis tripteris*)
- white lady-slipper (*Cypripedium candidum*)*
- bottle gentian (*Gentiana andrewsii*)
- small fringed gentian (*Gentianopsis virgata*)
- sneezeweed (*Helenium autumnale*)
- tall sunflower (*Helianthus giganteus*)
- marsh blazing-star (*Liatris spicata*)
- Michigan lily (*Lilium michiganense*)
- small yellow flax (*Linum medium*)
- pale spiked lobelia (*Lobelia spicata*)
- whorled loosestrife (*Lysimachia quadriflora*)
- winged loosestrife (*Lythrum alatum*)

- balsam ragwort (*Packera paupercula*)
- swamp-betony (*Pedicularis lanceolata*)
- foxglove beard-tongue (*Penstemon digitalis*)
- prairie fringed orchid (*Platanthera leucophaea*)*
- silverweed (*Potentilla anserina*)
- common mountain mint (*Pycnanthemum virginianum*)
- blue-eyed grass (*Sisyrinchium* spp.)
- goldenrods (*Solidago gigantea*, *S. ohioensis*, and *S. riddellii*)
- nodding ladies'-tresses (*Spiranthes cernua* and *S. magnicamporum*)
- asters (*Symphyotrichum ericoides*, *S. lanceolatum*, and *S. novae-angliae*)
- wingstem (*Verbesina alternifolia*)
- Missouri ironweed (*Vernonia missurica*)
- Culver's root (*Veronicastrum virginicum*)
- golden alexanders (*Zizia aurea*)

SHRUBS
- dogwoods (*Cornus* spp.)
- shrubby cinquefoil (*Dasiphora fruticosa*)
- Kalm's St. John's-wort (*Hypericum kalmianum*)
- prairie rose (*Rosa setigera*)
- dewberries and raspberries (*Rubus* spp.)
- willows (*Salix* spp.)
- meadowsweet (*Spiraea alba*)

PLACES TO VISIT
- BERRIEN: Grand Mere, Grand Mere State Park
- ST. CLAIR: Algonac, Algonac State Park
- ST. CLAIR: Harsen's Island, St. Clair Flats State Wildlife Area
- TUSCOLA: Sebewaing Bay, Fish Point State Game Area
- TUSCOLA: Thomas Prairie, Fish Point State Game Area

Purple milkweed (*Asclepias purpurascens*) is a characteristic species of lakeplain wet-mesic prairie

FEN GROUP

Fens are diverse open minerotrophic peatlands that are dominated by graminoids, forbs, shrubs, and stunted conifers and are found throughout Michigan. Fens occur primarily on glacial outwash plains, outwash channels, lakeplains, and kettle depressions in outwash plains and moraines. The saturated soils typically range from slightly acidic to alkaline peats and can also include alkaline marl. Fens are peat-accumulating wetlands that receive water that has been in contact with mineral soils or bedrock. Natural processes that influence species composition and community structure of Fens are groundwater seepage, fluctuating water levels, lateral flow, peat accumulation and erosion, fire, insect outbreaks, windthrow, and flooding by beaver.

Five natural community types fall within the Fen group, including poor fen, patterned fen, northern fen, prairie fen, and coastal fen. Classification of these Fen types is based on species composition, community structure, differences (often subtle) in soil chemistry and composition, hydrology, geographic distribution, and landscape setting.

Northern fen, Presque Isle County
JOSHUA G. COHEN

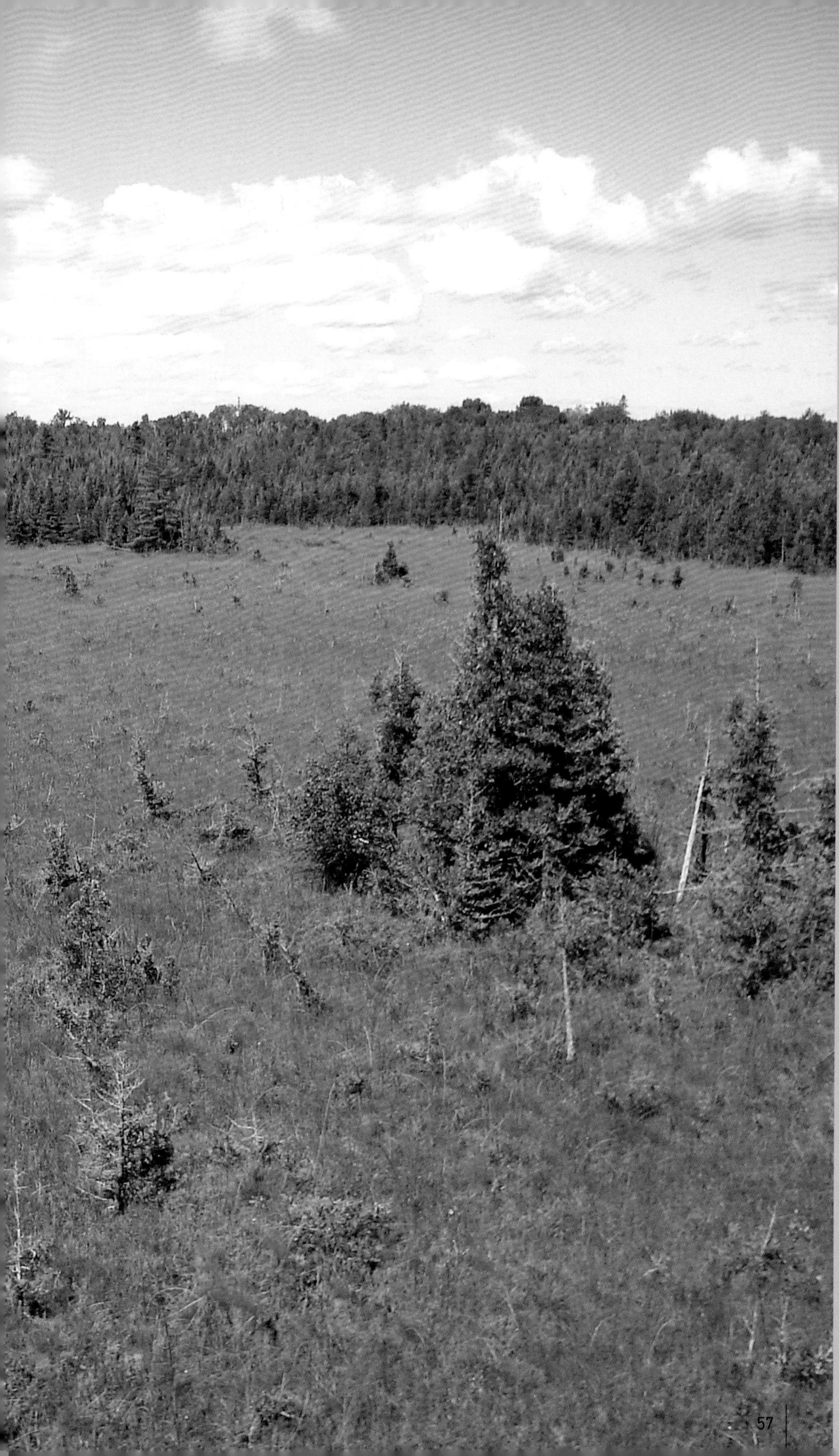

S3 POOR FEN

Poor fen is a wetland dominated by sedges, shrubs, and stunted conifers, and moderately influenced by groundwater. The community occurs within kettle depressions in outwash plains and moraines, and in mild depressions on glacial outwash plains and glacial lakeplain primarily in the Upper Peninsula and northern Lower Peninsula and rarely in the southern Lower Peninsula. Poor fen typically develops on slightly acidic to strongly acidic peat. Natural processes that influence species composition and community structure

include groundwater seepage and lateral flow, peat accumulation, flooding by beaver, insect outbreaks, and occasional fires. Dominant sedges include wiregrass sedge (*Carex lasiocarpa*) and few-seed sedge (*C. oligosperma*) with ground cover associates typically including

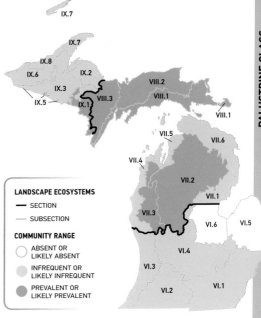

twig-rush (*Cladium mariscoides*), three-way sedge (*Dulichium arundinaceum*), cotton-grasses (*Eriophorum* spp.), white beak-rush (*Rhynchospora alba*), tufted bulrush (*Trichophorum cespitosum*), rush aster (*Symphyotrichum boreale*), bog buckbean (*Menyanthes trifoliata*), marsh cinquefoil (*Comarum palustre*), false mayflower (*Maianthemum trifolium*), round-leaved sundew (*Drosera rotundifolia*), pitcher-plant (*Sarracenia purpurea*), and bog goldenrod (*Solidago uliginosa*). In addition, many poor fens support a continuous carpet of sphagnum mosses and widely scattered, slightly raised peat ridges or mounds with low ericaceous, evergreen shrubs and stunted conifer trees. Characteristic shrubs include bog rosemary (*Andromeda glaucophylla*), leatherleaf (*Chamaedaphne calyculata*), bog laurel (*Kalmia polifolia*), Labrador-tea (*Rhododendron groenlandicum*), large cranberry (*Vaccinium macro-carpon*), small cranberry (*V. oxycoccos*), and black chokeberry (*Aronia*

JOSHUA G. COHEN

prunifolia), while black spruce (*Picea mariana*) and tamarack (*Larix laricina*) are characteristic trees.

CHARACTERISTIC PLANTS

GRAMINOIDS

- sedges (*Carex chordorrhiza, C. exilis, C. lasiocarpa, C. limosa, C. livida, C. oligosperma, C. pauciflora,* and others)
- twig-rush (*Cladium mariscoides*)
- three-way sedge (*Dulichium arundinaceum*)
- cotton-grasses (*Eriophorum angustifolium, E. vaginatum,* and *E. virginicum*)
- white beak-rush (*Rhynchospora alba*)
- tufted bulrush (*Trichophorum cespitosum*)

MICHAEL A. KOST

Few-seed sedge (*Carex oligosperma*) is a common dominant of poor fen and bog

FORBS

- marsh cinquefoil (*Comarum palustre*)
- spatulate-leaved sundew (*Drosera intermedia*)
- round-leaved sundew (*Drosera rotundifolia*)
- fringed willow-herb (*Epilobium ciliatum*)
- grass-leaved goldenrod (*Euthamia graminifolia*)
- wild blue flag (*Iris versicolor*)
- swamp candles (*Lysimachia terrestris*)
- false mayflower (*Maianthemum trifolium*)
- bog buckbean (*Menyanthes trifoliata*)
- bog aster (*Oclemena nemoralis*)
- pitcher-plant (*Sarracenia purpurea*)
- arrow-grass (*Scheuchzeria palustris*)
- bog goldenrod (*Solidago uliginosa*)
- rush aster (*Symphyotrichum boreale*)
- common bog arrow-grass (*Triglochin maritima*)
- bladderworts (*Utricularia cornuta* and *U. intermedia*)

MOSSES

- sphagnum mosses (*Sphagnum* spp.)

SHRUBS

- bog rosemary (*Andromeda glaucophylla*)
- black chokeberry (*Aronia prunifolia*)
- bog birch (*Betula pumila*)
- leatherleaf (*Chamaedaphne calyculata*)
- Kalm's St. John's-wort (*Hypericum kalmianum*)
- mountain holly (*Ilex mucronata*)
- bog laurel (*Kalmia polifolia*)
- sweet gale (*Myrica gale*)
- Labrador-tea (*Rhododendron groenlandicum*)
- bog willow (*Salix pedicellaris*)
- meadowsweet (*Spiraea alba*)
- steeplebush (*Spiraea tomentosa*)
- large cranberry (*Vaccinium macrocarpon*)
- small cranberry (*Vaccinium oxycoccos*)
- wild-raisin (*Viburnum cassinoides*)

TREES

- tamarack (*Larix laricina*)
- black spruce (*Picea mariana*)
- jack pine (*Pinus banksiana*)
- white pine (*Pinus strobus*)

PLACES TO VISIT

- BARRY: Snow Lake Fen, Barry State Game Area
- CHIPPEWA: Tahquamenon River Mouth Fen, Tahquamenon Falls State Park
- CRAWFORD: Lovell's Fen, Grayling State Forest Management Unit
- DELTA: Nahma Fen, Hiawatha National Forest
- MARQUETTE: Cyr Swamp, Escanaba State Forest Management Unit
- ROSCOMMON: Nine Mile Fen, Roscommon State Forest Management Unit
- SCHOOLCRAFT: Creighton Marsh, Shingleton State Forest Management Unit

Poor fen, Tahquamenon Falls State Park, Chippewa County

S2 PATTERNED FEN

Patterned fen[3] is a wetland characterized by a series of peat ridges (strings) and hollows (flarks) oriented parallel to the slope of the wetland and perpendicular to the flow of groundwater. Patterned fen occurs on glacial lakeplains, outwash plains, and outwash channels primarily in the eastern Upper Peninsula. Species composition and community structure are influenced by many factors, including peat accumulation and erosion, seasonal flooding, surface water and groundwater flow regimes, insect outbreaks, and occasional fires. The strings vary in height, width, and spacing, but are generally less than one meter tall and dominated by sphagnum mosses, sedges,

shrubs, and scattered, stunted trees. Characteristic species of the strings include sedges (*Carex oligosperma, C. sterilis,* and *C. lasiocarpa*), round-leaved sundew (*Drosera rotundifolia*), royal fern (*Osmunda regalis*), bog aster (*Oclemena nemoralis*), bog goldenrod (*Solidago uliginosa*), pitcher-plant (*Sarracenia purpurea*), tufted bulrush (*Trichophorum cespitosum*), bog birch (*Betula pumila*), shrubby cinquefoil (*Dasiphora fruticosa*), bog rosemary (*Andromeda glaucophylla*), leatherleaf (*Chamaedaphne calyculata*), black chokeberry (*Aronia prunifolia*), bog willow (*Salix pedicellaris*), and bog laurel (*Kalmia polifolia*). Scattered trees along the strings can include tamarack

(*Larix laricina*), black spruce (*Picea mariana*), and northern white cedar (*Thuja occidentalis*). The flarks are saturated to inundated open lawns of sedges and rushes. Prevalent species within the flarks are sedges (*Carex limosa, C. livida, C. lasiocarpa,* and *C. exilis*), spatulate-leaved sundew (*Drosera intermedia*), white beak-rush (*Rhynchospora alba*), large cranberry (*Vaccinium macrocarpon*), twig-rush (*Cladium mariscoides*), bog buckbean (*Menyanthes trifoliata*), arrow-grass (*Scheuchzeria palustris*), three-way sedge (*Dulichium arundinaceum*), and flat-leaved bladderwort (*Utricularia intermedia*).

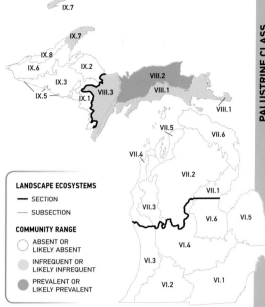

LANDSCAPE ECOSYSTEMS
— SECTION
— SUBSECTION

COMMUNITY RANGE
○ ABSENT OR LIKELY ABSENT
◐ INFREQUENT OR LIKELY INFREQUENT
● PREVALENT OR LIKELY PREVALENT

CHARACTERISTIC PLANTS

GRAMINOIDS

- blue-joint (*Calamagrostis canadensis*)
- sedges (*Carex buxbaumii, C. echinata, C. exilis, C. lasiocarpa, C. limosa, C. livida, C. oligosperma, C. sterilis,* and *C. stricta*)
- twig-rush (*Cladium mariscoides*)
- three-way sedge (*Dulichium arundinaceum*)
- golden-seeded spike-rush (*Eleocharis elliptica*)
- narrow-leaved cotton-grass (*Eriophorum angustifolium*)
- green-keeled cotton-grass (*Eriophorum viridi-carinatum*)
- Canadian rush (*Juncus canadensis*)
- common reed (*Phragmites australis* subsp. *americanus*)
- beak-rushes (*Rhynchospora alba* and *R. fusca*)
- submergent bulrush (*Schoenoplectus subterminalis*)
- alpine bulrush (*Trichophorum alpinum*)
- tufted bulrush (*Trichophorum cespitosum*)

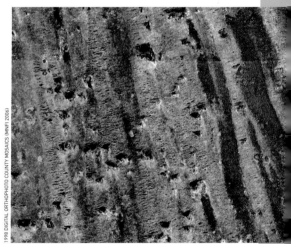

1998 DIGITAL ORTHOPHOTO COUNTY MOSAICS (MNFI 2006)

An aerial photograph of a patterned fen exhibiting several water tracks separated by bands of shrubs and trees; the elongated, dark features in the water tracks are the flarks

FORBS

- wood anemone (*Anemone quinquefolia*)
- dragon's mouth (*Arethusa bulbosa*)
- marsh cinquefoil (*Comarum palustre*)
- flat-topped white aster (*Doellingeria umbellata*)
- round-leaved sundew (*Drosera rotundifolia*)
- false mayflower (*Maianthemum trifolium*)
- bog buckbean (*Menyanthes trifoliata*)

63

- bog aster (*Oclemena nemoralis*)
- rose pogonia (*Pogonia ophioglossoides*)
- glaucous white lettuce (*Prenanthes racemosa*)
- round-leaved pyrola (*Pyrola americana*)
- pitcher-plant (*Sarracenia purpurea*)
- arrow-grass (*Scheuchzeria palustris*)
- bog goldenrod (*Solidago uliginosa*)
- rush aster (*Symphyotrichum boreale*)
- purple meadow-rue (*Thalictrum dasycarpum*)
- St. John's-wort (*Triadenum fraseri*)
- common bog arrow-grass (*Triglochin maritima*)
- bladderworts (*Utricularia cornuta, U. intermedia,* and *U. vulgaris*)

FERNS
- sensitive fern (*Onoclea sensibilis*)
- royal fern (*Osmunda regalis*)
- marsh fern (*Thelypteris palustris*)

FERN ALLIES
- water horsetail (*Equisetum fluviatile*)

MOSSES
- ribbed bog moss (*Aulacomnium palustre*)
- calliergon moss (*Calliergon trifarium*)
- campylium mosses (*Campylium* spp.)
- fork mosses (*Dicranum* spp.)
- haircap mosses (*Polytrichum* spp.)
- scorpidium moss (*Scorpidium scorpioides*)
- sphagnum mosses (*Sphagnum* spp.)

SHRUBS
- tag alder (*Alnus incana*)
- bog rosemary (*Andromeda glaucophylla*)
- black chokeberry (*Aronia prunifolia*)
- bog birch (*Betula pumila*)
- leatherleaf (*Chamaedaphne calyculata*)
- shrubby cinquefoil (*Dasiphora fruticosa*)
- mountain holly (*Ilex mucronata*)
- bog laurel (*Kalmia polifolia*)

In Michigan, dwarf raspberry (*Rubus acaulis*) occurs in patterned fen, northern fen, and poor fen

Patterned fens are characterized by ladder-like arrangements of alternating peat ridges (strings) and pools (flarks) oriented perpendicular to the direction of water flow and the orientation of the water track

- mountain fly honeysuckle (*Lonicera villosa*)
- alder-leaved buckthorn (*Rhamnus alnifolia*)
- Labrador-tea (*Rhododendron groenlandicum*)
- dwarf raspberry (*Rubus acaulis*)*
- bog willow (*Salix pedicellaris*)
- blueberries (*Vaccinium angustifolium* and *V. myrtilloides*)
- cranberries (*Vaccinium macrocarpon* and *V. oxycoccos*)

TREES
- tamarack (*Larix laricina*)
- black spruce (*Picea mariana*)
- white pine (*Pinus strobus*)
- northern white-cedar (*Thuja occidentalis*)

PLACES TO VISIT
- CHIPPEWA: Park Patterned Peatland, Tahquamenon Falls State Park
- CHIPPEWA: Black Creek (Tokar's Patterned Fen), Newberry State Forest Management Unit
- LUCE: McMahon Lake, Newberry State Forest Management Unit and The Nature Conservancy (McMahon Lake Preserve)
- LUCE: Sleeper Lake, Newberry State Forest Management Unit and The Nature Conservancy (McMahon Lake Preserve)
- SCHOOLCRAFT: Creighton Marsh, Shingleton State Forest Management Unit
- SCHOOLCRAFT: Marsh Creek (Seney Strangmoor), Seney National Wildlife Refuge and Shingleton State Forest Management Unit

S3 NORTHERN FEN

Northern fen is a groundwater-influenced wetland community dominated by graminoids, forbs, shrubs, and stunted conifers. The community occurs on circumneutral to moderately alkaline peat and marl in the Upper and northern Lower Peninsulas. Although primarily found where calcareous bedrock underlies a thin mantle of glacial drift within glacial lakeplains, northern fen may also occur on glacial outwash plains and in kettle depressions on pitted outwash plains and moraines. Northern fen is often associated with headwater streams and cold,

calcareous, groundwater-fed springs. Natural processes that influence species composition and community structure include calcareous groundwater seepage and lateral flow, flooding by beaver, and occasional fires. Variation in the flow rate and volume of groundwater moving through the community results in distinct vegetation zones, some of which support a diversity of calciphilic plants. Dominant sedges and grasses can include wiregrass sedge (*Carex lasiocarpa*), dioecious sedge (*C. sterilis*), twig-rush (*Cladium mariscoides*), white beak-rush (*Rhynchospora alba*),

JOSHUA G. COHEN

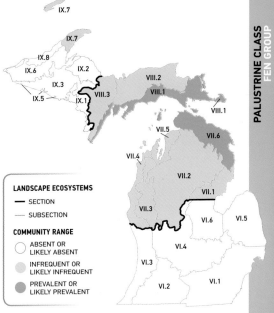

beak-rush (*R. capillacea*), blue-joint (*Calamagrostis canadensis*), spike-rushes (*Eleocharis* spp.), and tufted bulrush (*Trichophorum cespitosum*). Characteristic forbs include flat-topped white aster (*Doellingeria umbellata*), Kalm's lobelia (*Lobelia kalmii*), grass-of-Parnassus (*Parnassia glauca*), pitcher-plant (*Sarracenia purpurea*), Ohio goldenrod (*Solidago ohioensis*), and false asphodel (*Triantha glutinosa*). Important woody species are shrubby cinquefoil (*Dasiphora fruticosa*), bog birch (*Betula pumila*), northern white-cedar (*Thuja occidentalis*), and tamarack (*Larix laricina*).

LANDSCAPE ECOSYSTEMS
— SECTION
⋯ SUBSECTION

COMMUNITY RANGE
○ ABSENT OR LIKELY ABSENT
◔ INFREQUENT OR LIKELY INFREQUENT
● PREVALENT OR LIKELY PREVALENT

CHARACTERISTIC PLANTS

GRAMINOIDS

- blue-joint (*Calamagrostis canadensis*)
- sedges (*Carex aquatilis, C. buxbaumii, C. chordorrhiza, C. exilis, C. flava, C. interior, C. lasiocarpa, C. leptalea, C. limosa, C. livida, C. sterilis, C. stricta,* and others)
- twig-rush (*Cladium mariscoides*)
- tufted hair grass (*Deschampsia cespitosa*)
- panic grass (*Dichanthelium lindheimeri*)
- three-way sedge (*Dulichium arundinaceum*)
- spike-rushes (*Eleocharis elliptica, E. rostellata,* and others)
- cotton-grasses (*Eriophorum angustifolium* and *E. viridi-carinatum*)
- rush (*Juncus brachycephalus*)
- marsh wild-timothy (*Muhlenbergia glomerata*)
- common reed (*Phragmites australis* subsp. *americanus*)
- white beak-rush (*Rhynchospora alba*)
- beak-rush (*Rhynchospora capillacea*)
- alpine bulrush (*Trichophorum alpinum*)
- tufted bulrush (*Trichophorum cespitosum*)

BRADFORD S. SLAUGHTER

Dragon's mouth (*Arethusa bulbosa*), one of the characteristic orchids of northern fens, flowers in June

67

Northern fens are characterized by diverse herbaceous and shrub layers and scattered or clumped stunted conifers

FORBS

- white camas (*Anticlea elegans*)
- dragon's mouth (*Arethusa bulbosa*)
- flat-topped white aster (*Doellingeria umbellata*)
- round-leaved sundew (*Drosera rotundifolia*)
- small fringed gentian (*Gentianopsis virgata*)
- wild blue flag (*Iris versicolor*)
- Kalm's lobelia (*Lobelia kalmii*)
- bog buckbean (*Menyanthes trifoliata*)
- balsam ragwort (*Packera paupercula*)
- grass-of-Parnassus (*Parnassia glauca*)
- tall white bog orchid (*Platanthera dilatata*)
- silverweed (*Potentilla anserina*)
- bird's-eye primrose (*Primula mistassinica*)
- round-leaved pyrola (*Pyrola americana*)

- pitcher-plant (*Sarracenia purpurea*)
- Ohio goldenrod (*Solidago ohioensis*)
- bog goldenrod (*Solidago uliginosa*)
- nodding ladies'-tresses (*Spiranthes cernua*)
- rush aster (*Symphyotrichum boreale*)
- false asphodel (*Triantha glutinosa*)
- marsh St. John's-wort (*Triadenum fraseri*)
- common bog arrow-grass (*Triglochin maritima*)

MOSSES

- brown mosses (Family Amblystegiaceae)
- sphagnum mosses (*Sphagnum* spp.)

SHRUBS

- tag alder (*Alnus incana*)

- bog birch (*Betula pumila*)
- shrubby cinquefoil (*Dasiphora fruticosa*)
- Kalm's St. John's-wort (*Hypericum kalmianum*)
- creeping juniper (*Juniperus horizontalis*)
- sweet gale (*Myrica gale*)
- alder-leaved buckthorn (*Rhamnus alnifolia*)
- sage willow (*Salix candida*)
- bog willow (*Salix pedicellaris*)
- meadowsweet (*Spiraea alba*)

TREES
- tamarack (*Larix laricina*)
- black spruce (*Picea mariana*)
- northern white-cedar (*Thuja occidentalis*)

PLACES TO VISIT

- GRAND TRAVERSE: Sand Lakes, Sand Lakes Quiet Area, Traverse City State Forest Management Unit
- MACKINAC: Horseshoe Bay, Horseshoe Bay Wilderness Area, Hiawatha National Forest
- MACKINAC: Summerby Fen, Hiawatha National Forest
- MENOMINEE: Wiregrass Lake (Carney Fen Natural Area), Escanaba State Forest Management Unit
- OGEMAW: Pintail Pond, Rifle River State Recreation Area
- PRESQUE ISLE: Thompson's Harbor, Thompson's Harbor State Park

Northern fen occurring on marl, Thompson's Harbor State Park, Presque Isle County

S3 PRAIRIE FEN

Prairie fen is a groundwater-influenced wetland community dominated by graminoids, forbs, and shrubs. The community occurs in glacial outwash plains and outwash channels on moderately alkaline peat and marl in the southern Lower Peninsula. Prairie fen is often associated with headwater streams and cold, calcareous, groundwater-fed springs at the margins of steep end moraine ridges. Natural processes that determine species composition and community structure include calcareous groundwater seepage and lateral flow, fire, insect outbreaks, and flooding by beaver. Variation in the flow rate and groundwater volume influences vegetation patterning and results in distinct zones of vegetation, some of which support a diversity of calciphilic plants. Dominant sedges and grasses can include wiregrass sedge (*Carex lasiocarpa*), dioecious sedge (*C. sterilis*), tussock sedge (*C. stricta*), water sedge (*C. aquatilis*), twig-rush (*Cladium mariscoides*), spike-rushes (*Eleocharis elliptica* and *E. rostellata*), bulrushes (*Schoenoplectus* spp.), big bluestem (*Andropogon gerardii*), and little bluestem (*Schizachyrium*

MICHAEL A. KOST

scoparium). Characteristic herbs include swamp-betony (*Pedicularis lanceolata*), common mountain mint (*Pycnanthemum virginianum*), black-eyed Susan (*Rudbeckia hirta*), goldenrods (*Solidago ohioensis, S. riddellii,* and *S. uliginosa*), asters (*Symphyotrichum* spp. and *Doellingeria umbellata*), false asphodel (*Triantha glutinosa*), and marsh fern (*Thelypteris palustris*). Important woody species are shrubby cinquefoil (*Dasiphora fruticosa*), bog birch (*Betula pumila*), poison sumac (*Toxicodendron vernix*), and tamarack (*Larix laricina*).

LANDSCAPE ECOSYSTEMS
— SECTION
--- SUBSECTION

COMMUNITY RANGE
○ ABSENT OR LIKELY ABSENT
◔ INFREQUENT OR LIKELY INFREQUENT
● PREVALENT OR LIKELY PREVALENT

CHARACTERISTIC PLANTS

GRAMINOIDS

- big bluestem (*Andropogon gerardii*)
- fringed brome (*Bromus ciliatus*)
- blue-joint (*Calamagrostis canadensis*)
- sedges (*Carex aquatilis, C. buxbaumii, C. cryptolepis, C. diandra, C. flava, C. interior, C. lasiocarpa, C. leptalea, C. meadii, C. prairea, C. sterilis, C. stricta, C. tetanica, C. viridistellata,* and others)
- twig-rush (*Cladium mariscoides*)
- spike-rushes (*Eleocharis elliptica, E. rostellata,* and others)
- slender wheat grass (*Elymus trachycaulus*)
- sweet grass (*Hierochloe hirta*)
- rush (*Juncus brachycephalus*)
- marsh wild-timothy (*Muhlenbergia glomerata*)
- beak-rushes (*Rhynchospora alba* and *R. capillacea*)
- little bluestem (*Schizachyrium scoparium*)
- hardstem bulrush (*Schoenoplectus acutus*)
- threesquare (*Schoenoplectus pungens*)
- nut-rush (*Scleria verticillata*)
- Indian grass (*Sorghastrum nutans*)

FORBS

- swamp agrimony (*Agrimonia parviflora*)
- white camas (*Anticlea elegans*)
- tuberous Indian plantain (*Arnoglossum plantagineum*)*
- swamp thistle (*Cirsium muticum*)
- white lady-slipper (*Cypripedium candidum*)*
- showy lady-slipper (*Cypripedium reginae*)
- flat-topped white aster (*Doellingeria umbellata*)
- round-leaved sundew (*Drosera rotundifolia*)
- common boneset (*Eupatorium perfoliatum*)
- joe-pye-weed (*Eutrochium maculatum*)
- small fringed gentian (*Gentianopsis virgata*)
- marsh blazing-star (*Liatris spicata*)
- Kalm's lobelia (*Lobelia kalmii*)
- whorled loosestrife (*Lysimachia quadriflora*)
- grass-of-Parnassus (*Parnassia glauca*)
- swamp-betony (*Pedicularis lanceolata*)
- glaucous white lettuce (*Prenanthes racemosa*)
- common mountain mint (*Pycnanthemum virginianum*)
- black-eyed Susan (*Rudbeckia hirta*)
- pitcher-plant (*Sarracenia purpurea*)
- rosin weed (*Silphium integrifolium*)*

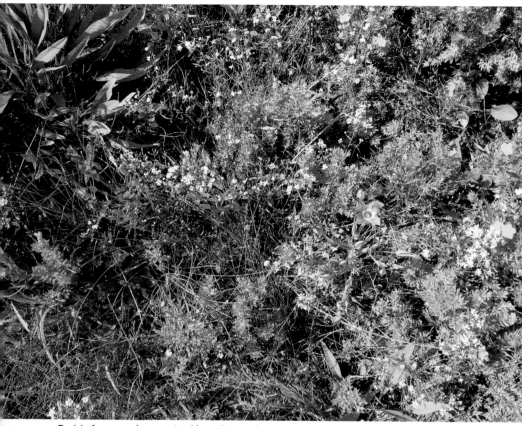

Prairie fens are characterized by a diverse herbaceous layer

- goldenrods (*Solidago ohioensis, S. riddellii, S. uliginosa*, and others)
- nodding ladies'-tresses (*Spiranthes cernua*)
- asters (*Symphyotrichum boreale, S. firmum, S. lateriflorum*, and others)
- false asphodel (*Triantha glutinosa*)
- common bog arrow-grass (*Triglochin maritima*)
- bladderwort (*Utricularia cornuta* and *U. intermedia*)
- bog valerian (*Valeriana uliginosa*)
- golden alexanders (*Zizia aurea*)

FERNS
- sensitive fern (*Onoclea sensibilis*)
- marsh fern (*Thelypteris palustris*)

FERN ALLIES
- selaginella (*Selaginella eclipes*)

MOSSES
- brown mosses (Family Amblystegiaceae)
- star campylium moss (*Campylium stellatum*)
- scorpidium moss (*Scorpidium scorpioides*)
- sphagnum mosses (*Sphagnum* spp.)

SHRUBS
- bog birch (*Betula pumila*)
- dogwoods (*Cornus* spp.)
- shrubby cinquefoil (*Dasiphora fruticosa*)
- ninebark (*Physocarpus opulifolius*)
- alder-leaved buckthorn (*Rhamnus alnifolia*)
- willows (*Salix bebbiana, S. candida,*

S. discolor, S. lucida, S. petiolaris, and others)

- meadowsweet (*Spiraea alba*)
- poison sumac (*Toxicodendron vernix*)

TREES

- red maple (*Acer rubrum*)
- red-cedar (*Juniperus virginiana*)
- tamarack (*Larix laricina*)
- American elm (*Ulmus americana*)

PLACES TO VISIT

- BARRY: Hill Creek Fen (Great Fen) and Shaw Lake Fen, Barry State Game Area

- LAPEER: Algoe Lake Fen, Ortonville State Recreation Area
- LENAWEE: Ives Road Fen Preserve, The Nature Conservancy
- LENAWEE: Little Goose Lake Fen, Michigan Nature Association (Goose Creek Grasslands Nature Sanctuary)
- OAKLAND: Brandt Road Fen and Halstead Lake, Holly State Recreation Area
- OAKLAND: Long Lake Fen, Springfield Township (Shiawassee Basin Preserve)
- VAN BUREN: Paw Paw Prairie Fen Preserve, The Nature Conservancy
- WASHTENAW: Park Lyndon Fen, Pinckney State Recreation Area and Washtenaw County Park

Prairie fens are often associated with groundwater springs and headwater streams

S2 COASTAL FEN

Coastal fen is a sedge-, rush-, and shrub-dominated wetland that occurs on calcareous substrates along Lake Huron and Lake Michigan in the Upper Peninsula and northern Lower Peninsula. The community occurs where marl and organic soils accumulate in protected coves and abandoned coastal embayments and on moderately alkaline fine-textured sands and clays lakeward. Sediments along the lakeshore are typically fine-textured and rich in calcium and magnesium carbonates. Natural processes that influence species composition and community structure include fluctuating Great Lakes water levels and groundwater seepage and lateral flow. Vegetation is comprised

primarily of calciphilic species capable of growing on wet alkaline substrates. Dominant species include beak-rush (*Rhynchospora capillacea*), twig-rush (*Cladium mariscoides*), beaked spike-rush (*Eleocharis rostellata*), shrubby cinquefoil (*Dasiphora fruticosa*), Kalm's St. John's-wort (*Hypericum kalmianum*), Ohio goldenrod (*Solidago ohioensis*),

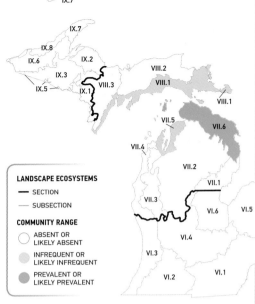

LANDSCAPE ECOSYSTEMS
— SECTION
— SUBSECTION

COMMUNITY RANGE
○ ABSENT OR LIKELY ABSENT
◑ INFREQUENT OR LIKELY INFREQUENT
● PREVALENT OR LIKELY PREVALENT

BRADFORD S. SLAUGHTER

Kalm's lobelia (*Lobelia kalmii*), limestone calamint (*Clinopodium arkansanum*), bird's-eye primrose (*Primula mistassinica*), and Baltic rush (*Juncus balticus*).

CHARACTERISTIC PLANTS

GRAMINOIDS
- blue-joint (*Calamagrostis canadensis*)
- sedges (*Carex buxbaumii*, *C. capillaris*, *C. crawei*, *C. eburnea*, *C. flava*, *C. garberi*, *C. lasiocarpa*, *C. viridula*, and others)
- twig-rush (*Cladium mariscoides*)
- tufted hair grass (*Deschampsia cespitosa*)
- Lindheimer panic grass (*Dichanthelium lindheimeri*)
- spike-rushes (*Eleocharis elliptica*, *E. quinqueflora*, and *E. rostellata*)
- Baltic rush (*Juncus balticus*)
- marsh wild-timothy (*Muhlenbergia glomerata*)
- beak-rushes (*Rhynchospora alba* and *R. capillacea*)
- bulrushes (*Schoenoplectus acutus* and *S. pungens*)

Diverse microhabitats, such as marl flats and low peat mounds, generate small-scale heterogeneity within coastal fens that contributes to their high floristic diversity

- nut-rush (*Scleria verticillata*)
- tufted bulrush (*Trichophorum cespitosum*)

FORBS

- purple false foxglove (*Agalinis purpurea*)
- white camas (*Anticlea elegans*)
- Indian paintbrush (*Castilleja coccinea*)
- limestone calamint (*Clinopodium arkansanum*)
- bastard-toadflax (*Comandra umbellata*)
- sundews (*Drosera linearis* and *D. rotundifolia*)
- small fringed gentian (*Gentianopsis virgata*)
- Kalm's lobelia (*Lobelia kalmii*)
- balsam ragwort (*Packera paupercula*)
- grass-of-Parnassus (*Parnassia glauca*)
- butterwort (*Pinguicula vulgaris*)*
- gay-wings (*Polygala paucifolia*)

- Seneca snakeroot (*Polygala senega*)
- silverweed (*Potentilla anserina*)
- bird's-eye primrose (*Primula mistassinica*)
- pitcher-plant (*Sarracenia purpurea*)
- Ohio goldenrod (*Solidago ohioensis*)
- bog goldenrod (*Solidago uliginosa*)
- nodding ladies'-tresses (*Spiranthes cernua*)
- rush aster (*Symphyotrichum boreale*)
- false asphodel (*Triantha glutinosa*)
- common bog arrow-grass (*Triglochin maritima*)
- bladderworts (*Utricularia cornuta* and *U. intermedia*)

FERN ALLIES

- variegated scouring rush (*Equisetum variegatum*)
- selaginella (*Selaginella eclipes*)

- spikemoss (*Selaginella selaginoides*)

MOSSES

- calliergon moss (*Calliergon trifarium*)
- star campylium moss (*Campylium polygamum*)
- cinclidium moss (*Cinclidium stygium*)
- scorpidium moss (*Scorpidium scorpioides*)
- sphagnum mosses (*Sphagnum* spp.)

SHRUBS

- shrubby cinquefoil (*Dasiphora fruticosa*)
- Kalm's St. John's-wort (*Hypericum kalmianum*)
- creeping juniper (*Juniperus horizontalis*)
- sweet gale (*Myrica gale*)
- alder-leaved buckthorn (*Rhamnus alnifolia*)

TREES

- paper birch (*Betula papyrifera*)
- tamarack (*Larix laricina*)
- balsam poplar (*Populus balsamifera*)
- northern white-cedar (*Thuja occidentalis*)

PLACES TO VISIT

- ALPENA: El Cajon Bay and Misery Bay, Atlanta State Forest Management Unit
- MACKINAC: Horseshoe Bay Grosse Point, Horseshoe Bay Wilderness Area, Hiawatha National Forest
- MACKINAC: Voight Bay, Little Traverse Conservancy (Aldo Leopold Preserve)
- PRESQUE ISLE: Thompson's Harbor, Thompson's Harbor State Park

Coastal fens are restricted to flat glacial lakeplains along the shorelines of Lake Huron and Lake Michigan

BOG GROUP

Bogs are open ombrotrophic peatlands that are characterized by a continuous carpet of sphagnum moss, a species-poor herbaceous layer, low ericaceous, evergreen shrubs, and scattered and stunted conifers. Found throughout Michigan but concentrated in northern Michigan, Bogs occur primarily in kettle depressions within pitted outwash plains and moraines and in shallow depressions on glacial outwash plains and glacial lakeplains. Soils are extremely acidic to very strongly acidic, saturated peats that are often deep. Natural processes that influence species composition and community structure include peat accumulation, insect outbreaks, flooding by beaver, windthrow, and occasional fires.

Two natural community types fall within the Bog group: bog and muskeg. Classification of these Bog types is based on species composition, community structure, geographic distribution, and landscape setting.

Bog, Luce County

JOSHUA G. COHEN

S4 BOG

Bog is a nutrient-poor peatland characterized by a continuous carpet of sphagnum moss, a species-poor herbaceous layer, low ericaceous, evergreen shrubs, and widely scattered and stunted conifers. Though much more prevalent in the north, bogs occur throughout Michigan in kettle depressions within pitted outwash plains and moraines and in shallow depressions on glacial outwash plains and glacial lakeplains. Bogs often develop on the margins of lakes and slowly colonize the lake basin. Soils are extremely acidic to very strongly acidic, saturated peat. Natural processes that influence species composition and community structure include peat accumulation, insect outbreaks, flooding by beaver, windthrow, and occasional fires. Bogs are dominated by sphagnum mosses (*Sphagnum* spp.), few-seed sedge (*Carex oligosperma*), ericaceous shrubs such as leatherleaf (*Chamaedaphne calyculata*), bog rosemary (*Andromeda glaucophylla*), bog laurel (*Kalmia polifolia*), low sweet blueberry (*Vaccinium angustifolium*), highbush blueberry (*V. corymbosum*), large cranberry (*V. macrocarpon*), and small cranberry (*V. oxycoccos*), and scattered trees, especially conifers

such as black spruce (*Picea mariana*), tamarack (*Larix laricina*), and pines (*Pinus* spp.). Insectivorous plants are characteristic of bogs and include round-leaved sundew (*Drosera rotundifolia*), pitcher-plant (*Sarracenia purpurea*), and bog bladderwort (*Utricularia geminiscapa*).

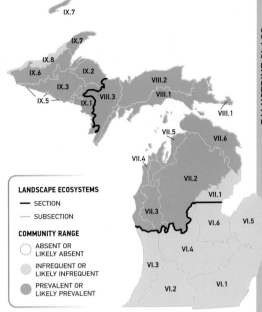

LANDSCAPE ECOSYSTEMS
— SECTION
— SUBSECTION

COMMUNITY RANGE
○ ABSENT OR LIKELY ABSENT
◐ INFREQUENT OR LIKELY INFREQUENT
● PREVALENT OR LIKELY PREVALENT

CHARACTERISTIC PLANTS

GRAMINOIDS

- few-seed sedge (*Carex oligosperma*)
- few-flower sedge (*Carex pauciflora*)
- cotton-grasses (*Eriophorum angustifolium*, *E. vaginatum*, *E. virginicum*, and others)
- white beak-rush (*Rhynchospora alba*)
- wool-grass (*Scirpus cyperinus*)

Insectivorous plants such as pitcher-plant (*Sarracenia purpurea*) have developed carnivorous adaptations to cope with the low nutrient availability in bogs

FORBS

- wild calla (*Calla palustris*)
- grass-pink (*Calopogon tuberosus*)
- marsh cinquefoil (*Comarum palustre*)
- pink lady-slipper (*Cypripedium acaule*)
- spatulate-leaved sundew (*Drosera intermedia*)
- round-leaved sundew (*Drosera rotundifolia*)
- bog buckbean (*Menyanthes trifoliata*)
- white fringed orchid (*Platanthera blephariglottis*)

Grass-pink (*Calopogon tuberosus*) is a characteristic orchid of bogs

81

Sphagnum peat, which forms a continuous mat in bogs, is characterized by extreme acidity, cool temperatures, high water-retaining capacity, low nutrient availability, and low oxygen levels

- rose pogonia (*Pogonia ophioglossoides*)
- pitcher-plant (*Sarracenia purpurea*)
- arrow-grass (*Scheuchzeria palustris*)
- bog goldenrod (*Solidago uliginosa*)
- horned bladderwort (*Utricularia cornuta*)
- bog bladderwort (*Utricularia geminiscapa*)
- yellow-eyed grasses (*Xyris montana* and *X. torta*)

FERNS
- Virginia chain-fern (*Woodwardia virginica*)

MOSSES
- sphagnum mosses (*Sphagnum* spp.)

SHRUBS
- bog rosemary (*Andromeda glaucophylla*)
- black chokeberry (*Aronia prunifolia*)
- buttonbush (*Cephalanthus occidentalis*)

- leatherleaf (*Chamaedaphne calyculata*)
- mountain holly (*Ilex mucronata*)
- winterberry (*Ilex verticillata*)
- sheep laurel (*Kalmia angustifolia*)
- bog laurel (*Kalmia polifolia*)
- Labrador-tea (*Rhododendron groenlandicum*)
- bog willow (*Salix pedicellaris*)
- low sweet blueberry (*Vaccinium angustifolium*)
- highbush blueberry (*Vaccinium corymbosum*)
- large cranberry (*Vaccinium macrocarpon*)
- Canada blueberry (*Vaccinium myrtilloides*)
- small cranberry (*Vaccinium oxycoccos*)
- wild-raisin (*Viburnum cassinoides*)

TREES
- red maple (*Acer rubrum*)
- tamarack (*Larix laricina*)
- black spruce (*Picea mariana*)

- jack pine (*Pinus banksiana*)
- red pine (*Pinus resinosa*)
- white pine (*Pinus strobus*)

PLACES TO VISIT

- ALLEGAN: Miner Lake or Fennville Bog, Allegan State Game Area
- GOGEBIC: Sylvania Bogs, Sylvania Wilderness and Recreation Area, Ottawa National Forest
- GRAND TRAVERSE: Long Lake, Traverse City State Forest Management Unit
- JACKSON: Race Road Bog, Waterloo State Recreation Area
- KALAMAZOO: West Lake Bog and Bishop's Bog Preserve, City of Portage
- KENT: Saul Lake Bog Nature Preserve, Land Conservancy of West Michigan
- LUCE: Stuart Lake, The Nature Conservancy (McMahon Lake Preserve)
- MASON: Green Road Bogs, Manistee National Forest
- NEWAYGO: Richmond Lake, Manistee National Forest
- SANILAC: Minden Bog, Minden City State Game Area
- ST. JOSEPH: Purgatory Bog, Three Rivers State Game Area

A bog occurring on a floating mat, Luce County

MUSKEG

Muskeg is a nutrient-poor peatland characterized by acidic, saturated peat and scattered or clumped, stunted conifers set in a matrix of sphagnum mosses and ericaceous shrubs. Muskeg occurs in large expanses of flat glacial outwash plains and sandy glacial lakeplains primarily in the Upper Peninsula and occasionally in the northern Lower Peninsula. Fire occurs

naturally during droughts and can alter the hydrology, mat surface, and floristic composition of muskegs. In addition to occasional fires, other natural processes that influence species composition and

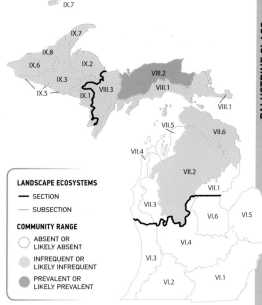

LANDSCAPE ECOSYSTEMS
— SECTION
— SUBSECTION

COMMUNITY RANGE
○ ABSENT OR LIKELY ABSENT
◔ INFREQUENT OR LIKELY INFREQUENT
● PREVALENT OR LIKELY PREVALENT

community structure include windthrow, flooding by beaver, and insect outbreaks. Dominant species include few-seed sedge (*Carex oligosperma*), leatherleaf (*Chamaedaphne calyculata*), bog rosemary (*Andromeda glaucophylla*), bog-laurel (*Kalmia polifolia*), Labrador-tea (*Rhododendron groenlandicum*), low sweet blueberry (*Vaccinium angustifolium*), and small cranberry (*V. oxycoccos*), and scattered conifers, especially black spruce (*Picea mariana*), tamarack (*Larix laricina*), and pines (*Pinus* spp.).

CHARACTERISTIC PLANTS

GRAMINOIDS

- sedges (*Carex oligosperma, C. pauciflora, C. trisperma,* and others)
- cotton-grasses (*Eriophorum angustifolium, E. vaginatum,* and *E. virginicum*)
- white beak-rush (*Rhynchospora alba*)

FORBS

- goldthread (*Coptis trifolia*)
- pink lady-slipper (*Cypripedium acaule*)

JOSHUA G. COHEN

Muskeg is characterized by acidic, saturated peat, and scattered or clumped, stunted conifer trees set in a matrix of sphagnum mosses, graminoids, and ericaceous shrubs

- spatulate-leaved sundew (*Drosera intermedia*)
- round-leaved sundew (*Drosera rotundifolia*)
- false mayflower (*Maianthemum trifolium*)
- bog buckbean (*Menyanthes trifoliata*)
- bog aster (*Oclemena nemoralis*)
- pitcher-plant (*Sarracenia purpurea*)
- arrow-grass (*Scheuchzeria palustris*)
- starflower (*Trientalis borealis*)

MOSSES

- ribbed bog moss (*Aulacomnium palustre*)
- big red stem moss (*Pleurozium schreberi*)
- pohlia moss (*Pohlia nutans*)
- sphagnum mosses (*Sphagnum* spp.)

SHRUBS

- bog rosemary (*Andromeda glaucophylla*)
- black chokeberry (*Aronia prunifolia*)
- leatherleaf (*Chamaedaphne calyculata*)
- creeping snowberry (*Gaultheria hispidula*)
- wintergreen (*Gaultheria procumbens*)
- mountain holly (*Ilex mucronata*)
- bog laurel (*Kalmia polifolia*)
- Labrador-tea (*Rhododendron groenlandicum*)
- low sweet blueberry (*Vaccinium angustifolium*)
- large cranberry (*Vaccinium macrocarpon*)
- Canada blueberry (*Vaccinium myrtilloides*)
- small cranberry (*Vaccinium oxycoccos*)

TREES

- tamarack (*Larix laricina*)
- black spruce (*Picea mariana*)
- jack pine (*Pinus banksiana*)
- red pine (*Pinus resinosa*)
- white pine (*Pinus strobus*)

PLACES TO VISIT

- CHIPPEWA: Betchler Tamarack Flats Candidate Research Natural Area, Hiawatha National Forest

- GOGEBIC: Sylvania, Sylvania Wilderness and Recreation Area, Ottawa National Forest
- LUCE: Dawson Creek Muskeg, Newberry State Forest Management Unit and The Nature Conservancy (Two-Hearted River Forest Reserve)
- LUCE: No Muskeg for Old Men, Newberry State Forest Management Unit
- LUCE & CHIPPEWA: Prison Camp Muskeg, Tahquamenon Falls State Park and Newberry State Forest Management Unit
- ROSCOMMON: Nine Mile Muskeg, Roscommon State Forest Management Unit

Muskeg, Tahquamenon Falls State Park, Luce County

SHRUB WETLAND GROUP

Shrub Wetlands occur throughout Michigan and are characterized by dominance of tall shrubs, which typically contribute greater than 50% of the overall cover. Shrub Wetlands occur in kettles and depressions on a variety of landforms, and develop on saturated to inundated organic or mineral soils of variable depth. Natural processes that influence species composition and community structure include fluctuating water levels, flooding by beaver, and windthrow.

Three natural community types fall within the Shrub Wetland group, including inundated shrub swamp, northern shrub thicket, and southern shrub-carr. Classification of these Shrub Wetland types is based on species composition, community structure, soil characteristics, hydrology, geographic distribution, and landscape setting.

Northern shrub thicket, Au Sable River, Crawford County

JOSHUA G. COHEN

S3   INUNDATED SHRUB SWAMP

Inundated shrub swamp[4] is a shrub-dominated wetland that occurs in small kettles and depressions throughout the southern Lower Peninsula. The community typically develops on shallow, saturated or inundated mucks over a variety of mineral soils from sands to silty or sandy clays.

Water depth varies seasonally and from year to year. Natural processes that influence species composition and community structure include

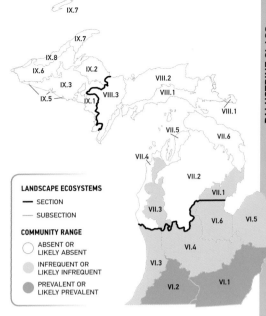

LANDSCAPE ECOSYSTEMS
— SECTION
— SUBSECTION

COMMUNITY RANGE
○ ABSENT OR LIKELY ABSENT
◯ INFREQUENT OR LIKELY INFREQUENT
● PREVALENT OR LIKELY PREVALENT

JOSHUA G. COHEN

water-level fluctuations and prolonged flooding. Inundated shrub swamp is dominated by buttonbush (*Cephalanthus occidentalis*). The community is often surrounded by a shallow moat of open water covered by small duckweed (*Lemna minor*) and ringed by a band of wetland trees. Herbaceous cover varies with depth and duration of inundation.

CHARACTERISTIC PLANTS

GRAMINOIDS
- short-awned foxtail (*Alopecurus aequalis*)
- blue-joint (*Calamagrostis canadensis*)
- sedges (*Carex crinita, C. intumescens, C. lacustris, C. radiata, C. retrorsa, C. stricta,* and others)
- three-way sedge (*Dulichium arundinaceum*)
- rattlesnake grass (*Glyceria canadensis*)
- floating manna grass (*Glyceria septentrionalis*)
- fowl manna grass (*Glyceria striata*)
- wool-grass (*Scirpus cyperinus*)
- puccinellia (*Torreyochloa pallida*)

The distinctive inflorescence of buttonbush (*Cephalanthus occidentalis*)

FORBS

- swamp milkweed (*Asclepias incarnata*)
- nodding bur-marigold (*Bidens cernua*)
- common beggar-ticks (*Bidens frondosa*)
- false nettle (*Boehmeria cylindrica*)
- water hemlock (*Cicuta bulbifera*)
- jewelweed (*Impatiens capensis*)
- southern blue flag (*Iris virginica*)
- small duckweed (*Lemna minor*)
- common water horehound (*Lycopus americanus*)
- northern bugle weed (*Lycopus uniflorus*)
- tufted loosestrife (*Lysimachia thyrsiflora*)
- clearweed (*Pilea pumila*)
- mad-dog skullcap (*Scutellaria lateriflora*)
- water parsnip (*Sium suave*)
- bur-reeds (*Sparganium* spp.)
- skunk-cabbage (*Symplocarpus foetidus*)
- common cat-tail (*Typha latifolia*)

FERNS

- sensitive fern (*Onoclea sensibilis*)
- cinnamon fern (*Osmunda cinnamomea*)
- Virginia chain-fern (*Woodwardia virginica*)

WOODY VINES

- poison-ivy (*Toxicodendron radicans*)

SHRUBS

- black chokeberry (*Aronia prunifolia*)

- buttonbush (*Cephalanthus occidentalis*)
- silky dogwood (*Cornus amomum*)
- gray dogwood (*Cornus foemina*)
- red-osier dogwood (*Cornus sericea*)
- whorled loosestrife (*Decodon verticillatus*)
- winterberry (*Ilex verticillata*)
- swamp rose (*Rosa palustris*)
- swamp dewberry (*Rubus hispidus*)
- Bebb's willow (*Salix bebbiana*)
- pussy willow (*Salix discolor*)
- highbush blueberry (*Vaccinium corymbosum*)

TREES

- red maple (*Acer rubrum*)
- silver maple (*Acer saccharinum*)
- yellow birch (*Betula alleghaniensis*)
- musclewood (*Carpinus caroliniana*)
- ashes (*Fraxinus nigra* and *F. pennsylvanica*)

- black gum (*Nyssa sylvatica*)
- cottonwood (*Populus deltoides*)
- swamp white oak (*Quercus bicolor*)
- pin oak (*Quercus palustris*)
- black willow (*Salix nigra*)
- American elm (*Ulmus americana*)

PLACES TO VISIT

- CASS: Crane Pond State Game Area
- CASS & ST. JOSEPH: Three Rivers State Game Area
- OAKLAND: Trout Lake, Bald Mountain State Recreation Area
- ST. CLAIR: Black River Shrub Swamp, Port Huron State Game Area
- WASHTENAW: Crooked Lake Shrub Swamp, Pinckney State Recreation Area

Inundated shrub swamp, Pinckney State Recreation Area, Washtenaw County

S5 NORTHERN SHRUB THICKET

Northern shrub thicket is a shrub-dominated wetland located in the Upper Peninsula and northern Lower Peninsula. Northern shrub thicket frequently occurs along streams but can also be found adjacent to lakes and beaver floodings. The saturated, nutrient-rich, organic soils are composed of

medium acidic to circumneutral sapric peat or, less frequently, mineral soil. Natural processes that influence species composition and community structure

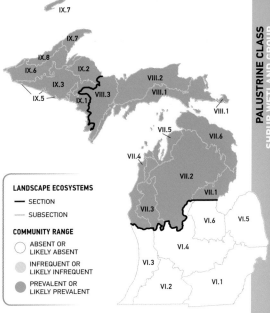

LANDSCAPE ECOSYSTEMS
— SECTION
--- SUBSECTION

COMMUNITY RANGE
○ ABSENT OR
   LIKELY ABSENT
◔ INFREQUENT OR
   LIKELY INFREQUENT
● PREVALENT OR
   LIKELY PREVALENT

include fluctuating water levels, flooding by beaver, and windthrow. The community is typically dominated by tag alder (*Alnus incana*), often associated with dogwoods (*Cornus* spp.), winterberry (*Ilex verticillata*), willows (*Salix* spp.), and wild-raisin (*Viburnum cassinoides*).

CHARACTERISTIC PLANTS

GRAMINOIDS
- blue-joint (*Calamagrostis canadensis*)
- lake sedge (*Carex lacustris*)
- retrorse sedge (*Carex retrorsa*)
- tussock sedge (*Carex stricta*)
- rattlesnake grass (*Glyceria canadensis*)
- fowl manna grass (*Glyceria striata*)
- cut grass (*Leersia oryzoides*)
- fowl meadow grass (*Poa palustris*)
- green bulrush (*Scirpus atrovirens*)

FORBS
- marsh-marigold (*Caltha palustris*)
- marsh bellflower (*Campanula aparinoides*)
- marsh cinquefoil (*Comarum palustre*)

JOSHUA G. COHEN

Tag alder (*Alnus incana*) and associated shrubs form seemingly impenetrable thickets; floristic diversity of these systems decreases with shrub canopy closure

- common boneset (*Eupatorium perfoliatum*)
- joe-pye-weed (*Eutrochium maculatum*)
- rough bedstraw (*Galium asprellum*)
- jewelweed (*Impatiens capensis*)
- wild blue flag (*Iris versicolor*)
- northern bugle weed (*Lycopus uniflorus*)
- wild mint (*Mentha canadensis*)
- monkey-flower (*Mimulus ringens*)
- golden ragwort (*Packera aurea*)
- great water dock (*Rumex orbiculatus*)
- common skullcap (*Scutellaria galericulata*)
- mad-dog skullcap (*Scutellaria lateriflora*)
- Canada goldenrod (*Solidago canadensis*)
- late goldenrod (*Solidago gigantea*)
- rough goldenrod (*Solidago rugosa*)
- panicled aster (*Symphyotrichum lanceolatum*)
- swamp aster (*Symphyotrichum puniceum*)
- skunk-cabbage (*Symplocarpus foetidus*)
- purple meadow-rue (*Thalictrum dasycarpum*)

FERNS
- sensitive fern (*Onoclea sensibilis*)
- cinnamon fern (*Osmunda cinnamomea*)
- royal fern (*Osmunda regalis*)
- marsh fern (*Thelypteris palustris*)

FERN ALLIES
- common horsetail (*Equisetum arvense*)

SHRUBS
- tag alder (*Alnus incana*)
- black chokeberry (*Aronia prunifolia*)
- bog birch (*Betula pumila*)
- silky dogwood (*Cornus amomum*)

- red-osier dogwood (*Cornus sericea*)
- winterberry (*Ilex verticillata*)
- sweet gale (*Myrica gale*)
- wild black currant (*Ribes americanum*)
- swamp rose (*Rosa palustris*)
- swamp dewberry (*Rubus hispidus*)
- dwarf raspberry (*Rubus pubescens*)
- wild red raspberry (*Rubus strigosus*)
- willows (*Salix bebbiana, S. discolor, S. exigua,* and *S. petiolaris*)
- meadowsweet (*Spiraea alba*)
- wild-raisin (*Viburnum cassinoides*)
- American highbush-cranberry (*Viburnum trilobum*)

TREES
- balsam fir (*Abies balsamea*)

- red maple (*Acer rubrum*)
- black ash (*Fraxinus nigra*)
- tamarack (*Larix laricina*)
- black spruce (*Picea mariana*)
- white pine (*Pinus strobus*)
- northern white-cedar (*Thuja occidentalis*)

PLACES TO VISIT

- ALGER: Laughing Whitefish River, Laughing Whitefish Falls State Park
- CRAWFORD: Au Sable River, Hartwick Pines State Park
- LUCE: Little Two-Hearted River, Tahquamenon Falls State Park
- ONTONAGON: Carp River, Porcupine Mountains Wilderness State Park

Northern shrub thicket along Laughing Whitefish River, Laughing Whitefish Falls State Park, Alger County

S5 SOUTHERN SHRUB-CARR

Southern shrub-carr is a shrub-dominated wetland that occurs throughout the southern Lower Peninsula. The community typically occurs on saturated organic soils within depressions on a variety of landforms. Natural processes that influence species composition and community structure

include fluctuating water levels, flooding by beaver, and windthrow. Southern shrub-carr is successively intermediate between a variety of open

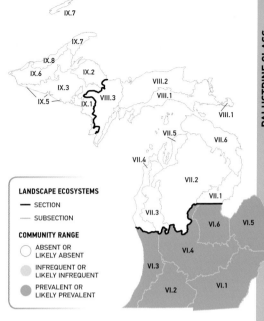

LANDSCAPE ECOSYSTEMS
— SECTION
— SUBSECTION

COMMUNITY RANGE
○ ABSENT OR LIKELY ABSENT
◔ INFREQUENT OR LIKELY INFREQUENT
● PREVALENT OR LIKELY PREVALENT

BRADFORD S. SLAUGHTER

herbaceous and forested wetlands. It frequently occurs where tall shrubs have colonized open wetlands in the absence of fire and prolonged flooding. Dominant shrub species can include willows (e.g., *Salix bebbiana*, *S. discolor*, *S. exigua*, and *S. petiolaris*), dogwoods (e.g., *Cornus sericea*, *C. foemina*, and *C. amomum*), and winterberry (*Ilex verticillata*), and common associates include poison sumac (*Toxicodendron vernix*) and spicebush (*Lindera benzoin*).

CHARACTERISTIC PLANTS

GRAMINOIDS
- blue-joint (*Calamagrostis canadensis*)
- sedges (*Carex comosa*, *C. hystericina*, *C. lacustris*, *C. leptalea*, *C. stricta*, and others)
- rattlesnake grass (*Glyceria canadensis*)
- fowl manna grass (*Glyceria striata*)
- cut grass (*Leersia oryzoides*)
- fowl meadow grass (*Poa palustris*)
- softstem bulrush (*Schoenoplectus tabernaemontani*)
- bulrush (*Scirpus pendulus*)

Southern shrub-carr, Williams Lake, Yankee Springs State Recreation Area, Barry County

FORBS

- water plantain (*Alisma subcordatum*)
- Canada anemone (*Anemone canadensis*)
- thimbleweed (*Anemone virginiana*)
- swamp milkweed (*Asclepias incarnata*)
- marsh-marigold (*Caltha palustris*)
- hedge bindweed (*Calystegia sepium*)
- marsh bellflower (*Campanula aparinoides*)
- spotted water hemlock (*Cicuta maculata*)
- willow-herbs (*Epilobium* spp.)
- marsh fleabane (*Erigeron philadelphicus*)
- common boneset (*Eupatorium perfoliatum*)
- joe-pye-weed (*Eutrochium maculatum*)
- bedstraws (*Galium asprellum, G. boreale, G. triflorum,* and others)
- purple avens (*Geum rivale*)
- great blue lobelia (*Lobelia siphilitica*)
- northern bugle weed (*Lycopus uniflorus*)
- golden ragwort (*Packera aurea*)
- clearweed (*Pilea pumila*)
- great water dock (*Rumex orbiculatus*)
- common skullcap (*Scutellaria galericulata*)
- mad-dog skullcap (*Scutellaria lateriflora*)
- Canada goldenrod (*Solidago canadensis*)

- swamp goldenrod (*Solidago patula*)
- rough goldenrod (*Solidago rugosa*)
- skunk-cabbage (*Symplocarpus foetidus*)

FERNS
- marsh fern (*Thelypteris palustris*)

FERN ALLIES
- water horsetail (*Equisetum fluviatile*)

SHRUBS
- black chokeberry (*Aronia prunifolia*)
- bog birch (*Betula pumila*)
- buttonbush (*Cephalanthus occidentalis*)
- silky dogwood (*Cornus amomum*)
- gray dogwood (*Cornus foemina*)
- red-osier dogwood (*Cornus sericea*)
- American hazelnut (*Corylus americana*)
- shrubby cinquefoil (*Dasiphora fruticosa*)
- winterberry (*Ilex verticillata*)
- swamp gooseberry (*Ribes hirtellum*)
- swamp rose (*Rosa palustris*)
- dwarf raspberry (*Rubus pubescens*)
- wild red raspberry (*Rubus strigosus*)
- Bebb's willow (*Salix bebbiana*)

- pussy willow (*Salix discolor*)
- willow (*Salix eriocephala*)
- sandbar willow (*Salix exigua*)
- slender willow (*Salix petiolaris*)
- autumn willow (*Salix serissima*)
- elderberry (*Sambucus canadensis*)
- meadowsweet (*Spiraea alba*)
- poison sumac (*Toxicodendron vernix*)
- highbush blueberry (*Vaccinium corymbosum*)
- nannyberry (*Viburnum lentago*)

TREES
- red maple (*Acer rubrum*)
- black ash (*Fraxinus nigra*)
- green ash (*Fraxinus pennsylvanica*)
- tamarack (*Larix laricina*)
- American elm (*Ulmus americana*)

PLACES TO VISIT

- BARRY: Williams Lake, Yankee Springs State Recreation Area
- OAKLAND: Chamberlain Lakes, Bald Mountain State Recreation Area

FORESTED WETLAND GROUP

Forested Wetlands occur throughout Michigan and are characterized by dominance of trees, which typically contribute greater than 50% of the overall canopy cover. Forested Wetlands occur on a variety of landforms including depressions on glacial outwash plains, moraines, and lakeplains; outwash channels; poorly drained lakeplain; and within kettles on pitted outwash plains and ice-contact topography. Soils that support Forested Wetlands include both organics and mineral soils and range from shallow to deep, acidic to alkaline, and saturated to seasonally inundated. Natural processes that influence species composition and community structure include groundwater seepage, seasonal flooding, drought, windthrow, flooding by beaver, insect outbreaks, and occasional fires.

Eight natural community types fall within the Forested Wetland group: poor conifer swamp, rich conifer swamp, rich tamarack swamp, hardwood-conifer swamp, floodplain forest, northern hardwood swamp, southern hardwood swamp, and wet-mesic flatwoods. Classification of these Forested Wetland types is based on species composition, community structure, differences in soil chemistry and composition, hydrology, geographic distribution, and landscape setting.

Rich conifer swamp, Luce County
BRADFORD S. SLAUGHTER

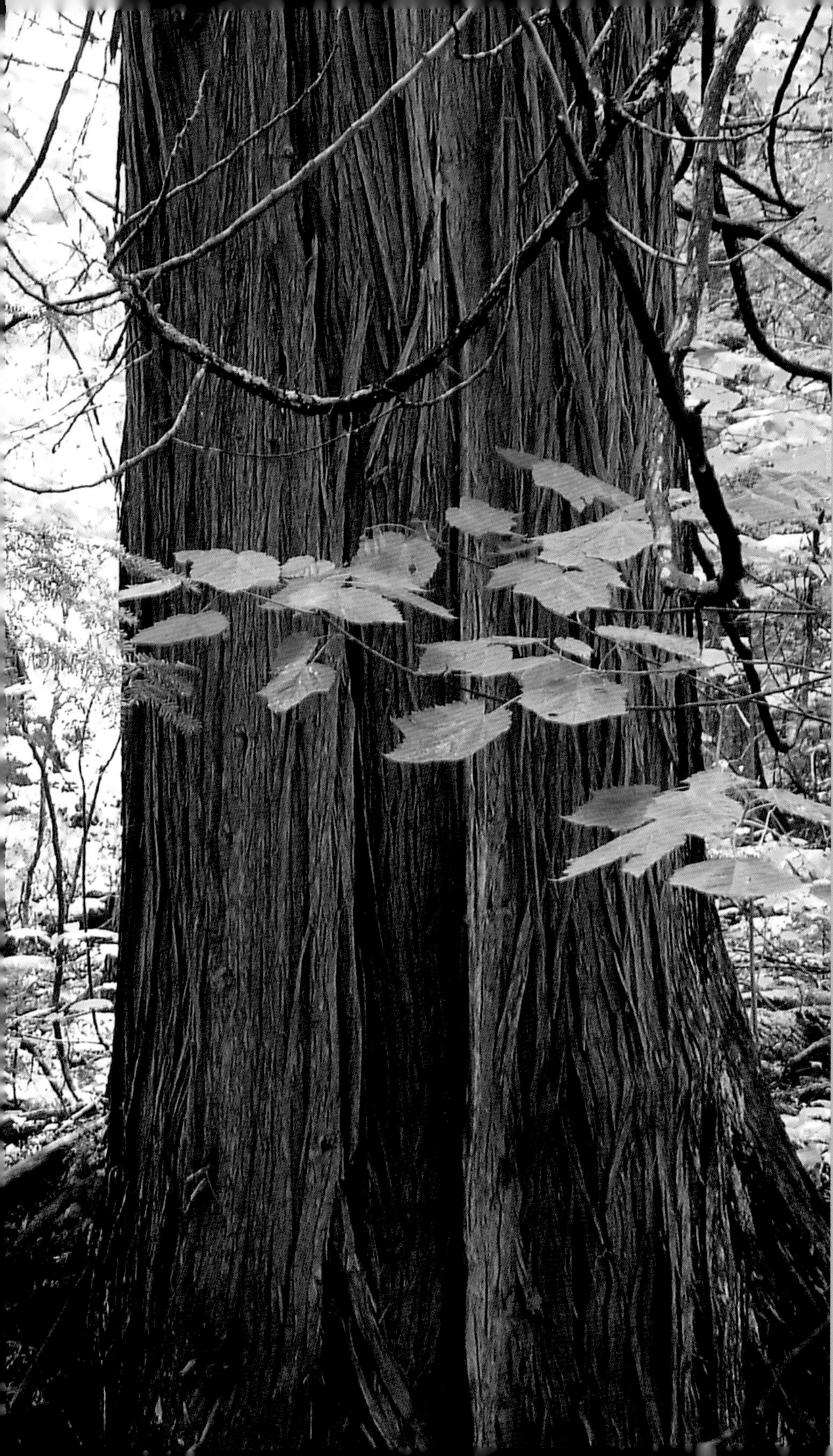

S4 POOR CONIFER SWAMP

Poor conifer swamp is a nutrient-poor forested peatland that occurs most commonly in the Upper Peninsula and northern Lower Peninsula and infrequently in the southern Lower Peninsula. Poor conifer swamp develops on extremely acidic, saturated peat in depressions on glacial outwash plains,

moraines, and sandy glacial lakeplains, and within kettles on pitted outwash plains and ice-contact topography. Natural processes that influence species

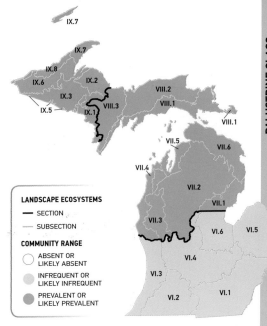

LANDSCAPE ECOSYSTEMS
— SECTION
— SUBSECTION

COMMUNITY RANGE
○ ABSENT OR LIKELY ABSENT
◐ INFREQUENT OR LIKELY INFREQUENT
● PREVALENT OR LIKELY PREVALENT

composition and community structure include windthrow, flooding by beaver, insect outbreaks, peat accumulation, and occasional fires. The community is characterized by the prevalence of coniferous trees, ericaceous shrubs, and sphagnum mosses. Dominant trees can include black spruce (*Picea mariana*), tamarack (*Larix laricina*), and jack pine (*Pinus banksiana*), and prevalent shrubs include leatherleaf (*Chamaedaphne calyculata*) and Labrador-tea (*Rhododendron groenlandicum*).

CHARACTERISTIC PLANTS

GRAMINOIDS
- sedges (*Carex oligosperma, C. pauciflora, C. trisperma*, and others)
- sheathed cotton-grass (*Eriophorum vaginatum*)
- tawny cotton-grass (*Eriophorum virginicum*)
- wool-grass (*Scirpus cyperinus*)

FORBS
- wild calla (*Calla palustris*)
- bluebead lily (*Clintonia borealis*)

JOSHUA G. COHEN

105

Poor conifer swamps are dominated by black spruce (*Picea mariana*)

- goldthread (*Coptis trifolia*)
- pink lady-slipper (*Cypripedium acaule*)
- round-leaved sundew (*Drosera rotundifolia*)
- wild blue flag (*Iris versicolor*)
- Canada mayflower (*Maianthemum canadense*)
- false mayflower (*Maianthemum trifolium*)
- pitcher-plant (*Sarracenia purpurea*)
- starflower (*Trientalis borealis*)

FERNS
- sensitive fern (*Onoclea sensibilis*)
- royal fern (*Osmunda regalis*)
- Virginia chain-fern (*Woodwardia virginica*)

MOSSES
- ribbed bog moss (*Aulacomnium palustre*)
- big red stem moss (*Pleurozium schreberi*)
- pohlia moss (*Pohlia nutans*)
- sphagnum mosses (*Sphagnum* spp.)

SHRUBS
- bog rosemary (*Andromeda glaucophylla*)
- black chokeberry (*Aronia prunifolia*)
- leatherleaf (*Chamaedaphne calyculata*)
- bunchberry (*Cornus canadensis*)
- creeping snowberry (*Gaultheria hispidula*)
- wintergreen (*Gaultheria procumbens*)
- huckleberry (*Gaylussacia baccata*)

- mountain holly (*Ilex mucronata*)
- winterberry (*Ilex verticillata*)
- sheep laurel (*Kalmia angustifolia*)
- bog laurel (*Kalmia polifolia*)
- Labrador-tea (*Rhododendron groenlandicum*)
- blueberries (*Vaccinium angustifolium,
  V. corymbosum,* and *V. myrtilloides*)
- small cranberry (*Vaccinium oxycoccos*)
- wild-raisin (*Viburnum cassinoides*)

TREES
- balsam fir (*Abies balsamea*)
- paper birch (*Betula papyrifera*)
- tamarack (*Larix laricina*)
- black spruce (*Picea mariana*)

- jack pine (*Pinus banksiana*)
- white pine (*Pinus strobus*)

PLACES TO VISIT
- CHIPPEWA: Tahqua Trail Swamp,
  Tahquamenon Falls State Park
- GOGEBIC: Sylvania, Sylvania Wilderness and
  Recreation Area, Ottawa National Forest
- JACKSON: Waterloo Black Spruce Bog,
  Waterloo State Recreation Area
- LUCE: Prison Camp Swamp, Tahquamenon
  Falls State Park
- ROSCOMMON: Nine Mile Swamp, Roscommon
  State Forest Management Unit

Dense ericaceous shrubs often characterize the low shrub layer of poor conifer swamp

S3 RICH CONIFER SWAMP

Rich conifer swamp[5] is a diverse groundwater-influenced, forested wetland dominated by northern white-cedar (*Thuja occidentalis*) that occurs primarily in the Upper Peninsula and northern Lower Peninsula. The community is found in outwash channels and in depressions on outwash plains, lakeplains, and moraines. Rich conifer swamp typically develops on saturated, circumneutral to moderately alkaline peats that may be acidic near the surface where sphagnum mosses are locally prevalent. The community is often associated with headwater streams and cold, calcareous, groundwater-fed springs. Natural processes that influence species composition and community structure include groundwater seepage, seasonal water-level fluctuations, windthrow, flooding by beaver, sphagnum hummock and hollow development, and infrequent fires. In addition to northern white-cedar, prevalent canopy species include tamarack (*Larix laricina*), white pine (*Pinus strobus*), spruce (*Picea* spp.), red maple (*Acer rubrum*), and black ash (*Fraxinus nigra*), and tag alder (*Alnus incana*) is characteristic of the understory.

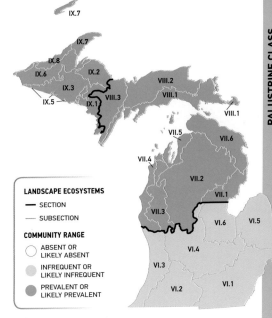

CHARACTERISTIC PLANTS

GRAMINOIDS

- blue-joint (*Calamagrostis canadensis*)
- sedges (*Carex disperma, C. eburnea, C. gynocrates, C. interior, C. leptalea, C. pedunculata, C. trisperma, C. vaginata,* and others)
- fowl manna grass (*Glyceria striata*)
- cut grass (*Leersia oryzoides*)
- fowl meadow grass (*Poa palustris*)

FORBS

- wild sarsaparilla (*Aralia nudicaulis*)
- Jack-in-the-pulpit (*Arisaema triphyllum*)
- marsh-marigold (*Caltha palustris*)
- small enchanter's-nightshade (*Circaea alpina*)
- bluebead lily (*Clintonia borealis*)
- goldthread (*Coptis trifolia*)
- lady-slippers (*Cypripedium* spp.)
- willow-herbs (*Epilobium* spp.)
- fragrant bedstraw (*Galium triflorum*)
- purple avens (*Geum rivale*)
- creeping rattlesnake plantain (*Goodyera repens*)
- tesselated rattlesnake plantain (*Goodyera tesselata*)
- jewelweed (*Impatiens capensis*)
- wild blue flag (*Iris versicolor*)
- twinflower (*Linnaea borealis*)
- Canada mayflower (*Maianthemum canadense*)
- false mayflower (*Maianthemum trifolium*)
- partridge berry (*Mitchella repens*)
- naked miterwort (*Mitella nuda*)
- one-flowered pyrola (*Moneses uniflora*)
- broad-leaved twayblade (*Neottia convallarioides*)
- heartleaf twayblade (*Neottia cordata*)
- one-sided pyrola (*Orthilia secunda*)
- sweet-coltsfoot (*Petasites frigidus*)
- northern green orchid (*Platanthera aquilonis*)
- club-spur orchid (*Platanthera clavellata*)
- Lake Huron green orchid (*Platanthera huronensis*)
- blunt-leaved orchid (*Platanthera obtusata*)
- gay-wings (*Polygala paucifolia*)
- pyrolas (*Pyrola americana* and *P. asarifolia*)
- common skullcap (*Scutellaria galericulata*)
- mad-dog skullcap (*Scutellaria lateriflora*)
- starflower (*Trientalis borealis*)
- violets (*Viola* spp.)

FERNS

- bulblet fern (*Cystopteris bulbifera*)
- woodferns (*Dryopteris* spp.)
- oak fern (*Gymnocarpium dryopteris*)
- sensitive fern (*Onoclea sensibilis*)
- cinnamon fern (*Osmunda cinnamomea*)
- northern beech fern (*Phegopteris connectilis*)
- marsh fern (*Thelypteris palustris*)

FERN ALLIES

- water horsetail (*Equisetum fluviatile*)
- dwarf scouring rush (*Equisetum scirpoides*)
- woodland horsetail (*Equisetum sylvaticum*)

MOSSES

- ribbed bog moss (*Aulacomnium palustre*)
- calliergon moss (*Calliergon cordifolium*)

LANDSCAPE ECOSYSTEMS

— SECTION
--- SUBSECTION

COMMUNITY RANGE

- ABSENT OR LIKELY ABSENT
- INFREQUENT OR LIKELY INFREQUENT
- PREVALENT OR LIKELY PREVALENT

Windthrow is an important disturbance factor in rich conifer swamps

- big red stem moss (*Pleurozium schreberi*)
- sphagnum mosses (*Sphagnum* spp.)

WOODY VINES
- red honeysuckle (*Lonicera dioica*)
- hairy honeysuckle (*Lonicera hirsuta*)
- poison-ivy (*Toxicodendron radicans*)

SHRUBS
- tag alder (*Alnus incana*)
- bunchberry (*Cornus canadensis*)
- round-leaved dogwood (*Cornus rugosa*)
- red-osier dogwood (*Cornus sericea*)
- creeping snowberry (*Gaultheria hispidula*)

- wintergreen (*Gaultheria procumbens*)
- huckleberry (*Gaylussacia baccata*)
- mountain holly (*Ilex mucronata*)
- winterberry (*Ilex verticillata*)
- Canadian fly honeysuckle (*Lonicera canadensis*)
- swamp fly honeysuckle (*Lonicera oblongifolia*)
- alder-leaved buckthorn (*Rhamnus alnifolia*)
- Labrador-tea (*Rhododendron groenlandicum*)
- currants (*Ribes americanum, R. hirtellum, R. hudsonianum, R. lacustre,* and *R. triste*)
- dwarf raspberry (*Rubus pubescens*)
- blueberries (*Vaccinium* spp.)

TREES

- balsam fir (*Abies balsamea*)
- red maple (*Acer rubrum*)
- yellow birch (*Betula alleghaniensis*)
- paper birch (*Betula papyrifera*)
- black ash (*Fraxinus nigra*)
- tamarack (*Larix laricina*)
- black spruce (*Picea mariana*)
- white spruce (*Picea glauca*)
- white pine (*Pinus strobus*)
- balsam poplar (*Populus balsamifera*)
- quaking aspen (*Populus tremuloides*)
- northern white-cedar (*Thuja occidentalis*)
- hemlock (*Tsuga canadensis*)
- American elm (*Ulmus americana*)

PLACES TO VISIT

- BARRY: Pierce Cedar Creek Institute
- CHIPPEWA: Gogomain Swamp, Sault Sainte Marie State Forest Management Unit
- EMMET: Bear River Swamp, Gaylord State Forest Management Unit
- EMMET: Minnehaha Creek, Gaylord State Forest Management Unit
- KALKASKA: Watson Swamp, Traverse City State Forest Management Unit
- OAKLAND: Lakeville Swamp Nature Sanctuary, Michigan Nature Association
- OTSEGO & MONTMORENCY: Green Swamp, Atlanta State Forest Management Unit
- ROSCOMMON: Deadstream Swamp, Roscommon State Forest Management Unit

Bear River Swamp, Gaylord State Forest Management Unit, Emmet County

S3 RICH TAMARACK SWAMP

Rich tamarack swamp[6] is a diverse groundwater-influenced, forested wetland dominated by tamarack (*Larix laricina*) that occurs primarily in the southern Lower Peninsula and occasionally in the northern Lower Peninsula and Upper Peninsula. The community is found on circumneutral to mildly alkaline deep peat soils in outwash channels, in depressions

and kettles on outwash plains and moraines, and on poorly drained glacial outwash plains and lakeplains. Rich tamarack swamp often occurs in areas of groundwater seepage associated

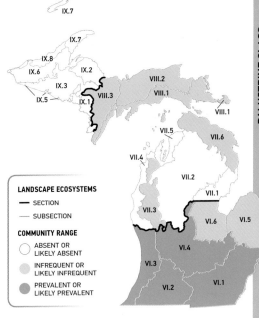

LANDSCAPE ECOSYSTEMS
— SECTION
--- SUBSECTION

COMMUNITY RANGE
○ ABSENT OR LIKELY ABSENT
◌ INFREQUENT OR LIKELY INFREQUENT
● PREVALENT OR LIKELY PREVALENT

BRADFORD S. SLAUGHTER

with headwater streams and lakes. Natural processes that influence species composition and community structure include groundwater seepage, seasonal water-level fluctuation, insect outbreaks, windthrow, flooding by beaver, and occasional fires. In addition to tamarack, prevalent canopy trees include red maple (*Acer rubrum*), black ash (*Fraxinus nigra*), yellow birch (*Betula alleghaniensis*), and white pine (*Pinus strobus*), while poison sumac (*Toxicodendron vernix*) and winterberry (*Ilex verticillata*) are characteristic of the dense understory.

CHARACTERISTIC PLANTS

GRAMINOIDS

- blue-joint (*Calamagrostis canadensis*)
- sedges (*Carex bromoides*, *C. comosa*, *C. disperma*, *C. hystericina*, *C. lacustris*, *C. leptalea*, *C. stricta*, and others)
- wood reedgrass (*Cinna arundinacea*)
- fowl manna grass (*Glyceria striata*)
- cut grass (*Leersia oryzoides*)
- fowl meadow grass (*Poa palustris*)

FORBS

- jack-in-the-pulpit (*Arisaema triphyllum*)
- nodding bur-marigold (*Bidens cernua*)
- tall swamp-marigold (*Bidens trichosperma*)
- false nettle (*Boehmeria cylindrica*)
- marsh-marigold (*Caltha palustris*)
- spring cress (*Cardamine bulbosa*)
- Pennsylvania bitter cress (*Cardamine pensylvanica*)
- cuckoo-flower (*Cardamine pratensis*)
- turtlehead (*Chelone glabra*)
- water hemlock (*Cicuta bulbifera*)
- goldthread (*Coptis trifolia*)
- small yellow lady-slipper (*Cypripedium parviflorum* var. *makasin*)
- flat-topped white aster (*Doellingeria umbellata*)
- willow-herbs (*Epilobium* spp.)
- bedstraws (*Galium asprellum, G. labradoricum, G. tinctorium,* and others)
- northern bugle weed (*Lycopus uniflorus*)
- tufted loosestrife (*Lysimachia thyrsiflora*)
- Canada mayflower (*Maianthemum canadense*)
- false mayflower (*Maianthemum trifolium*)
- swamp saxifrage (*Micranthes pensylvanica*)
- bishop's-cap (*Mitella diphylla*)
- golden ragwort (*Packera aurea*)
- clearweed (*Pilea pumila*)
- club-spur orchid (*Platanthera clavellata*)
- great water dock (*Rumex orbiculatus*)
- black snakeroot (*Sanicula marilandica*)
- pitcher-plant (*Sarracenia purpurea*)
- common skullcap (*Scutellaria galericulata*)

Rich tamarack swamps are often characterized by a partial overstory of tamarack (*Larix laricina*) and a dense and diverse understory

- mad-dog skullcap (*Scutellaria lateriflora*)
- goldenrods (*Solidago patula, S. rugosa*, and others)
- smooth swamp aster (*Symphyotrichum firmum*)
- panicled aster (*Symphyotrichum lanceolatum*)
- calico aster (*Symphyotrichum lateriflorum*)
- swamp aster (*Symphyotrichum puniceum*)
- skunk-cabbage (*Symplocarpus foetidus*)
- starflower (*Trientalis borealis*)
- violets (*Viola* spp.)

FERNS
- crested shield fern (*Dryopteris cristata*)
- sensitive fern (*Onoclea sensibilis*)
- cinnamon fern (*Osmunda cinnamomea*)
- royal fern (*Osmunda regalis*)
- marsh fern (*Thelypteris palustris*)

FERN ALLIES
- water horsetail (*Equisetum fluviatile*)

MOSSES
- brown mosses (Family Amblystegiaceae)
- sphagnum mosses (*Sphagnum* spp.)

WOODY VINES
- virgin's bower (*Clematis virginiana*)
- red honeysuckle (*Lonicera dioica*)
- Virginia creeper (*Parthenocissus quinquefolia*)
- poison-ivy (*Toxicodendron radicans*)
- riverbank grape (*Vitis riparia*)

SHRUBS
- black chokeberry (*Aronia prunifolia*)
- bog birch (*Betula pumila*)
- dogwoods (*Cornus amomum, C. foemina*, and *C. sericea*)
- American hazelnut (*Corylus americana*)
- winterberry (*Ilex verticillata*)

- alder-leaved buckthorn (*Rhamnus alnifolia*)
- swamp gooseberry (*Ribes hirtellum*)
- swamp rose (*Rosa palustris*)
- dwarf raspberry (*Rubus pubescens*)
- wild red raspberry (*Rubus strigosus*)
- willows (*Salix bebbiana, S. discolor, S. serissima*, and others)
- poison sumac (*Toxicodendron vernix*)
- highbush blueberry (*Vaccinium corymbosum*)
- nannyberry (*Viburnum lentago*)

TREES
- red maple (*Acer rubrum*)
- yellow birch (*Betula alleghaniensis*)
- musclewood (*Carpinus caroliniana*)
- black ash (*Fraxinus nigra*)
- red-cedar (*Juniperus virginiana*)
- tamarack (*Larix laricina*)
- white pine (*Pinus strobus*)
- quaking aspen (*Populus tremuloides*)
- swamp white oak (*Quercus bicolor*)
- American elm (*Ulmus americana*)

PLACES TO VISIT
- BARRY: Pierce Cedar Creek Institute
- JACKSON: Leeke Lake Swamp, Waterloo State Recreation Area
- JACKSON: Little Portage Lake Swamp, Waterloo State Recreation Area
- MONTMORENCY: Lower Tomahawk Lake, Atlanta State Forest Management Unit
- OAKLAND: Tamarack Trail Swamp, Kensington Metropark
- SCHOOLCRAFT: East Branch Fox River, Shingleton State Forest Management Unit
- WASHTENAW: Embury Road Swamp, Waterloo State Recreation Area and Park Lyndon (Washtenaw County Park)
- WASHTENAW: Hudson Mills Tamarack Swamp, Hudson Mills Metropark

HARDWOOD-CONIFER SWAMP

Hardwood-conifer swamp is a diverse groundwater-influenced forested wetland dominated by a mixture of lowland hardwoods and conifers. The community occurs on peat and poorly drained mineral soils on a variety of landforms throughout Michigan. Hardwood-conifer swamp is often

associated with headwater streams and areas of groundwater seepage. Natural processes that influence species composition and community

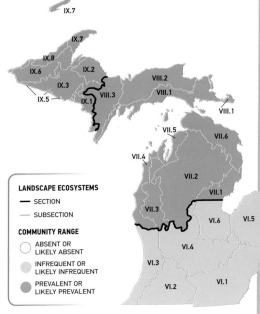

LANDSCAPE ECOSYSTEMS
— SECTION
— SUBSECTION

COMMUNITY RANGE
○ ABSENT OR LIKELY ABSENT
◔ INFREQUENT OR LIKELY INFREQUENT
● PREVALENT OR LIKELY PREVALENT

BRADFORD S. SLAUGHTER

structure include windthrow, fluctuating water levels, and flooding by beaver. Species composition and dominance patterns vary regionally, but dominant trees typically include red maple (*Acer rubrum*), yellow birch (*Betula alleghaniensis*), white pine (*Pinus strobus*), northern white-cedar (*Thuja occidentalis*), and hemlock (*Tsuga canadensis*).

CHARACTERISTIC PLANTS

GRAMINOIDS

- sedges (*Carex bromoides*, *C. crinita*, *C. disperma*, *C. folliculata*, *C. gracillima*, *C. hystericina*, *C. intumescens*, *C. lacustris*, *C. lupulina*, *C. stricta*, and others)
- wood reedgrasses (*Cinna arundinacea* and *C. latifolia*)
- Virginia wild-rye (*Elymus virginicus*)
- fowl manna grass (*Glyceria striata*)
- rice cut grass (*Leersia oryzoides*)
- bog bluegrass (*Poa paludigena*)*
- fowl meadow grass (*Poa palustris*)

Hemlock (*Tsuga canadensis*) and yellow birch (*Betula alleghaniensis*) are frequent canopy codominants of hardwood-conifer swamp

FORBS

- wild sarsaparilla (*Aralia nudicaulis*)
- jack-in-the-pulpit (*Arisaema triphyllum*)
- beggar-ticks (*Bidens* spp.)
- marsh-marigold (*Caltha palustris*)
- spring cress (*Cardamine bulbosa*)
- Pennsylvania bitter cress (*Cardamine pensylvanica*)
- cuckoo-flower (*Cardamine pratensis*)
- turtlehead (*Chelone glabra*)
- golden saxifrage (*Chrysosplenium americanum*)
- small enchanter's-nightshade (*Circaea alpina*)
- virgin's bower (*Clematis virginiana*)
- bluebead lily (*Clintonia borealis*)
- goldthread (*Coptis trifolia*)
- lady-slippers (*Cypripedium* spp.)
- flat-topped white aster (*Doellingeria umbellata*)
- willow-herbs (*Epilobium* spp.)
- jewelweed (*Impatiens capensis*)
- twinflower (*Linnaea borealis*)
- northern bugle weed (*Lycopus uniflorus*)
- tufted loosestrife (*Lysimachia thyrsiflora*)
- Canada mayflower (*Maianthemum canadense*)
- partridge berry (*Mitchella repens*)
- bishop's-cap (*Mitella diphylla*)
- naked miterwort (*Mitella nuda*)
- northern wood sorrel (*Oxalis acetosella*)

- golden ragwort (*Packera aurea*)
- smartweeds (*Persicaria* spp.)
- gay-wings (*Polygala paucifolia*)
- water-parsnip (*Sium suave*)
- goldenrods (*Solidago patula, S. rugosa*, and others)
- calico aster (*Symphyotrichum lateriflorum*)
- swamp aster (*Symphyotrichum puniceum*)
- skunk-cabbage (*Symplocarpus foetidus*)
- starflower (*Trientalis borealis*)
- violets (*Viola* spp.)

FERNS
- woodferns (*Dryopteris* spp.)
- oak fern (*Gymnocarpium dryopteris*)
- sensitive fern (*Onoclea sensibilis*)
- cinnamon fern (*Osmunda cinnamomea*)
- interrupted fern (*Osmunda claytoniana*)
- royal fern (*Osmunda regalis*)
- New York fern (*Thelypteris noveboracensis*)

FERN ALLIES
- horsetails (*Equisetum* spp.)

WOODY VINES
- red honeysuckle (*Lonicera dioica*)
- Virginia creeper (*Parthenocissus quinquefolia*)
- poison-ivy (*Toxicodendron radicans*)
- riverbank grape (*Vitis riparia*)

MOSSES
- callicladium moss (*Callicladium haldanianum*)
- big red stem moss (*Pleurozium schreberi*)
- sphagnum mosses (*Sphagnum* spp.)

SHRUBS
- tag alder (*Alnus incana*)
- bunchberry (*Cornus canadensis*)
- dogwoods (*Cornus foemina* and *C. sericea*)
- creeping snowberry (*Gaultheria hispidula*)

- winterberry (*Ilex verticillata*)
- spicebush (*Lindera benzoin*)
- Canadian fly honeysuckle (*Lonicera canadensis*)
- alder-leaved buckthorn (*Rhamnus alnifolia*)
- swamp red currant (*Ribes triste*)
- dwarf raspberry (*Rubus pubescens*)
- poison sumac (*Toxicodendron vernix*)

TREES
- balsam fir (*Abies balsamea*)
- red maple (*Acer rubrum*)
- mountain maple (*Acer spicatum*)
- yellow birch (*Betula alleghaniensis*)
- paper birch (*Betula papyrifera*)
- musclewood (*Carpinus caroliniana*)
- black ash (*Fraxinus nigra*)
- green ash (*Fraxinus pennsylvanica*)
- tamarack (*Larix laricina*)
- white spruce (*Picea glauca*)
- black spruce (*Picea mariana*)
- white pine (*Pinus strobus*)
- northern white-cedar (*Thuja occidentalis*)
- basswood (*Tilia americana*)
- hemlock (*Tsuga canadensis*)
- American elm (*Ulmus americana*)

PLACES TO VISIT
- BARRY: Long Lake, Yankee Springs State Recreation Area
- CASS & ST. JOSEPH: Mill Creek Swamp, Three Rivers State Game Area
- CHIPPEWA & LUCE: Tahquamenon River, Tahquamenon Falls State Park
- LUCE: Beavertown Lakes, Newberry State Forest Management Unit and The Nature Conservancy (Two-Hearted River Forest Reserve)
- OAKLAND: Clinton River Headwaters, Independence Oaks County Park, Oakland County Parks

S3 FLOODPLAIN FOREST

Floodplain forest is a diverse bottomland deciduous or deciduous-coniferous forest community occupying low-lying areas adjacent to large streams and rivers, and subject to periodic over-the-bank flooding and cycles of erosion and deposition. Floodplain forests occur along major rivers throughout Michigan but are most common in the southern Lower Peninsula. Floodplain soils are highly variable due to dynamic erosional and depositional fluvial processes. Species composition and community structure vary both regionally and within individual floodplain forests in response to flooding frequency and duration. Additional natural processes impacting floodplain forests include soil erosion and deposition, ice scour,

windthrow, and infrequent fires. Hydrogeomorphic processes such as over-the-bank flooding, transport and deposition of sediment, and erosive and abrasive water movement cause the floodplains of large rivers to exhibit a variety of fluvial landforms, each of which supports a particular vegetation assemblage. Among the most characteristic fluvial landforms are natural levee, first bottom, second bottom, backswamp, meander-scar swamp, oxbow, and terrace.

Floodplain bottoms, typically the most prevalent zones within floodplain forests, are overwhelmingly dominated by silver maple (*Acer saccharinum*) and green ash (*Fraxinus pennsylvanica*), although the introduced emerald ash borer has locally decimated canopy

ash in southern Lower Michigan. Characteristic canopy trees of the levee include silver maple, black willow (*Salix nigra*), cottonwood (*Populus deltoides*), basswood (*Tilia americana*), swamp white oak (*Quercus bicolor*), bur oak (*Q. macrocarpa*), sycamore (*Platanus occidentalis*), hackberry (*Celtis occidentalis*), box elder (*Acer negundo*), and shagbark hickory (*Carya ovata*). Terraces, fluvial landforms within the floodplain but above the influence of most floodwaters, are often dominated by American beech (*Fagus grandifolia*) and sugar maple (*Acer saccharum*), often with black maple (*Acer nigrum*), oaks (*Quercus* spp.), and hickories (*Carya* spp.) in the southern Lower Peninsula, and hemlock (*Tsuga canadensis*), oaks, and white pine (*Pinus strobus*) in the northern Lower and Upper Peninsulas. Backswamps and meander-scar swamps are often dominated by black ash (*Fraxinus nigra*), yellow birch (*Betula alleghaniensis*), red maple (*Acer rubrum*), tamarack (*Larix laricina*), northern white-cedar (*Thuja occidentalis*), white pine, and hemlock, with conifer cover especially high in the northern part of the state and typically lacking in southern Lower Michigan.

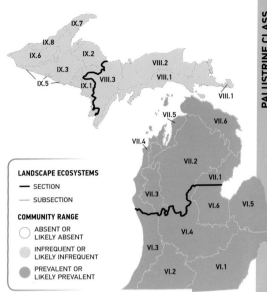

LANDSCAPE ECOSYSTEMS
— SECTION
– SUBSECTION

COMMUNITY RANGE
○ ABSENT OR LIKELY ABSENT
◑ INFREQUENT OR LIKELY INFREQUENT
● PREVALENT OR LIKELY PREVALENT

CHARACTERISTIC PLANTS

GRAMINOIDS
- blue-joint (*Calamagrostis canadensis*)
- sedges (*Carex crinita, C. grayi, C. hirtifolia, C. intumescens, C. lacustris, C. lupulina, C. muskingumensis, C. stricta, C. tuckermanii,* and others)
- wood reedgrass (*Cinna arundinacea*)
- beak grass (*Diarrhena obovata*)*

- riverbank wild-rye (*Elymus riparius*)
- Virginia wild-rye (*Elymus virginicus*)
- fowl manna grass (*Glyceria striata*)
- cut grass (*Leersia oryzoides*)
- white grass (*Leersia virginica*)

FORBS
- wild leeks (*Allium burdickii* and *A. tricoccum*)
- wild garlic (*Allium canadense*)
- green dragon (*Arisaema dracontium*)
- jack-in-the-pulpit (*Arisaema triphyllum*)
- wild ginger (*Asarum canadense*)
- false nettle (*Boehmeria cylindrica*)
- blue cohoshes (*Caulophyllum giganteum* and *C. thalictroides*)
- turtlehead (*Chelone glabra*)
- honewort (*Cryptotaenia canadensis*)
- flat-topped white aster (*Doellingeria umbellata*)
- white trout lily (*Erythronium albidum*)
- yellow trout lily (*Erythronium americanum*)
- green-stemmed joe-pye-weed (*Eutrochium purpureum*)
- false mermaid (*Floerkea proserpinacoides*)
- wild geranium (*Geranium maculatum*)
- white avens (*Geum canadense*)
- Jerusalem-artichoke (*Helianthus tuberosus*)

Virginia bluebells (*Mertensia virginica*) locally dominating the ground layer of a floodplain bottom

- cow-parsnip (*Heracleum maximum*)
- great waterleaf (*Hydrophyllum appendiculatum*)
- Canada waterleaf (*Hydrophyllum canadense*)
- Virginia waterleaf (*Hydrophyllum virginianum*)
- jewelweed (*Impatiens capensis*)
- southern blue flag (*Iris virginica*)
- wood nettle (*Laportea canadensis*)
- Michigan lily (*Lilium michiganense*)
- cardinal flower (*Lobelia cardinalis*)
- fringed loosestrife (*Lysimachia ciliata*)
- Virginia bluebells (*Mertensia virginica*)*
- golden ragwort (*Packera aurea*)
- arrow-arum (*Peltandra virginica*)

- jumpseed (*Persicaria virginiana*)
- clearweed (*Pilea pumila*)
- Solomon-seal (*Polygonatum biflorum*)
- pickerel-weed (*Pontederia cordata*)
- swamp buttercup (*Ranunculus hispidus*)
- water dock (*Rumex verticillatus*)
- black snakeroots (*Sanicula marilandica* and *S. odorata*)
- lizard's tail (*Saururus cernuus*)
- carrion flower (*Smilax ecirrata*)
- goldenrods (*Solidago* spp.)
- side-flowering aster (*Symphyotrichum lateriflorum*)
- skunk-cabbage (*Symplocarpus foetidus*)
- wood-sage (*Teucrium canadense*)
- purple meadow-rue (*Thalictrum dasycarpum*)
- drooping trillium (*Trillium flexipes*)
- common trillium (*Trillium grandiflorum*)
- stinging nettle (*Urtica dioica*)
- violets (*Viola* spp.)

FERNS
- maidenhair fern (*Adiantum pedatum*)
- bulblet fern (*Cystopteris bulbifera*)
- woodferns (*Dryopteris* spp.)
- ostrich fern (*Matteuccia struthiopteris*)
- sensitive fern (*Onoclea sensibilis*)
- royal fern (*Osmunda regalis*)
- New York fern (*Thelypteris noveboracensis*)

FERN ALLIES
- field horsetail (*Equisetum arvense*)

WOODY VINES
- American bittersweet (*Celastrus scandens*)
- wild yam (*Dioscorea villosa*)
- moonseed (*Menispermum canadense*)
- Virginia creeper (*Parthenocissus quinquefolia*)
- poison-ivy (*Toxicodendron radicans*)
- riverbank grape (*Vitis riparia*)

SHRUBS

- buttonbush (*Cephalanthus occidentalis*)
- dogwoods (*Cornus* spp.)
- whorled loosestrife (*Decodon verticillatus*)
- wahoo (*Euonymus atropurpurea*)*
- spicebush (*Lindera benzoin*)
- choke cherry (*Prunus virginiana*)
- sandbar willow (*Salix exigua*)
- bladdernut (*Staphylea trifolia*)
- black-haw (*Viburnum prunifolium*)*
- prickly ash (*Zanthoxylum americanum*)

TREES

- box elder (*Acer negundo*)
- black maple (*Acer nigrum*)
- red maple (*Acer rubrum*)
- silver maple (*Acer saccharinum*)
- sugar maple (*Acer saccharum*)
- pawpaw (*Asimina triloba*)
- yellow birch (*Betula alleghaniensis*)
- musclewood (*Carpinus caroliniana*)
- bitternut hickory (*Carya cordiformis*)
- shagbark hickory (*Carya ovata*)
- hackberry (*Celtis occidentalis*)
- redbud (*Cercis canadensis*)
- hawthorns (*Crataegus* spp.)
- beech (*Fagus grandifolia*)
- black ash (*Fraxinus nigra*)
- green ash (*Fraxinus pennsylvanica*)
- pumpkin ash (*Fraxinus profunda*)*
- blue ash (*Fraxinus quadrangulata*)
- honey locust (*Gleditsia triacanthos*)
- Kentucky coffee-tree (*Gymnocladus dioicus*)
- butternut (*Juglans cinerea*)
- black walnut (*Juglans nigra*)
- red mulberry (*Morus rubra*)*
- white pine (*Pinus strobus*)
- sycamore (*Platanus occidentalis*)
- cottonwood (*Populus deltoides*)
- swamp white oak (*Quercus bicolor*)
- bur oak (*Quercus macrocarpa*)
- red oak (*Quercus rubra*)

- peach-leaf willow (*Salix amygdaloides*)
- black willow (*Salix nigra*)
- northern white-cedar (*Thuja occidentalis*)
- basswood (*Tilia americana*)
- hemlock (*Tsuga canadensis*)
- American elm (*Ulmus americana*)

PLACES TO VISIT

- BERRIEN: Warren Woods, Warren Woods State Park
- CLARE: Muskegon River, Gladwin State Forest Management Unit
- CLINTON: Maple River Floodplain, Maple River State Game Area
- DELTA: Sturgeon River, Hiawatha National Forest
- MANISTEE: Manistee River Floodplain, Manistee River State Game Area
- OCEANA: White River, Manistee National Forest
- OTTAWA: Aman Park, City of Grand Rapids
- ST. CLAIR: Black River Floodplain Forest, Port Huron State Game Area
- WAYNE: Haggerty Road Floodplain, Lower Huron Metropark

Levee of the Muskegon River floodplain forest, Gladwin State Forest Management Unit, Clare County

123

S3 NORTHERN HARDWOOD SWAMP

Northern hardwood swamp is a seasonally inundated deciduous forested wetland typically dominated by black ash (*Fraxinus nigra*). The community is found primarily in depressions on glacial lakeplains, fine- and medium-textured glacial tills, and outwash plains. Northern hardwood swamp occurs on circumneutral to slightly acidic mineral soils and shallow mucks in the Upper Peninsula and northern Lower Peninsula. Natural processes that influence species composition and community structure include seasonal flooding, flooding by beaver, and windthrow. In addition to black ash, prevalent canopy species include red maple (*Acer rubrum*) and yellow birch (*Betula alleghaniensis*).

CHARACTERISTIC PLANTS

GRAMINOIDS
- sedges (*Carex crinita*, *C. intumescens*, *C. lupulina*, and others)
- wood reedgrasses (*Cinna arundinacea* and *C. latifolia*)
- Virginia wild-rye (*Elymus virginicus*)
- fowl manna grass (*Glyceria striata*)
- rice cut grass (*Leersia oryzoides*)
- fowl meadow grass (*Poa palustris*)

FORBS

- jack-in-the-pulpit (*Arisaema triphyllum*)
- false nettle (*Boehmeria cylindrica*)
- marsh-marigold (*Caltha palustris*)
- Pennsylvania bitter cress (*Cardamine pensylvanica*)
- turtlehead (*Chelone glabra*)
- small enchanter's-nightshade (*Circaea alpina*)
- goldthread (*Coptis trifolia*)
- flat-topped white aster (*Doellingeria umbellata*)
- willow-herbs (*Epilobium* spp.)
- fragrant bedstraw (*Galium triflorum*)

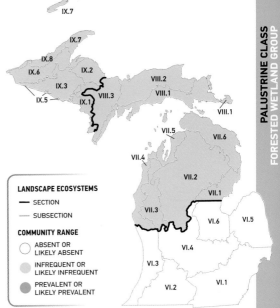

LANDSCAPE ECOSYSTEMS
— SECTION
— SUBSECTION

COMMUNITY RANGE
○ ABSENT OR LIKELY ABSENT
◐ INFREQUENT OR LIKELY INFREQUENT
● PREVALENT OR LIKELY PREVALENT

Northern hardwood swamps are characterized by overstory dominance by black ash (*Fraxinus nigra*), patches of shrubs, and a diverse ground cover, with ferns, forbs, and graminoids well represented

Black ash (*Fraxinus nigra*) is tolerant of seasonal flooding

- jewelweed (*Impatiens capensis*)
- wild blue flag (*Iris versicolor*)
- wood nettle (*Laportea canadensis*)
- northern bugle weed (*Lycopus uniflorus*)
- tufted loosestrife (*Lysimachia thyrsiflora*)
- Canada mayflower (*Maianthemum canadense*)
- partridge berry (*Mitchella repens*)
- naked miterwort (*Mitella nuda*)
- smartweeds (*Persicaria* spp.)
- clearweed (*Pilea pumila*)
- mad-dog skullcap (*Scutellaria lateriflora*)
- water parsnip (*Sium suave*)
- goldenrods (*Solidago patula*, *S. rugosa*, and others)
- calico aster (*Symphyotrichum lateriflorum*)

- swamp aster (*Symphyotrichum puniceum*)
- skunk-cabbage (*Symplocarpus foetidus*)

FERNS
- oak fern (*Gymnocarpium dryopteris*)
- ostrich fern (*Matteuccia struthiopteris*)
- sensitive fern (*Onoclea sensibilis*)
- cinnamon fern (*Osmunda cinnamomea*)
- royal fern (*Osmunda regalis*)

FERN ALLIES
- horsetails (*Equisetum* spp.)

WOODY VINES
- Virginia creeper (*Parthenocissus quinquefolia*)

SHRUBS
- tag alder (*Alnus incana*)
- winterberry (*Ilex verticillata*)
- dwarf raspberry (*Rubus pubescens*)

TREES
- balsam fir (*Abies balsamea*)
- red maple (*Acer rubrum*)
- silver maple (*Acer saccharinum*)
- yellow birch (*Betula alleghaniensis*)
- black ash (*Fraxinus nigra*)
- green ash (*Fraxinus pennsylvanica*)
- northern white-cedar (*Thuja occidentalis*)

- basswood (*Tilia americana*)
- American elm (*Ulmus americana*)

PLACES TO VISIT

- CHARLEVOIX: Walloon Lake Swamp, Gaylord State Forest Management Unit
- GOGEBIC & ONTONAGON: Porcupine Mountains, Porcupine Mountains Wilderness State Park
- LAKE & MASON: Bear Swamp, Manistee National Forest
- MANISTEE & MASON: Hopper's Swamp, Manistee National Forest

Filtered light through the open black ash (*Fraxinus nigra*) canopy allows for a dense and diverse ground-cover layer to develop following the recession of seasonal flooding

S3 SOUTHERN HARDWOOD SWAMP

Southern hardwood swamp is a groundwater-influenced forested wetland dominated by a mixture of lowland hardwoods that occurs in the southern Lower Peninsula. Southern hardwood swamp occupies shallow depressions and small stream drainages on a variety of landforms. On

lakeplains and within depressions on fine- to medium-textured moraines, an underlying impermeable clay lens is often present and allows for prolonged

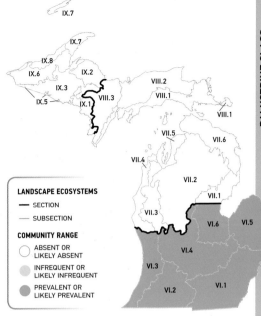

LANDSCAPE ECOSYSTEMS
— SECTION
— SUBSECTION

COMMUNITY RANGE
○ ABSENT OR LIKELY ABSENT
◐ INFREQUENT OR LIKELY INFREQUENT
● PREVALENT OR LIKELY PREVALENT

MICHAEL A. KOST

seasonal flooding. The community occurs on a variety of mineral and organic soils that range from acidic to alkaline but are generally circumneutral. Natural processes that influence species composition and community structure include seasonal flooding, flooding by beaver, and windthrow. Canopy dominants include silver maple (*Acer saccharinum*), red maple (*A. rubrum*), swamp white oak (*Quercus bicolor*), and historically, green ash (*Fraxinus pennsylvanica*), black ash (*F. nigra*), and American elm (*Ulmus americana*), which are now largely restricted to the understory due to canopy die-off caused by the introduced emerald ash borer (*Agrilus planipennis*) and Dutch elm disease.

CHARACTERISTIC PLANTS

GRAMINOIDS
- sedges (*Carex bromoides, C. gracillima, C. intumescens, C. lupulina, C. radiata, C. stipata,* and others)

Southern hardwood swamp, Highland State Recreation Area, Oakland County

- wood reedgrass (*Cinna arundinacea*)
- fowl manna grass (*Glyceria striata*)
- cut grass (*Leersia oryzoides*)
- fowl meadow grass (*Poa palustris*)

FORBS
- jack-in-the-pulpit (*Arisaema triphyllum*)
- beggar-ticks (*Bidens* spp.)
- false nettle (*Boehmeria cylindrica*)
- marsh-marigold (*Caltha palustris*)
- spring cresses (*Cardamine bulbosa* and *C. douglassii*)
- turtlehead (*Chelone glabra*)
- golden saxifrage (*Chrysosplenium americanum*)
- enchanter's-nightshade (*Circaea canadensis*)

- goldthread (*Coptis trifolia*)
- small yellow lady-slipper (*Cypripedium parviflorum* var. *makasin*)
- flat-topped white aster (*Doellingeria umbellata*)
- willow-herbs (*Epilobium* spp.)
- jewelweed (*Impatiens capensis*)
- southern blue flag (*Iris virginica*)
- wood nettle (*Laportea canadensis*)
- Michigan lily (*Lilium michiganense*)
- cardinal-flower (*Lobelia cardinalis*)
- northern bugle weed (*Lycopus uniflorus*)
- tufted loosestrife (*Lysimachia thyrsiflora*)
- Canada mayflower (*Maianthemum canadense*)
- swamp saxifrage (*Micranthes pensylvanica*)

- bishop's cap (*Mitella diphylla*)
- golden ragwort (*Packera aurea*)
- smartweeds (*Persicaria* spp.)
- clearweed (*Pilea pumila*)
- purple fringed orchid (*Platanthera psycodes*)
- swamp buttercup (*Ranunculus hispidus*)
- black snakeroots (*Sanicula marilandica* and *S. odorata*)
- mad-dog skullcap (*Scutellaria lateriflora*)
- water-parsnip (*Sium suave*)
- goldenrods (*Solidago patula*, *S. rugosa*, and others)
- calico aster (*Symphyotrichum lateriflorum*)
- swamp aster (*Symphyotrichum puniceum*)
- skunk-cabbage (*Symplocarpus foetidus*)
- purple meadow-rue (*Thalictrum dasycarpum*)

FERNS

- maidenhair fern (*Adiantum pedatum*)
- woodferns (*Dryopteris* spp.)
- sensitive fern (*Onoclea sensibilis*)
- cinnamon fern (*Osmunda cinnamomea*)
- marsh fern (*Thelypteris palustris*)

WOODY VINES

- moonseed (*Menispermum canadense*)
- Virginia creeper (*Parthenocissus quinquefolia*)
- poison-ivy (*Toxicodendron radicans*)
- riverbank grape (*Vitis riparia*)

SHRUBS

- buttonbush (*Cephalanthus occidentalis*)
- dogwoods (*Cornus amomum* and *C. foemina*)

- winterberry (*Ilex verticillata*)
- spicebush (*Lindera benzoin*)
- wild black currant (*Ribes americanum*)
- prickly gooseberry (*Ribes cynosbati*)
- dwarf raspberry (*Rubus pubescens*)
- elderberry (*Sambucus canadensis*)
- highbush blueberry (*Vaccinium corymbosum*)
- nannyberry (*Viburnum lentago*)

TREES

- red maple (*Acer rubrum*)
- silver maple (*Acer saccharinum*)
- yellow birch (*Betula alleghaniensis*)
- musclewood (*Carpinus caroliniana*)
- hackberry (*Celtis occidentalis*)
- black ash (*Fraxinus nigra*)
- green ash (*Fraxinus pennsylvanica*)
- tulip tree (*Liriodendron tulipifera*)
- sycamore (*Platanus occidentalis*)
- cottonwood (*Populus deltoides*)
- swamp white oak (*Quercus bicolor*)
- bur oak (*Quercus macrocarpa*)
- pin oak (*Quercus palustris*)
- basswood (*Tilia americana*)
- American elm (*Ulmus americana*)

PLACES TO VISIT

- BAY: Tobico Swamp, Tobico State Game Area
- OAKLAND: Haven Hill, Highland State Recreation Area
- OAKLAND: Huron Swamp, Indian Springs Metropark
- OAKLAND: Sheldon Forest, Stony Creek Metropark

S2 WET-MESIC FLATWOODS

Wet-mesic flatwoods is a wet to mesic forest on seasonally wet, poorly aerated mineral soils dominated by a highly diverse mixture of upland and lowland hardwoods. The community occurs almost exclusively on poorly drained glacial clay lakeplain or clay/sand lakeplain in the southeastern Lower

Peninsula. Surface soils are typically medium to slightly acidic sandy loam to loam and overlay mildly to moderately alkaline sandy clay loam, clay loam, or

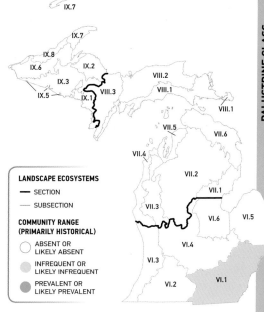

LANDSCAPE ECOSYSTEMS

— SECTION

— SUBSECTION

COMMUNITY RANGE (PRIMARILY HISTORICAL)

○ ABSENT OR LIKELY ABSENT

◐ INFREQUENT OR LIKELY INFREQUENT

● PREVALENT OR LIKELY PREVALENT

JOSHUA G. COHEN

clay. An underlying impermeable clay lens is often present, which allows for prolonged pooling of water. Natural processes that influence species composition and community structure include seasonal inundation and desiccation, windthrow, and occasional fires. Canopy dominants include oaks (*Quercus* spp.), hickories (*Carya* spp.), maples (*Acer* spp.), basswood (*Tilia americana*), American beech (*Fagus grandifolia*), and historically ashes (*Fraxinus* spp.) and American elm (*Ulmus americana*), which are now largely restricted to the understory due to canopy die-off caused by the introduced emerald ash borer (*Agrilus planipennis*) and Dutch elm disease.

CHARACTERISTIC PLANTS

GRAMINOIDS

- sedges (*Carex grayi*, *C. intumescens*, *C. lupulina*, *C. muskingumensis*, *C. tuckermanii*, and others)
- fowl manna grass (*Glyceria striata*)

Wet-mesic flatwoods with Shumard's oak (*Quercus shumardii*), Wolcott Mill Metropark, Macomb County

FORBS

- jack-in-the-pulpit (*Arisaema triphyllum*)
- spotted water hemlock (*Cicuta maculata*)
- enchanter's-nightshade (*Circaea canadensis*)
- wild geranium (*Geranium maculatum*)
- southern blue flag (*Iris virginica*)
- common water horehound (*Lycopus americanus*)
- northern bugle weed (*Lycopus uniflorus*)
- jumpseed (*Persicaria virginiana*)
- clearweed (*Pilea pumila*)
- may apple (*Podophyllum peltatum*)
- bluestem goldenrod (*Solidago caesia*)
- broad-leaved goldenrod (*Solidago flexicaulis*)

FERNS

- woodferns (*Dryopteris* spp.)
- sensitive fern (*Onoclea sensibilis*)
- royal fern (*Osmunda regalis*)
- New York fern (*Thelypteris noveboracensis*)

WOODY VINES

- Virginia creeper (*Parthenocissus quinquefolia*)
- poison-ivy (*Toxicodendron radicans*)
- riverbank grape (*Vitis riparia*)

SHRUBS

- rough-leaved dogwood (*Cornus drummondii*)

- witch-hazel (*Hamamelis virginiana*)
- winterberry (*Ilex verticillata*)
- spicebush (*Lindera benzoin*)
- maple-leaved arrow-wood (*Viburnum acerifolium*)
- prickly ash (*Zanthoxylum americanum*)

TREES
- black maple (*Acer nigrum*)
- red maple (*Acer rubrum*)
- silver maple (*Acer saccharinum*)
- sugar maple (*Acer saccharum*)
- musclewood (*Carpinus caroliniana*)
- bitternut hickory (*Carya cordiformis*)
- shellbark hickory (*Carya laciniosa*)
- shagbark hickory (*Carya ovata*)
- hackberry (*Celtis occidentalis*)
- hawthorns (*Crataegus* spp.)
- American beech (*Fagus grandifolia*)
- white ash (*Fraxinus americana*)
- green ash (*Fraxinus pennsylvanica*)

- pumpkin ash (*Fraxinus profunda*)*
- ironwood (*Ostrya virginiana*)
- sycamore (*Platanus occidentalis*)
- cottonwood (*Populus deltoides*)
- white oak (*Quercus alba*)
- swamp white oak (*Quercus bicolor*)
- bur oak (*Quercus macrocarpa*)
- chinquapin oak (*Quercus muehlenbergii*)
- pin oak (*Quercus palustris*)
- red oak (*Quercus rubra*)
- Shumard's oak (*Quercus shumardii*)*
- basswood (*Tilia americana*)
- American elm (*Ulmus americana*)

PLACES TO VISIT
- MACOMB: Kuntsman Road Swamp, Wolcott Mill Metropark
- WAYNE: Belle Isle Flatwoods, Belle Isle Park
- WAYNE: Salamander Woods, Oakwoods Metropark

Wet-mesic flatwoods, Belle Isle Park, Wayne County

135

Old-growth mesic northern forest, Porcupine Mountains Wilderness State Park, Gogebic and Ontonagon Counties

MICHAEL A. KOST

Terrestrial Class

PRAIRIE GROUP

Prairies are diverse, fire-dependent native grassland communities that occur infrequently in the Lower Peninsula and rarely in the Upper Peninsula but were historically abundant in southern Lower Michigan and infrequent farther north. Prairies occur on glacial outwash plains, pitted outwash plains, lakeplains, coarse-textured end moraines, and glacial till plains on a variety of soils, including sands, loamy sands, sandy loams, loams, and silt loams. Natural processes that influence species composition and community structure include fire, fluctuating water levels, and drought, and for prairies occurring in northern Michigan, growing-season frosts and low-nutrient soils. Prairies are dominated by warm-season grasses and herbs with no or few trees.

Five natural community types fall within the Prairie group, including hillside prairie, dry sand prairie, dry-mesic prairie, mesic prairie, and mesic sand prairie. Classification of these Prairie types is based on species composition; differences (often subtle) in soil chemistry, moisture, and composition; hydrology; geographic distribution; and landscape setting.

Dry sand prairie, Manistee National Forest, Newaygo County

MICHAEL A. KOST

HILLSIDE PRAIRIE

Hillside prairie is a native prairie community that occurs on moderate to steep exposed slopes and crests of hills associated with river valleys, streams, or kettle lakes. The community is almost always found on south- to west-facing slopes, where exposure to sunlight is highest, and is usually surrounded by oak savanna or oak forest. Hillside prairie typically occurs on strongly acidic to circumneutral loamy sands or sandy loams that are often mixed with gravel. Soil erosion and occasional fire maintain species composition and open

conditions. Dominant species are little bluestem (*Schizachyrium scoparium*), porcupine grass (*Hesperostipa spartea*), and big bluestem (*Andropogon gerardii*). These species are associated with a variety of graminoids, forbs, shrubs, and occasional trees, including Pennsylvania

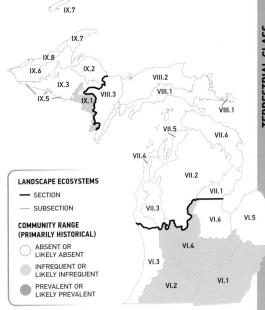

LANDSCAPE ECOSYSTEMS
— SECTION
— SUBSECTION

COMMUNITY RANGE
(PRIMARILY HISTORICAL)
○ ABSENT OR LIKELY ABSENT
◐ INFREQUENT OR LIKELY INFREQUENT
● PREVALENT OR LIKELY PREVALENT

JOSHUA G. COHEN

sedge (*Carex pensylvanica*), summer grape (*Vitis aestivalis*), flowering dogwood (*Cornus florida*), white oak (*Quercus alba*), harebell (*Campanula rotundifolia*), kitten-tails (*Besseya bullii*), round-lobed hepatica (*Hepatica americana*), bastard-toadflax (*Comandra umbellata*), and side-oats grama (*Bouteloua curtipendula*). Today, hillside prairie is nearly extirpated from Michigan due to changes in land use and colonization by shrubs and trees.

CHARACTERISTIC PLANTS

GRAMINOIDS
- big bluestem (*Andropogon gerardii*)
- side-oats grama (*Bouteloua curtipendula*)*
- Pennsylvania sedge (*Carex pensylvanica*)
- poverty grass (*Danthonia spicata*)
- porcupine grass (*Hesperostipa spartea*)
- wood-rushes (*Luzula acuminata* and *L. multiflora*)
- little bluestem (*Schizachyrium scoparium*)
- Indian grass (*Sorghastrum nutans*)

FORBS
- thimbleweed (*Anemone cylindrica*)

141

Kitten-tails (*Besseya bullii*) is a characteristic species of hillside prairies

- wild columbine (*Aquilegia canadensis*)
- milkweeds (*Asclepias amplexicaulis*, *A. verticillata*, and others)
- kitten-tails (*Besseya bullii*)*
- harebell (*Campanula rotundifolia*)
- spring-beauty (*Claytonia virginica*)
- bastard-toadflax (*Comandra umbellata*)
- common whitlow-grass (*Draba reptans*)*
- robin's-plantain (*Erigeron pulchellus*)
- flowering spurge (*Euphorbia corollata*)
- American columbo (*Frasera caroliniensis*)
- northern bedstraw (*Galium boreale*)
- pale avens (*Geum virginianum*)*
- round-leaved hepatica (*Hepatica americana*)
- alum roots (*Heuchera americana* and *H. richardsonii*)
- cylindrical blazing-star (*Liatris cylindracea*)
- northern blazing-star (*Liatris scariosa*)
- hoary puccoon (*Lithospermum canescens*)
- false spikenard (*Maianthemum racemosum*)
- prairie ragwort (*Packera paupercula*)

- hairy beard-tongue (*Penstemon hirsutus*)
- Seneca snakeroot (*Polygala senega*)
- early buttercup (*Ranunculus fascicularis*)
- old-field goldenrod (*Solidago nemoralis*)
- elm-leaved goldenrod (*Solidago ulmifolia*)
- asters (*Symphyotrichum laeve*, *S. sericeum*, and *S. urophyllum**)
- yellow-pimpernel (*Taenidia integerrima*)
- early meadow-rue (*Thalictrum dioicum*)
- rue-anemone (*Thalictrum thalictroides*)
- birdfoot violet (*Viola pedata*)
- prairie golden alexanders (*Zizia aptera*)*

WOODY VINES
- summer grape (*Vitis aestivalis*)

SHRUBS
- New Jersey tea (*Ceanothus americanus*)
- dogwoods (*Cornus* spp.)
- American hazelnut (*Corylus americana*)
- witch-hazel (*Hamamelis virginiana*)
- winged sumac (*Rhus copallina*)
- staghorn sumac (*Rhus typhina*)

TREES
- juneberry (*Amelanchier arborea*)
- pignut hickory (*Carya glabra*)
- flowering dogwood (*Cornus florida*)
- red-cedar (*Juniperus virginiana*)
- ironwood (*Ostrya virginiana*)
- white pine (*Pinus strobus*)
- quaking aspen (*Populus tremuloides*)
- white oak (*Quercus alba*)
- black oak (*Quercus velutina*)
- sassafras (*Sassafras albidum*)

PLACES TO VISIT

- JACKSON: MacCready Reserve, Michigan State University
- MENOMINEE: Pemene Falls, Escanaba State Forest Management Unit

Hillside prairie, Washtenaw County

S2 DRY SAND PRAIRIE

Dry sand prairie is a native grassland community that occurs on acidic loamy sands and sands on well-drained to excessively well-drained, sandy glacial outwash plains, pitted outwash plains, and lakebeds. Although it can occur throughout Michigan, dry sand prairie is most common in the northern Lower

Peninsula. Droughty, low-nutrient soils, growing-season frost, and occasional fire maintain species composition and community structure. Vegetation

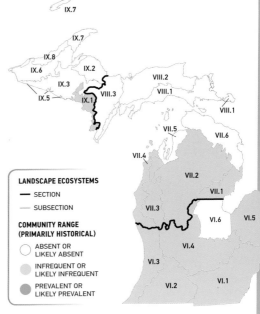

LANDSCAPE ECOSYSTEMS
— SECTION
— SUBSECTION

COMMUNITY RANGE
(PRIMARILY HISTORICAL)
○ ABSENT OR LIKELY ABSENT
◐ INFREQUENT OR LIKELY INFREQUENT
● PREVALENT OR LIKELY PREVALENT

MICHAEL A. KOST

is patchy and short in comparison to other prairie communities, and areas of exposed soil are common. The community is dominated by little bluestem (*Schizachyrium scoparium*), big bluestem (*Andropogon gerardii*), and Pennsylvania sedge (*Carex pensylvanica*). Other common grasses and forbs include poverty grass (*Danthonia spicata*), June grass (*Koeleria macrantha*), three-awned grass (*Aristida purpurascens*), sand dropseed (*Sporobolus cryptandrus*), rough blazing star (*Liatris aspera*), wild lupine (*Lupinus perennis*), horse mint (*Monarda punctata*), and milkweeds (*Asclepias* spp.).

CHARACTERISTIC PLANTS

GRAMINOIDS
- big bluestem (*Andropogon gerardii*)
- fork-tipped three-awned grass (*Aristida basiramea*)
- three-awned grass (*Aristida purpurascens*)
- wavy hair grass (*Avenella flexuosa*)

Wild lupine (*Lupinus perennis*) is a characteristic species of dry sand prairie and oak barrens

BRADFORD S. SLAUGHTER

- Pennsylvania sedge (*Carex pensylvanica*)
- slender sand sedge (*Cyperus lupulinus*)
- poverty grass (*Danthonia spicata*)
- Scribner's panic grass (*Dichanthelium oligosanthes*)
- fall witch grass (*Digitaria cognata*)
- purple love grass (*Eragrostis spectabilis*)
- rough fescue (*Festuca altaica*)*
- June grass (*Koeleria macrantha*)
- rice grass (*Piptatherum pungens*)
- little bluestem (*Schizachyrium scoparium*)
- sand dropseed (*Sporobolus cryptandrus*)

FORBS
- pale agoseris (*Agoseris glauca*)*
- smooth pussytoes (*Antennaria parlinii*)
- wormwood (*Artemisia campestris*)
- clasping milkweed (*Asclepias amplexicaulis*)
- butterfly-weed (*Asclepias tuberosa*)
- green milkweed (*Asclepias viridiflora*)
- harebell (*Campanula rotundifolia*)
- Hill's thistle (*Cirsium hillii*)*
- common rockrose (*Crocanthemum canadense*)
- prairie cinquefoil (*Drymocallis arguta*)
- flowering spurge (*Euphorbia corollata*)
- wild strawberry (*Fragaria virginiana*)
- prairie-smoke (*Geum triflorum*)*
- western sunflower (*Helianthus occidentalis*)
- long-bearded hawkweed (*Hieracium longipilum*)
- long-leaved bluets (*Houstonia longifolia*)
- hairy bush-clover (*Lespedeza hirta*)
- rough blazing-star (*Liatris aspera*)
- cylindrical blazing-star (*Liatris cylindracea*)
- northern blazing-star (*Liatris scariosa*)
- hoary puccoon (*Lithospermum canescens*)
- hairy puccoon (*Lithospermum caroliniense*)
- wild lupine (*Lupinus perennis*)
- wild bergamot (*Monarda fistulosa*)
- horse mint (*Monarda punctata*)
- blue toadflax (*Nuttallanthus canadensis*)
- prickly-pear (*Opuntia humifusa*)
- hairy beard-tongue (*Penstemon hirsutus*)
- prairie phlox (*Phlox pilosa*)
- jointweed (*Polygonella articulata*)
- early buttercup (*Ranunculus fascicularis*)
- black-eyed Susan (*Rudbeckia hirta*)
- old-field goldenrod (*Solidago nemoralis*)
- prairie heart-leaved aster (*Symphyotrichum oolentangiense*)
- silky aster (*Symphyotrichum sericeum*)*
- goats-rue (*Tephrosia virginiana*)
- birdfoot violet (*Viola pedata*)

SHRUBS

- bearberry (*Arctostaphylos uva-ursi*)
- New Jersey tea (*Ceanothus americanus*)
- sweetfern (*Comptonia peregrina*)
- sand cherry (*Prunus pumila*)
- Alleghany plum (*Prunus umbellata*)*
- northern dewberry (*Rubus flagellaris*)
- low sweet blueberry (*Vaccinium angustifolium*)

TREES

- jack pine (*Pinus banksiana*)
- red pine (*Pinus resinosa*)
- white pine (*Pinus strobus*)
- white oak (*Quercus alba*)
- northern pin oak (*Quercus ellipsoidalis*)
- black oak (*Quercus velutina*)

PLACES TO VISIT

- CRAWFORD: Shupac Lake, Grayling State Forest Management Unit
- LAKE: Tussing Prairie, Manistee National Forest
- NEWAYGO: Coolbough Natural Areas, Brooks Township
- NEWAYGO: Indian Lake Southwest and Newaygo Prairie, Manistee National Forest
- NEWAYGO: Newaygo Prairie Nature Sanctuary, Michigan Nature Association
- OCEANA: Sischo Prairies, Manistee National Forest

Newaygo Prairie, Manistee National Forest, Newaygo County

S1 DRY-MESIC PRAIRIE

Dry-mesic prairie[7] is a fire-dependent, native grassland community that occurs on sandy loams or loamy sands on level to gently sloping sites on glacial outwash plains, coarse-textured end moraine, and glacial till plain. Dry-mesic prairie represents stands of open grassland that once occurred in association with

oak openings throughout much of the southern Lower Peninsula. Historically, frequent fires helped maintain species composition and open conditions of

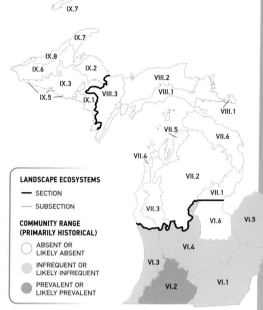

BRADFORD S. SLAUGHTER

dry-mesic prairie. The community is dominated by big bluestem (*Andropogon gerardii*), little bluestem (*Schizachyrium scoparium*), and Indian grass (*Sorghastrum nutans*). Associated forbs and occasional shrubs can include butterfly-weed (*Asclepias tuberosa*), thimbleweed (*Anemone cylindrica*), flowering spurge (*Euphorbia corollata*), smooth aster (*Symphyotrichum laeve*), black-eyed Susan (*Rudbeckia hirta*), leadplant (*Amorpha canescens*), round-headed bush-clover (*Lespedeza capitata*), daisy fleabane (*Erigeron strigosus*), and wild bergamot (*Monarda fistulosa*). Today, dry-mesic prairie is nearly extirpated from Michigan due to changes in land use and colonization by shrubs and trees.

CHARACTERISTIC PLANTS

GRAMINOIDS

- big bluestem (*Andropogon gerardii*)
- Bicknell's sedge (*Carex bicknellii*)
- Pennsylvania sedge (*Carex pensylvanica*)

- little bluestem (*Schizachyrium scoparium*)
- Indian grass (*Sorghastrum nutans*)

FORBS
- thimbleweed (*Anemone cylindrica*)
- smooth pussytoes (*Antennaria parlinii*)
- pale Indian plantain (*Arnoglossum atriplicifolium*)

- milkweeds (*Asclepias purpurascens,** *A. syriaca, A. tuberosa, A. verticillata, A. viridiflora,* and others)
- white false indigo (*Baptisia lactea*)*
- false boneset (*Brickellia eupatorioides*)*
- bastard-toadflax (*Comandra umbellata*)
- prairie coreopsis (*Coreopsis palmata*)*
- tall coreopsis (*Coreopsis tripteris*)

Dry-mesic prairie, Calhoun County

- tick-trefoils (*Desmodium canadense, D. illinoense,* and *D. marilandicum*)
- daisy fleabanes (*Erigeron annuus* and *E. strigosus*)
- flowering spurge (*Euphorbia corollata*)
- wild strawberry (*Fragaria virginiana*)
- American columbo (*Frasera caroliniensis*)
- western sunflower (*Helianthus occidentalis*)

- tall lettuce (*Lactuca canadensis*)
- round-headed bush-clover (*Lespedeza capitata*)
- hairy bush-clover (*Lespedeza hirta*)
- hoary puccoon (*Lithospermum canescens*)
- false spikenard (*Maianthemum racemosum*)
- wild bergamot (*Monarda fistulosa*)
- Solomon-seal (*Polygonatum biflorum*)
- old-field cinquefoil (*Potentilla simplex*)
- yellow coneflower (*Ratibida pinnata*)
- black-eyed Susan (*Rudbeckia hirta*)
- goldenrods (*Solidago juncea, S. nemoralis, S. rigida,* and *S. speciosa*)
- asters (*Symphyotrichum laeve, S. oolentangiense,* and *S. pilosum*)
- yellow-pimpernel (*Taenidia integerrima*)
- spiderwort (*Tradescantia ohiensis*)
- Culver's-root (*Veronicastrum virginicum*)

SHRUBS
- leadplant (*Amorpha canescens*)*
- New Jersey tea (*Ceanothus americanus*)
- American hazelnut (*Corylus americana*)
- winged sumac (*Rhus copallina*)
- smooth sumac (*Rhus glabra*)
- pasture rose (*Rosa carolina*)
- northern dewberry (*Rubus flagellaris*)
- prairie willow (*Salix humilis*)

TREES
- white oak (*Quercus alba*)
- bur oak (*Quercus macrocarpa*)
- dwarf chinquapin oak (*Quercus prinoides*)
- black oak (*Quercus velutina*)

PLACES TO VISIT
- ST. JOSEPH: Sauk Indian Trail Plant Preserve, Michigan Nature Association
- WASHTENAW: Foster Prairie, City of Ann Arbor

BRADFORD S. SLAUGHTER

S1 MESIC PRAIRIE

Mesic prairie is a fire-dependent, native grassland community that occurs on sandy loam, loam, or silt loam soils on level or slightly undulating glacial outwash plains primarily in the southwestern Lower Peninsula. Historically, frequent fires maintained species composition and

open conditions. The community is dominated by big bluestem (*Andropogon gerardii*), little bluestem (*Schizachyrium scoparium*), and Indian

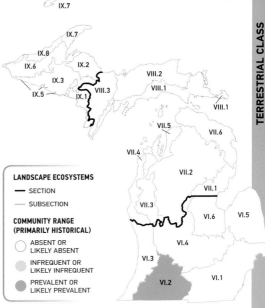

LANDSCAPE ECOSYSTEMS
— SECTION
— SUBSECTION

COMMUNITY RANGE (PRIMARILY HISTORICAL)
○ ABSENT OR LIKELY ABSENT
◐ INFREQUENT OR LIKELY INFREQUENT
● PREVALENT OR LIKELY PREVALENT

BRADFORD S. SLAUGHTER

grass (*Sorghastrum nutans*). Associated forbs and occasional shrubs can include New Jersey tea (*Ceanothus americanus*), American hazelnut (*Corylus americana*), prairie coreopsis (*Coreopsis palmata*), tall coreopsis (*C. tripteris*), northern bedstraw (*Galium boreale*), Culver's root (*Veronicastrum virginicum*), stiff goldenrod (*Solidago rigida*), wild geranium (*Geranium maculatum*), rattlesnake-master (*Eryngium yuccifolium*), and golden alexanders (*Zizia aurea*). Today, mesic prairie is nearly extirpated from Michigan due to changes in land use and colonization by shrubs and trees.

CHARACTERISTIC PLANTS

GRAMINOIDS
- big bluestem (*Andropogon gerardii*)
- Bicknell's sedge (*Carex bicknellii*)
- Leiberg's panic grass (*Dichanthelium leibergii*)*
- panic grass (*Dichanthelium oligosanthes*)
- porcupine grass (*Hesperostipa spartea*)

153

- switch grass (*Panicum virgatum*)
- little bluestem (*Schizachyrium scoparium*)
- Indian grass (*Sorghastrum nutans*)
- cordgrass (*Spartina pectinata*)
- prairie dropseed (*Sporobolus heterolepis*)*

FORBS

- thimbleweed (*Anemone cylindrica*)
- pale Indian plantain (*Arnoglossum atriplicifolium*)
- butterfly-weed (*Asclepias tuberosa*)
- white false indigo (*Baptisia lactea*)*
- false boneset (*Brickellia eupatorioides*)*
- bastard-toadflax (*Comandra umbellata*)
- prairie coreopsis (*Coreopsis palmata*)*
- tall coreopsis (*Coreopsis tripteris*)
- prairie tick-trefoil (*Desmodium illinoense*)
- wild yam (*Dioscorea villosa*)
- rattlesnake-master (*Eryngium yuccifolium*)*
- flowering spurge (*Euphorbia corollata*)
- American columbo (*Frasera caroliniensis*)
- bedstraws (*Galium boreale* and *G. pilosum*)
- wild geranium (*Geranium maculatum*)
- western sunflower (*Helianthus occidentalis*)
- pale-leaved sunflower (*Helianthus strumosus*)
- alum root (*Heuchera americana*)
- tall lettuce (*Lactuca canadensis*)
- round-headed bush-clover (*Lespedeza capitata*)
- hairy bush-clover (*Lespedeza hirta*)
- hoary puccoon (*Lithospermum canescens*)
- false spikenard (*Maianthemum racemosum*)
- wild bergamot (*Monarda fistulosa*)
- prairie phlox (*Phlox pilosa*)

- early buttercup (*Ranunculus fascicularis*)
- yellow coneflower (*Ratibida pinnata*)
- black-eyed Susan (*Rudbeckia hirta*)
- rosin weed (*Silphium integrifolium*)*
- prairie dock (*Silphium terebinthinaceum*)
- stiff goldenrod (*Solidago rigida*)
- smooth aster (*Symphyotrichum laeve*)
- prairie heart-leaved aster (*Symphyotrichum oolentangiense*)
- yellow pimpernel (*Taenidia integerrima*)
- purple meadow-rue (*Thalictrum dasycarpum*)
- common spiderwort (*Tradescantia ohiensis*)
- Culver's root (*Veronicastrum virginicum*)
- prairie violet (*Viola pedatifida*)*
- golden alexanders (*Zizia aurea*)

SHRUBS

- leadplant (*Amorpha canescens*)*
- New Jersey tea (*Ceanothus americanus*)
- American hazelnut (*Corylus americana*)
- pasture rose (*Rosa carolina*)
- prairie willow (*Salix humilis*)

TREES
- bur oak (*Quercus macrocarpa*)

PLACES TO VISIT

- No remaining sites occur on lands accessible to the public. However, readers may be able to find remnants of mesic prairie along railroad tracks and adjacent to cemeteries in southwestern Michigan.

Rattlesnake-master (*Eryngium yuccifolium*) is a characteristic species of mesic prairies

S1 MESIC SAND PRAIRIE

Mesic sand prairie is a native grassland community that occurs on sandy loam, loamy sand, or sand soils on nearly level glacial outwash plains and lakeplains in the Lower Peninsula. Mesic sand prairie is characterized by fluctuating water levels, which allow wetland plant species to coexist with dominant upland

species. In addition to fluctuating water levels, frequent fires historically served to maintain species composition and open conditions of mesic sand prairie.

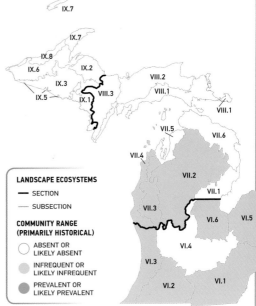

LANDSCAPE ECOSYSTEMS
— SECTION
— SUBSECTION

COMMUNITY RANGE
(PRIMARILY HISTORICAL)
○ ABSENT OR LIKELY ABSENT
◐ INFREQUENT OR LIKELY INFREQUENT
● PREVALENT OR LIKELY PREVALENT

BRADFORD S. SLAUGHTER

The community is dominated by little bluestem (*Schizachyrium scoparium*), big bluestem (*Andropogon gerardii*), and Indian grass (*Sorghastrum nutans*). Associated forbs and occasional shrubs can include tall coreopsis (*Coreopsis tripteris*), spreading dogbane (*Apocynum androsaemifolium*), butterfly-weed (*Asclepias tuberosa*), showy tick-trefoil (*Desmodium canadense*), field milkwort (*Polygala sanguinea*), false dandelion (*Krigia biflora*), round-headed bush-clover (*Lespedeza capitata*), and meadowsweet (*Spiraea alba*).

CHARACTERISTIC PLANTS

GRAMINOIDS

- big bluestem (*Andropogon gerardii*)
- blue-joint (*Calamagrostis canadensis*)
- Pennsylvania sedge (*Carex pensylvanica*)
- poverty grass (*Danthonia spicata*)
- rushes (*Juncus canadensis* and *J. tenuis*)
- little bluestem (*Schizachyrium scoparium*)
- Indian grass (*Sorghastrum nutans*)
- prairie dropseed (*Sporobolus heterolepis*)*

Mesic sand prairie dominated by big bluestem (*Andropogon gerardii*) and Indian grass (*Sorghastrum nutans*), Washtenaw County

FORBS

- colic root (*Aletris farinosa*)
- thimbleweed (*Anemone cylindrica*)
- spreading dogbane (*Apocynum androsaemifolium*)
- tall green milkweed (*Asclepias hirtella*)*
- butterfly-weed (*Asclepias tuberosa*)
- white false indigo (*Baptisia lactea*)*
- wild indigo (*Baptisia tinctoria*)
- Indian paintbrush (*Castilleja coccinea*)
- bastard-toadflax (*Comandra umbellata*)
- tall coreopsis (*Coreopsis tripteris*)
- common rockrose (*Crocanthemum canadense*)
- showy tick-trefoil (*Desmodium canadense*)
- flat-topped white aster (*Doellingeria umbellata*)
- rattlesnake-master (*Eryngium yuccifolium*)*
- flowering spurge (*Euphorbia corollata*)
- northern bedstraw (*Galium boreale*)
- bottle gentian (*Gentiana andrewsii*)
- tall sunflower (*Helianthus giganteus*)
- alum root (*Heuchera americana*)
- false dandelions (*Krigia biflora* and *K. virginica*)
- round-headed bush-clover (*Lespedeza capitata*)
- blazing-stars (*Liatris aspera*, *L. scariosa*, and *L. spicata*)
- pale spiked lobelia (*Lobelia spicata*)
- wild lupine (*Lupinus perennis*)
- wild bergamot (*Monarda fistulosa*)

- balsam ragwort (*Packera paupercula*)
- prairie phlox (*Phlox pilosa*)
- field milkwort (*Polygala sanguinea*)
- old-field cinquefoil (*Potentilla simplex*)
- common mountain mint (*Pycnanthemum virginianum*)
- black-eyed Susan (*Rudbeckia hirta*)
- stiff goldenrod (*Solidago rigida*)
- smooth aster (*Symphyotrichum laeve*)
- prairie heart-leaved aster (*Symphyotrichum oolentangiense*)
- Missouri ironweed (*Vernonia missurica*)
- arrow-leaved violet (*Viola sagittata*)

FERN ALLIES
- smooth scouring rush (*Equisetum laevigatum*)

SHRUBS
- American hazelnut (*Corylus americana*)
- winged sumac (*Rhus copallina*)
- pasture rose (*Rosa carolina*)
- northern dewberry (*Rubus flagellaris*)
- prairie willow (*Salix humilis*)
- meadowsweet (*Spiraea alba*)

PLACES TO VISIT

- MONROE: Minong Prairie, Petersburg State Game Area
- OAKLAND: Teeple Lake, Highland State Recreation Area
- WASHTENAW: Pinckney Prairie, Pinckney State Recreation Area

Mesic sand prairie, Highland State Recreation Area, Oakland County

SAVANNA GROUP

Savannas are fire-dependent upland systems that are characterized by a scattered overstory of oaks and sometimes conifers and a graminoid-dominated ground layer. The canopy cover is typically less than 60%. Savannas are now infrequent but were once widespread throughout Michigan on a variety of landforms including sandy outwash plains, sandy glacial lakeplains, coarse-textured end moraines, and kettle-kame topography. Savannas occur on a variety of soils, including sands, loamy sands, sandy loams, and loams, and soil moisture ranges from droughty to mesic. Natural processes that influence species composition and community structure include fire, fluctuating water levels, and drought, and for savannas occurring in northern Michigan, growing-season frosts and low-nutrient soils.

Six natural community types fall within the Savanna group including pine barrens, oak-pine barrens, oak barrens, oak openings, lakeplain oak openings, and bur oak plains. Classification of these Savanna types is based on species composition; differences in soil chemistry, moisture, and composition; hydrology; geographic distribution; and landscape setting.

Recently burned oak barrens, Pinckney State Recreation Area, Washtenaw County
JOSHUA G. COHEN

S2 PINE BARRENS

Pine barrens is a coniferous, fire-dependent savanna community that occurs on level sandy outwash plains and sandy glacial lakeplains in the northern Lower Peninsula and infrequently in the Upper Peninsula. Pine barrens is found on very strongly to strongly acidic, droughty sands with

very poor water-retaining capacity and low nutrient availability. Fire, severe growing-season frosts, and droughty, low-nutrient soils maintain

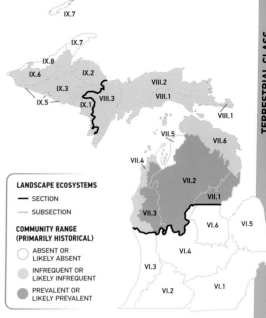

LANDSCAPE ECOSYSTEMS
— SECTION
— SUBSECTION

COMMUNITY RANGE (PRIMARILY HISTORICAL)
○ ABSENT OR LIKELY ABSENT
◐ INFREQUENT OR LIKELY INFREQUENT
● PREVALENT OR LIKELY PREVALENT

JOSHUA G. COHEN

species composition and community structure. The community consists of scattered and clumped jack pine (*Pinus banksiana*), frequently associated with northern pin oak (*Quercus ellipsoidalis*). Characteristic shrubs and herbaceous species include low sweet blueberry (*Vaccinium angustifolium*), sweet-fern (*Comptonia peregrina*), sand cherry (*Prunus pumila*), poverty grass (*Danthonia spicata*), little bluestem (*Schizachyrium scoparium*), and Pennsylvania sedge (*Carex pensylvanica*).

CHARACTERISTIC PLANTS

GRAMINOIDS
- big bluestem (*Andropogon gerardii*)
- wavy hair grass (*Avenella flexuosa*)
- prairie brome (*Bromus kalmii*)
- Pennsylvania sedge (*Carex pensylvanica*)
- slender sand sedge (*Cyperus lupulinus*)
- poverty grass (*Danthonia spicata*)
- panic grasses (*Dichanthelium* spp.)
- slender wheat grass (*Elymus trachycaulus*)

163

BRADFORD S. SLAUGHTER

Hill's thistle (*Cirsium hillii*) is a characteristic species of pine barrens and oak-pine barrens

- purple love grass (*Eragrostis spectabilis*)
- rough fescue (*Festuca altaica*)*
- June grass (*Koeleria macrantha*)
- rough-leaved rice grass (*Oryzopsis asperifolia*)
- rice grass (*Piptatherum pungens*)
- little bluestem (*Schizachyrium scoparium*)

FORBS
- pale agoseris (*Agoseris glauca*)*
- pussytoes (*Antennaria howellii* and *A. parlinii*)
- wormwood (*Artemisia campestris*)
- harebell (*Campanula rotundifolia*)
- Hill's thistle (*Cirsium hillii*)*

- common rockrose (*Crocanthemum canadense*)
- wild strawberry (*Fragaria virginiana*)
- western sunflower (*Helianthus occidentalis*)
- hawkweeds (*Hieracium kalmii* and *H. venosum*)
- long-leaved bluets (*Houstonia longifolia*)
- rough blazing-star (*Liatris aspera*)
- cylindrical blazing-star (*Liatris cylindracea*)
- northern blazing-star (*Liatris scariosa*)
- hoary puccoon (*Lithospermum canescens*)
- hairy puccoon (*Lithospermum caroliniense*)
- cow-wheat (*Melampyrum lineare*)
- horse mint (*Monarda punctata*)
- blue toadflax (*Nuttallanthus canadensis*)
- racemed milkwort (*Polygala polygama*)
- jointweed (*Polygonella articulata*)
- goldenrods (*Solidago hispida*, *S. nemoralis*, and *S. ptarmicoides*)
- slender ladies'-tresses (*Spiranthes lacera*)
- smooth aster (*Symphyotrichum laeve*)
- birdfoot violet (*Viola pedata*)

FERNS
- bracken fern (*Pteridium aquilinum*)

LICHENS
- reindeer lichens (*Cladina* spp.)

SHRUBS
- serviceberries (*Amelanchier spicata* and others)
- bearberry (*Arctostaphylos uva-ursi*)
- sweetfern (*Comptonia peregrina*)
- trailing arbutus (*Epigaea repens*)
- sand cherry (*Prunus pumila*)
- Alleghany plum (*Prunus umbellata*)*
- northern dewberry (*Rubus flagellaris*)
- prairie willow (*Salix humilis*)
- low sweet blueberry (*Vaccinium angustifolium*)
- Canada blueberry (*Vaccinium myrtilloides*)

TREES

- jack pine (*Pinus banksiana*)
- red pine (*Pinus resinosa*)
- white pine (*Pinus strobus*)
- aspens (*Populus grandidentata* and *P. tremuloides*)
- black cherry (*Prunus serotina*)
- northern pin oak (*Quercus ellipsoidalis*)

PLACES TO VISIT

- BARAGA: Baraga Plains, Baraga State Forest Management Unit
- CHIPPEWA: Raco Plains, Sault Sainte Marie State Forest Management Unit
- CRAWFORD: Frog Lake Barrens, Grayling State Forest Management Unit
- CRAWFORD: Shupac Lake Barrens, Grayling State Forest Management Unit
- OTSEGO: Little Bear Lake Barrens, Gaylord State Forest Management Unit

Pine barrens is characterized by scattered or clumped jack pine (*Pinus banksiana*)

S2 OAK-PINE BARRENS

Oak-pine barrens is a fire-dependent savanna community that occurs on well-drained sandy glacial outwash, sandy glacial lakeplains, and less often on sandy areas in coarse-textured moraines. The community is found primarily in the northern Lower and Upper Peninsulas and occasionally

in the southern Lower Peninsula. The soils of oak-pine barrens are medium to slightly acidic, droughty, low-nutrient sands or loamy sands. Fire, severe

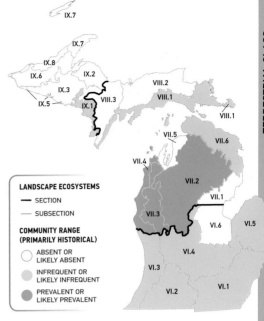

LANDSCAPE ECOSYSTEMS
— SECTION
-- SUBSECTION

COMMUNITY RANGE
(PRIMARILY HISTORICAL)
○ ABSENT OR LIKELY ABSENT
◐ INFREQUENT OR LIKELY INFREQUENT
● PREVALENT OR LIKELY PREVALENT

JOSHUA G. COHEN

growing-season frosts, and droughty, low-nutrient soils maintain species composition and the open community structure. Oak-pine barrens consists of scattered and clumped oaks and pines, including white oak (*Quercus alba*), black oak (*Q. velutina*), northern pin oak (*Q. ellipsoidalis*), jack pine (*Pinus banksiana*), red pine (*P. resinosa*), and white pine (*P. strobus*). Prevalent woody understory species are serviceberries (*Amelanchier* spp.), sweet-fern (*Comptonia peregrina*), and low sweet blueberry (*Vaccinium angustifolium*). The graminoid-dominated ground layer contains plant species associated with both prairie and forest, including little bluestem (*Schizachyrium scoparium*), big bluestem (*Andropogon gerardii*), Pennsylvania sedge (*Carex pensylvanica*), poverty oats (*Danthonia spicata*), and hair grass (*Avenella flexuosa*).

167

Oak-pine barrens grading to dry sand prairie, Newaygo County

CHARACTERISTIC PLANTS

GRAMINOIDS

- big bluestem (*Andropogon gerardii*)
- fork-tipped three-awned grass (*Aristida basiramea*)
- three-awned grass (*Aristida purpurascens*)
- wavy hair grass (*Avenella flexuosa*)
- Pennsylvania sedge (*Carex pensylvanica*)
- slender sand sedge (*Cyperus lupulinus*)
- poverty grass (*Danthonia spicata*)
- panic grasses (*Dichanthelium* spp.)
- fall witch grass (*Digitaria cognata*)
- purple love grass (*Eragrostis spectabilis*)
- porcupine grass (*Hesperostipa spartea*)
- June grass (*Koeleria macrantha*)
- black oatgrass (*Piptochaetium avenaceum*)
- little bluestem (*Schizachyrium scoparium*)

FORBS

- pussytoes (*Antennaria howellii* and *A. parlinii*)
- wormwood (*Artemisia campestris*)
- milkweeds (*Asclepias amplexicaulis*, *A. syriaca*, *A. tuberosa*, and *A. viridiflora*)
- false foxgloves (*Aureolaria flava*, *A. pedicularia*, and *A. virginica*)

- harebell (*Campanula rotundifolia*)
- Hill's thistle (*Cirsium hillii*)*
- sand coreopsis (*Coreopsis lanceolata*)
- common rockrose (*Crocanthemum canadense*)
- prairie cinquefoil (*Drymocallis arguta*)
- flowering spurge (*Euphorbia corollata*)
- wild strawberry (*Fragaria virginiana*)
- woodland sunflower (*Helianthus divaricatus*)
- western sunflower (*Helianthus occidentalis*)
- hawkweeds (*Hieracium kalmii* and *H. venosum*)
- long-leaved bluets (*Houstonia longifolia*)
- false dandelion (*Krigia biflora*)
- dwarf dandelion (*Krigia virginica*)
- hairy bush-clover (*Lespedeza hirta*)
- rough blazing-star (*Liatris aspera*)
- cylindrical blazing-star (*Liatris cylindracea*)
- northern blazing-star (*Liatris scariosa*)
- hoary puccoon (*Lithospermum canescens*)
- hairy puccoon (*Lithospermum caroliniense*)
- wild lupine (*Lupinus perennis*)
- wild bergamot (*Monarda fistulosa*)
- horse mint (*Monarda punctata*)
- blue toadflax (*Nuttallanthus canadensis*)
- prickly-pear (*Opuntia humifusa*)
- wood-betony (*Pedicularis canadensis*)
- prairie phlox (*Phlox pilosa*)
- racemed milkwort (*Polygala polygama*)
- jointweed (*Polygonella articulata*)
- early buttercup (*Ranunculus fascicularis*)
- goldenrods (*Solidago caesia, S. hispida, S. juncea, S. nemoralis,* and *S. speciosa*)
- prairie heart-leaved aster (*Symphyotrichum oolentangiense*)
- yellow-pimpernel (*Taenidia integerrima*)
- goats-rue (*Tephrosia virginiana*)
- birdfoot violet (*Viola pedata*)

FERNS

- bracken fern (*Pteridium aquilinum*)

SHRUBS

- serviceberries (*Amelanchier* spp.)
- bearberry (*Arctostaphylos uva-ursi*)
- New Jersey tea (*Ceanothus americanus*)
- sweetfern (*Comptonia peregrina*)
- hazelnuts (*Corylus americana* and *C. cornuta*)
- huckleberry (*Gaylussacia baccata*)
- American plum (*Prunus americana*)
- sand cherry (*Prunus pumila*)
- choke cherry (*Prunus virginiana*)
- pasture rose (*Rosa carolina*)
- northern dewberry (*Rubus flagellaris*)
- prairie willow (*Salix humilis*)
- low sweet blueberry (*Vaccinium angustifolium*)

TREES

- red maple (*Acer rubrum*)
- juneberry (*Amelanchier arborea*)
- flowering dogwood (*Cornus florida*)
- hawthorns (*Crataegus* spp.)
- jack pine (*Pinus banksiana*)
- red pine (*Pinus resinosa*)
- white pine (*Pinus strobus*)
- big-toothed aspen (*Populus grandidentata*)
- quaking aspen (*Populus tremuloides*)
- black cherry (*Prunus serotina*)
- white oak (*Quercus alba*)
- northern pin oak (*Quercus ellipsoidalis*)
- black oak (*Quercus velutina*)

PLACES TO VISIT

- ALLEGAN: Allegan Oak-Pine Barrens, Allegan State Game Area
- HURON: Sleeper Barrens, Albert E. Sleeper State Park and Rush Lake State Game Area
- MENOMINEE: Shakey Lakes, Escanaba State Forest Management Unit

S1 OAK BARRENS

Oak barrens is a fire-dependent savanna community that occurs in the southern Lower Peninsula on nearly level to slightly undulating sandy glacial outwash plains and less frequently on coarse-textured moraines and kettle-kame topography. The community is found on medium to slightly acidic,

droughty, low-nutrient sands or loamy sands. Historically, frequent fires and droughty, low-nutrient soils maintained species composition and

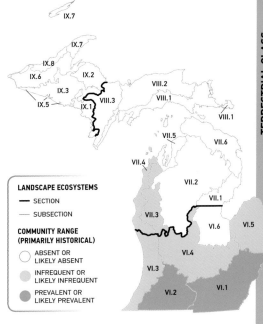

LANDSCAPE ECOSYSTEMS
— SECTION
— SUBSECTION

**COMMUNITY RANGE
(PRIMARILY HISTORICAL)**

○ ABSENT OR LIKELY ABSENT

◐ INFREQUENT OR LIKELY INFREQUENT

● PREVALENT OR LIKELY PREVALENT

JOSHUA G. COHEN

community structure. Oak barrens is dominated by scattered and clumped black oak (*Quercus velutina*) and white oak (*Q. alba*). Prevalent woody understory species are hazelnuts (*Corylus americana*), New Jersey tea (*Ceanothus americanus*), and cherries (*Prunus* spp.). The graminoid-dominated ground layer contains plant species associated with both prairie and forest, including little bluestem (*Schizachyrium scoparium*), big bluestem (*Andropogon gerardii*), Pennsylvania sedge (*Carex pensylvanica*), asters (*Symphyotrichum* spp.), false foxglove (*Aureolaria* spp.), blazing stars (*Liatris* spp.), hairy bush-clover (*Lespedeza hirta*), wild lupine (*Lupinus perennis*), wood-betony (*Pedicularis canadensis*), and milkweeds (*Asclepias* spp.). Today, oak barrens is rare in Michigan due to changes in land use and colonization by shrubs and trees.

Northern blazing-star (*Liatris scariosa*) occurring in oak barrens, Proud Lake State Recreation Area, Oakland County

JOSHUA G. COHEN

GRAMINOIDS

- big bluestem (*Andropogon gerardii*)
- fork-tipped three-awned grass (*Aristida basiramea*)
- three-awned grass (*Aristida purpurascens*)
- wavy hair grass (*Avenella flexuosa*)

- sedges (*Carex bicknellii, C. pensylvanica, C. siccata,* and others)
- slender sand sedge (*Cyperus lupulinus*)
- poverty grass (*Danthonia spicata*)
- panic grasses (*Dichanthelium* spp.)
- fall witch grass (*Digitaria cognata*)
- purple love grass (*Eragrostis spectabilis*)
- porcupine grass (*Hesperostipa spartea*)
- June grass (*Koeleria macrantha*)
- black oatgrass (*Piptochaetium avenaceum*)
- little bluestem (*Schizachyrium scoparium*)

FORBS

- pussytoes (*Antennaria howellii* and *A. parlinii*)
- wormwood (*Artemisia campestris*)
- milkweeds (*Asclepias amplexicaulis, A. tuberosa, A. verticillata, A. viridiflora,* and others)
- false foxgloves (*Aureolaria flava, A. pedicularia,* and *A. virginica*)
- white false indigo (*Baptisia lactea*)*
- false boneset (*Brickellia eupatorioides*)*
- bastard-toadflax (*Comandra umbellata*)
- sand coreopsis (*Coreopsis lanceolata*)
- frostweeds (*Crocanthemum bicknellii* and *C. canadense*)
- tick-trefoils (*Desmodium* spp.)
- flowering spurge (*Euphorbia corollata*)
- wild strawberry (*Fragaria virginiana*)
- American columbo (*Frasera caroliniensis*)
- woodland sunflower (*Helianthus divaricatus*)
- western sunflower (*Helianthus occidentalis*)
- dwarf dandelion (*Krigia virginica*)
- bush-clovers (*Lespedeza capitata, L. frutescens, L. hirta, L. violacea,* and *L. virginica*)
- rough blazing-star (*Liatris aspera*)
- cylindrical blazing-star (*Liatris cylindracea*)
- northern blazing-star (*Liatris scariosa*)
- hoary puccoon (*Lithospermum canescens*)
- hairy puccoon (*Lithospermum caroliniense*)

- wild lupine (*Lupinus perennis*)
- four-leaved loosestrife (*Lysimachia quadrifolia*)
- wild bergamot (*Monarda fistulosa*)
- horse mint (*Monarda punctata*)
- blue toadflax (*Nuttallanthus canadensis*)
- prickly-pear (*Opuntia humifusa*)
- wood-betony (*Pedicularis canadensis*)
- prairie phlox (*Phlox pilosa*)
- racemed milkwort (*Polygala polygama*)
- jointweed (*Polygonella articulata*)
- early buttercup (*Ranunculus fascicularis*)
- goldenrods (*Solidago caesia, S. juncea, S. nemoralis, S. rigida*, and *S. speciosa*)
- asters (*Symphyotrichum laeve, S. oolentangiense*, and *S. pilosum*)
- goats-rue (*Tephrosia virginiana*)
- common spiderwort (*Tradescantia ohiensis*)
- birdfoot violet (*Viola pedata*)

FERNS
- bracken fern (*Pteridium aquilinum*)

SHRUBS
- serviceberry (*Amelanchier interior*)
- leadplant (*Amorpha canescens*)*
- bearberry (*Arctostaphylos uva-ursi*)
- New Jersey tea (*Ceanothus americanus*)
- sweetfern (*Comptonia peregrina*)
- dogwoods (*Cornus* spp.)
- American hazelnut (*Corylus americana*)
- huckleberry (*Gaylussacia baccata*)

- American plum (*Prunus americana*)
- sand cherry (*Prunus pumila*)
- choke cherry (*Prunus virginiana*)
- shining sumac (*Rhus copallina*)
- pasture rose (*Rosa carolina*)
- northern dewberry (*Rubus flagellaris*)
- prairie willow (*Salix humilis*)
- low sweet blueberry (*Vaccinium angustifolium*)

TREES
- serviceberries (*Amelanchier arborea* and *A. laevis*)
- pignut hickory (*Carya glabra*)
- flowering dogwood (*Cornus florida*)
- hawthorns (*Crataegus* spp.)
- black cherry (*Prunus serotina*)
- white oak (*Quercus alba*)
- northern pin oak (*Quercus ellipsoidalis*)
- dwarf chinquapin oak (*Quercus prinoides*)
- black oak (*Quercus velutina*)
- sassafras (*Sassafras albidum*)

PLACES TO VISIT

- LIVINGSTON: Huron River Barrens, Island Lake State Recreation Area
- OAKLAND: Proud Lake Barrens, Proud Lake State Recreation Area
- WASHTENAW: Pickerel Lake Complex, Pinckney State Recreation Area

S1 OAK OPENINGS

Oak openings is a fire-dependent savanna community that occurs on slightly acidic to circumneutral, well-drained, moderately fertile sandy loams or loams on level to rolling topography of glacial outwash plains and coarse-textured end moraines in the southern Lower Peninsula.

Historically, frequent fires maintained species composition and community structure. The community is dominated by white oak (*Quercus alba*), with bur

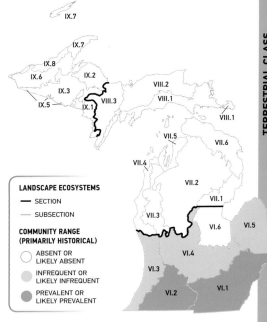

LANDSCAPE ECOSYSTEMS

— SECTION
— SUBSECTION

COMMUNITY RANGE (PRIMARILY HISTORICAL)

○ ABSENT OR LIKELY ABSENT
◐ INFREQUENT OR LIKELY INFREQUENT
● PREVALENT OR LIKELY PREVALENT

BRADFORD S. SLAUGHTER

oak (*Q. macrocarpa*) and chinquapin oak (*Q. muehlenbergii*) as frequent codominants. Prevalent woody understory species are American hazelnut (*Corylus americana*), New Jersey tea (*Ceanothus americanus*), prairie willow (*Salix humilis*), and leadplant (*Amorpha canescens*). The graminoid-dominated ground layer is composed of species associated with both prairie and forest, including big bluestem (*Andropogon gerardii*), little bluestem (*Schizachyrium scoparium*), Indian grass (*Sorghastrum nutans*), thimbleweed (*Anemone cylindrica*), milkweeds (*Asclepias* spp.), prairie coreopsis (*Coreopsis palmata*), bush-clovers (*Lespedeza capitata* and *L. hirta*), asters (*Symphyotrichum* spp.), upland boneset (*Eupatorium sessilifolium*), black-eyed Susan (*Rudbeckia hirta*), Culver's root (*Veronicastrum virginicum*), yellow coneflower (*Ratibida pinnata*), tick-trefoils (*Desmodium* spp.), and golden alexanders (*Zizia aurea*). Today, oak

175

Open-grown oak within an oak openings remnant, Barry County

openings is nearly extirpated from Michigan due to changes in land use and colonization by shrubs and trees.

CHARACTERISTIC PLANTS

GRAMINOIDS

- big bluestem (*Andropogon gerardii*)
- sedges (*Carex bicknellii, C. brevior, C.meadii,* and others)
- panic grasses (*Dichanthelium* spp.)
- porcupine grass (*Hesperostipa spartea*)
- switch grass (*Panicum virgatum*)
- little bluestem (*Schizachyrium scoparium*)
- Indian grass (*Sorghastrum nutans*)

FORBS

- hog-peanut (*Amphicarpaea bracteata*)
- thimbleweed (*Anemone cylindrica*)
- pussytoes (*Antennaria howellii* and *A. parlinii*)
- spreading dogbane (*Apocynum androsaemifolium*)
- pale Indian plantain (*Arnoglossum atriplicifolium*)
- milkweeds (*Asclepias purpurascens,** *A. syriaca, A. tuberosa, A. verticillata,* and *A. viridiflora*)
- white false indigo (*Baptisia lactea*)*
- false boneset (*Brickellia eupatorioides*)*
- bastard-toadflax (*Comandra umbellata*)

- prairie coreopsis (*Coreopsis palmata*)*
- tall coreopsis (*Coreopsis tripteris*)
- tick-trefoils (*Desmodium* spp.)
- daisy fleabane (*Erigeron strigosus*)
- upland boneset (*Eupatorium sessilifolium*)*
- flowering spurge (*Euphorbia corollata*)
- wild strawberry (*Fragaria virginiana*)
- American columbo (*Frasera caroliniensis*)
- northern bedstraw (*Galium boreale*)
- white gentian (*Gentiana alba*)*
- wild geranium (*Geranium maculatum*)
- woodland sunflower (*Helianthus divaricatus*)
- western sunflower (*Helianthus occidentalis*)
- pale-leaved sunflower (*Helianthus strumosus*)
- veiny pea (*Lathyrus venosus*)
- bush-clovers (*Lespedeza capitata, L. frutescens, L. hirta, L. violacea,* and *L. virginica*)
- hoary puccoon (*Lithospermum canescens*)
- wild lupine (*Lupinus perennis*)
- false spikenard (*Maianthemum racemosum*)
- wild-bergamot (*Monarda fistulosa*)
- wood-betony (*Pedicularis canadensis*)
- prairie phlox (*Phlox pilosa*)
- Solomon-seal (*Polygonatum biflorum*)
- common mountain mint (*Pycnanthemum virginianum*)
- early buttercup (*Ranunculus fascicularis*)
- yellow coneflower (*Ratibida pinnata*)
- black-eyed Susan (*Rudbeckia hirta*)
- starry campion (*Silene stellata*)*
- goldenrods (*Solidago caesia, S. juncea, S. nemoralis, S. rigida,* and *S. speciosa*)
- asters (*Symphyotrichum laeve, S. oolentangiense,* and *S. pilosum*)
- yellow pimpernel (*Taenidia integerrima*)
- feverwort (*Triosteum perfoliatum*)
- Culver's root (*Veronicastrum virginicum*)
- American vetch (*Vicia americana*)
- pale vetch (*Vicia caroliniana*)
- golden alexanders (*Zizia aurea*)

FERNS
- bracken fern (*Pteridium aquilinum*)

WOODY VINES
- Virginia creeper (*Parthenocissus quinquefolia*)
- bristly greenbrier (*Smilax hispida*)
- poison-ivy (*Toxicodendron radicans*)
- summer grape (*Vitis aestivalis*)
- riverbank grape (*Vitis riparia*)

SHRUBS
- leadplant (*Amorpha canescens*)*
- New Jersey tea (*Ceanothus americanus*)
- gray dogwood (*Cornus foemina*)
- American hazelnut (*Corylus americana*)
- American plum (*Prunus americana*)
- pasture rose (*Rosa carolina*)
- northern dewberry (*Rubus flagellaris*)
- sumacs (*Rhus copallina, R. glabra,* and *R. typhina*)
- prairie willow (*Salix humilis*)

TREES
- pignut hickory (*Carya glabra*)
- shagbark hickory (*Carya ovata*)
- white oak (*Quercus alba*)
- bur oak (*Quercus macrocarpa*)
- chinquapin oak (*Quercus muehlenbergii*)
- dwarf chinquapin oak (*Quercus prinoides*)
- red oak (*Quercus rubra*)
- black oak (*Quercus velutina*)

PLACES TO VISIT
- No remaining sites occur on lands accessible to the public. However, readers may be able to find remnants of oak openings along railroad tracks and adjacent to cemeteries in southwestern Michigan.

S1 LAKEPLAIN OAK OPENINGS

Lakeplain oak openings is a fire-dependent savanna community that occurs on glacial lakeplains on sand ridges, level sandplains, and adjacent depressions in the southern Lower Peninsula. The community develops on strongly acidic to mildly alkaline very fine sandy loams, loamy sands, or sands. Historically, frequent fires and seasonal flooding in depressions maintained species composition and community structure. The sandy ridges are dominated by black oak (*Quercus velutina*) and white oak (*Q. alba*). Characteristic shrubs and herbaceous species include New Jersey tea (*Ceanothus americanus*), American hazelnut (*Corylus americana*), blueberries (*Vaccinium* spp.), big bluestem (*Andropogon gerardii*), Pennsylvania sedge (*Carex pensylvanica*), blazing star (*Liatris* spp.), little bluestem (*Schizachyrium scoparium*), and Indian grass (*Sorghastrum nutans*). The depressions or swales are dominated by bur oak (*Quercus macrocarpa*), pin

oak (*Q. palustris*), and swamp white oak (*Q. bicolor*). Common species in the depressions can include dogwoods (*Cornus* spp.), willows (*Salix* spp.), blue-joint (*Calamagrostis canadensis*), tussock sedge (*Carex stricta*), water sedge (*C. aquatilis*), twig-rush (*Cladium mariscoides*), switch grass (*Panicum virgatum*), common mountain mint (*Pycnanthemum virginianum*), and cordgrass (*Spartina pectinata*). Today, lakeplain oak openings is nearly extirpated from Michigan due to changes in land use and colonization by shrubs and trees.

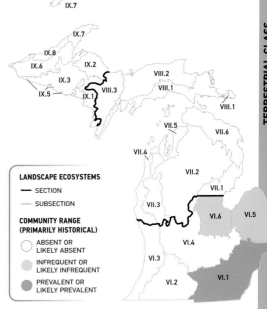

LANDSCAPE ECOSYSTEMS
— SECTION
— SUBSECTION

COMMUNITY RANGE
(PRIMARILY HISTORICAL)
○ ABSENT OR LIKELY ABSENT
◓ INFREQUENT OR LIKELY INFREQUENT
● PREVALENT OR LIKELY PREVALENT

CHARACTERISTIC PLANTS

GRAMINOIDS

- big bluestem (*Andropogon gerardii*)
- blue-joint (*Calamagrostis canadensis*)
- sedges (*Carex aquatilis, C. pensylvanica, C. stricta*, and others)
- twig-rush (*Cladium mariscoides*)
- panic grasses (*Dichanthelium* spp.)
- switch grass (*Panicum virgatum*)
- little bluestem (*Schizachyrium scoparium*)
- Indian grass (*Sorghastrum nutans*)
- cordgrass (*Spartina pectinata*)

FORBS

- purple false foxglove (*Agalinis purpurea*)
- common false foxglove (*Agalinis tenuifolia*)
- colic root (*Aletris farinosa*)
- hog-peanut (*Amphicarpaea bracteata*)
- Canada anemone (*Anemone canadensis*)
- thimbleweed (*Anemone virginiana*)
- milkweeds (*Asclepias incarnata, A. purpurascens,* * *A. syriaca, A. tuberosa, A. verticillata*, and others)
- false foxgloves (*Aureolaria flava, A. pedicularia,* and *A. virginica*)

- wild indigo (*Baptisia tinctoria*)
- bastard-toadflax (*Comandra umbellata*)
- sand coreopsis (*Coreopsis lanceolata*)
- tall coreopsis (*Coreopsis tripteris*)
- tick-trefoils (*Desmodium* spp.)
- flowering spurge (*Euphorbia corollata*)
- wild strawberry (*Fragaria virginiana*)
- northern bedstraw (*Galium boreale*)
- woodland sunflower (*Helianthus divaricatus*)
- tall sunflower (*Helianthus giganteus*)
- hairy bush-clover (*Lespedeza hirta*)
- rough blazing-star (*Liatris aspera*)
- cylindrical blazing-star (*Liatris cylindracea*)
- marsh blazing-star (*Liatris spicata*)
- Michigan lily (*Lilium michiganense*)
- wood lily (*Lilium philadelphicum*)
- hairy puccoon (*Lithospermum caroliniense*)
- wild lupine (*Lupinus perennis*)
- false spikenard (*Maianthemum racemosum*)
- wild bergamot (*Monarda fistulosa*)
- common mountain mint (*Pycnanthemum virginianum*)
- goldenrods (*Solidago altissima, S. ohioensis, S. riddellii, S. rugosa*, and others)
- prairie heart-leaved aster (*Symphyotrichum oolentangiense*)

The partially open canopy conditions of lakeplain oak openings allow for a diverse array of understory forbs and graminoids

- yellow-pimpernel (*Taenidia integerrima*)
- Culver's root (*Veronicastrum virginicum*)

FERNS
- bracken fern (*Pteridium aquilinum*)

WOODY VINES
- Virginia creeper (*Parthenocissus quinquefolia*)

- greenbriers (*Smilax hispida* and *S. rotundifolia*)
- poison-ivy (*Toxicodendron radicans*)
- summer grape (*Vitis aestivalis*)
- riverbank grape (*Vitis riparia*)

SHRUBS
- serviceberries (*Amelanchier* spp.)
- bearberry (*Arctostaphylos uva-ursi*)
- black chokeberry (*Aronia prunifolia*)
- New Jersey tea (*Ceanothus americanus*)
- buttonbush (*Cephalanthus occidentalis*)
- sweetfern (*Comptonia peregrina*)
- dogwoods (*Cornus amomum, C. foemina,* and *C. sericea*)
- American hazelnut (*Corylus americana*)
- shrubby cinquefoil (*Dasiphora fruticosa*)
- wintergreen (*Gaultheria procumbens*)
- huckleberry (*Gaylussacia baccata*)
- winterberry (*Ilex verticillata*)
- cherries and plums (*Prunus americana, P. pumila,* and *P. virginiana*)
- sumacs (*Rhus copallina* and *R. typhina*)
- pasture rose (*Rosa carolina*)
- prairie rose (*Rosa setigera*)
- northern dewberry (*Rubus flagellaris*)
- swamp dewberry (*Rubus hispidus*)
- willows (*Salix eriocephala, S. humilis,* and *S. myricoides*)
- blueberries (*Vaccinium angustifolium* and *V. myrtilloides*)
- maple-leaved arrow-wood (*Viburnum acerifolium*)

TREES
- red maple (*Acer rubrum*)
- silver maple (*Acer saccharinum*)
- juneberry (*Amelanchier arborea*)
- bitternut hickory (*Carya cordiformis*)
- pignut hickory (*Carya glabra*)
- shagbark hickory (*Carya ovata*)
- hawthorns (*Crataegus* spp.)

- green ash (*Fraxinus pennsylvanica*)
- cottonwood (*Populus deltoides*)
- black cherry (*Prunus serotina*)
- white oak (*Quercus alba*)
- swamp white oak (*Quercus bicolor*)
- bur oak (*Quercus macrocarpa*)
- pin oak (*Quercus palustris*)
- black oak (*Quercus velutina*)
- sassafras (*Sassafras albidum*)

PLACES TO VISIT

- BAY: Killarney Beach, Bay City State Recreation Area
- HURON: Wildfowl Bay Islands, Wildfowl Bay Wildlife Area
- ST. CLAIR: Algonac, Algonac State Park
- ST. CLAIR: Dickinson Island, St. Clair Flats State Wildlife Area

Lakeplain oak openings restoration, Algonac State Park, St. Clair County

SX BUR OAK PLAINS

Bur oak plains was a fire-dependent savanna community that occurred on fertile, circumneutral, mesic loam soils on river terraces and level to slightly undulating sandy glacial outwash plains in the southern Lower Peninsula. Fire maintained species composition and community structure. The community

44

was dominated by bur oak (*Quercus macrocarpa*) and occasionally white oak (*Q. alba*). The graminoid-dominated ground layer was composed of species

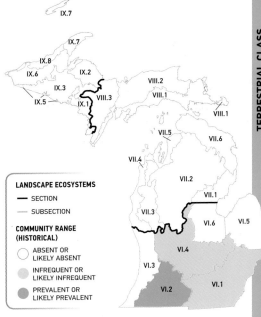

LANDSCAPE ECOSYSTEMS

— SECTION

---- SUBSECTION

COMMUNITY RANGE (HISTORICAL)

○ ABSENT OR LIKELY ABSENT

◐ INFREQUENT OR LIKELY INFREQUENT

● PREVALENT OR LIKELY PREVALENT

JOSHUA G. COHEN

associated with both prairie and forest communities, including big bluestem (*Andropogon gerardii*), little bluestem (*Schizachyrium scoparium*), Indian grass (*Sorghastrum nutans*), thimbleweed (*Anemone cylindrica*), milkweeds (*Asclepias* spp.), flowering spurge (*Euphorbia corollata*), prairie coreopsis (*Coreopsis palmata*), white gentian (*Gentiana alba*), round-headed bush-clover (*Lespedeza capitata*), asters (*Symphyotrichum* spp.), upland boneset (*Eupatorium sessilifolium*), starry campion (*Silene stellata*), yellow pimpernel (*Taenidia integerrima*), horse-gentian (*Triosteum aurantiacum*), feverwort (*Triosteum perfoliatum*), Culver's root (*Veronicastrum virginicum*), and golden alexanders (*Zizia aurea*). Prevalent woody understory species were American hazelnut (*Corylus americana*), New Jersey tea (*Ceanothus americanus*), prairie willow (*Salix humilis*), and leadplant (*Amorpha canescens*). Bur oak plains has been extirpated from Michigan and is now

Bur oak plains has been extirpated from Michigan

known only from historical literature and data derived from severely disturbed sites.

CHARACTERISTIC PLANTS

GRAMINOIDS

- big bluestem (*Andropogon gerardii*)
- blue-joint (*Calamagrostis canadensis*)
- Bicknell's sedge (*Carex bicknellii*)
- Leiberg's panic grass (*Dichanthelium leibergii*)*
- panic grass (*Dichanthelium oligosanthes*)
- porcupine grass (*Hesperostipa spartea*)
- switch grass (*Panicum virgatum*)
- little bluestem (*Schizachyrium scoparium*)
- Indian grass (*Sorghastrum nutans*)
- cordgrass (*Spartina pectinata*)
- prairie dropseed (*Sporobolus heterolepis*)*

FORBS

- hog-peanut (*Amphicarpaea bracteata*)
- milkweeds (*Asclepias purpurascens,* *A. syriaca, A. tuberosa,* and *A. verticillata*)
- white false indigo (*Baptisia lactea*)*
- false boneset (*Brickellia eupatorioides*)*
- prairie coreopsis (*Coreopsis palmata*)*
- tall coreopsis (*Coreopsis tripteris*)

- showy tick-trefoil (*Desmodium canadense*)
- prairie tick-trefoil (*Desmodium illinoense*)
- rattlesnake-master (*Eryngium yuccifolium*)*
- flowering spurge (*Euphorbia corollata*)
- wild strawberry (*Fragaria virginiana*)
- American columbo (*Frasera caroliniensis*)
- northern bedstraw (*Galium boreale*)
- wild geranium (*Geranium maculatum*)
- white gentian (*Gentiana alba*)*
- woodland sunflower (*Helianthus divaricatus*)
- western sunflower (*Helianthus occidentalis*)
- pale-leaved sunflower (*Helianthus strumosus*)
- alum root (*Heuchera americana*)
- tall lettuce (*Lactuca canadensis*)
- veiny pea (*Lathyrus venosus*)
- round-headed bush-clover (*Lespedeza capitata*)
- hairy bush-clover (*Lespedeza hirta*)
- hoary puccoon (*Lithospermum canescens*)
- false spikenard (*Maianthemum racemosum*)
- wild-bergamot (*Monarda fistulosa*)
- prairie phlox (*Phlox pilosa*)
- common mountain mint (*Pycnanthemum virginianum*)
- early buttercup (*Ranunculus fascicularis*)
- yellow coneflower (*Ratibida pinnata*)
- black-eyed Susan (*Rudbeckia hirta*)
- starry campion (*Silene stellata*)*
- rosin weed (*Silphium integrifolium*)*
- prairie dock (*Silphium terebinthinaceum*)
- goldenrods (*Solidago caesia, S. juncea, S. nemoralis, S. rigida,* and *S. speciosa*)
- asters (*Symphyotrichum laeve, S. oolentangiense,* and *S. pilosum*)
- yellow pimpernel (*Taenidia integerrima*)
- purple meadow-rue (*Thalictrum dasycarpum*)

- common spiderwort (*Tradescantia ohiensis*)
- horse-gentian (*Triosteum aurantiacum*)
- feverwort (*Triosteum perfoliatum*)
- Culver's root (*Veronicastrum virginicum*)
- American vetch (*Vicia americana*)
- pale vetch (*Vicia caroliniana*)
- prairie violet (*Viola pedatifida*)*
- golden alexanders (*Zizia aurea*)

WOODY VINES
- Virginia creeper (*Parthenocissus quinquefolia*)
- bristly greenbrier (*Smilax hispida*)
- poison-ivy (*Toxicodendron radicans*)
- summer grape (*Vitis aestivalis*)
- riverbank grape (*Vitis riparia*)

SHRUBS
- leadplant (*Amorpha canescens*)*
- New Jersey tea (*Ceanothus americanus*)
- gray dogwood (*Cornus foemina*)
- American hazelnut (*Corylus americana*)
- American plum (*Prunus americana*)
- sumacs (*Rhus copallina, R. glabra,* and *R. typhina*)
- pasture rose (*Rosa carolina*)
- prairie willow (*Salix humilis*)

TREES
- pignut hickory (*Carya glabra*)
- shagbark hickory (*Carya ovata*)
- white oak (*Quercus alba*)
- bur oak (*Quercus macrocarpa*)
- black oak (*Quercus velutina*)

PLACES TO VISIT
- Extirpated.

185

FOREST GROUP

Forests are tree-dominated uplands that occur throughout Michigan. The canopy cover of Forests is typically greater than 60%. A variety of landforms support Forests, including glacial outwash plains, glacial lakeplains, coarse-textured ground and end moraines, thin glacial drift over bedrock or cobble, kettle-kame topography, and stabilized sand dunes. Forests develop on a variety of soils, including droughty to mesic, acidic to alkaline sands, loamy sands, sandy loams, silty loams, clay loams, loams, and clays. Natural processes that influence species composition and community structure include windthrow, insect outbreaks, growing-season frosts, drought, and fires.

Seven natural community types fall within the Forest group, including dry northern forest, dry-mesic northern forest, mesic northern forest, boreal forest, dry southern forest, dry-mesic southern forest, and mesic southern forest. Classification of these Forest types is based on species composition; differences in soil chemistry, moisture, and composition; hydrology; geographic distribution; and landscape setting.

Old-growth mesic northern forest dominated by sugar maple (*Acer saccharum*), Porcupine Mountains Wilderness State Park, Gogebic and Ontonagon Counties

JOSHUA G. COHEN

S3 DRY NORTHERN FOREST

Dry northern forest is a pine or pine-hardwood forest found throughout the Upper Peninsula and northern Lower Peninsula. The community occurs primarily on sandy glacial outwash plains and lakeplains, and also commonly on upland sand ridges within peatlands on poorly drained glacial outwash plains or

lakeplains. Dry northern forest develops on excessively drained, extremely to very strongly acidic sands with low nutrient content. Historically, dry northern

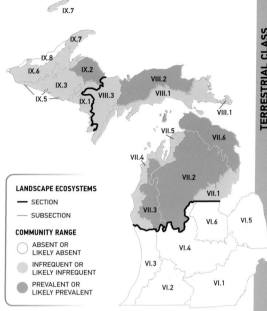

LANDSCAPE ECOSYSTEMS

— SECTION

--- SUBSECTION

COMMUNITY RANGE

○ ABSENT OR LIKELY ABSENT

◌ INFREQUENT OR LIKELY INFREQUENT

● PREVALENT OR LIKELY PREVALENT

JOSHUA G. COHEN

forest dominated by jack pine (*Pinus banksiana*) typically originated in the wake of catastrophic fire. Frequent low-intensity ground fires maintained red pine (*P. resinosa*) systems by removing competing hardwoods. In addition to fire, natural processes that influence species composition and community structure include windthrow, insect outbreaks, and severe growing-season frosts. Overstory dominants include jack pine and red pine, which are frequently associated with northern pin oak (*Quercus ellipsoidalis*).

CHARACTERISTIC PLANTS

GRAMINOIDS
- wavy hair grass (*Avenella flexuosa*)
- long-awned wood grass (*Brachyelytrum aristosum*)
- sedges (*Carex foenea, C. pensylvanica, C. siccata,* and others)
- poverty grass (*Danthonia spicata*)
- rough-leaved rice grass (*Oryzopsis asperifolia*)
- rice grass (*Piptatherum pungens*)

Dry northern forest dominated by red pine (*Pinus resinosa*) frequently occurs on inland dune ridges within peatland complexes in the Upper Peninsula

FORBS

- spreading dogbane (*Apocynum androsaemifolium*)
- wild sarsaparilla (*Aralia nudicaulis*)
- bluebell (*Campanula rotundifolia*)
- fireweed (*Chamerion angustifolium*)
- pink lady-slipper (*Cypripedium acaule*)
- large-leaved aster (*Eurybia macrophylla*)
- rattlesnake weed (*Hieracium venosum*)
- twinflower (*Linnaea borealis*)
- Canada mayflower (*Maianthemum canadense*)
- cow-wheat (*Melampyrum lineare*)
- partridge berry (*Mitchella repens*)
- hairy goldenrod (*Solidago hispida*)
- starflower (*Trientalis borealis*)

FERNS

- bracken fern (*Pteridium aquilinum*)

LICHENS

- reindeer lichens (*Cladina mitis* and *C. rangiferina*)

MOSSES

- fork mosses (*Dicranum* spp.)
- Hypnum mosses (*Hypnum* spp.)
- big red stem moss (*Pleurozium schreberi*)

SHRUBS

- running serviceberry (*Amelanchier spicata*)
- bearberry (*Arctostaphylos uva-ursi*)
- pipsissewa (*Chimaphila umbellata*)
- sweetfern (*Comptonia peregrina*)
- bunchberry (*Cornus canadensis*)
- bush honeysuckle (*Diervilla lonicera*)
- trailing arbutus (*Epigaea repens*)
- wintergreen (*Gaultheria procumbens*)
- huckleberry (*Gaylussacia baccata*)

- sand cherry (*Prunus pumila*)
- northern dewberry (*Rubus flagellaris*)
- prairie willow (*Salix humilis*)
- low sweet blueberry (*Vaccinium angustifolium*)
- Canada blueberry (*Vaccinium myrtilloides*)

TREES
- balsam fir (*Abies balsamea*)
- red maple (*Acer rubrum*)
- paper birch (*Betula papyrifera*)
- white spruce (*Picea glauca*)
- black spruce (*Picea mariana*)
- jack pine (*Pinus banksiana*)
- red pine (*Pinus resinosa*)
- white pine (*Pinus strobus*)
- big-toothed aspen (*Populus grandidentata*)

- trembling aspen (*Populus tremuloides*)
- black cherry (*Prunus serotina*)
- northern pin oak (*Quercus ellipsoidalis*)

PLACES TO VISIT
- CHIPPEWA & LUCE: Clark Lake Pine Ridges, Tahquamenon Falls State Park
- CRAWFORD: Crawford Red Pines, Grayling Forest Management Unit
- CRAWFORD: Hartwick Pines, Hartwick Pines State Park
- LUCE: Barclay Lake Jack Pines, Newberry State Forest Management Unit
- ROSCOMMON: Roscommon Red Pines, Roscommon Forest Management Unit

Fire scar on a red pine (*Pinus resinosa*), Luce County

S3 DRY-MESIC NORTHERN FOREST

Dry-mesic northern forest is a pine or pine-hardwood forest found throughout the Upper Peninsula and northern Lower Peninsula and locally in southern Michigan. The community occurs principally on sandy glacial outwash plains, sandy glacial lakeplains, and less often on inland dune ridges,

coarse-textured moraines, and thin glacial drift over bedrock. Dry-mesic northern forest develops on extremely to very strongly acidic sands or loamy sands.

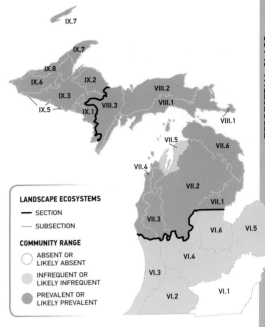

LANDSCAPE ECOSYSTEMS

— SECTION

--- SUBSECTION

COMMUNITY RANGE

○ ABSENT OR LIKELY ABSENT

INFREQUENT OR LIKELY INFREQUENT

PREVALENT OR LIKELY PREVALENT

JOSHUA G. COHEN

Dry-mesic northern forest historically originated in the wake of catastrophic fire and was maintained by frequent low-intensity ground fires. Natural processes that influence species composition and community structure include fire, windthrow, and insect outbreaks. The canopy is dominated by white pine (*Pinus strobus*) with associates including red pine (*P. resinosa*), hemlock (*Tsuga canadensis*), white oak (*Quercus alba*), and red oak (*Q. rubra*).

CHARACTERISTIC PLANTS

GRAMINOIDS

- wavy hair grass (*Avenella flexuosa*)
- long-awned wood grass (*Brachyelytrum aristosum*)
- Pennsylvania sedge (*Carex pensylvanica*)
- poverty oats (*Danthonia spicata*)
- rice grass (*Oryzopsis asperifolia*)

FORBS

- wild columbine (*Aquilegia canadensis*)
- wild sarsaparilla (*Aralia nudicaulis*)

Dry-mesic northern forest dominated by hemlock (*Tsuga canadensis*) and white pine (*Pinus strobus*)

- poke milkweed (*Asclepias exaltata*)
- blue-bead lily (*Clintonia borealis*)
- goldthread (*Coptis trifolia*)
- coral-root orchids (*Corallorhiza maculata* and *C. trifida*)
- pink lady-slipper (*Cypripedium acaule*)
- large-leaved aster (*Eurybia macrophylla*)
- rattlesnake plantains (*Goodyera oblongifolia* and *G. pubescens*)
- pinesap (*Hypopitys monotropa*)
- twinflower (*Linnaea borealis*)
- Canada mayflower (*Maianthemum canadense*)
- partridge berry (*Mitchella repens*)
- Indian-pipe (*Monotropa uniflora*)
- gay-wings (*Polygala paucifolia*)
- pine-drops (*Pterospora andromedea*)*
- large-leaved shinleaf (*Pyrola elliptica*)
- starflower (*Trientalis borealis*)

FERNS
- woodferns (*Dryopteris* spp.)
- bracken fern (*Pteridium aquilinum*)

FERN ALLIES
- ground-pine (*Dendrolycopodium obscurum*)

SHRUBS
- serviceberries (*Amelanchier* spp.)
- pipsissewa (*Chimaphila umbellata*)
- bunchberry (*Cornus canadensis*)
- beaked hazelnut (*Corylus cornuta*)
- bush honeysuckle (*Diervilla lonicera*)
- trailing arbutus (*Epigaea repens*)
- wintergreen (*Gaultheria procumbens*)
- huckleberry (*Gaylussacia baccata*)
- witch-hazel (*Hamamelis virginiana*)
- Canadian fly honeysuckle (*Lonicera canadensis*)

- choke cherry (*Prunus virginiana*)
- blueberries (*Vaccinium angustifolium* and *V. myrtilloides*)

TREES
- balsam fir (*Abies balsamea*)
- striped maple (*Acer pensylvanicum*)
- red maple (*Acer rubrum*)
- serviceberries (*Amelanchier arborea* and *A. laevis*)
- paper birch (*Betula papyrifera*)
- white spruce (*Picea glauca*)
- black spruce (*Picea mariana*)
- red pine (*Pinus resinosa*)
- white pine (*Pinus strobus*)
- big-toothed aspen (*Populus grandidentata*)
- quaking aspen (*Populus tremuloides*)
- white oak (*Quercus alba*)
- red oak (*Quercus rubra*)

- black oak (*Quercus velutina*)
- hemlock (*Tsuga canadensis*)

PLACES TO VISIT
- BARRY: Turner Creek Forest, Barry State Game Area
- CRAWFORD: Hartwick Pines, Hartwick Pines State Park
- EMMET: Nebo Trail, Wilderness State Park
- KEWEENAW: Estivant Pines Nature Sanctuary, Michigan Nature Association
- LUCE: Swamp Lakes, Newberry State Forest Management Unit and The Nature Conservancy (Swamp Lakes Preserve)
- LUCE: Two-Hearted Lakes, The Nature Conservancy (Two-Hearted River Forest Reserve)

Dry-mesic northern forest often occurs along the margins of inland lakes

S3 MESIC NORTHERN FOREST

Mesic northern forest is a hardwood or hardwood-conifer forest found throughout the Upper and northern Lower Peninsulas and locally southward along the Lake Michigan shoreline and in the Thumb. The community occurs on a wide variety of landforms and soil types but is primarily found on loamy sand to sandy loam on coarse-textured ground and end moraines. Frequent small-scale windthrow events (i.e., gap-phase dynamics) promote species diversity and allow for the regeneration of shade-tolerant canopy species. Historically, mesic northern forest occurred as a matrix system, dominating vast areas of mesic uplands in the Great Lakes region. These forests were multi-generational, with old-growth conditions lasting many centuries. Mesic northern

forest is characterized by the dominance of northern hardwoods, particularly sugar maple (*Acer saccharum*) and American beech (*Fagus grandifolia*).[8] Frequent canopy associates include yellow birch (*Betula alleghaniensis*), basswood (*Tilia americana*), and red oak (*Quercus rubra*), and conifers such as hemlock (*Tsuga canadensis*), white pine (*Pinus strobus*), and, near lakeshores and wetlands, northern white-cedar (*Thuja occidentalis*).

LANDSCAPE ECOSYSTEMS
— SECTION
---- SUBSECTION

COMMUNITY RANGE
○ ABSENT OR LIKELY ABSENT
◔ INFREQUENT OR LIKELY INFREQUENT
● PREVALENT OR LIKELY PREVALENT

CHARACTERISTIC PLANTS

GRAMINOIDS

- long-awned wood grass (*Brachyelytrum aristosum*)
- sedges (*Carex albursina, C. arctata, C. deweyana, C. hirtifolia, C. intumescens, C. leptonervia, C. pedunculata, C. plantaginea, C. radiata, C. rosea, C. woodii*, and others)
- bottlebrush grass (*Elymus hystrix*)
- western fescue (*Festuca occidentalis*)
- wood millet (*Milium effusum*)
- rough-leaved rice-grass (*Oryzopsis asperifolia*)
- bluegrasses (*Poa alsodes* and *P. saltuensis*)
- false melic (*Schizachne purpurascens*)

FORBS

- baneberries (*Actaea pachypoda* and *A. rubra*)
- wild leek (*Allium tricoccum*)
- wild sarsaparilla (*Aralia nudicaulis*)
- jack-in-the-pulpit (*Arisaema triphyllum*)
- blue cohoshes (*Caulophyllum giganteum* and *C. thalictroides*)
- enchanter's-nightshade (*Circaea canadensis*)
- Carolina spring-beauty (*Claytonia caroliniana*)
- blue-bead lily (*Clintonia borealis*)
- goldthread (*Coptis trifolia*)
- coral-root orchids (*Corallorhiza* spp.)
- squirrel-corn (*Dicentra canadensis*)
- Dutchman's breeches (*Dicentra cucullaria*)
- beech drops (*Epifagus virginiana*)
- yellow trout lily (*Erythronium americanum*)
- bedstraw (*Galium triflorum*)
- Canada mayflower (*Maianthemum canadense*)
- false spikenard (*Maianthemum racemosum*)
- Indian cucumber-root (*Medeola virginiana*)
- partridge berry (*Mitchella repens*)
- Indian-pipes (*Monotropa uniflora*)
- hairy sweet cicely (*Osmorhiza claytonii*)
- northern wood-sorrel (*Oxalis acetosella*)
- downy Solomon seal (*Polygonatum pubescens*)
- twisted-stalks (*Streptopus* spp.)
- starflower (*Trientalis borealis*)
- common trillium (*Trillium grandiflorum*)
- large-flowered bellwort (*Uvularia grandiflora*)
- sweet white violet (*Viola blanda*)
- Canada violet (*Viola canadensis*)
- yellow violet (*Viola pubescens*)
- great-spurred violet (*Viola selkirkii*)
- common blue violet (*Viola sororia*)

Mesic northern forest dominated by sugar maple (*Acer saccharum*) (*above*). The dense, shade-tolerant canopy of mesic northern forest is periodically and patchily opened by small-scale windthrow events that generate canopy gaps (*below*) critical for tree regeneration

FERNS
- maidenhair fern (*Adiantum pedatum*)
- lady fern (*Athyrium filix-femina*)
- rattlesnake fern (*Botrypus virginianus*)
- spinulose woodfern (*Dryopteris carthusiana*)
- glandular woodfern (*Dryopteris intermedia*)

- marginal woodfern (*Dryopteris marginalis*)
- oak fern (*Gymnocarpium dryopteris*)
- ostrich fern (*Matteuccia struthiopteris*)
- sensitive fern (*Onoclea sensibilis*)
- northern beech-fern (*Phegopteris connectilis*)

FERN ALLIES
- ground-pines (*Dendrolycopodium dendroideum* and *D. obscurum*)
- shining clubmoss (*Huperzia lucidula*)
- running ground-pine (*Lycopodium clavatum*)
- stiff clubmoss (*Spinulum annotinum*)

SHRUBS
- bunchberry (*Cornus canadensis*)
- beaked hazelnut (*Corylus cornuta*)
- leatherwood (*Dirca palustris*)
- Canadian fly honeysuckle (*Lonicera canadensis*)
- prickly gooseberry (*Ribes cynosbati*)
- red elderberry (*Sambucus racemosa*)
- maple-leaved arrow-wood (*Viburnum acerifolium*)

TREES
- balsam fir (*Abies balsamea*)
- striped maple (*Acer pensylvanicum*)
- red maple (*Acer rubrum*)
- sugar maple (*Acer saccharum*)
- mountain maple (*Acer spicatum*)
- yellow birch (*Betula alleghaniensis*)
- paper birch (*Betula papyrifera*)
- alternate-leaved dogwood (*Cornus alternifolia*)
- American beech (*Fagus grandifolia*)
- white ash (*Fraxinus americana*)
- ironwood (*Ostrya virginiana*)
- white pine (*Pinus strobus*)
- red oak (*Quercus rubra*)
- northern white-cedar (*Thuja occidentalis*)
- basswood (*Tilia americana*)
- hemlock (*Tsuga canadensis*)

PLACES TO VISIT

- ALGER: Pictured Rocks, Pictured Rocks National Lakeshore
- CHARLEVOIX: Walloon Lake, Gaylord State Forest Management Unit
- GOGEBIC: Lake Gogebic, Lake Gogebic State Park
- GOGEBIC: Sylvania, Sylvania Wilderness and Recreation Area, Ottawa National Forest
- GOGEBIC & ONTONAGON: Porcupine Mountains, Porcupine Mountains Wilderness State Park
- LEELANAU: Sleeping Bear Dunes, Sleeping Bear Dunes National Lakeshore
- LUCE & CHIPPEWA: Betsy Lake, Tahquamenon Falls State Park
- MARQUETTE: McCormick Tract, McCormick Research Natural Area, Ottawa National Forest
- OAKLAND: Murphy Lake Hemlocks, Murphy Lake State Game Area
- OTTAWA & MUSKEGON: P. J. Hoffmaster State Park
- ST. CLAIR: Port Huron Mesic Northern Forest, Port Huron State Game Area

Old-growth mesic northern forest, Porcupine Mountains Wilderness State Park, Gogebic and Ontonagon Counties

S3 BOREAL FOREST

Boreal forest is a conifer or conifer-hardwood forest that occupies upland sites along shores of the northern Great Lakes, on islands in the northern Great Lakes, and locally inland in the Upper Peninsula. Boreal forest occurs primarily on sand dunes, glacial lakeplains, and thin soil over bedrock or cobble. Soils vary widely, ranging from sands to clay loams and acidic to alkaline. Proximity to the Great Lakes results in high levels of windthrow and climatic conditions characterized by low summer temperatures and high levels of humidity, snowfall, and summer fog and mist. Infrequent fire and insect outbreaks are additional natural processes that influence species composition and community structure. Boreal forest is characterized by species dominant in the Canadian boreal forest. Dominant trees typically include northern white-cedar (*Thuja occidentalis*), white spruce (*Picea glauca*), and balsam fir (*Abies balsamea*).

CHARACTERISTIC PLANTS

GRAMINOIDS

- sedges (*Carex deweyana* and *C. eburnea*)
- blue wild-rye (*Elymus glaucus*)*
- false melic (*Schizachne purpurascens*)

FORBS

- red baneberry (*Actaea rubra*)
- trail-plant (*Adenocaulon bicolor*)
- wild sarsaparilla (*Aralia nudicaulis*)
- calypso (*Calypso bulbosa*)*
- bluebead lily (*Clintonia borealis*)
- goldthread (*Coptis trifolia*)
- ram's head lady-slipper (*Cypripedium arietinum*)*
- large-leaved aster (*Eurybia macrophylla*)
- fragrant bedstraw (*Galium triflorum*)
- Menzie's rattlesnake plantain (*Goodyera oblongifolia*)
- creeping rattlesnake plantain (*Goodyera repens*)
- twinflower (*Linnaea borealis*)
- Canada mayflower (*Maianthemum canadense*)
- starry false Solomon-seal (*Maianthemum stellatum*)
- false mayflower (*Maianthemum trifolium*)
- partridge berry (*Mitchella repens*)
- naked miterwort (*Mitella nuda*)
- one-flowered pyrola (*Moneses uniflora*)
- broad-leaved twayblade (*Neottia convallarioides*)
- one-sided pyrola (*Orthilia secunda*)
- northern wood-sorrel (*Oxalis acetosella*)
- sweet-coltsfoot (*Petasites frigidus*)
- gay-wings (*Polygala paucifolia*)
- green shinleaf (*Pyrola chlorantha*)
- lesser pyrola (*Pyrola minor*)
- twisted-stalks (*Streptopus* spp.)
- starflower (*Trientalis borealis*)

FERNS

- woodferns (*Dryopteris* spp.)
- oak fern (*Gymnocarpium dryopteris*)
- bracken fern (*Pteridium aquilinum*)

FERN ALLIES

ground-pines (*Dendrolycopodium*

dendroideum and *D. obscurum*)
- shining clubmoss (*Huperzia lucidula*)
- running ground-pine (*Lycopodium clavatum*)
- stiff clubmoss (*Spinulum annotinum*)

LICHENS

- usnea lichens (*Usnea* spp.)

Boreal forest along the Garden Peninsula: juxtaposition near the Great Lakes results in modified climate with cool, even temperature, a short growing season, abundant available moisture during the growing season, and deep snows in the winter

Proximity to the Great Lakes and coniferous canopy coverage generate moisture conditions suitable for a diverse array of nonvascular flora such as usnea lichens (*Usnea* spp.)

MOSSES

- dicranum moss (*Dicranum montanum*)
- stair step moss (*Hylocomium splendens*)
- largetooth calcareous moss (*Mnium spinulosum*)
- oncophorus moss (*Oncophorus wahlenbergii*)
- big red stem moss (*Pleurozium schreberi*)
- ostrich-plume moss (*Ptilium crista-castrensis*)
- shaggy moss (*Rhytidiadelphus triquetrus*)

SHRUBS

- tag alder (*Alnus incana*)
- mountain alder (*Alnus viridis*)
- bearberry (*Arctostaphylos uva-ursi*)
- bunchberry (*Cornus canadensis*)
- round-leaved dogwood (*Cornus rugosa*)
- bush honeysuckle (*Diervilla lonicera*)
- wintergreen (*Gaultheria procumbens*)
- common juniper (*Juniperus communis*)
- Canadian fly honeysuckle (*Lonicera canadensis*)
- prickly gooseberry (*Ribes cynosbati*)
- skunk currant (*Ribes glandulosum*)
- thimbleberry (*Rubus parviflorus*)
- dwarf raspberry (*Rubus pubescens*)
- soapberry (*Shepherdia canadensis*)
- snowberry (*Symphoricarpos albus*)
- Canada yew (*Taxus canadensis*)
- tall bilberry (*Vaccinium membranaceum*)
- Canada blueberry (*Vaccinium myrtilloides*)
- oval-leaved bilberry (*Vaccinium ovalifolium*)

TREES

- balsam fir (*Abies balsamea*)
- striped maple (*Acer pensylvanicum*)

- red maple (*Acer rubrum*)
- mountain maple (*Acer spicatum*)
- paper birch (*Betula papyrifera*)
- white spruce (*Picea glauca*)
- black spruce (*Picea mariana*)
- jack pine (*Pinus banksiana*)
- red pine (*Pinus resinosa*)
- white pine (*Pinus strobus*)
- balsam poplar (*Populus balsamifera*)
- quaking aspen (*Populus tremuloides*)
- American mountain-ash (*Sorbus americana*)
- mountain-ash (*Sorbus decora*)
- northern white-cedar (*Thuja occidentalis*)
- hemlock (*Tsuga canadensis*)

PLACES TO VISIT

- BENZIE: Point Betsie, The Nature Conservancy (Zetterberg Preserve at Point Betsie)
- EMMET: Cap's Cabin and Waugoshance Point, Wilderness State Park
- KEWEENAW: Isle Royale National Park
- KEWEENAW: Keweenaw Point, Baraga State Forest Management Unit
- MACKINAC: Lighthouse Point Boreal Forest (Bois Blanc Island), Gaylord State Forest Management Unit

Large stretches of boreal forest occur along the Lake Superior shoreline of the Keweenaw Peninsula

S3 DRY SOUTHERN FOREST

Dry southern forest is an oak-dominated, fire-dependent forest that occurs in the southern Lower Peninsula on glacial outwash plains and kettle-kame topography and less frequently on sand dunes, sandy glacial lakeplains, and coarse-textured moraines. The community is found

on well-drained, medium to strongly acidic sands, loamy sands, or sandy loams with low nutrient content. Historically, frequent fires maintained

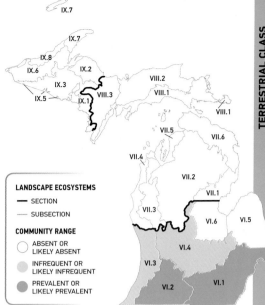

LANDSCAPE ECOSYSTEMS

— SECTION
— SUBSECTION

COMMUNITY RANGE

○ ABSENT OR LIKELY ABSENT
◔ INFREQUENT OR LIKELY INFREQUENT
● PREVALENT OR LIKELY PREVALENT

semi-open conditions and promoted oak regeneration and plant diversity. In addition to fire, windthrow, droughty low-nutrient soils, and insect outbreaks and pathogens associated with oak decline influence species composition and community structure. Dry southern forest is dominated by oaks, particularly black oak (*Quercus velutina*) and white oak (*Q. alba*).

CHARACTERISTIC PLANTS

GRAMINOIDS
- wavy hair grass (*Avenella flexuosa*)
- long-awned wood grass (*Brachyelytrum erectum*)
- sedges (*Carex cephalophora, C. muehlenbergii, C. pensylvanica,* and others)
- poverty grass (*Danthonia spicata*)

FORBS
- hog-peanut (*Amphicarpaea bracteata*)
- false foxgloves (*Aureolaria* spp.)
- large-leaved aster (*Eurybia macrophylla*)

JOSHUA G. COHEN

Dry southern forest dominated by black oak (*Quercus velutina*)

- wild geranium (*Geranium maculatum*)
- beggars lice (*Hackelia virginiana*)
- woodland sunflower (*Helianthus divaricatus*)
- pointed-leaf tick-trefoil (*Hylodesmum glutinosum*)
- naked-flower tick-trefoil (*Hylodesmum nudiflorum*)
- pale vetchling (*Lathyrus ochroleucus*)
- four-leaved loosestrife (*Lysimachia quadrifolia*)
- Canada mayflower (*Maianthemum canadense*)

- false spikenard (*Maianthemum racemosum*)
- black snakeroots (*Sanicula* spp.)
- bluestem goldenrod (*Solidago caesia*)
- yellow-pimpernel (*Taenidia integerrima*)
- pale vetch (*Vicia caroliniana*)

WOODY VINES
- summer grape (*Vitis aestivalis*)

SHRUBS
- serviceberries (*Amelanchier* spp.)
- New Jersey tea (*Ceanothus americanus*)

- spotted wintergreen (*Chimaphila maculata*)
- pipsissewa (*Chimaphila umbellata*)
- gray dogwood (*Cornus foemina*)
- American hazelnut (*Corylus americana*)
- hawthorn (*Crataegus* spp.)
- wintergreen (*Gaultheria procumbens*)
- huckleberry (*Gaylussacia baccata*)
- witch-hazel (*Hamamelis virginiana*)
- sand cherry (*Prunus pumila*)
- choke cherry (*Prunus virginiana*)
- common blackberry (*Rubus allegheniensis*)
- northern dewberry (*Rubus flagellaris*)
- low sweet blueberry (*Vaccinium angustifolium*)
- Canada blueberry (*Vaccinium myrtilloides*)
- hillside blueberry (*Vaccinium pallidum*)

TREES
- red maple (*Acer rubrum*)

- serviceberries (*Amelanchier arborea*, *A. interior*, and *A. laevis*)
- pignut hickory (*Carya glabra*)
- flowering dogwood (*Cornus florida*)
- hawthorns (*Crataegus* spp.)
- black cherry (*Prunus serotina*)
- white oak (*Quercus alba*)
- northern pin oak (*Quercus ellipsoidalis*)
- black oak (*Quercus velutina*)
- sassafras (*Sassafras albidum*)

PLACES TO VISIT

- BARRY: Bassett Lake Woods, Barry State Game Area
- JACKSON: Moeckel Road Woods, Waterloo State Recreation Area
- JACKSON & WASHTENAW: Crooked Lake Forest, Waterloo State Recreation Area

S3 DRY-MESIC SOUTHERN FOREST

Dry-mesic southern forest is an oak-dominated, fire-dependent forest that occurs in the southern Lower Peninsula on glacial outwash plains, coarse-textured moraines, sandy lakeplains, kettle-kame topography, and sand dunes. The community is found on slightly acidic to circumneutral sandy loams or loams. Historically, frequent fires maintained semi-open conditions and promoted oak regeneration and plant diversity.

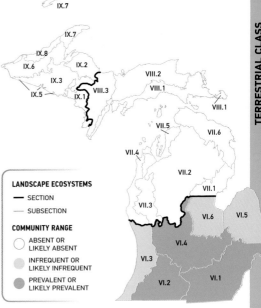

LANDSCAPE ECOSYSTEMS
— SECTION
— SUBSECTION

COMMUNITY RANGE
○ ABSENT OR LIKELY ABSENT
◔ INFREQUENT OR LIKELY INFREQUENT
● PREVALENT OR LIKELY PREVALENT

JOSHUA G. COHEN

Windthrow and insect outbreaks and pathogens associated with oak decline also influence species composition and community structure. Dry-mesic southern forest is dominated by oaks or oaks and hickories, particularly white oak (*Quercus alba*), black oak (*Q. velutina*), red oak (*Q. rubra*), pignut hickory (*Carya glabra*), and shagbark hickory (*C. ovata*).

CHARACTERISTIC PLANTS

GRAMINOIDS

- autumn bent (*Agrostis perennans*)
- long-awned wood grass (*Brachyelytrum erectum*)
- Canada brome (*Bromus pubescens*)
- sedges (*Carex albursina, C. cephalophora, C. communis, C. digitalis, C. pensylvanica, C. rosea,* and others)
- poverty grass (*Danthonia spicata*)
- panic grasses (*Dichanthelium* spp.)
- bottlebrush grass (*Elymus hystrix*)
- nodding fescue (*Festuca subverticillata*)
- cut-leaved rice-grass (*Oryzopsis asperifolia*)

Dry-mesic southern forest, Waterloo State Recreation Area, Washtenaw County

FORBS
- doll's eyes (*Actaea pachypoda*)
- tall agrimony (*Agrimonia gryposepala*)
- hog-peanut (*Amphicarpaea bracteata*)
- wild columbine (*Aquilegia canadensis*)
- wild sarsaparilla (*Aralia nudicaulis*)
- poke milkweed (*Asclepias exaltata*)
- false foxglove (*Aureolaria* spp.)
- enchanter's-nightshade (*Circaea canadensis*)
- wild yam (*Dioscorea villosa*)
- large-leaved aster (*Eurybia macrophylla*)
- bedstraws (*Galium circaezans, G. triflorum,* and others)
- wild geranium (*Geranium maculatum*)
- round-leaved hepatica (*Hepatica americana*)
- pointed-leaf tick-trefoil (*Hylodesmum glutinosum*)
- naked-flower tick-trefoil (*Hylodesmum nudiflorum*)
- Canada mayflower (*Maianthemum canadense*)
- false spikenard (*Maianthemum racemosum*)

- hairy sweet cicely (*Osmorhiza claytonii*)
- jumpseed (*Persicaria virginiana*)
- lopseed (*Phryma leptostachya*)
- may apple (*Podophyllum peltatum*)
- large-leaved shinleaf (*Pyrola elliptica*)
- black snakeroots (*Sanicula* spp.)
- bluestem goldenrod (*Solidago caesia*)
- elm-leaved goldenrod (*Solidago ulmifolia*)
- early meadow-rue (*Thalictrum dioicum*)
- rue-anemone (*Thalictrum thalictroides*)
- common trillium (*Trillium grandiflorum*)
- large-flowered bellwort (*Uvularia grandiflora*)
- merrybells (*Uvularia sessilifolia*)
- downy yellow violet (*Viola pubescens*)

FERNS

- rattlesnake fern (*Botrypus virginianus*)
- bracken fern (*Pteridium aquilinum*)

WOODY VINES

- Virginia creeper (*Parthenocissus quinquefolia*)
- bristly greenbrier (*Smilax hispida*)
- poison-ivy (*Toxicodendron radicans*)
- summer grape (*Vitis aestivalis*)
- riverbank grape (*Vitis riparia*)

SHRUBS

- serviceberries (*Amelanchier* spp.)
- gray dogwood (*Cornus foemina*)
- American hazelnut (*Corylus americana*)
- wintergreen (*Gaultheria procumbens*)
- huckleberry (*Gaylussacia baccata*)
- witch-hazel (*Hamamelis virginiana*)
- choke cherry (*Prunus virginiana*)
- prickly gooseberry (*Ribes cynosbati*)
- common blackberry (*Rubus allegheniensis*)
- black raspberry (*Rubus occidentalis*)
- wild red raspberry (*Rubus strigosus*)
- maple-leaved arrow-wood (*Viburnum acerifolium*)

- low sweet blueberry (*Vaccinium angustifolium*)
- Canada blueberry (*Vaccinium myrtilloides*)
- hillside blueberry (*Vaccinium pallidum*)

TREES

- red maple (*Acer rubrum*)
- juneberry (*Amelanchier arborea*)
- bitternut hickory (*Carya cordiformis*)
- pignut hickory (*Carya glabra*)
- shagbark hickory (*Carya ovata*)
- alternate-leaved dogwood (*Cornus alternifolia*)
- flowering dogwood (*Cornus florida*)
- white ash (*Fraxinus americana*)
- ironwood (*Ostrya virginiana*)
- black cherry (*Prunus serotina*)
- white oak (*Quercus alba*)
- northern pin oak (*Quercus ellipsoidalis*)
- red oak (*Quercus rubra*)
- black oak (*Quercus velutina*)
- sassafras (*Sassafras albidum*)
- basswood (*Tilia americana*)

PLACES TO VISIT

- BARRY: Norris Road Woods (Devil's Soupbowl) and Hall Lake, Yankee Springs State Recreation Area
- BARRY: The Hills and Gun Lake Woods, Barry State Game Area
- CASS: Forked Lake Woods and Mann Street Woods, Crane Pond State Game Area
- OAKLAND: Haven Hill, Highland State Recreation Area
- OAKLAND: Seven Lakes, Seven Lakes State Park
- OTTAWA: Aman Park, City of Grand Rapids
- WASHTENAW: Pickerel Lake Complex, Pinckney State Recreation Area

S3 MESIC SOUTHERN FOREST

Mesic southern forest is a hardwood forest found throughout the southern Lower Peninsula on a wide variety of landforms. The community is most prevalent on gently rolling ground moraine but also occurs on flat glacial outwash plains and lakeplains, kettle-kame topography, and sand dunes. Soils vary widely but are typically well-drained loams with high water-holding capacity and high nutrient content. Frequent small-scale windthrow

events (i.e., gap-phase dynamics) promote species diversity and allow for the regeneration of shade-tolerant canopy species. Historically, mesic southern forest occurred as a matrix system, dominating vast areas of level

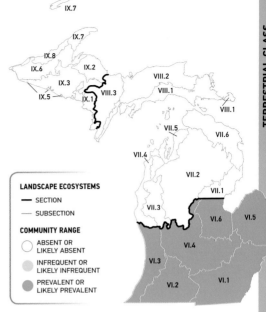

LANDSCAPE ECOSYSTEMS
— SECTION
— SUBSECTION

COMMUNITY RANGE
○ ABSENT OR LIKELY ABSENT
◐ INFREQUENT OR LIKELY INFREQUENT
● PREVALENT OR LIKELY PREVALENT

BRADFORD S. SLAUGHTER

to rolling, loamy uplands of southern Lower Michigan. These forests were multigenerational, with old-growth conditions lasting many centuries. Mesic southern forest is dominated by American beech (*Fagus grandifolia*) and sugar maple (*Acer saccharum*).

CHARACTERISTIC PLANTS

GRAMINOIDS
- autumn bent (*Agrostis perennans*)
- sedges (*Carex albursina*, *C. arctata*, *C. blanda*, *C. communis*, *C. gracilescens*, *C. grisea*, *C. hirtifolia*, *C. jamesii*, *C. pedunculata*, *C. plantaginea*, *C. rosea*, *C. woodii*, and others)
- nodding fescue (*Festuca subverticillata*)
- wood millet (*Milium effusum*)
- bluegrasses (*Poa alsodes* and *P. sylvestris*)

FORBS
- baneberries (*Actaea pachypoda* and *A. rubra*)
- wild leeks (*Allium burdickii* and *A. tricoccum*)
- Jack-in-the-pulpit (*Arisaema triphyllum*)
- wild ginger (*Asarum canadense*)

Mesic southern forest, Warren Woods State Park, Berrien County

- cut-leaved toothwort (*Cardamine concatenata*)
- blue cohoshes (*Caulophyllum giganteum* and *C. thalictroides*)
- enchanter's-nightshade (*Circaea canadensis*)
- spring beauty (*Claytonia virginica*)
- squirrel-corn (*Dicentra canadensis*)
- Dutchman's breeches (*Dicentra cucullaria*)
- false rue anemone (*Enemion biternatum*)
- beech drops (*Epifagus virginiana*)
- harbinger-of-spring (*Erigenia bulbosa*)
- yellow trout lily (*Erythronium americanum*)
- false mermaid (*Floerkea proserpinacoides*)
- wild geranium (*Geranium maculatum*)
- sharp-lobed hepatica (*Hepatica acutiloba*)

- great waterleaf (*Hydrophyllum appendiculatum*)
- Canada waterleaf (*Hydrophyllum canadense*)
- Virginia waterleaf (*Hydrophyllum virginianum*)
- pale touch-me-not (*Impatiens pallida*)
- wood nettle (*Laportea canadensis*)
- Canada mayflower (*Maianthemum canadense*)
- false spikenard (*Maianthemum racemosum*)
- bishop's-cap (*Mitella diphylla*)
- hairy sweet cicely (*Osmorhiza claytonii*)
- dwarf ginseng (*Panax trifolius*)
- May apple (*Podophyllum peltatum*)
- downy Solomon seal (*Polygonatum pubescens*)

- white lettuces (*Prenanthes alba* and *P. altissima*)
- bloodroot (*Sanguinaria canadensis*)
- upright carrion-flower (*Smilax ecirrata*)
- bluestem goldenrod (*Solidago caesia*)
- common trillium (*Trillium grandiflorum*)
- large-flowered bellwort (*Uvularia grandiflora*)
- violets (*Viola* spp.)

FERNS
- maidenhair fern (*Adiantum pedatum*)
- lady fern (*Athyrium filix-femina*)
- rattlesnake fern (*Botrypus virginianus*)
- silvery spleenwort (*Deparia acrostichoides*)
- spinulose woodfern (*Dryopteris carthusiana*)
- Goldie's woodfern (*Dryopteris goldiana*)
- evergreen woodfern (*Dryopteris intermedia*)
- marginal woodfern (*Dryopteris marginalis*)
- narrow-leaved spleenwort (*Homalosorus pycnocarpos*)
- broad beech-fern (*Phegopteris hexagonoptera*)
- Christmas fern (*Polystichum acrostichoides*)
- New York fern (*Thelypteris noveboracensis*)

WOODY VINES
- Virginia creeper (*Parthenocissus quinquefolia*)
- greenbriers (*Smilax* spp.)
- poison-ivy (*Toxicodendron radicans*)
- riverbank grape (*Vitis riparia*)

SHRUBS
- leatherwood (*Dirca palustris*)
- witch hazel (*Hamamelis virginiana*)
- spicebush (*Lindera benzoin*)
- Canadian fly honeysuckle (*Lonicera canadensis*)
- prickly gooseberry (*Ribes cynosbati*)
- red elderberry (*Sambucus racemosa*)
- maple-leaved arrow-wood (*Viburnum acerifolium*)

TREES
- sugar maple (*Acer saccharum*)
- pawpaw (*Asimina triloba*)
- musclewood (*Carpinus caroliniana*)
- bitternut hickory (*Carya cordiformis*)
- shagbark hickory (*Carya ovata*)
- alternate-leaved dogwood (*Cornus alternifolia*)
- flowering dogwood (*Cornus florida*)
- American beech (*Fagus grandifolia*)
- white ash (*Fraxinus americana*)
- tulip tree (*Liriodendron tulipifera*)
- ironwood (*Ostrya virginiana*)
- black cherry (*Prunus serotina*)
- white oak (*Quercus alba*)
- chinquapin oak (*Quercus muehlenbergii*)
- red oak (*Quercus rubra*)
- basswood (*Tilia americana*)
- American elm (*Ulmus americana*)

PLACES TO VISIT
- BERRIEN: Warren Dunes,[9] Warren Dunes State Park
- BERRIEN: Warren Woods, Warren Woods State Park
- CASS: Crane Hills, Crane Pond State Game Area
- CASS: Russ Forest, Michigan State University
- INGHAM: Baker Woodlot, Michigan State University
- INGHAM: Sanford Woods, Michigan State University
- OAKLAND: Haven Hill, Highland State Recreation Area
- OTTAWA: Grand Valley Ravines, Grand Valley State University
- WASHTENAW: Sharon Hollow, The Nature Conservancy (Nan Weston Nature Preserve at Sharon Hollow)

Wooded dune and swale complex, Gulliver
Lake Dunes, Shingleton State Forest
Management Unit, Schoolcraft County

JOSHUA G. COHEN

Palustrine/Terrestrial Class

WOODED DUNE & SWALE GROUP

The Palustrine/Terrestrial class is a unique class that includes the ecological group of Wooded Dune and Swale and the wooded dune and swale complex natural community type. Wooded dune and swale complex has characteristics of both wetlands and uplands. The community occurs on a repeated pattern of alternating dunes and swales adjacent to the Great Lakes and supports a mixture of upland and wetland communities. Floodplain forest, wet-mesic flatwoods, and lakeplain oak openings can contain wetland and upland zones. However, floodplain forest and wet-mesic flatwoods fall within the Palustrine class since they tend to be primarily dominated by wetland conditions and species, and lakeplain oak openings falls within the Terrestrial class since it tends to be primarily dominated by upland conditions and species.

Wooded dune and swale complex, Grand Traverse Bay, Baraga State Forest Management Unit, Houghton and Keweenaw Counties
MICHAEL A. KOST

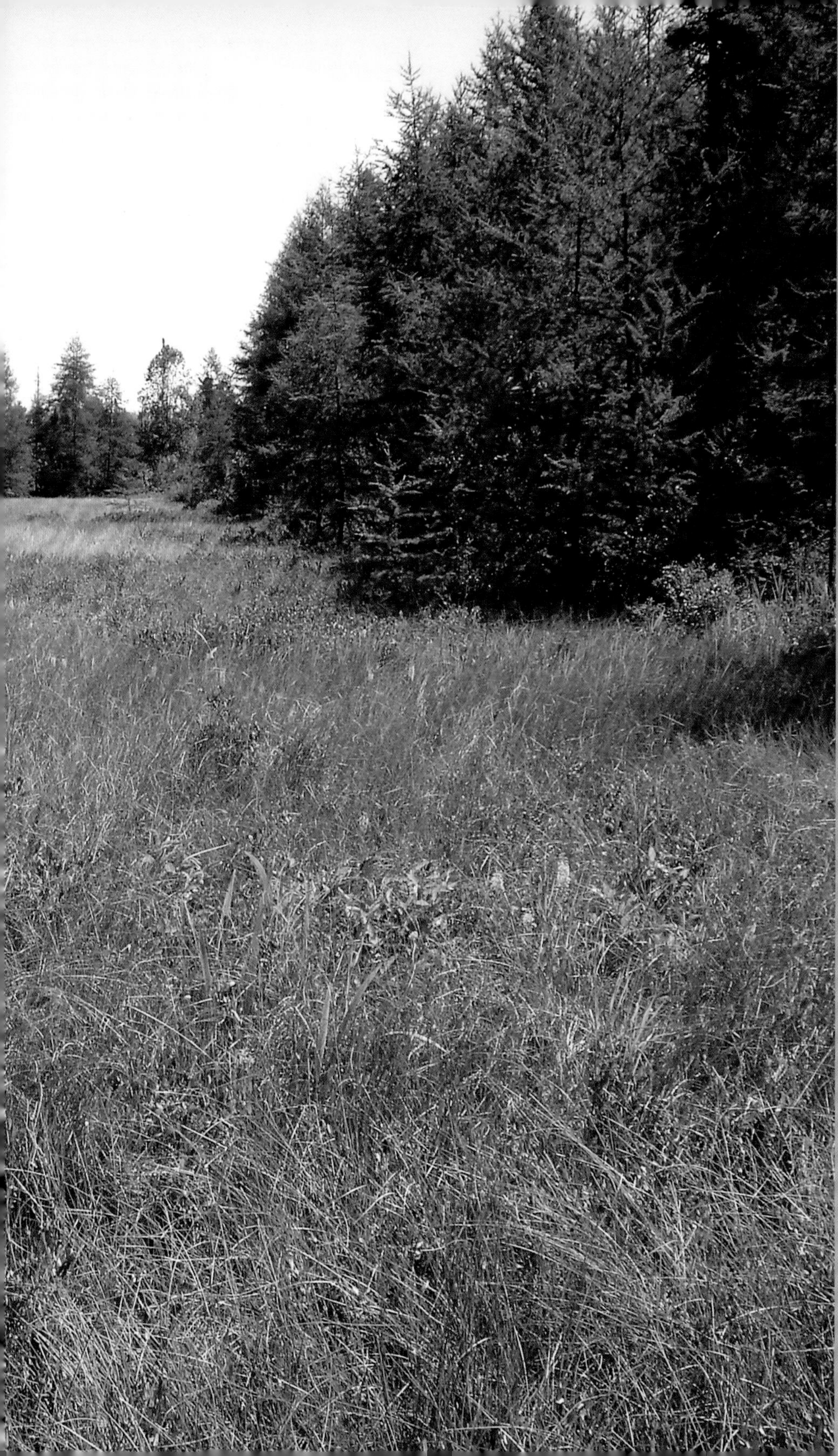

S3 WOODED DUNE & SWALE COMPLEX

Wooded dune and swale complex consists of a series of parallel wetland swales and upland beach ridges (dunes) found in coastal embayments and on large sand spits along the shorelines of the Great Lakes. The community occurs primarily in the Upper and northern Lower Peninsulas and locally in the Thumb region. Wooded dune and swale complex develops on a variety of lacustrine soils, ranging from calcareous sands on the foredunes to shallow to deep acidic peat or alkaline marl in the swales. Natural processes that influence species composition and community structure include insect outbreaks, surface water and groundwater flow regimes, windthrow, flooding by beaver, and infrequent fires. Wooded dune and swale complexes formed as a result of receding Great Lakes water levels in combination with post-glacial uplift that created a series of parallel, arcuate sand ridges and swales. The upland dune ridges are often dominated by pines (*Pinus* spp.), but a diversity of upland trees can be dominant. The swales support a variety of herbaceous or forested wetland types, with open wetlands more common near the shoreline and forested wetlands more prevalent farther from the lake.

CHARACTERISTIC PLANTS

DUNE RIDGES
GRAMINOIDS
- wavy hair grass (*Avenella flexuosa*)
- Pennsylvania sedge (*Carex pensylvanica*)
- poverty grass (*Danthonia spicata*)

FORBS
- wild sarsaparilla (*Aralia nudicaulis*)
- goldthread (*Coptis trifolia*)
- large-leaved aster (*Eurybia macrophylla*)
- twinflower (*Linnaea borealis*)
- Canada mayflower (*Maianthemum canadense*)
- cow-wheat (*Melampyrum lineare*)
- partridge berry (*Mitchella repens*)
- gay-wings (*Polygala paucifolia*)
- starflower (*Trientalis borealis*)

FERNS
- bracken fern (*Pteridium aquilinum*)

FERN ALLIES
- ground-pine (*Dendrolycopodium obscurum*)
- running ground-pine (*Lycopodium clavatum*)
- stiff clubmoss (*Spinulum annotinum*)

SHRUBS
- bearberry (*Arctostaphylos uva-ursi*)
- bunchberry (*Cornus canadensis*)
- wintergreen (*Gaultheria procumbens*)
- huckleberry (*Gaylussacia baccata*)
- common juniper (*Juniperus communis*)
- creeping juniper (*Juniperus horizontalis*)
- soapberry (*Shepherdia canadensis*)
- low sweet blueberry (*Vaccinium angustifolium*)
- Canada blueberry (*Vaccinium myrtilloides*)

TREES
- balsam fir (*Abies balsamea*)
- red maple (*Acer rubrum*)

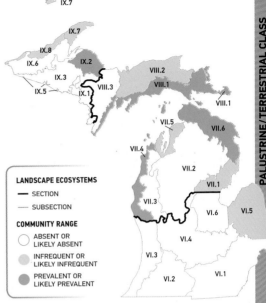

LANDSCAPE ECOSYSTEMS
- — SECTION
- — SUBSECTION

COMMUNITY RANGE
- ○ ABSENT OR LIKELY ABSENT
- INFREQUENT OR LIKELY INFREQUENT
- PREVALENT OR LIKELY PREVALENT

1998 DIGITAL ORTHOPHOTO COUNTY MOSAICS (MNFI 2006)

Aerial photo of wooded dune and swale complex on the north shore of Lake Michigan

- paper birch (*Betula papyrifera*)
- white spruce (*Picea glauca*)
- jack pine (*Pinus banksiana*)
- red pine (*Pinus resinosa*)
- white pine (*Pinus strobus*)
- big-toothed aspen (*Populus grandidentata*)
- quaking aspen (*Populus tremuloides*)
- white oak (*Quercus alba*)
- red oak (*Quercus rubra*)
- hemlock (*Tsuga canadensis*)

221

Forested dune ridge dominated by hemlock (*Tsuga canadensis*)

SWALES

GRAMINOIDS

- blue-joint (*Calamagrostis canadensis*)
- sedges (*Carex aquatilis, C. disperma, C. intumescens, C. lasiocarpa, C. leptalea, C. oligosperma, C. stricta, C. trisperma,* and others)
- twig-rush (*Cladium mariscoides*)
- tawny cotton-grass (*Eriophorum virginicum*)
- fowl manna grass (*Glyceria striata*)
- rushes (*Juncus* spp.)
- common reed (*Phragmites australis* subsp. *americanus*)
- hardstem bulrush (*Schoenoplectus acutus*)
- threesquare (*Schoenoplectus pungens*)
- wool-grass (*Scirpus cyperinus*)

FORBS

- marsh-marigold (*Caltha palustris*)
- marsh cinquefoil (*Comarum palustre*)
- Kalm's lobelia (*Lobelia kalmii*)
- swamp candles (*Lysimachia terrestris*)
- grass-of-Parnassus (*Parnassia glauca*)
- false asphodel (*Triantha glutinosa*)

FERNS

- oak fern (*Gymnocarpium dryopteris*)
- sensitive fern (*Onoclea sensibilis*)
- cinnamon fern (*Osmunda cinnamomea*)
- royal fern (*Osmunda regalis*)
- marsh fern (*Thelypteris palustris*)

FERN ALLIES

- woodland horsetail (*Equisetum sylvaticum*)

MOSSES

- sphagnum mosses (*Sphagnum* spp.)

SHRUBS

- tag alder (*Alnus incana*)
- black chokeberry (*Aronia prunifolia*)
- bog birch (*Betula pumila*)
- dogwoods (*Cornus* spp.)
- leatherleaf (*Chamaedaphne calyculata*)
- shrubby cinquefoil (*Dasiphora fruticosa*)
- sweet gale (*Myrica gale*)
- dwarf raspberry (*Rubus pubescens*)
- willows (*Salix candida*, *S. pedicellaris*, *S. petiolaris*, and others)
- cranberries (*Vaccinium macrocarpon* and *V. oxycoccos*)

TREES

- red maple (*Acer rubrum*)
- black ash (*Fraxinus nigra*)
- tamarack (*Larix laricina*)
- black spruce (*Picea mariana*)
- northern white-cedar (*Thuja occidentalis*)

PLACES TO VISIT

- BENZIE: Platte Bay, Sleeping Bear Dunes National Lakeshore
- CHIPPEWA: Whitefish Point, Newberry State Forest Management Unit
- EMMET: Sturgeon Bay, Wilderness State Park
- HURON: Port Crescent, Port Crescent State Park
- MACKINAC: Big Knob Campground, Sault Sainte Marie State Forest Management Unit
- MACKINAC: Pointe Aux Chenes, Hiawatha National Forest
- MACKINAC: Scott Point, Sault Sainte Marie State Forest Management Unit
- MARQUETTE: Little Presque Isle, Gwinn State Forest Management Unit
- SCHOOLCRAFT: Gulliver Lake Dunes, Shingleton State Forest Management Unit

Wooded dune and swale complex, Big Knob Campground, Sault Sainte Marie State Forest Management Unit, Mackinac County

223

Granite bedrock glade, Gwinn Forest
Management Unit, Marquette County

JOSHUA G. COHEN

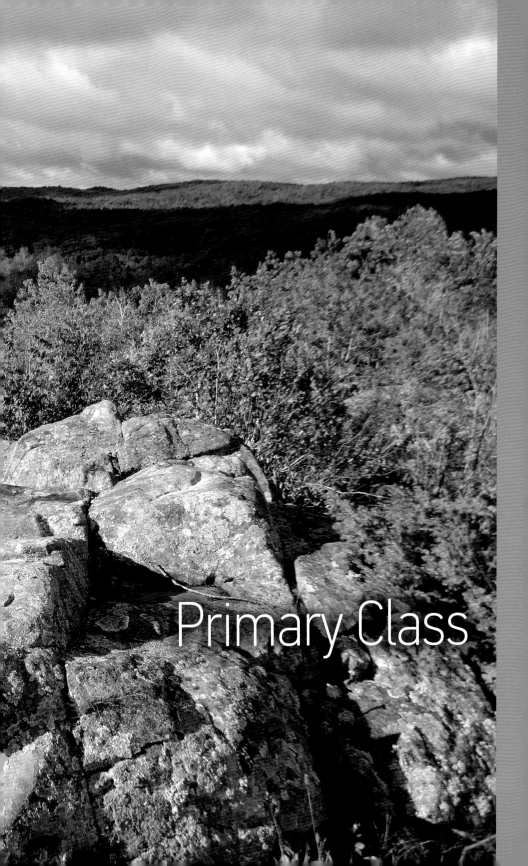

Primary Class

DUNES GROUP

Dunes occur on wind-deposited sand formations near the shorelines of the Great Lakes. Dunes are characterized by little soil development and exposed, neutral to alkaline dune sands. Natural processes that influence species composition and community structure include wind-mediated sand deposition and erosion, sand burial and abrasion, desiccation, and infrequent fire.

Two natural community types fall within the Dunes group, including open dunes and Great Lakes barrens. Classification of these Dunes types is based on shoreline processes, species composition, community structure, and landscape setting.

Open dunes, North Manitou Island, Sleeping Bear Dunes National Lakeshore, Leelanau County

JOSHUA G. COHEN

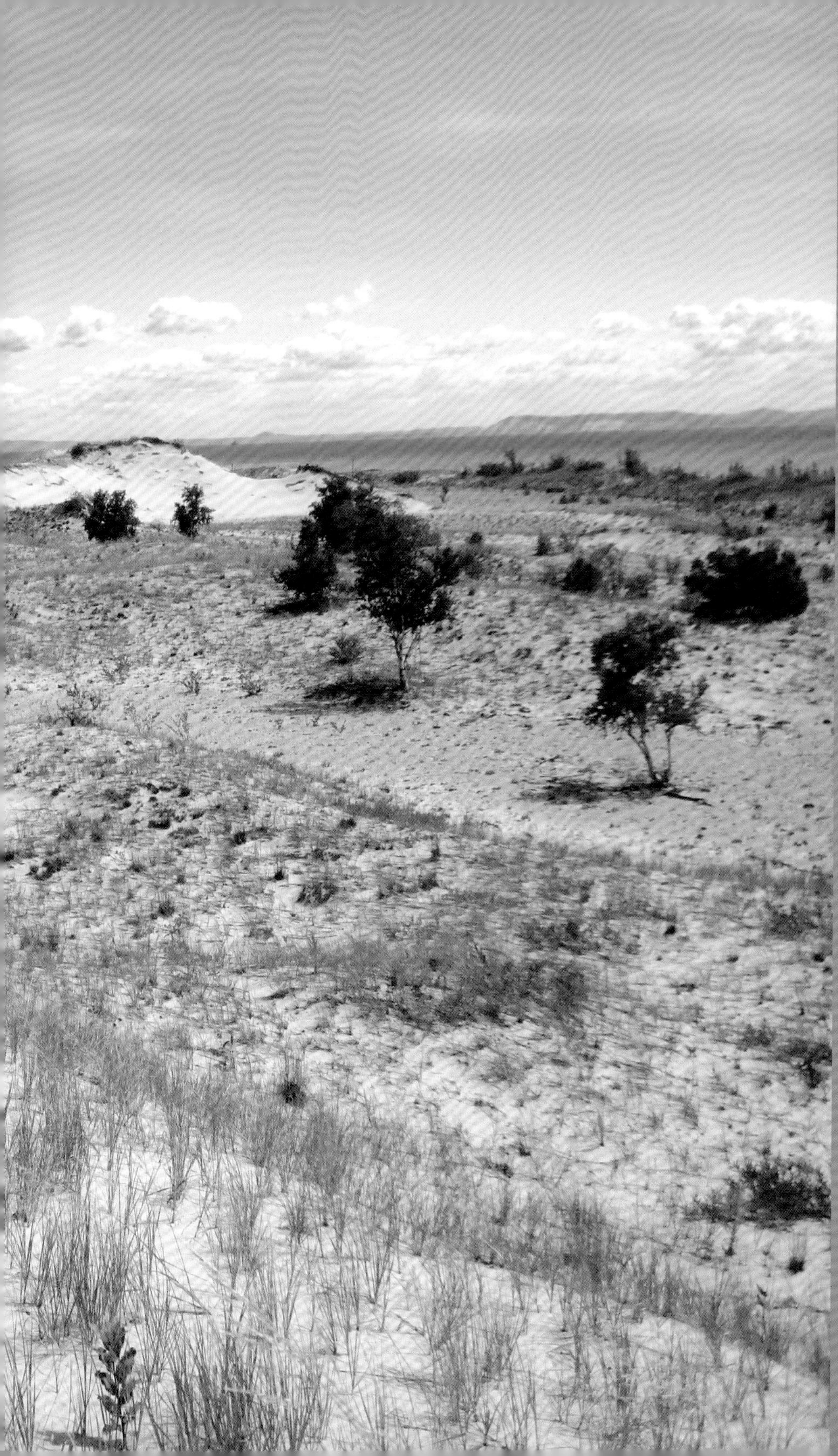

S3 · OPEN DUNES

Open dunes is a grass- and shrub-dominated community located on wind-deposited sand formations near the shorelines of the Great Lakes. The greatest concentration of open dunes occurs along the eastern and northern shorelines of Lake Michigan, with the largest dunes along the eastern shoreline

due to strong prevailing southwest winds. Open dunes develop on circumneutral to slightly alkaline sands. Blowouts, sand burial and abrasion,

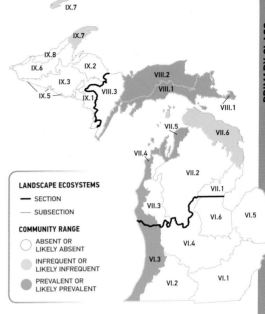

LANDSCAPE ECOSYSTEMS
— SECTION
----- SUBSECTION

COMMUNITY RANGE
○ ABSENT OR LIKELY ABSENT
◔ INFREQUENT OR LIKELY INFREQUENT
● PREVALENT OR LIKELY PREVALENT

JOSHUA G. COHEN

excessively well-drained and droughty soils, desiccating winds, and occasional fires maintain open conditions. Dominant species typically include marram grass (*Ammophila breviligulata*) and sand reed grass (*Calamovilfa longifolia*). Characteristic associates include little bluestem (*Schizachyrium scoparium*), bearberry (*Arctostaphylos uva-ursi*), creeping juniper (*Juniperus horizontalis*), common juniper (*J. communis*), sand cherry (*Prunus pumila*), willows (*Salix cordata, S. exigua, S. serissima,* and *S. myricoides*), beach pea (*Lathyrus japonicus*), plains puccoon (*Lithospermum caroliniense*), wormwood (*Artemisia campestris*), harebell (*Campanula rotundifolia*), Pitcher's thistle (*Cirsium pitcheri*), and common milkweed (*Asclepias syriaca*).

CHARACTERISTIC PLANTS

GRAMINOIDS

- marram grass (*Ammophila breviligulata*)
- sand reed grass (*Calamovilfa longifolia*)

Open dunes dominated by marram grass (*Ammophila breviligulata*)

- rough sand sedge (*Cyperus schweinitzii*)
- wheat grasses (*Elymus lanceolatus* and *E. trachycaulus*)
- Rocky Mountain fescue (*Festuca saximontana*)
- June grass (*Koeleria macrantha*)
- switch grass (*Panicum virgatum*)
- little bluestem (*Schizachyrium scoparium*)

FORBS
- red anemone (*Anemone multifida*)
- sand cress (*Arabidopsis lyrata*)
- wormwood (*Artemisia campestris*)
- common milkweed (*Asclepias syriaca*)

- sea rocket (*Cakile edentula*)
- harebell (*Campanula rotundifolia*)
- Pitcher's thistle (*Cirsium pitcheri*)*
- sand coreopsis (*Coreopsis lanceolata*)
- bugseeds (*Corispermum americanum* and *C. pallasii*)
- flowering spurge (*Euphorbia corollata*)
- seaside spurge (*Euphorbia polygonifolia*)
- beach pea (*Lathyrus japonicus*)
- plains puccoon (*Lithospermum caroliniense*)
- starry false Solomon-seal (*Maianthemum stellatum*)
- horse mint (*Monarda punctata*)
- jointweed (*Polygonella articulata*)

- silverweed (*Potentilla anserina*)
- Gillman's goldenrod (*Solidago simplex*)
- Lake Huron tansy (*Tanacetum bipinnatum*)*

WOODY VINES

- American bittersweet (*Celastrus scandens*)
- poison-ivy (*Toxicodendron radicans*)
- riverbank grape (*Vitis riparia*)

SHRUBS

- bearberry (*Arctostaphylos uva-ursi*)
- bunchberry (*Cornus canadensis*)
- round-leaved dogwood (*Cornus rugosa*)
- red-osier dogwood (*Cornus sericea*)
- shrubby cinquefoil (*Dasiphora fruticosa*)
- beach heath (*Hudsonia tomentosa*)
- common juniper (*Juniperus communis*)
- creeping juniper (*Juniperus horizontalis*)
- sand cherry (*Prunus pumila*)
- hop tree (*Ptelea trifoliata*)
- wild roses (*Rosa acicularis* and *R. blanda*)
- pasture rose (*Rosa carolina*)
- willows (*Salix cordata, S. exigua,
  S. myricoides,* and *S. serissima*)
- poison-ivy (*Toxicodendron rydbergii*)
- blueberries (*Vaccinium angustifolium* and
  V. myrtilloides)

TREES

- balsam fir (*Abies balsamea*)
- paper birch (*Betula papyrifera*)
- white ash (*Fraxinus americana*)
- white spruce (*Picea glauca*)
- pines (*Pinus banksiana, P. resinosa,* and
  P. strobus)
- balsam poplar (*Populus balsamifera*)
- cottonwood (*Populus deltoides*)
- big-toothed aspen (*Populus grandidentata*)
- quaking aspen (*Populus tremuloides*)
- red oak (*Quercus rubra*)
- black oak (*Quercus velutina*)
- sassafras (*Sassafras albidum*)

- northern white-cedar (*Thuja occidentalis*)
- basswood (*Tilia americana*)

PLACES TO VISIT

- ALGER: Grand Sable Dunes, Pictured Rocks
  National Lakeshore
- ALLEGAN: Saugatuck Dunes, Saugatuck
  Dunes State Park
- BERRIEN: Grand Mere, Grand Mere State Park
- BERRIEN: Warren Dunes, Warren Dunes State
  Park
- LEELANAU: North Manitou Island, Sleeping
  Bear Dunes National Lakeshore
- LEELANAU: Pyramid Point, Sleeping Bear
  Dunes National Lakeshore
- LEELANAU: Sleeping Bear Dunes, Sleeping
  Bear Dunes National Lakeshore
- LEELANAU: South Manitou Island, Sleeping
  Bear Dunes National Lakeshore
- MASON: Nordhouse Dunes, Ludington State
  Park and Manistee National Forest
- MUSKEGON: Muskegon Dunes, Muskegon
  State Park
- OTTAWA & MUSKEGON: P. J. Hoffmaster State
  Park

JOSHUA G. COHEN

**Nordhouse Dunes, Ludington State Park,
Mason County**

231

S2 GREAT LAKES BARRENS

Great Lakes barrens is a coniferous savanna community of scattered and clumped trees and an often dense, low or creeping shrub layer. The community occurs on circumneutral sands along the shores of the Great Lakes, where it is often associated with interdunal wetland and open dunes. Natural processes that influence species composition and community

structure include episodes of sand movement and vegetation burial, growing-season frosts, fluctuating water levels, and occasional fires. Dominant species typically include jack

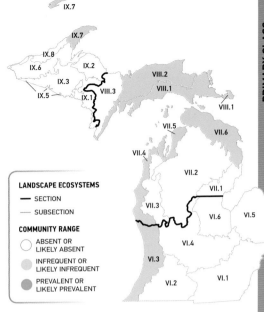

LANDSCAPE ECOSYSTEMS

— SECTION

---- SUBSECTION

COMMUNITY RANGE

○ ABSENT OR LIKELY ABSENT

◐ INFREQUENT OR LIKELY INFREQUENT

● PREVALENT OR LIKELY PREVALENT

pine (*Pinus banksiana*), white pine (*P. strobus*), red pine (*P. resinosa*), white spruce (*Picea glauca*), northern white-cedar (*Thuja occidentalis*), bearberry (*Arctostaphylos uva-ursi*), common juniper (*Juniperus communis*), creeping juniper (*J. horizontalis*), sand reed grass (*Calamovilfa longifolia*), and little bluestem (*Schizachyrium scoparium*).

CHARACTERISTIC PLANTS

GRAMINOIDS

- marram grass (*Ammophila breviligulata*)
- wavy hair grass (*Avenella flexuosa*)
- sand reed grass (*Calamovilfa longifolia*)
- ebony sedge (*Carex eburnea*)
- rough sand sedge (*Cyperus schweinitzii*)
- poverty grass (*Danthonia spicata*)
- wheat grass (*Elymus lanceolatus*)
- slender wheat grass (*Elymus trachycaulus*)
- Rocky Mountain fescue (*Festuca saximontana*)
- June grass (*Koeleria macrantha*)
- rough-leaved rice-grass (*Oryzopsis asperifolia*)

JOSHUA G. COHEN

233

Great Lakes barrens is characterized by scattered and clumped trees and a dense, low shrub layer

- switch grass (*Panicum virgatum*)
- little bluestem (*Schizachyrium scoparium*)

FORBS
- wormwood (*Artemisia campestris*)
- common milkweed (*Asclepias syriaca*)
- harebell (*Campanula rotundifolia*)
- lance-leaved coreopsis (*Coreopsis lanceolata*)
- wild strawberry (*Fragaria virginiana*)
- hairy bedstraw (*Galium pilosum*)
- plains puccoon (*Lithospermum caroliniense*)
- Canada mayflower (*Maianthemum canadense*)
- starry false Solomon-seal (*Maianthemum stellatum*)

- cow-wheat (*Melampyrum lineare*)
- rock sandwort (*Minuartia michauxii*)
- horse mint (*Monarda punctata*)
- clammy cudweed (*Pseudognaphalium macounii*)
- smooth aster (*Symphyotrichum laeve*)

LICHENS
- reindeer lichens (*Cladina mitis* and *C. rangiferina*)
- British soldiers lichen (*Cladonia cristatella*)

MOSSES
- Leucobryum moss (*Leucobryum glaucum*)
- tortured tortella moss (*Tortella tortuosa*)

WOODY VINES
- poison-ivy (*Toxicodendron radicans*)
- riverbank grape (*Vitis riparia*)

SHRUBS
- bearberry (*Arctostaphylos uva-ursi*)
- pipsissewa (*Chimaphila umbellata*)
- beach heath (*Hudsonia tomentosa*)
- common juniper (*Juniperus communis*)
- creeping juniper (*Juniperus horizontalis*)
- sand cherry (*Prunus pumila*)
- soapberry (*Shepherdia canadensis*)
- poison-ivy (*Toxicodendron rydbergii*)

TREES
- paper birch (*Betula papyrifera*)
- white spruce (*Picea glauca*)

- jack pine (*Pinus banksiana*)
- red pine (*Pinus resinosa*)
- white pine (*Pinus strobus*)
- balsam poplar (*Populus balsamifera*)
- cottonwood (*Populus deltoides*)
- red oak (*Quercus rubra*)
- northern white-cedar (*Thuja occidentalis*)

PLACES TO VISIT

- BENZIE: Platte Bay, Sleeping Bear Dunes National Lakeshore
- EMMET: Sturgeon Bay, Wilderness State Park
- LEELANAU: Cathead Bay, Leelanau State Park
- MASON: Nordhouse Dunes, Ludington State Park and Manistee National Forest

Great Lakes barrens, Cathead Bay, Leelanau State Park, Leelanau County

SAND/COBBLE SHORE GROUP

Sand/Cobble Shores are sparsely vegetated communities that occur along the Great Lakes shoreline. Substrate types that support Sand/Cobble Shore include sand and gravel, limestone cobble, sandstone cobble, and volcanic cobble. Soils of sand and gravel Sand/Cobble Shore are neutral to alkaline sands and gravels. The soils of bedrock-derived Sand/Cobble Shores are typically limited to sand and gravel deposits occurring between and beneath the cobble, but shallow organic sediments can accumulate in protected inner portions of the shore. Vegetation is typically sparse because storm waves are prevalent and soil development and suitable substrates for plant establishment are limited. Natural processes that influence species composition and community structure include wind and wave action, Great Lakes water level fluctuation, winter ice scour, and desiccation.

Four natural community types fall within the Sand/Cobble Shore group, including sand and gravel beach, limestone cobble shore, sandstone cobble shore, and volcanic cobble shore. Classification of these Sand/Cobble Shore types is based primarily on differences in substrate composition, although species composition and community structure also vary by substrate.

Limestone cobble shore, Mackinac County

JOSHUA G. COHEN

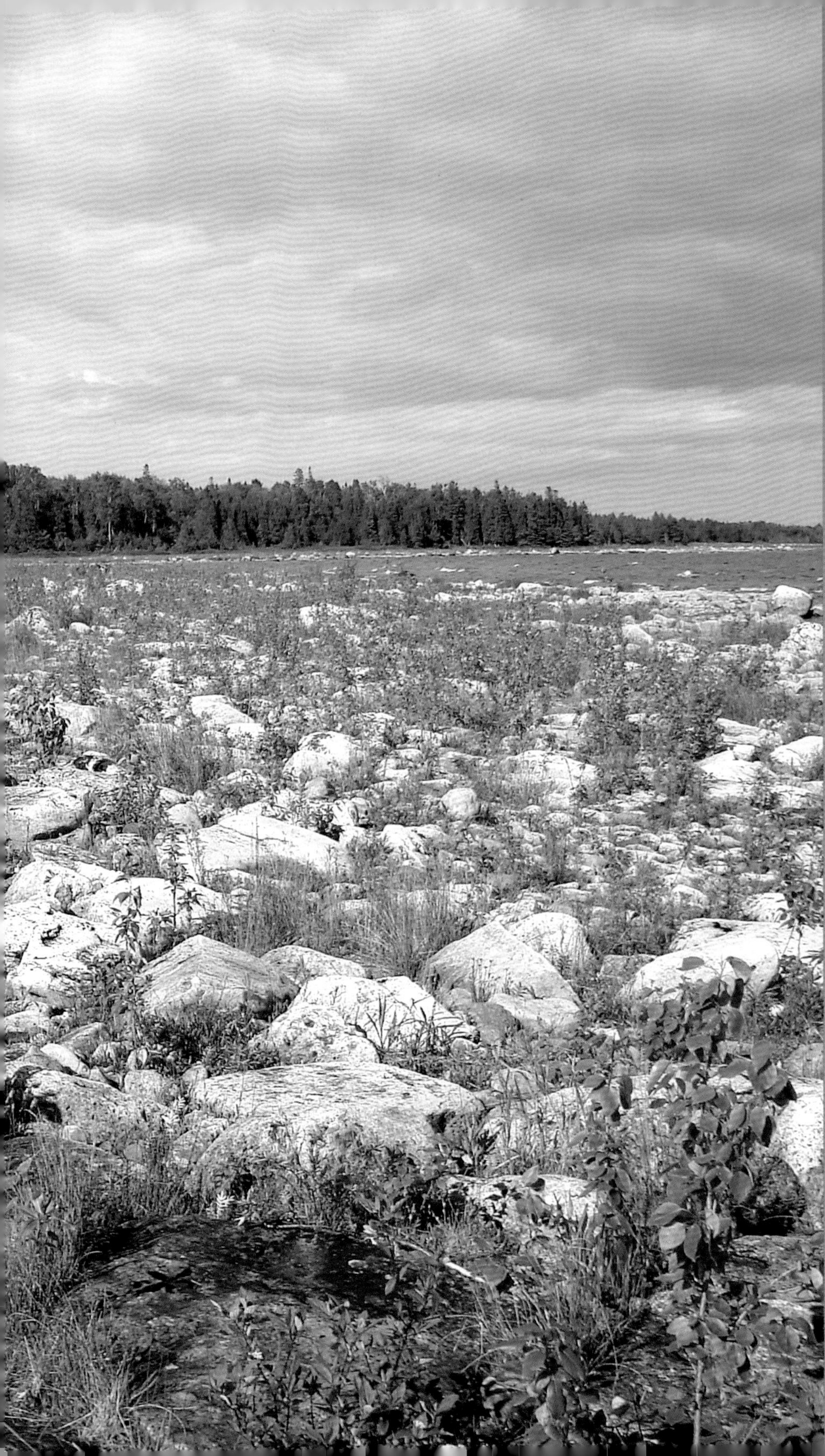

S3 SAND & GRAVEL BEACH

Sand and gravel beach occurs along the shorelines of the Great Lakes, where wind, waves, and ice abrasion maintain an open beach. Soils are circumneutral to alkaline sands and gravels. Because of the high levels of natural disturbance, sand and gravel beach is mostly open, with only

scattered vegetation. Wind, waves, and winter ice scour strongly influence species composition and community structure. Characteristic species of this

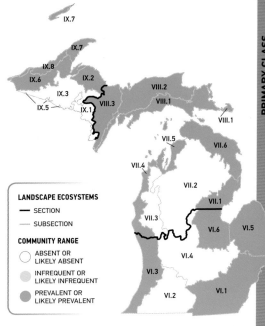

LANDSCAPE ECOSYSTEMS
— SECTION
— SUBSECTION

COMMUNITY RANGE
○ ABSENT OR LIKELY ABSENT
◐ INFREQUENT OR LIKELY INFREQUENT
● PREVALENT OR LIKELY PREVALENT

open shoreline community include sea rocket (*Cakile edentula*), seaside spurge (*Euphorbia polygonifolia*), Baltic rush (*Juncus balticus*), silverweed (*Potentilla anserina*), marram grass (*Ammophila breviligulata*), and beach pea (*Lathyrus japonicus*).

CHARACTERISTIC PLANTS

GRAMINOIDS
- marram grass (*Ammophila breviligulata*)
- Baltic rush (*Juncus balticus*)
- hardstem bulrush (*Schoenoplectus acutus*)
- threesquare (*Schoenoplectus pungens*)

FORBS
- sea rocket (*Cakile edentula*)
- Pitcher's thistle (*Cirsium pitcheri*)*
- bugseeds (*Corispermum americanum* and *C. pallasii*)
- seaside spurge (*Euphorbia polygonifolia*)
- beach pea (*Lathyrus japonicus*)
- silverweed (*Potentilla anserina*)
- Lake Huron tansy (*Tanacetum bipinnatum*)*

JOSHUA G. COHEN

239

Sand and gravel beach along the Lake Superior shoreline

SHRUBS
- sand dune willow (*Salix cordata*)
- sandbar willow (*Salix exigua*)
- blue-leaf willow (*Salix myricoides*)

- ALGER: Pictured Rocks, Pictured Rocks National Lakeshore
- ALGER: Twelve Mile Beach, Pictured Rocks National Lakeshore
- LEELANAU: Sleeping Bear Dunes, Sleeping Bear Dunes National Lakeshore
- LEELANAU: South Manitou Island, Sleeping Bear Dunes National Lakeshore
- MARQUETTE: Little Presque Isle, Gwinn State Forest Management Unit
- MASON: Nordhouse Dunes, Ludington State Park and Manistee National Forest
- ONTONAGON: Misery Bay and Sleeping Bay, Baraga State Forest Management Unit

Sand and gravel beach, Sleeping Bay, Baraga State Forest Management Unit, Ontonagon County

Sand and gravel beach, Luce County

LIMESTONE COBBLE SHORE

Limestone cobble shore is a sparsely vegetated community of scattered herbs, graminoids, shrubs, saplings, and stunted trees growing between limestone or dolomite cobbles along the shorelines of Lake Michigan and Lake Huron in the Upper Peninsula and northern Lower Peninsula. The

community expands and contracts in size in accordance with periodic changes in Great Lakes water levels. Plants typically root in alkaline sands

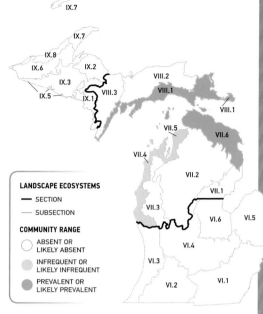

LANDSCAPE ECOSYSTEMS

— SECTION

— SUBSECTION

COMMUNITY RANGE

○ ABSENT OR LIKELY ABSENT

◑ INFREQUENT OR LIKELY INFREQUENT

● PREVALENT OR LIKELY PREVALENT

JOSHUA G. COHEN

and gravel that accumulate between the cobbles, or in shallow organic sediments that accumulate in protected inner portions of the shore. Vegetation is typically sparse because cobbles cover most of the surface, soil development is limited, and storm waves prevent the establishment of a persistent plant community. Characteristic forbs and graminoids include harebell (*Campanula rotundifolia*), grass-leaved goldenrod (*Euthamia graminifolia*), Kalm's lobelia (*Lobelia kalmii*), bird's-eye primrose (*Primula mistassinica*), silverweed (*Potentilla anserina*), limestone calamint (*Clinopodium arkansanum*), rushes (*Juncus* spp.), spike-rushes (*Eleocharis* spp.), sedges (*Carex* spp.), and goldenrods (*Solidago* spp.). Scattered woody species include northern white-cedar (*Thuja occidentalis*), paper birch (*Betula papyrifera*), balsam poplar (*Populus balsamifera*), shrubby cinquefoil (*Dasiphora fruticosa*), Kalm's St. John's-wort (*Hypericum kalmianum*), and soapberry (*Shepherdia canadensis*).

▶

243

JOSHUA G. COHEN

Limestone cobble shore is characterized by sparse vegetation

CHARACTERISTIC PLANTS

GRAMINOIDS

- ticklegrass (*Agrostis scabra*)
- narrow-leaved reedgrass (*Calamagrostis stricta*)
- sedges (*Carex crawei, C. eburnea,* and *C. viridula*)
- twig-rush (*Cladium mariscoides*)
- tufted hair grass (*Deschampsia cespitosa*)
- Lindheimer panic grass (*Dichanthelium lindheimeri*)
- golden-seeded spike-rush (*Eleocharis elliptica*)
- spike-rush (*Eleocharis quinqueflora*)
- beaked spike-rush (*Eleocharis rostellata*)
- rushes (*Juncus balticus, J. brachycephalus, J. brevicaudatus, J. dudleyi,* and *J. nodosus*)
- common reed (*Phragmites australis* subsp. *americanus*)
- beak-rush (*Rhynchospora capillacea*)
- hardstem bulrush (*Schoenoplectus acutus*)
- threesquare (*Schoenoplectus pungens*)

FORBS

- purple false foxglove (*Agalinis purpurea*)
- white camas (*Anticlea elegans*)
- wild columbine (*Aquilegia canadensis*)
- harebell (*Campanula rotundifolia*)
- Indian paintbrush (*Castilleja coccinea*)
- limestone calamint (*Clinopodium arkansanum*)
- common boneset (*Eupatorium perfoliatum*)
- grass-leaved goldenrod (*Euthamia graminifolia*)
- small fringed gentian (*Gentianopsis virgata*)
- Kalm's lobelia (*Lobelia kalmii*)
- balsam ragwort (*Packera paupercula*)
- grass-of-Parnassus (*Parnassia glauca*)
- silverweed (*Potentilla anserina*)
- bird's-eye primrose (*Primula mistassinica*)
- Houghton's goldenrod (*Solidago houghtonii*)*
- Ohio goldenrod (*Solidago ohioensis*)
- upland white goldenrod (*Solidago ptarmicoides*)
- bog goldenrod (*Solidago uliginosa*)
- panicled aster (*Symphyotrichum lanceolatum*)
- false asphodel (*Triantha glutinosa*)
- common bog arrow-grass (*Triglochin maritima*)
- slender bog arrow-grass (*Triglochin palustris*)
- broad-leaved cat-tail (*Typha latifolia*)

FERN ALLIES

- variegated scouring rush (*Equisetum variegatum*)
- selaginella (*Selaginella eclipes*)

SHRUBS

- tag alder (*Alnus incana*)
- red-osier dogwood (*Cornus sericea*)
- shrubby cinquefoil (*Dasiphora fruticosa*)
- Kalm's St. John's-wort (*Hypericum kalmianum*)

- sweet gale (*Myrica gale*)
- slender willow (*Salix petiolaris*)
- soapberry (*Shepherdia canadensis*)

TREES
- paper birch (*Betula papyrifera*)
- green ash (*Fraxinus pennsylvanica*)
- tamarack (*Larix laricina*)
- white spruce (*Picea glauca*)
- balsam poplar (*Populus balsamifera*)
- quaking aspen (*Populus tremuloides*)
- northern white-cedar (*Thuja occidentalis*)

PLACES TO VISIT
- EMMET: Waugoshance Point, Wilderness State Park
- MACKINAC: Horseshoe Bay Grosse Point, Horseshoe Bay Wilderness Area, Hiawatha National Forest
- MACKINAC: Seiner's Point, Sault Sainte Marie State Forest Management Unit
- MACKINAC: St. Martin Point, Hiawatha National Forest
- PRESQUE ISLE: Thompson's Harbor, Thompson's Harbor State Park

Limestone cobble shore intergrading with Great Lakes marsh, Wilderness State Park, Emmet County

S2 SANDSTONE COBBLE SHORE

Sandstone cobble shore is a sparsely vegetated community of scattered herbs, shrubs, saplings, and stunted trees growing between sandstone cobbles along the shoreline of Lake Superior. The community expands and contracts in size in accordance with periodic changes in

Great Lakes water levels. Sandstone cobble shore primarily occupies coves and gently curving bays and may be nearly level with a diversity

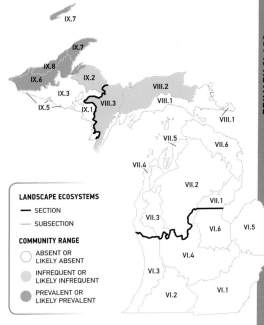

LANDSCAPE ECOSYSTEMS

— SECTION

— SUBSECTION

COMMUNITY RANGE

○ ABSENT OR LIKELY ABSENT

◐ INFREQUENT OR LIKELY INFREQUENT

● PREVALENT OR LIKELY PREVALENT

MICHAEL A. KOST

of herbaceous plants, or relatively steep and terraced with vegetation mostly limited to the highest cobble beach ridge. Plants typically root in scattered sand and gravel deposits that accumulate between and beneath sandstone cobble. Vegetation is typically sparse because cobbles cover most of the surface, soil development is limited, and storm waves prevent the establishment of a persistent plant community. Characteristic herbaceous species include sedges (*Carex* spp.), fireweed (*Chamerion angustifolium*), common horsetail (*Equisetum arvense*), grass-leaved goldenrod (*Euthamia graminifolia*), common boneset (*Eupatorium perfoliatum*), jewelweed (*Impatiens capensis*), common water horehound (*Lycopus americanus*), northern bugle weed (*Lycopus uniflorus*), balsam ragwort (*Packera paupercula*), common skullcap (*Scutellaria galericulata*), and goldenrods (*Solidago* spp.). Scattered woody species along the upper

Sandstone cobble shore, Porcupine Mountains Wilderness State Park, Ontonagon County

margin of the cobble shore include thimbleberry (*Rubus parviflorus*), ninebark (*Physocarpus opulifolius*), mountain alder (*Alnus viridis*), paper birch (*Betula papyrifera*), northern white-cedar (*Thuja occidentalis*), balsam poplar (*Populus balsamifera*), and green ash (*Fraxinus pennsylvanica*).

CHARACTERISTIC PLANTS

GRAMINOIDS

- fringed sedge (*Carex crinita*)
- little green sedge (*Carex viridula*)
- tufted hair grass (*Deschampsia cespitosa*)
- rattlesnake grass (*Glyceria canadensis*)
- Baltic rush (*Juncus balticus*)
- knotted rush (*Juncus nodosus*)

FORBS

- water plantain (*Alisma triviale*)
- fireweed (*Chamerion angustifolium*)
- water hemlocks (*Cicuta bulbifera*)
- spotted water hemlock (*Cicuta maculata*)
- common boneset (*Eupatorium perfoliatum*)
- grass-leaved goldenrod (*Euthamia graminifolia*)
- joe-pye-weed (*Eutrochium maculatum*)
- wild strawberry (*Fragaria virginiana*)
- jewelweed (*Impatiens capensis*)

- marsh pea (*Lathyrus palustris*)
- common water horehound (*Lycopus americanus*)
- northern bugle weed (*Lycopus uniflorus*)
- balsam ragwort (*Packera paupercula*)
- smartweeds (*Persicaria* spp.)
- common arrowhead (*Sagittaria latifolia*)
- common skullcap (*Scutellaria galericulata*)
- water parsnip (*Sium suave*)
- upland white goldenrod (*Solidago ptarmicoides*)
- Gillman's goldenrod (*Solidago simplex*)

FERN ALLIES
- common horsetail (*Equisetum arvense*)

SHRUBS
- mountain alder (*Alnus viridis*)
- ninebark (*Physocarpus opulifolius*)
- thimbleberry (*Rubus parviflorus*)

- wild red raspberry (*Rubus strigosus*)
- American highbush-cranberry (*Viburnum trilobum*)

TREES
- paper birch (*Betula papyrifera*)
- green ash (*Fraxinus pennsylvanica*)
- balsam poplar (*Populus balsamifera*)
- quaking aspen (*Populus tremuloides*)
- northern white-cedar (*Thuja occidentalis*)

PLACES TO VISIT
- BARAGA: Point Abbaye, Baraga State Forest Management Unit
- ONTONAGON: Misery Bay and Sleeping Bay, Baraga State Forest Management Unit
- ONTONAGON: Porcupine Shore, Porcupine Mountains Wilderness State Park

Sandstone cobble shore, Porcupine Mountains Wilderness State Park, Ontonagon County

S3 VOLCANIC COBBLE SHORE

Volcanic cobble shore is a sparsely vegetated community of scattered herbs, shrubs, saplings, and stunted trees growing between volcanic cobbles along the shoreline of Lake Superior. The community primarily occupies coves and gently curving bays between rocky points and expands and contracts

in size in accordance with periodic changes in Great Lakes water levels. These mostly unvegetated shores are often terraced, with the highest cobble

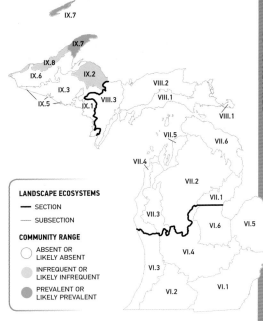

LANDSCAPE ECOSYSTEMS

— SECTION

— SUBSECTION

COMMUNITY RANGE

○ ABSENT OR LIKELY ABSENT

INFREQUENT OR LIKELY INFREQUENT

PREVALENT OR LIKELY PREVALENT

JOSHUA G. COHEN

beach ridge typically supporting a shrub zone several meters above Lake Superior. Vegetation is typically sparse because cobbles cover most of the surface, soil development is limited, and storm waves prevent the establishment of a persistent plant community. Plants typically root in scattered sand and gravel deposits that accumulate between and beneath the volcanic cobble. Characteristic herbaceous species include sedges (*Carex* spp.), marsh pea (*Lathyrus palustris*), blue wild-rye (*Elymus glaucus*), evening primrose (*Oenothera oakesiana*), scouring rush (*Equisetum hyemale*), blue-joint (*Calamagrostis canadensis*), and grass-leaved goldenrod (*Euthamia graminifolia*). Scattered woody species along the upper margin of the cobble shore include ninebark (*Physocarpus opulifolius*), mountain alder (*Alnus viridis*), mountain ash (*Sorbus decora*), paper birch (*Betula papyrifera*), and northern white-cedar (*Thuja occidentalis*).

▶

251

CHARACTERISTIC PLANTS

GRAMINOIDS

- blue-joint (*Calamagrostis canadensis*)
- tufted hair grass (*Deschampsia cespitosa*)

- blue wild-rye (*Elymus glaucus*)*

FORBS

- fireweed (*Chamerion angustifolium*)

Volcanic cobble shore, Keweenaw Peninsula, Keweenaw County

- grass-leaved goldenrod (*Euthamia graminifolia*)
- marsh pea (*Lathyrus palustris*)
- evening primrose (*Oenothera biennis*)

FERN ALLIES
- scouring rush (*Equisetum hyemale*)

SHRUBS
- mountain alder (*Alnus viridis*)
- red-osier dogwood (*Cornus sericea*)
- bush honeysuckle (*Diervilla lonicera*)
- ninebark (*Physocarpus opulifolius*)
- northern gooseberry (*Ribes oxyacanthoides*)*
- wild rose (*Rosa acicularis*)
- wild red raspberry (*Rubus strigosus*)
- soapberry (*Shepherdia canadensis*)

TREES
- balsam fir (*Abies balsamea*)
- paper birch (*Betula papyrifera*)
- white spruce (*Picea glauca*)
- quaking aspen (*Populus tremuloides*)
- mountain-ash (*Sorbus decora*)
- northern white-cedar (*Thuja occidentalis*)

PLACES TO VISIT
- KEWEENAW: High Rock Bay, Baraga State Forest Management Unit
- KEWEENAW: Isle Royale National Park
- KEWEENAW: Keweenaw Point, Baraga State Forest Management Unit
- ONTONAGON: Porcupine Shore, Porcupine Mountains Wilderness State Park

JOSHUA G. COHEN

BEDROCK LAKESHORE GROUP

Bedrock Lakeshores are sparsely vegetated communities with scattered herbs, graminoids, shrubs, and stunted trees growing on flat to gently sloping bedrock exposures along the Great Lakes shorelines of the Upper Peninsula and northern Lower Peninsula. Bedrock types that support Bedrock Lakeshore include limestone, sandstone, granite, and volcanics. Soil development and plant establishment are generally limited to cracks, joints, vesicles, and depressions in the bedrock, where small amounts of organic matter and finer sediments accumulate. Natural processes that influence species composition and community structure include wind and wave action, Great Lakes water level fluctuation, winter ice scour, and desiccation.

Four natural community types fall within the Bedrock Lakeshore group, including limestone bedrock lakeshore, sandstone bedrock lakeshore, granite bedrock lakeshore, and volcanic bedrock lakeshore. Classification of these Bedrock Lakeshore types is based primarily on differences in bedrock composition, although species composition and community structure also vary by substrate.

Volcanic bedrock lakeshore composed of conglomerate, Porters Island, Fort Wilkins State Historic Park, Keweenaw County

JOSHUA G. COHEN

S2 LIMESTONE BEDROCK LAKESHORE

Limestone bedrock lakeshore[10] is a sparsely vegetated community that occurs on broad, flat, horizontally bedded expanses of limestone or dolomite bedrock. The community occurs on the shorelines of Lake Michigan and Lake Huron in the Upper Peninsula and northern Lower

Peninsula. Soil development is generally limited to cracks, joints, and depressions in the bedrock, where small amounts of organic matter, cobble, and finer

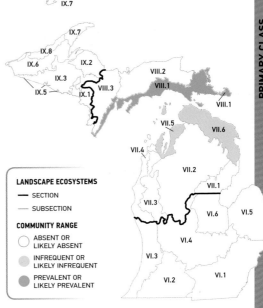

LANDSCAPE ECOSYSTEMS
— SECTION
— SUBSECTION

COMMUNITY RANGE
○ ABSENT OR LIKELY ABSENT
◐ INFREQUENT OR LIKELY INFREQUENT
● PREVALENT OR LIKELY PREVALENT

JOSHUA G. COHEN

sediments accumulate. The thin soils are typically mildly alkaline. Storms, wind, winter ice scour, fluctuating Great Lakes water levels, and desiccation also limit vegetation establishment and growth. Mosses and lichens are common on the exposed bedrock, but herbaceous and woody plants are typically limited to cracks, joints, and depressions in the bedrock. Characteristic forbs and graminoids include limestone calamint (*Clinopodium arkansanum*), hair grasses (*Avenella flexuosa* and *Deschampsia cespitosa*), Baltic rush (*Juncus balticus*), silverweed (*Potentilla anserina*), harebell (*Campanula rotundifolia*), bird's-eye primrose (*Primula mistassinica*), and grass-leaved goldenrod (*Euthamia graminifolia*). Scattered woody species include Kalm's St. John's-wort (*Hypericum kalmianum*), shrubby cinquefoil (*Dasiphora fruticosa*), balsam poplar (*Populus balsamifera*), paper birch (*Betula papyrifera*), white spruce (*Picea glauca*), and northern white-cedar (*Thuja occidentalis*).

257

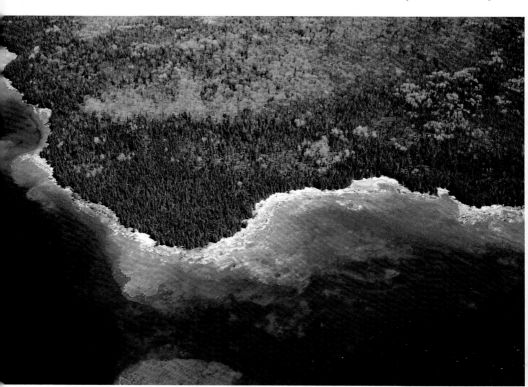

Along the Garden Peninsula in Delta County, limestone bedrock lakeshore occurs along the northern Lake Michigan shoreline with a band of boreal forest inland

Limestone bedrock lakeshore with stunted northern white-cedar (*Thuja occidentalis*) and white spruce (*Picea glauca*)

JOSHUA G. COHEN

CHARACTERISTIC PLANTS

GRAMINOIDS

- ticklegrass (*Agrostis scabra*)
- wavy hair grass (*Avenella flexuosa*)
- narrow-leaved reedgrass (*Calamagrostis stricta*)
- beauty sedge (*Carex concinna*)
- Crawe's sedge (*Carex crawei*)
- ebony sedge (*Carex eburnea*)
- sedge (*Carex garberi*)
- Richardson's sedge (*Carex richardsonii*)*
- bulrush sedge (*Carex scirpoidea*)*
- little green sedge (*Carex viridula*)
- poverty grass (*Danthonia spicata*)
- tufted hair grass (*Deschampsia cespitosa*)
- Lindheimer panic grass (*Dichanthelium lindheimeri*)

- golden-seeded spike-rush (*Eleocharis elliptica*)
- slender wheat grass (*Elymus trachycaulus*)
- Baltic rush (*Juncus balticus*)
- beak-rush (*Rhynchospora capillacea*)

FORBS
- purple false foxglove (*Agalinis purpurea*)
- white camas (*Anticlea elegans*)
- wild columbine (*Aquilegia canadensis*)
- harebell (*Campanula rotundifolia*)
- Indian paintbrush (*Castilleja coccinea*)
- limestone calamint (*Clinopodium arkansanum*)
- large yellow lady-slipper (*Cypripedium parviflorum* var. *pubescens*)
- flat-topped white aster (*Doellingeria umbellata*)
- large-leaved aster (*Eurybia macrophylla*)
- grass-leaved goldenrod (*Euthamia graminifolia*)
- wild strawberry (*Fragaria virginiana*)
- dwarf lake iris (*Iris lacustris*)*
- Kalm's lobelia (*Lobelia kalmii*)
- common water horehound (*Lycopus americanus*)
- balsam ragwort (*Packera paupercula*)
- silverweed (*Potentilla anserina*)
- bird's-eye primrose (*Primula mistassinica*)
- Houghton's goldenrod (*Solidago houghtonii*)*
- Ohio goldenrod (*Solidago ohioensis*)
- nodding ladies'-tresses (*Spiranthes cernua*)
- smooth aster (*Symphyotrichum laeve*)
- false asphodel (*Triantha glutinosa*)
- northern bog violet (*Viola nephrophylla*)

SHRUBS
- bearberry (*Arctostaphylos uva-ursi*)
- shrubby cinquefoil (*Dasiphora fruticosa*)
- Kalm's St. John's-wort (*Hypericum kalmianum*)
- common juniper (*Juniperus communis*)

- ninebark (*Physocarpus opulifolius*)
- soapberry (*Shepherdia canadensis*)

TREES
- balsam fir (*Abies balsamea*)
- paper birch (*Betula papyrifera*)
- white spruce (*Picea glauca*)
- balsam poplar (*Populus balsamifera*)
- northern white-cedar (*Thuja occidentalis*)

PLACES TO VISIT

- CHARLEVOIX: Fisherman's Island, Fisherman's Island State Park
- CHIPPEWA: Drummond Island (Bass Cove, Huron Bay, Grand Marais Lake, and Seaman's Point), Sault Sainte Marie State Forest Management Unit
- DELTA: Point De Tour, Shingleton State Forest Management Unit

JOSHUA G. COHEN

Limestone bedrock lakeshore occurs along the shorelines of northern Lake Michigan and Lake Huron on broad, flat, horizontally bedded expanses of limestone or dolomite bedrock that support sparse vegetation concentrated in cracks and depressions in the bedrock

SANDSTONE BEDROCK LAKESHORE

Sandstone bedrock lakeshore is a sparsely vegetated community that occurs on flat to tilted, horizontally bedded sandstone bedrock along the shoreline of Lake Superior in the central and western Upper Peninsula. Soil development and plant establishment are limited to cracks,

joints, and depressions in the bedrock where small amounts of slightly acidic to alkaline sands and organic matter accumulate. Storms, wind, winter ice

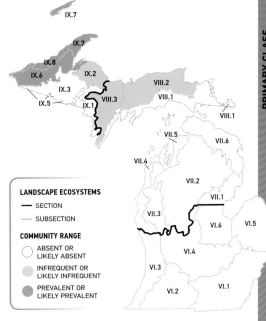

LANDSCAPE ECOSYSTEMS
— SECTION
— SUBSECTION

COMMUNITY RANGE
○ ABSENT OR LIKELY ABSENT
◔ INFREQUENT OR LIKELY INFREQUENT
● PREVALENT OR LIKELY PREVALENT

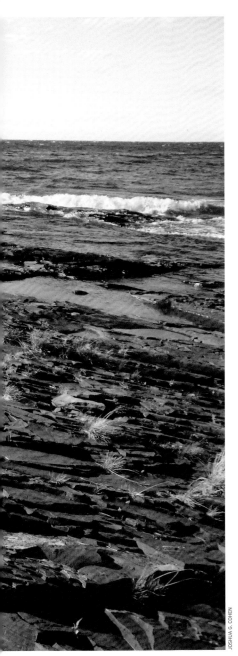

JOSHUA G. COHEN

scour, fluctuating Great Lakes water levels, and desiccation also limit vegetation establishment and growth. Mosses and lichens are common on the exposed bedrock, but herbaceous and woody plants are typically limited to cracks, joints, and depressions in the bedrock. Characteristic ground cover species include harebell (*Campanula rotundifolia*), sedges (*Carex* spp.), fireweed (*Chamerion angustifolium*), hair grass (*Deschampsia cespitosa*), grass-leaved goldenrod (*Euthamia graminifolia*), jewelweed (*Impatiens capensis*), rushes (*Juncus* spp.), balsam ragwort (*Packera paupercula*), and goldenrods (*Solidago* spp.). Scattered woody species include thimbleberry (*Rubus parviflorus*), ninebark (*Physocarpus opulifolius*), mountain alder (*Alnus viridis*), paper birch (*Betula papyrifera*), northern white-cedar (*Thuja occidentalis*), and balsam poplar (*Populus balsamifera*).

Harebell (*Campanula rotundifolia*) is a characteristic species of sandstone bedrock lakeshore, occurring in cracks and crevices

JOSHUA G. COHEN

CHARACTERISTIC PLANTS

GRAMINOIDS

- little green sedge (*Carex viridula*)
- tufted hair grass (*Deschampsia cespitosa*)
- Baltic rush (*Juncus balticus*)
- knotted rush (*Juncus nodosus*)

FORBS

- harebell (*Campanula rotundifolia*)
- fireweed (*Chamerion angustifolium*)
- common boneset (*Eupatorium perfoliatum*)
- grass-leaved goldenrod (*Euthamia graminifolia*)
- joe-pye-weed (*Eutrochium maculatum*)
- wild strawberry (*Fragaria virginiana*)
- jewelweed (*Impatiens capensis*)
- Kalm's lobelia (*Lobelia kalmii*)
- northern bugle weed (*Lycopus uniflorus*)
- balsam ragwort (*Packera paupercula*)
- mad-dog skullcap (*Scutellaria lateriflora*)
- upland white goldenrod (*Solidago ptarmicoides*)

- Gillman's goldenrod (*Solidago simplex*)
- purple meadow-rue (*Thalictrum dasycarpum*)

SHRUBS

- mountain alder (*Alnus viridis*)
- serviceberries (*Amelanchier* spp.)
- bush honeysuckle (*Diervilla lonicera*)
- Canadian fly honeysuckle (*Lonicera canadensis*)
- sweet gale (*Myrica gale*)
- ninebark (*Physocarpus opulifolius*)
- choke cherry (*Prunus virginiana*)
- wild rose (*Rosa acicularis*)
- thimbleberry (*Rubus parviflorus*)
- Bebb's willow (*Salix bebbiana*)
- pussy willow (*Salix discolor*)
- soapberry (*Shepherdia canadensis*)

TREES

- balsam fir (*Abies balsamea*)
- red maple (*Acer rubrum*)
- juneberry (*Amelanchier arborea*)
- yellow birch (*Betula alleghaniensis*)
- paper birch (*Betula papyrifera*)
- white ash (*Fraxinus americana*)
- green ash (*Fraxinus pennsylvanica*)
- white spruce (*Picea glauca*)
- white pine (*Pinus strobus*)
- balsam poplar (*Populus balsamifera*)
- quaking aspen (*Populus tremuloides*)
- northern white-cedar (*Thuja occidentalis*)

PLACES TO VISIT

- ALGER: Pictured Rocks, Pictured Rocks National Lakeshore
- BARAGA: Point Abbaye, Baraga State Forest Management Unit
- ONTONAGON: Misery Bay and Sleeping Bay, Baraga State Forest Management Unit
- ONTONAGON: Porcupine Shore, Porcupine Mountains Wilderness State Park

Sandstone bedrock lakeshore with sparse vegetation following the cracks in the bedrock

Sandstone bedrock lakeshore along the Lake Superior shoreline in Porcupine
Mountains Wilderness State Park, Ontonagon County

S2 GRANITE BEDROCK LAKESHORE

Granite bedrock lakeshore[11] is a sparsely vegetated community that occurs as small knobs of granitic or less frequently quartzite bedrock along the shoreline of Lake Superior in the west-central Upper Peninsula. Because the granitic rocks along the coast are highly polished and extremely resistant

to weathering and susceptible to storm waves and ice scour, very little soil development occurs. Some organic soil development takes place in cracks,

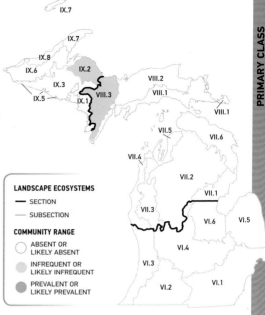

LANDSCAPE ECOSYSTEMS

—— SECTION

----- SUBSECTION

COMMUNITY RANGE

○ ABSENT OR
   LIKELY ABSENT

◔ INFREQUENT OR
   LIKELY INFREQUENT

● PREVALENT OR
   LIKELY PREVALENT

JOSHUA G. COHEN

under low shrubs, or in pools. Storms, wind, winter ice scour, fluctuating Great Lakes water levels, and desiccation also limit vegetation establishment and growth. Mosses and lichens are common on the exposed bedrock, and scattered herbs, shrubs, and tree saplings and stunted trees are restricted to areas above the strong influence of waves and ice scour. Characteristic ground cover species include ticklegrass (*Agrostis scabra*), wavy hair grass (*Avenella flexuosa*), poverty grass (*Danthonia spicata*), tufted hair grass (*Deschampsia cespitosa*), harebell (*Campanula rotundifolia*), fireweed (*Chamerion angustifolium*), yarrow (*Achillea millefolium*), grass-leaved goldenrod (*Euthamia graminifolia*), and three-toothed cinquefoil (*Sibbaldiopsis tridentata*). Scattered woody species include bearberry (*Arctostaphylos uva-ursi*), bush honeysuckle (*Diervilla lonicera*), common juniper (*Juniperus communis*), ninebark (*Physocarpus opulifolius*), pines (*Pinus* spp.), quaking

265

Vegetation is restricted to cracks in granite bedrock lakeshore

aspen (*Populus tremuloides*), northern white-cedar (*Thuja occidentalis*), and white spruce (*Picea glauca*).

CHARACTERISTIC PLANTS

GRAMINOIDS

- ticklegrass (*Agrostis scabra*)
- wavy hair grass (*Avenella flexuosa*)
- blue-joint (*Calamagrostis canadensis*)
- poverty grass (*Danthonia spicata*)
- tufted hair grass (*Deschampsia cespitosa*)
- wool-grass (*Scirpus cyperinus*)

FORBS

- yarrow (*Achillea millefolium*)
- harebell (*Campanula rotundifolia*)
- fireweed (*Chamerion angustifolium*)
- grass-leaved goldenrod (*Euthamia graminifolia*)
- wild strawberry (*Fragaria virginiana*)
- Kalm's lobelia (*Lobelia kalmii*)
- cow-wheat (*Melampyrum lineare*)
- three-toothed cinquefoil (*Sibbaldiopsis tridentata*)
- old-field goldenrod (*Solidago nemoralis*)

FERNS

- fragile fern (*Cystopteris fragilis*)
- common polypody (*Polypodium virginianum*)
- rusty woodsia (*Woodsia ilvensis*)

SHRUBS

- mountain alder (*Alnus viridis*)
- bearberry (*Arctostaphylos uva-ursi*)
- bush honeysuckle (*Diervilla lonicera*)
- common juniper (*Juniperus communis*)
- ninebark (*Physocarpus opulifolius*)
- wild rose (*Rosa acicularis*)
- low sweet blueberry (*Vaccinium angustifolium*)
- Canada blueberry (*Vaccinium myrtilloides*)

TREES

- paper birch (*Betula papyrifera*)
- white spruce (*Picea glauca*)
- jack pine (*Pinus banksiana*)
- red pine (*Pinus resinosa*)
- white pine (*Pinus strobus*)
- quaking aspen (*Populus tremuloides*)
- mountain-ash (*Sorbus decora*)
- northern white-cedar (*Thuja occidentalis*)

PLACES TO VISIT

- MARQUETTE: Harvey, Gwinn State Forest Management Unit
- MARQUETTE: Little Presque Isle, Gwinn State Forest Management Unit

Granite bedrock lakeshore, Little Presque Isle, Gwinn State Forest Management Unit, Marquette County

S2 VOLCANIC BEDROCK LAKESHORE

Volcanic bedrock lakeshore[12] is a sparsely vegetated community that occurs along the shoreline of Lake Superior, primarily on the Keweenaw Peninsula and Isle Royale. Soil development and plant establishment are limited to cracks, joints, vesicles, and depressions in the bedrock, where small amounts

of organic matter accumulate. Storms, wind, winter ice scour, fluctuating Great Lakes water levels, and desiccation also limit vegetation establishment

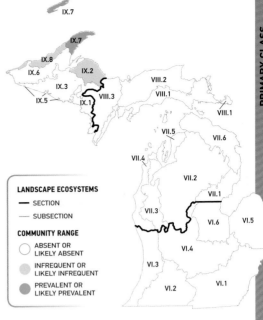

LANDSCAPE ECOSYSTEMS
— SECTION
— SUBSECTION

COMMUNITY RANGE
○ ABSENT OR LIKELY ABSENT
◑ INFREQUENT OR LIKELY INFREQUENT
● PREVALENT OR LIKELY PREVALENT

JOSHUA G. COHEN

and growth. Mosses and lichens are common on the exposed bedrock, and scattered herbs, shrubs, tree saplings, and stunted trees are restricted to areas above the strong influence of waves and ice scour. Characteristic ground cover species include harebell (*Campanula rotundifolia*), wild strawberry (*Fragaria virginiana*), three-toothed cinquefoil (*Sibbaldiopsis tridentata*), downy oat-grass (*Trisetum spicatum*), tufted hair grass (*Deschampsia cespitosa*), bird's-eye primrose (*Primula mistassinica*), balsam ragwort (*Packera paupercula*), grass-leaved goldenrod (*Euthamia graminifolia*), and yarrow (*Achillea millefolium*). Scattered woody species include bearberry (*Arctostaphylos uva-ursi*), common juniper (*Juniperus communis*), creeping juniper (*J. horizontalis*), ninebark (*Physocarpus opulifolius*), soapberry (*Shepherdia canadensis*), northern white-cedar (*Thuja occidentalis*), quaking aspen (*Populus tremuloides*), and white spruce (*Picea glauca*).

269

MICHAEL A. KOST

Clumps of tufted hair grass (*Deschampsia cespitosa*) occurring on basalt

CHARACTERISTIC PLANTS

GRAMINOIDS
- blue-joint (*Calamagrostis canadensis*)
- sedges (*Carex buxbaumii, C. castanea, C. cryptolepis,* and *C. rossii**)
- poverty grass (*Danthonia spicata*)
- tufted hair grass (*Deschampsia cespitosa*)
- blue wild-rye (*Elymus glaucus*)*
- Rocky Mountain fescue (*Festuca saximontana*)

JOSHUA G. COHEN

Twisted and stunted northern white-cedar (*Thuja occidentalis*) growing in crevices in volcanic conglomerate

- tufted bulrush (*Trichophorum cespitosum*)
- downy oat-grass (*Trisetum spicatum*)*

FORBS
- yarrow (*Achillea millefolium*)
- wormwood (*Artemisia campestris*)
- harebell (*Campanula rotundifolia*)
- pale Indian paintbrush (*Castilleja septentrionalis*)*
- fireweed (*Chamerion angustifolium*)
- prairie cinquefoil (*Drymocallis arguta*)
- large-leaved aster (*Eurybia macrophylla*)
- grass-leaved goldenrod (*Euthamia graminifolia*)
- wild strawberry (*Fragaria virginiana*)
- balsam ragwort (*Packera paupercula*)
- butterwort (*Pinguicula vulgaris*)*
- bird's-eye primrose (*Primula mistassinica*)
- pearlwort (*Sagina nodosa*)*
- three-toothed cinquefoil (*Sibbaldiopsis tridentata*)
- upland white goldenrod (*Solidago ptarmicoides*)
- Gillman's goldenrod (*Solidago simplex*)
- sand violet (*Viola adunca*)
- northern bog violet (*Viola nephrophylla*)

FERN ALLIES
- common horsetail (*Equisetum arvense*)

LICHENS
- map lichens (*Rhizocarpon* spp.)
- orange wall lichen (*Xanthoria* spp.)

MOSSES
- pseudoleskea mosses (*Pseudoleskea* spp.)
- schistidium mosses (*Schistidium* spp.)
- tortured tortella moss (*Tortella tortuosa*)

SHRUBS
- mountain alder (*Alnus viridis*)
- serviceberries (*Amelanchier* spp.)

- bearberry (*Arctostaphylos uva-ursi*)
- black hawthorn (*Crataegus douglasii*)*
- bush honeysuckle (*Diervilla lonicera*)
- common juniper (*Juniperus communis*)
- creeping juniper (*Juniperus horizontalis*)
- sweet gale (*Myrica gale*)
- ninebark (*Physocarpus opulifolius*)
- wild rose (*Rosa acicularis*)
- dwarf raspberry (*Rubus pubescens*)
- soapberry (*Shepherdia canadensis*)
- low sweet blueberry (*Vaccinium angustifolium*)
- alpine blueberry (*Vaccinium uliginosum*)*

TREES

- balsam fir (*Abies balsamea*)
- juneberry (*Amelanchier arborea*)
- paper birch (*Betula papyrifera*)
- white spruce (*Picea glauca*)
- white pine (*Pinus strobus*)

- quaking aspen (*Populus tremuloides*)
- northern white-cedar (*Thuja occidentalis*)

PLACES TO VISIT

- KEWEENAW: Bete Grise, Bear Bluff, and Big Bay West, Baraga State Forest Management Unit
- KEWEENAW: Copper Harbor Lighthouse and Porters Island, Fort Wilkins State Historic Park
- KEWEENAW: Horseshoe Harbor, The Nature Conservancy (Mary Macdonald Preserve at Horseshoe Harbor)
- KEWEENAW: Isle Royale National Park
- KEWEENAW: Keweenaw Point, High Rock Bay, and Keystone Bay, Baraga State Forest Management Unit
- ONTONAGON: Porcupine Shore, Porcupine Mountains Wilderness State Park

Volcanic bedrock lakeshore, Bete Grise, Baraga State Forest Management Unit, Keweenaw County

BEDROCK GRASSLAND GROUP

Bedrock Grassland is a unique group that includes one natural community type, alvar. Alvar is a grassland community that occurs on level exposures of limestone and dolomite bedrock and thin soils over these calcareous bedrock types. Alvar occurs on the Niagaran Cuesta in the eastern and south-central Upper Peninsula and northeastern Lower Peninsula. Alvar is characterized by the dominance of grasses and sedges with scattered shrubs and trees. Bedrock Grassland is differentiated from Bedrock Glade based on canopy cover. Bedrock Grasslands typically support less than 10% canopy cover whereas Bedrock Glades support between 10 and 60% canopy cover.

Alvar, Maxton Plains, Drummond Island, Chippewa County

BRADFORD S. SLAUGHTER

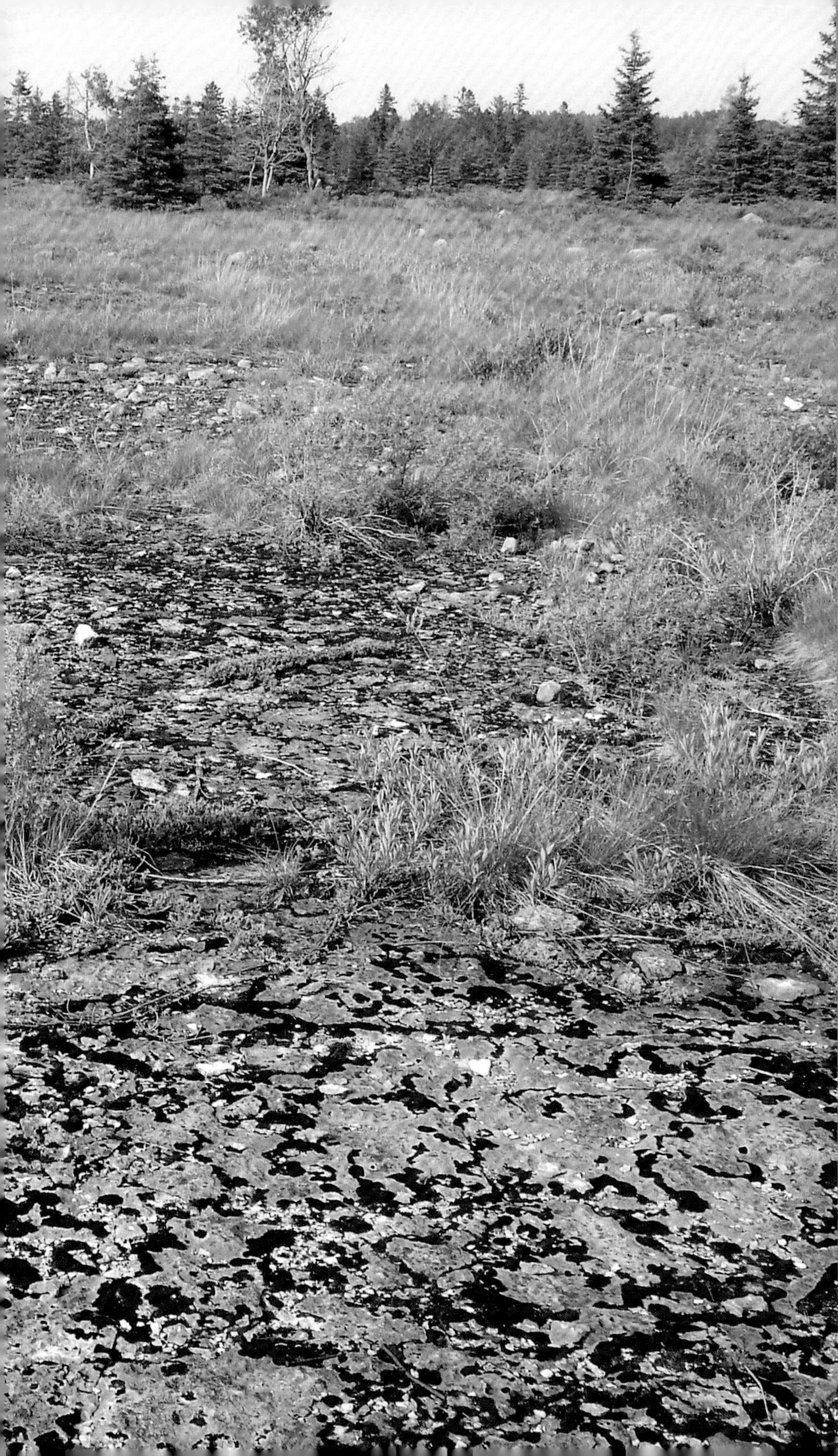

S1 ALVAR

Alvar is a grass- and sedge-dominated community that occurs on broad, flat expanses of calcareous bedrock (limestone or dolomite) near the shorelines of Lakes Huron and Michigan in the Upper Peninsula and northeastern Lower Michigan and locally along the Escanaba River in the central Upper

Peninsula. The calcareous bedrock is often covered by a thin veneer of mildly to moderately alkaline loamy sand or sandy loam, but areas of exposed

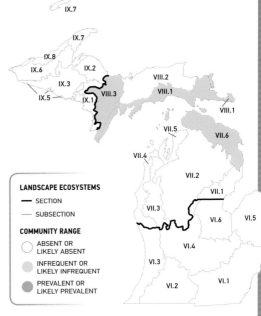

LANDSCAPE ECOSYSTEMS

━━ SECTION

┈┈ SUBSECTION

COMMUNITY RANGE

◯ ABSENT OR LIKELY ABSENT

◔ INFREQUENT OR LIKELY INFREQUENT

⬤ PREVALENT OR LIKELY PREVALENT

JOSHUA G. COHEN

limestone and dolomite are common. Natural processes that influence species composition and community structure include extreme fluctuations in soil moisture ranging from inundation in spring to drought in summer, windthrow, and occasional fires. In addition to grasses and sedges, alvar supports scattered patches of shrubs and trees, and mosses and lichens are locally prevalent. Characteristic species include little bluestem (*Schizachyrium scoparium*), prairie dropseed (*Sporobolus heterolepis*), bulrush sedge (*Carex scirpoidea*), flattened spike-rush (*Eleocharis compressa*), big bluestem (*Andropogon gerardii*), mat muhly (*Muhlenbergia richardsonis*), cordgrass (*Spartina pectinata*), ticklegrass (*Agrostis scabra*), common juniper (*Juniperus communis*), creeping juniper (*J. horizontalis*), shrubby cinquefoil (*Dasiphora fruticosa*), northern white-cedar (*Thuja occidentalis*), and quaking aspen (*Populus tremuloides*).

Alvar occurring as a thin band along the Escanaba River in Delta County

CHARACTERISTIC PLANTS

GRAMINOIDS

- ticklegrass (*Agrostis scabra*)
- big bluestem (*Andropogon gerardii*)
- prairie brome (*Bromus kalmii*)
- blue-joint (*Calamagrostis canadensis*)
- Crawe's sedge (*Carex crawei*)
- Richardson's sedge (*Carex richardsonii*)*
- bulrush sedge (*Carex scirpoidea*)*
- poverty grass (*Danthonia spicata*)
- tufted hair grass (*Deschampsia cespitosa*)
- flattened spike-rush (*Eleocharis compressa*)*
- golden-seeded spike-rush (*Eleocharis elliptica*)
- mat muhly (*Muhlenbergia richardsonis*)*
- little bluestem (*Schizachyrium scoparium*)
- cordgrass (*Spartina pectinata*)
- prairie dropseed (*Sporobolus heterolepis*)*

FORBS

- small pussytoes (*Antennaria howellii*)
- wild columbine (*Aquilegia canadensis*)
- hairy rock cress (*Arabis pycnocarpa*)
- harebell (*Campanula rotundifolia*)
- Indian paintbrush (*Castilleja coccinea*)
- field chickweed (*Cerastium arvense*)
- Hill's thistle (*Cirsium hillii*)*
- limestone calamint (*Clinopodium arkansanum*)
- bastard-toadflax (*Comandra umbellata*)
- prairie cinquefoil (*Drymocallis arguta*)
- wild strawberry (*Fragaria virginiana*)
- Carolina crane's-bill (*Geranium carolinianum*)
- prairie-smoke (*Geum triflorum*)*
- early saxifrage (*Micranthes virginiensis*)
- rock sandwort (*Minuartia michauxii*)
- wild bergamot (*Monarda fistulosa*)
- balsam ragwort (*Packera paupercula*)
- early buttercup (*Ranunculus fascicularis*)

- small skullcap (*Scutellaria parvula*)*
- old-field goldenrod (*Solidago nemoralis*)
- upland white goldenrod (*Solidago ptarmicoides*)

LICHENS
- reindeer lichens (*Cladina mitis* and *C. rangiferina*)
- felt lichen (*Peltigera canina*)

MOSSES
- schistidium mosses (*Schistidium* spp.)
- tortella moss (*Tortella* spp.)

SHRUBS
- serviceberries (*Amelanchier* spp.)
- shrubby cinquefoil (*Dasiphora fruticosa*)
- common juniper (*Juniperus communis*)
- creeping juniper (*Juniperus horizontalis*)
- sand cherry (*Prunus pumila*)

- choke cherry (*Prunus virginiana*)
- fragrant sumac (*Rhus aromatica*)
- soapberry (*Shepherdia canadensis*)
- snowberry (*Symphoricarpos albus*)

TREES
- paper birch (*Betula papyrifera*)
- white spruce (*Picea glauca*)
- white pine (*Pinus strobus*)
- quaking aspen (*Populus tremuloides*)
- northern white-cedar (*Thuja occidentalis*)

PLACES TO VISIT

- CHIPPEWA: Maxton Plains (Drummond Island), Sault Sainte Marie State Forest Management Unit and The Nature Conservancy (Maxton Plains Preserve)
- DELTA: Escanaba River, Escanaba State Forest Management Unit

Alvar occurs on broad, flat expanses of calcareous bedrock (limestone or dolomite) covered by a thin veneer of mineral soil

BEDROCK GLADE GROUP

Bedrock Glades are savanna or open woodland communities that occur on exposed bedrock and thin soils over bedrock. These systems are found primarily in the Upper Peninsula but also occur infrequently in the northeastern Lower Peninsula. Bedrock Glades are characterized by sparse vegetation consisting of scattered and stunted trees, scattered shrubs and shrub thickets, and a partial turf of herbs, grasses, sedges, mosses, and lichens. Canopy cover typically ranges from 10 to 60%. Bedrock types that support Bedrock Glade include limestone, granite, and volcanics. Bedrock Glades are found on flat expanses of limestone or dolomite and steep to stair-stepped slopes, knobs, and exposures of granite and volcanic bedrock. The soils of bedrock glades are shallow, restricted to cracks, crevices, ledges, and depressions, and range from acidic to alkaline depending on the bedrock type. Natural processes that influence species composition and community structure include seasonal patterns of soil saturation and desiccation, extreme winds, ice and snow abrasion, erosion, windthrow, exfoliation of rock slabs, and occasional fires.

Four natural community types fall within the Bedrock Glade group, including limestone bedrock glade, granite bedrock glade, volcanic bedrock glade, and northern bald. Classification of these Bedrock Glade types is based on differences in bedrock composition, species composition, community structure, natural processes, and landscape setting.

Volcanic bedrock glade, Fish Cove, Keweenaw County

MICHAEL A. KOST

S2 LIMESTONE BEDROCK GLADE

Limestone bedrock glade[13] is a savanna or open woodland community dominated by herbs, graminoids, and scattered clumps of shrubs and stunted trees that typically occurs on flat expanses of calcareous bedrock (limestone or dolomite) near the shorelines of Lake Huron and Lake

Michigan in the Upper Peninsula and near the Lake Huron shoreline in northern Lower Michigan. The calcareous bedrock is covered by a

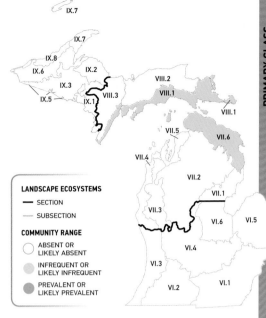

LANDSCAPE ECOSYSTEMS

— SECTION
---- SUBSECTION

COMMUNITY RANGE

○ ABSENT OR LIKELY ABSENT

◑ INFREQUENT OR LIKELY INFREQUENT

● PREVALENT OR LIKELY PREVALENT

thin veneer of mildly to moderately alkaline loamy sand or sandy loam. Areas of exposed bedrock are common. Natural processes that influence species composition and community structure include extreme fluctuations in soil moisture ranging from inundation in spring to drought in summer, windthrow, and occasional fires. Common trees and shrubs include northern white-cedar (*Thuja occidentalis*), balsam fir (*Abies balsamea*), quaking aspen (*Populus tremuloides*), common juniper (*Juniperus communis*), bearberry (*Arctostaphylos uva-ursi*), and soapberry (*Shepherdia canadensis*). Prevalent graminoids are poverty grass (*Danthonia spicata*), sedges (*Carex* spp.), and hair grass (*Deschampsia cespitosa*).

CHARACTERISTIC PLANTS

GRAMINOIDS

- Kalm's brome (*Bromus kalmii*)
- beauty sedge (*Carex concinna*)

JOSHUA G. COHEN

281

Limestone bedrock glade, Garden Peninsula, Delta County

- ebony sedge (*Carex eburnea*)
- sedge (*Carex garberi*)
- Richardson's sedge (*Carex richardsonii*)*
- poverty grass (*Danthonia spicata*)
- tufted hair grass (*Deschampsia cespitosa*)
- Lindheimer's panic grass (*Dichanthelium lindheimeri*)
- slender wheat grass (*Elymus trachycaulus*)
- rough-leaved rice grass (*Oryzopsis asperifolia*)
- little bluestem (*Schizachyrium scoparium*)

FORBS
- yarrow (*Achillea millefolium*)
- small pussytoes (*Antennaria howellii*)

- white camas (*Anticlea elegans*)
- wild columbine (*Aquilegia canadensis*)
- Cooper's milk-vetch (*Astragalus neglectus*)*
- harebell (*Campanula rotundifolia*)
- Indian paintbrush (*Castilleja coccinea*)
- Hill's thistle (*Cirsium hillii*)*
- limestone calamint (*Clinopodium arkansanum*)
- bastard-toadflax (*Comandra umbellata*)
- lance-leaved coreopsis (*Coreopsis lanceolata*)
- small yellow lady-slipper (*Cypripedium parviflorum* var. *makasin*)
- large yellow lady-slipper (*Cypripedium parviflorum* var. *pubescens*)

- large-leaved aster (*Eurybia macrophylla*)
- wild strawberry (*Fragaria virginiana*)
- barren-strawberry (*Geum fragarioides*)
- dwarf lake iris (*Iris lacustris*)*
- wood lily (*Lilium philadelphicum*)
- twinflower (*Linnaea borealis*)
- starry false Solomon-seal (*Maianthemum stellatum*)
- cow-wheat (*Melampyrum lineare*)
- rock sandwort (*Minuartia michauxii*)
- balsam ragwort (*Packera paupercula*)
- sweet-coltsfoot (*Petasites frigidus*)
- Alaska orchid (*Platanthera unalascensis*)*
- gay-wings (*Polygala paucifolia*)
- bird's-eye primrose (*Primula mistassinica*)
- early buttercup (*Ranunculus fascicularis*)
- black-eyed Susan (*Rudbeckia hirta*)
- old-field goldenrod (*Solidago nemoralis*)
- upland white goldenrod (*Solidago ptarmicoides*)
- smooth aster (*Symphyotrichum laeve*)

FERNS
- maidenhair spleenwort (*Asplenium trichomanes*)
- common polypody (*Polypodium virginianum*)
- bracken fern (*Pteridium aquilinum*)

LICHENS
- reindeer lichens (*Cladina mitis* and *C. rangiferina*)
- felt lichen (*Peltigera canina*)

MOSSES
- schistidium mosses (*Schistidium* spp.)
- tortella moss (*Tortella* spp.)

SHRUBS
- serviceberries (*Amelanchier* spp.)
- bearberry (*Arctostaphylos uva-ursi*)
- bunchberry (*Cornus canadensis*)
- red-osier dogwood (*Cornus sericea*)
- bush honeysuckle (*Diervilla lonicera*)
- Kalm's St. John's-wort (*Hypericum kalmianum*)
- common juniper (*Juniperus communis*)
- creeping juniper (*Juniperus horizontalis*)
- choke cherry (*Prunus virginiana*)
- alder-leaved buckthorn (*Rhamnus alnifolia*)
- wild rose (*Rosa blanda*)
- dwarf raspberry (*Rubus pubescens*)
- soapberry (*Shepherdia canadensis*)
- snowberry (*Symphoricarpos albus*)

TREES
- balsam fir (*Abies balsamea*)
- paper birch (*Betula papyrifera*)
- white spruce (*Picea glauca*)
- white pine (*Pinus strobus*)
- balsam poplar (*Populus balsamifera*)
- quaking aspen (*Populus tremuloides*)
- northern white-cedar (*Thuja occidentalis*)

PLACES TO VISIT
- CHIPPEWA: East Lake Glade, Hiawatha National Forest
- CHIPPEWA: Maxton Plains (Drummond Island), Sault Sainte Marie State Forest Management Unit and The Nature Conservancy (Maxton Plains Preserve)
- CHIPPEWA: The Rock (Drummond Island), Sault Saint Marie State Forest Management Unit
- DELTA: Kregg Bay Glade (Garden Peninsula), Shingleton State Forest Management Unit
- PRESQUE ISLE: Thompson's Harbor, Thompson's Harbor State Park

S2 GRANITE BEDROCK GLADE

Granite bedrock glade is a savanna or open woodland community characterized by sparse vegetation consisting of scattered open-grown trees, scattered shrubs or shrub thickets, and a partial turf of herbs, grasses, sedges, mosses, and lichens. The community occurs in the western

Upper Peninsula where knobs of granitic bedrock types are exposed at the surface. Granite bedrock glade typically occupies areas of steep to

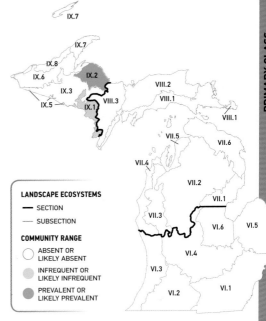

LANDSCAPE ECOSYSTEMS
— SECTION
— SUBSECTION

COMMUNITY RANGE
○ ABSENT OR LIKELY ABSENT
◔ INFREQUENT OR LIKELY INFREQUENT
● PREVALENT OR LIKELY PREVALENT

JOSHUA G. COHEN

stair-stepped slopes, with short cliffs, and exposed knobs of bedrock. Soil development is generally restricted to cracks and depressions within the rock, where shallow organic deposits and sand and gravel can accumulate. The thin soils are typically strongly acidic. Natural processes that influence species composition and community structure include erosion, windthrow, desiccation, exfoliation of rock slabs, and occasional fires. Characteristic species include red oak (*Quercus rubra*), pines (*Pinus* spp.), aspens (*Populus* spp.), paper birch (*Betula papyrifera*), serviceberries (*Amelanchier* spp.), blueberries (*Vaccinium* spp.), bearberry (*Arctostaphylos uva-ursi*), common juniper (*Juniperus communis*), large-leaved aster (*Eurybia macrophylla*), harebell (*Campanula rotundifolia*), poverty grass (*Danthonia spicata*), hair grasses (*Avenella flexuosa* and *Deschampsia cespitosa*), and common polypody (*Polypodium virginianum*).

▶

285

JOSHUA G. COHEN

Lichens and mosses are common on the granitic bedrock

CHARACTERISTIC PLANTS

GRAMINOIDS
- wavy hair grass (*Avenella flexuosa*)
- Pennsylvania sedge (*Carex pensylvanica*)
- poverty grass (*Danthonia spicata*)
- tufted hair grass (*Deschampsia cespitosa*)
- panic grasses (*Dichanthelium columbianum, D. depauperatum,* and *D. linearifolium*)
- rice grass (*Piptatherum pungens*)

FORBS
- yarrow (*Achillea millefolium*)
- small pussytoes (*Antennaria howellii*)
- spreading dogbane (*Apocynum androsaemifolium*)
- wild columbine (*Aquilegia canadensis*)
- bristly sarsaparilla (*Aralia hispida*)
- harebell (*Campanula rotundifolia*)
- pink corydalis (*Capnoides sempervirens*)
- trailing arbutus (*Epigaea repens*)
- large-leaved aster (*Eurybia macrophylla*)
- wild strawberry (*Fragaria virginiana*)
- cow-wheat (*Melampyrum lineare*)
- big-leaf sandwort (*Moehringia macrophylla*)*
- jumpseed (*Persicaria virginiana*)
- western smartweed (*Polygonum douglasii*)
- three-toothed cinquefoil (*Sibbaldiopsis tridentata*)
- slender ladies'-tresses (*Spiranthes lacera*)

FERNS
- maidenhair spleenwort (*Asplenium trichomanes*)
- spinulose woodfern (*Dryopteris carthusiana*)
- marginal woodfern (*Dryopteris marginalis*)
- common polypody (*Polypodium virginianum*)
- bracken fern (*Pteridium aquilinum*)
- rusty woodsia (*Woodsia ilvensis*)

LICHENS
- reindeer lichens (*Cladina* spp.)

MOSSES
- haircap mosses (*Polytrichum* spp.)

WOODY VINES
- poison-ivy (*Toxicodendron radicans*)
- riverbank grape (*Vitis riparia*)

SHRUBS
- serviceberries (*Amelanchier* spp.)
- bearberry (*Arctostaphylos uva-ursi*)
- bush honeysuckle (*Diervilla lonicera*)
- wintergreen (*Gaultheria procumbens*)
- common juniper (*Juniperus communis*)
- choke cherry (*Prunus virginiana*)
- smooth sumac (*Rhus glabra*)

- northern gooseberry (*Ribes oxyacanthoides*)*
- thimbleberry (*Rubus parviflorus*)
- wild red raspberry (*Rubus strigosus*)
- low sweet blueberry (*Vaccinium angustifolium*)
- Canada blueberry (*Vaccinium myrtilloides*)

TREES
- balsam fir (*Abies balsamea*)
- red maple (*Acer rubrum*)
- paper birch (*Betula papyrifera*)
- black hawthorn (*Crataegus douglasii*)*
- white spruce (*Picea glauca*)
- jack pine (*Pinus banksiana*)
- red pine (*Pinus resinosa*)

- white pine (*Pinus strobus*)
- big-toothed aspen (*Populus grandidentata*)
- quaking aspen (*Populus tremuloides*)
- pin cherry (*Prunus pensylvanica*)
- red oak (*Quercus rubra*)
- basswood (*Tilia americana*)

PLACES TO VISIT
- DICKINSON: Lost Lake Outcrops, Crystal Falls State Forest Management Unit
- MARQUETTE: Lost Creek Outcrops, Gwinn State Forest Management Unit
- MARQUETTE: Van Riper Glades, Van Riper State Park

Granite bedrock glade, Marquette County

VOLCANIC BEDROCK GLADE

Volcanic bedrock glade is a savanna or open woodland community characterized by sparse vegetation consisting of scattered open-grown trees, scattered shrubs or shrub thickets, and a partial turf of herbs, grasses, sedges, mosses, and lichens. The community primarily occurs in

the western Upper Peninsula and on Isle Royale where basaltic bedrock and volcanic conglomerates are exposed at the surface. The community frequently

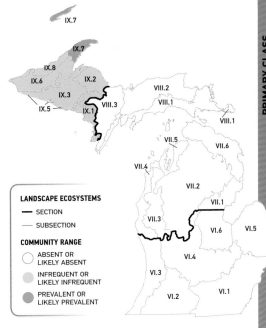

LANDSCAPE ECOSYSTEMS
— SECTION
— SUBSECTION

COMMUNITY RANGE
○ ABSENT OR LIKELY ABSENT
◐ INFREQUENT OR LIKELY INFREQUENT
● PREVALENT OR LIKELY PREVALENT

MICHAEL A. KOST

occupies areas of steep to stair-stepped slopes, with short cliffs, and exposed knobs of bedrock. Soil development is generally restricted to cracks, pockets, and vesicles within the volcanic rock where shallow organic deposits can accumulate. The thin soils are typically medium acidic to mildly alkaline. Natural processes that influence species composition and community structure include erosion, windthrow, desiccation, occasional fires, and sloughing of rock slabs. Characteristic species include pines (*Pinus* spp.), quaking aspen (*Populus tremuloides*), paper birch (*Betula papyrifera*), white spruce (*Picea glauca*), balsam fir (*Abies balsamea*), red oak (*Quercus rubra*), low sweet blueberry (*Vaccinium angustifolium*), tall bilberry (*V. membranaceum*), Canada blueberry (*V. myrtilloides*), bearberry (*Arctostaphylos uva-ursi*), common juniper (*Juniperus communis*), creeping juniper (*J. horizontalis*), soapberry (*Shepherdia canadensis*), thimbleberry (*Rubus parviflorus*), poverty grass

A diverse array of lichens and mosses occurs on the volcanic bedrock

(*Danthonia spicata*), hair grasses (*Avenella flexuosa* and *Deschampsia cespitosa*), yarrow (*Achillea millefolium*), large-leaved aster (*Eurybia macrophylla*), small blue-eyed Mary (*Collinsia parviflora*), small pussytoes (*Antennaria howellii*), low bindweed (*Calystegia spithamea*), and harebell (*Campanula rotundifolia*).

CHARACTERISTIC PLANTS

GRAMINOIDS
- wavy hair grass (*Avenella flexuosa*)
- poverty grass (*Danthonia spicata*)
- tufted hair grass (*Deschampsia cespitosa*)
- rough-leaved rice grass (*Oryzopsis asperifolia*)

FORBS
- yarrow (*Achillea millefolium*)
- small pussytoes (*Antennaria howellii*)
- wild columbine (*Aquilegia canadensis*)
- low bindweed (*Calystegia spithamea*)
- harebell (*Campanula rotundifolia*)
- pink corydalis (*Capnoides sempervirens*)

- small blue-eyed Mary (*Collinsia parviflora*)*
- bastard-toadflax (*Comandra umbellata*)
- prairie cinquefoil (*Drymocallis arguta*)
- large-leaved aster (*Eurybia macrophylla*)
- wild strawberry (*Fragaria virginiana*)
- geocaulon (*Geocaulon lividum*)
- twinflower (*Linnaea borealis*)
- Canada mayflower (*Maianthemum canadense*)
- cow-wheat (*Melampyrum lineare*)
- early saxifrage (*Micranthes virginiensis*)
- rough-leaved rice grass (*Oryzopsis asperifolia*)
- balsam ragwort (*Packera paupercula*)
- bracken fern (*Pteridium aquilinum*)
- old-field goldenrod (*Solidago nemoralis*)

FERNS
- male fern (*Dryopteris filix-mas*)*
- bracken fern (*Pteridium aquilinum*)

LICHENS
- reindeer lichens (*Cladina* spp.)
- usnea lichens (*Usnea* spp.)

MOSSES
- haircap mosses (*Polytrichum* spp.)

WOODY VINES
- red honeysuckle (*Lonicera dioica*)
- poison-ivy (*Toxicodendron radicans*)
- riverbank grape (*Vitis riparia*)

SHRUBS
- serviceberries (*Amelanchier* spp.)
- bearberry (*Arctostaphylos uva-ursi*)
- pipsissewa (*Chimaphila umbellata*)
- bush honeysuckle (*Diervilla lonicera*)
- trailing arbutus (*Epigaea repens*)
- wintergreen (*Gaultheria procumbens*)
- common juniper (*Juniperus communis*)
- creeping juniper (*Juniperus horizontalis*)

- wild rose (*Rosa acicularis*)
- thimbleberry (*Rubus parviflorus*)
- soapberry (*Shepherdia canadensis*)
- low sweet blueberry (*Vaccinium angustifolium*)
- tall bilberry (*Vaccinium membranaceum*)
- Canada blueberry (*Vaccinium myrtilloides*)

TREES
- balsam fir (*Abies balsamea*)
- juneberry (*Amelanchier arborea*)
- paper birch (*Betula papyrifera*)
- white spruce (*Picea glauca*)
- jack pine (*Pinus banksiana*)
- red pine (*Pinus resinosa*)
- white pine (*Pinus strobus*)
- quaking aspen (*Populus tremuloides*)
- red oak (*Quercus rubra*)

- mountain-ash (*Sorbus decora*)
- northern white-cedar (*Thuja occidentalis*)

PLACES TO VISIT
- KEWEENAW: Bare Bluff Glade, Michigan Nature Association (Grinnell Memorial Nature Sanctuary at Bare Bluff)
- KEWEENAW: Fish Cove, Baraga State Forest Management Unit
- KEWEENAW: Horseshoe Harbor, The Nature Conservancy (Mary Macdonald Preserve at Horseshoe Harbor)
- KEWEENAW: Isle Royale National Park
- ONTONAGON: Porcupine Mountain Glades, Porcupine Mountains Wilderness State Park
- ONTONAGON: Traps Hills Escarpment, Ottawa National Forest

Volcanic bedrock glade, Horseshoe Harbor, Keweenaw County

S1 NORTHERN BALD

Northern bald[14] is a dwarf shrub– and herb-dominated community restricted to large escarpments of volcanic bedrock ridges in the western Upper Peninsula.

The community is characterized by areas of exposed bedrock, thin, slightly acidic soils, and sparse vegetation, including scattered flagged trees and

trees distorted into a krummholz growth form by branch breakage due to heavy snow, thick ice, and extreme winds. Natural processes that influence species

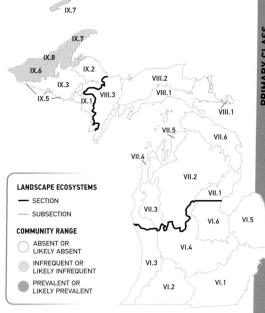

LANDSCAPE ECOSYSTEMS
— SECTION
--- SUBSECTION

COMMUNITY RANGE
○ ABSENT OR LIKELY ABSENT
◐ INFREQUENT OR LIKELY INFREQUENT
● PREVALENT OR LIKELY PREVALENT

JOSHUA G. COHEN

composition and community structure include extreme winds, ice and snow abrasion, desiccation, erosion, occasional fires, and sloughing of rock slabs. Common trees and shrubs include white pine (*Pinus strobus*), red oak (*Quercus rubra*), bearberry (*Arctostaphylos uva-ursi*), and common juniper (*Juniperus communis*). Characteristic ground cover species include poverty grass (*Danthonia spicata*), prairie cinquefoil (*Drymocallis arguta*), three-toothed cinquefoil (*Sibbaldiopsis tridentata*), small blue-eyed Mary (*Collinsia parviflora*), rusty woodsia (*Woodsia ilvensis*), and maidenhair spleenwort (*Asplenium trichomanes*).

CHARACTERISTIC PLANTS

GRAMINOIDS
- Pennsylvania sedge (*Carex pensylvanica*)
- poverty grass (*Danthonia spicata*)
- tufted hair grass (*Deschampsia cespitosa*)
- rice grass (*Piptatherum pungens*)

Trees growing on northern balds, like this northern white-cedar (*Thuja occidentalis*), are subject to heavy snow, thick ice, and extreme winds

JOSHUA G. COHEN

- large-leaved aster (*Eurybia macrophylla*)
- wild strawberry (*Fragaria virginiana*)
- false spikenard (*Maianthemum racemosum*)
- early saxifrage (*Micranthes virginiensis*)
- balsam ragwort (*Packera paupercula*)
- western smartweed (*Polygonum douglasii*)
- clammy cudweed (*Pseudognaphalium macounii*)
- three-toothed cinquefoil (*Sibbaldiopsis tridentata*)
- sand violet (*Viola adunca*)

FERNS

- maidenhair spleenwort (*Asplenium trichomanes*)
- male fern (*Dryopteris filix-mas*)*
- common polypody (*Polypodium virginianum*)
- Braun's holly-fern (*Polystichum braunii*)
- northern holly-fern (*Polystichum lonchitis*)
- rusty woodsia (*Woodsia ilvensis*)

FERN ALLIES

- ground-cedar (*Diphasiastrum tristachyum*)
- sand club moss (*Selaginella rupestris*)

SHRUBS

- serviceberries (*Amelanchier* spp.)
- bearberry (*Arctostaphylos uva-ursi*)
- New Jersey tea (*Ceanothus herbaceus*)
- common juniper (*Juniperus communis*)
- creeping juniper (*Juniperus horizontalis*)
- choke cherry (*Prunus virginiana*)
- staghorn sumac (*Rhus typhina*)
- wild rose (*Rosa acicularis*)
- soapberry (*Shepherdia canadensis*)
- snowberry (*Symphoricarpos albus*)
- low sweet blueberry (*Vaccinium angustifolium*)

TREES

- balsam fir (*Abies balsamea*)
- red maple (*Acer rubrum*)

FORBS

- yarrow (*Achillea millefolium*)
- small-leaved pussytoes (*Antennaria howellii*)
- wild columbine (*Aquilegia canadensis*)
- wormwood (*Artemisia campestris*)
- harebell (*Campanula rotundifolia*)
- small blue-eyed Mary (*Collinsia parviflora*)*
- rock whitlow-grass (*Draba arabisans*)*
- prairie cinquefoil (*Drymocallis arguta*)

- mountain maple (*Acer spicatum*)
- juneberry (*Amelanchier arborea*)
- paper birch (*Betula papyrifera*)
- white spruce (*Picea glauca*)
- red pine (*Pinus resinosa*)
- white pine (*Pinus strobus*)
- big-toothed aspen (*Populus grandidentata*)
- red oak (*Quercus rubra*)
- northern white-cedar (*Thuja occidentalis*)

PLACES TO VISIT

- KEWEENAW: Bare Bluff Bald, Michigan Nature Association (Grinnell Memorial Nature Sanctuary at Bare Bluff)
- KEWEENAW: Isle Royale National Park
- KEWEENAW: Mt. Lookout, Brockaway Mountain Drive
- ONTONAGON: Escarpment Trail, Porcupine Mountains Wilderness State Park

Northern bald, Escarpment Trail, Porcupine Mountains Wilderness State Park, Ontonagon County

LAKESHORE CLIFF/ BLUFF GROUP

Lakeshore Cliff/Bluff systems are sparsely vegetated communities on vertical or near-vertical exposures of bedrock or steeply sloping bluffs of clay along the Great Lakes shorelines or along rivers draining into the Great Lakes. Bedrock types that support Lakeshore Cliff/Bluff include limestone, sandstone, granite, and volcanics. There is almost no soil development on these bedrock cliffs except where shallow mineral and organic deposits accumulate along the narrow cliff summit and ledges, in crevices in the cliff face, and at the base of the cliff. Clay bluff is characterized by eroding alkaline clays. Although these Lakeshore Cliff/ Bluff systems experience high levels of moisture due to their proximity to the Great Lakes, plant growth and establishment are limited by the lack of suitable substrate, desiccation, constant erosion, and direct exposure to waves, wind, and ice.

Five natural community types fall within the Lakeshore Cliff/Bluff group, including clay bluff, limestone lakeshore cliff, sandstone lakeshore cliff, granite lakeshore cliff, and volcanic lakeshore cliff. Classification of these Lakeshore Cliff/Bluff types is based on differences in substrate composition, species composition, community structure, and natural processes.

Sandstone lakeshore cliff, Point Abbaye, Baraga State Forest Management Unit, Baraga County
JOSHUA G. COHEN

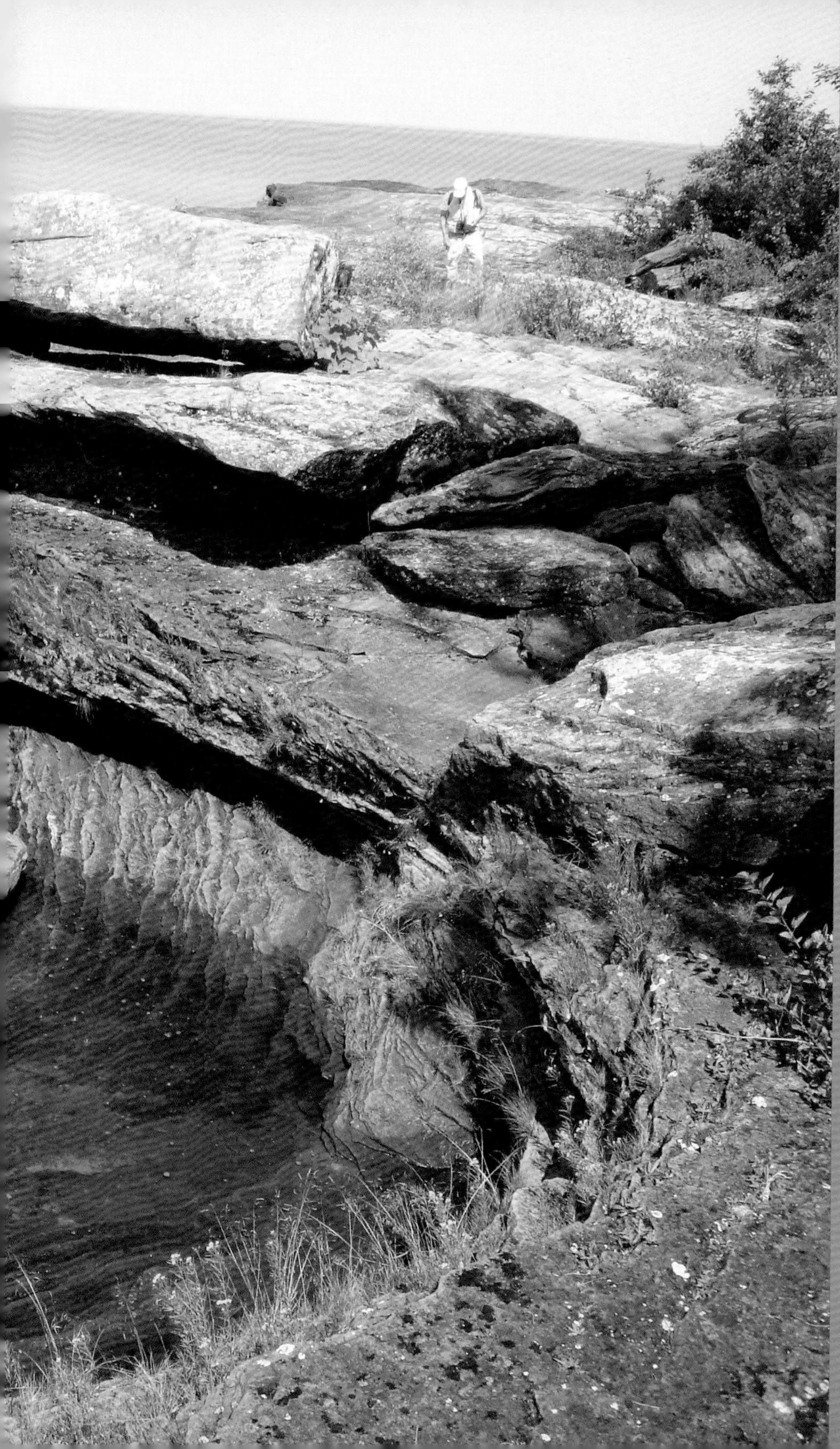

S2 CLAY BLUFF

Clay bluff is an erosion-dependent, forb-, graminoid-, and shrub-dominated community that occurs infrequently on steep to near-vertical clay slopes along the shorelines of Lake Michigan and Lake Superior. Clay bluff is less commonly found localized along eroding banks of rivers and streams that form ravines through clay soils and drain into these Great Lakes. The

community develops on alkaline clays that are locally exposed following landslide events. Species composition and vegetative structure of clay bluff is patterned by sloughing of clay slopes.

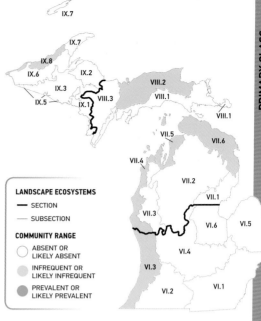

LANDSCAPE ECOSYSTEMS

— SECTION

---- SUBSECTION

COMMUNITY RANGE

○ ABSENT OR LIKELY ABSENT

◐ INFREQUENT OR LIKELY INFREQUENT

● PREVALENT OR LIKELY PREVALENT

JOSHUA G. COHEN

Active sloughing occurs following frost heave and spring thaw, and vegetation can vary from year to year. Clay bluff is characterized by sparse cover of forbs, graminoids, and low shrubs, dense patches of tall shrubs, and scattered and stunted overstory trees. Characteristic species include alders (*Alnus* spp.), willows (*Salix* spp.), northern white-cedar (*Thuja occidentalis*), paper birch (*Betula papyrifera*), Kalm's St. John's-wort (*Hypericum kalmianum*), soapberry (*Shepherdia canadensis*), scouring rushes (*Equisetum* spp.), grass-of-Parnassus (*Parnassia glauca*), goldenrods (*Solidago* spp.), small fringed gentian (*Gentianopsis virgata*), grass-leaved goldenrod (*Euthamia graminifolia*), jewelweed (*Impatiens capensis*), and rushes (*Juncus* spp.). Due to the frequency of disturbance and the shifting exposure of clay substrate, native and non-native ruderal species are common within clay bluff.

▶

Clay bluff along the Lake Michigan shoreline in Allegan County

CHARACTERISTIC PLANTS

GRAMINOIDS

- marram grass (*Ammophila breviligulata*)
- golden-fruited sedge (*Carex aurea*)
- rushes (*Juncus brachycephalus,
  J. canadensis, J. tenuis,* and *J. torreyi*)
- green bulrush (*Scirpus atrovirens*)

FORBS

- fireweed (*Chamerion angustifolium*)
- common boneset (*Eupatorium perfoliatum*)
- grass-leaved goldenrod (*Euthamia
  graminifolia*)
- wild strawberry (*Fragaria virginiana*)
- small fringed gentian (*Gentianopsis virgata*)
- jewelweed (*Impatiens capensis*)
- great blue lobelia (*Lobelia siphilitica*)
- grass-of-Parnassus (*Parnassia glauca*)

- goldenrods (*Solidago canadensis,
  S. nemoralis, S. rugosa,* and *S. uliginosa*)
- side-flowering aster (*Symphyotrichum
  lateriflorum*)

FERN ALLIES

- common horsetail (*Equisetum arvense*)
- scouring rush (*Equisetum hyemale*)
- variegated scouring rush (*Equisetum
  variegatum*)

SHRUBS

- tag alder (*Alnus incana*)
- red-osier dogwood (*Cornus sericea*)
- Kalm's St. John's-wort (*Hypericum kalmianum*)
- pin cherry (*Prunus pensylvanica*)
- choke cherry (*Prunus virginiana*)
- staghorn sumac (*Rhus typhina*)

- wild black currant (*Ribes americanum*)
- willows (*Salix myricoides* and others)
- soapberry (*Shepherdia canadensis*)

TREES
- sugar maple (*Acer saccharum*)
- paper birch (*Betula papyrifera*)
- white ash (*Fraxinus americana*)
- green ash (*Fraxinus pennsylvanica*)
- red-cedar (*Juniperus virginiana*)
- tulip tree (*Liriodendron tulipifera*)
- ironwood (*Ostrya virginiana*)
- cottonwood (*Populus deltoides*)
- quaking aspen (*Populus tremuloides*)
- mountain-ash (*Sorbus decora*)

- northern white-cedar (*Thuja occidentalis*)
- basswood (*Tilia americana*)
- hemlock (*Tsuga canadensis*)

PLACES TO VISIT

- ALLEGAN: Wau-Ke-Na, William Erby Smith Preserve, Southwest Michigan Land Conservancy
- GOGEBIC: Porcupine Mountains Clay Bluffs, Porcupine Mountains Wilderness State Park
- LEELANAU: Clay Cliffs Natural Area, Leland Township and Leelanau Conservancy
- LEELANAU: North Manitou Island, Sleeping Bear Dunes National Lakeshore

Clay bluff occurs along the Lake Superior shoreline in the Porcupine Mountains Wilderness State Park, Gogebic County

S1 LIMESTONE LAKESHORE CLIFF

Limestone lakeshore cliff consists of vertical or near-vertical exposures of limestone bedrock along the shorelines of Lake Michigan and Lake Huron in the Upper Peninsula. Documented limestone lakeshore cliffs range in height from 1.5 to 40 meters (5 to 130 ft). Soil development is primarily limited to

thin, mildly alkaline organic soils that form from decaying roots and other plant materials along the top of the cliff escarpment and ledges, in cracks

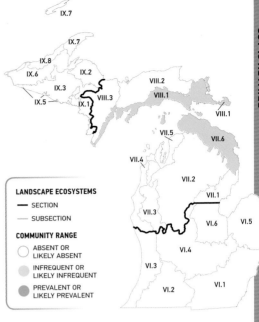

BRADFORD S. SLAUGHTER

and crevices in the bedrock, and at the base of the cliff. Although limestone lakeshore cliff experiences high levels of moisture due to its proximity to the Great Lakes, plant growth and establishment are limited by the lack of suitable substrate, desiccation, constant erosion, and direct exposure to waves, wind, and ice. Vegetation cover is sparse, but abundant cracks and crevices combined with calcareous conditions result in greater plant diversity and cover than on other lakeshore cliff types. The community typically supports less than 25% vascular plant cover, although some rock surfaces can be densely covered with lichens, mosses, and liverworts. Common herbaceous plants are common polypody (*Polypodium virginianum*), large-leaved aster (*Eurybia macrophylla*), wild sarsaparilla (*Aralia nudicaulis*), maidenhair spleenwort (*Asplenium trichomanes*), fragile fern (*Cystopteris fragilis*), oak fern (*Gymnocarpium dryopteris*),

303

Limestone lakeshore cliff, Fayette Historic State Park, Delta County

smooth cliff brake (*Pellaea glabella*), Oregon woodsia (*Woodsia oregana*), grass-leaved goldenrod (*Euthamia graminifolia*), herb Robert (*Geranium robertianum*), and wild columbine (*Aquilegia canadensis*). Scattered woody species include bush honeysuckle (*Diervilla lonicera*), thimbleberry (*Rubus parviflorus*), mountain maple (*Acer spicatum*), choke cherry (*Prunus virginiana*), red elderberry (*Sambucus racemosa*), paper birch (*Betula papyrifera*), and northern white-cedar (*Thuja occidentalis*).

CHARACTERISTIC PLANTS

GRAMINOIDS

- beauty sedge (*Carex concinna*)
- ebony sedge (*Carex eburnea*)

FORBS
- yarrow (*Achillea millefolium*)
- wild columbine (*Aquilegia canadensis*)
- wild sarsaparilla (*Aralia nudicaulis*)
- rock whitlow-grass (*Draba arabisans*)*
- large-leaved aster (*Eurybia macrophylla*)
- grass-leaved goldenrod (*Euthamia graminifolia*)
- wild strawberry (*Fragaria virginiana*)
- herb Robert (*Geranium robertianum*)
- Canada mayflower (*Maianthemum canadense*)

FERNS
- maidenhair spleenwort (*Asplenium trichomanes*)
- slender rock-brake (*Cryptogramma stelleri*)
- fragile fern (*Cystopteris fragilis*)
- oak fern (*Gymnocarpium dryopteris*)
- limestone oak fern (*Gymnocarpium robertianum*)*
- purple cliff-brake (*Pellaea atropurpurea*)*
- smooth cliff-brake (*Pellaea glabella*)
- common polypody (*Polypodium virginianum*)
- bracken fern (*Pteridium aquilinum*)
- Oregon woodsia (*Woodsia oregana*)

SHRUBS
- beaked hazelnut (*Corylus cornuta*)

- bush honeysuckle (*Diervilla lonicera*)
- Canadian fly honeysuckle (*Lonicera canadensis*)
- choke cherry (*Prunus virginiana*)
- thimbleberry (*Rubus parviflorus*)
- red elderberry (*Sambucus racemosa*)
- soapberry (*Shepherdia canadensis*)

TREES
- balsam fir (*Abies balsamea*)
- sugar maple (*Acer saccharum*)
- mountain maple (*Acer spicatum*)
- paper birch (*Betula papyrifera*)
- white pine (*Pinus strobus*)
- red oak (*Quercus rubra*)
- northern white-cedar (*Thuja occidentalis*)
- hemlock (*Tsuga canadensis*)

PLACES TO VISIT

- CHIPPEWA: Poe Point (Drummond Island), The Nature Conservancy (Maxton Plains Preserve)
- DELTA: Burnt Bluff (Garden Peninsula), Fayette Historic State Park
- DELTA: Middle Bluff (Garden Peninsula), Shingleton State Forest Management Unit and Fayette Historic State Park

SANDSTONE LAKESHORE CLIFF

Sandstone lakeshore cliff consists of sparsely vegetated vertical or near-vertical exposures of sandstone bedrock that occur primarily in the central and western Upper Peninsula along Lake Superior and also along a short stretch of the Lake Huron shoreline in the Thumb region of the Lower

Peninsula. Documented sandstone lakeshore cliffs range in height from 2 to 65 meters (6 to 200 ft). There is almost no soil development on the

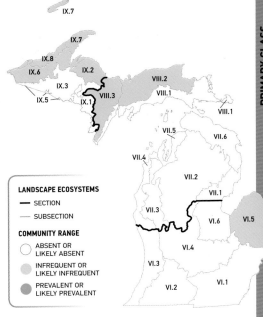

LANDSCAPE ECOSYSTEMS

—— SECTION

---- SUBSECTION

COMMUNITY RANGE

○ ABSENT OR LIKELY ABSENT

◐ INFREQUENT OR LIKELY INFREQUENT

● PREVALENT OR LIKELY PREVALENT

JOSHUA G. COHEN

cliffs except where shallow, organic deposits and sand particles accumulate along the narrow cliff summit and ledges, in crevices in the cliff face, and at the base of the cliff. Although the community experiences high levels of moisture due to its proximity to the Great Lakes, plant growth and establishment are limited by the lack of suitable substrate, desiccation, constant erosion, and direct exposure to waves, wind, and ice. Characteristic herbaceous species include hair grass (*Deschampsia cespitosa*), harebell (*Campanula rotundifolia*), fireweed (*Chamerion angustifolium*), grass-leaved goldenrod (*Euthamia graminifolia*), and yarrow (*Achillea millefolium*). Scattered woody species include bush honeysuckle (*Diervilla lonicera*), ninebark (*Physocarpus opulifolius*), mountain alder (*Alnus viridis*), serviceberries (*Amelanchier* spp.), paper birch (*Betula papyrifera*), northern white-cedar (*Thuja occidentalis*), balsam fir (*Abies balsamea*), and white pine

Grass-leaved goldenrod (*Euthamia graminifolia*) is common along ledges and in crevices of sandstone lakeshore cliff

(*Pinus strobus*). Lichens, mosses, and liverworts occur primarily in moist areas associated with seepages.

CHARACTERISTIC PLANTS

GRAMINOIDS
- tufted hair grass (*Deschampsia cespitosa*)

FORBS
- yarrow (*Achillea millefolium*)
- harebell (*Campanula rotundifolia*)
- fireweed (*Chamerion angustifolium*)
- grass-leaved goldenrod (*Euthamia graminifolia*)
- wild strawberry (*Fragaria virginiana*)
- hairy hawkweed (*Hieracium gronovii*)
- jewelweed (*Impatiens capensis*)
- marsh pea (*Lathyrus palustris*)

- Kalm's lobelia (*Lobelia kalmii*)
- northern bugle weed (*Lycopus uniflorus*)
- bird's-eye primrose (*Primula mistassinica*)
- three-toothed cinquefoil (*Sibbaldiopsis tridentata*)
- marsh violet (*Viola cucullata*)

FERNS
- lady fern (*Athyrium filix-femina*)
- fragile fern (*Cystopteris fragilis*)
- spinulose woodfern (*Dryopteris carthusiana*)
- northern beech fern (*Phegopteris connectilis*)

FERN ALLIES
- common horsetail (*Equisetum arvense*)

SHRUBS
- mountain alder (*Alnus viridis*)
- serviceberries (*Amelanchier* spp.)

- red-osier dogwood (*Cornus sericea*)
- bush honeysuckle (*Diervilla lonicera*)
- ninebark (*Physocarpus opulifolius*)
- choke cherry (*Prunus virginiana*)
- dwarf raspberry (*Rubus pubescens*)
- wild red raspberry (*Rubus strigosus*)
- willows (*Salix bebbiana, S. discolor*, and others)

TREES
- balsam fir (*Abies balsamea*)
- sugar maple (*Acer saccharum*)
- paper birch (*Betula papyrifera*)
- American beech (*Fagus grandifolia*)
- white spruce (*Picea glauca*)
- white pine (*Pinus strobus*)

- balsam poplar (*Populus balsamifera*)
- quaking aspen (*Populus tremuloides*)
- black cherry (*Prunus serotina*)
- northern white-cedar (*Thuja occidentalis*)
- hemlock (*Tsuga canadensis*)

PLACES TO VISIT
- ALGER: Pictured Rocks, Pictured Rocks National Lakeshore
- BARAGA: Point Abbaye, Baraga State Forest Management Unit
- HOUGHTON: Rabbit Bay, Baraga State Forest Management Unit
- MARQUETTE: Little Presque Isle, Gwinn State Forest Management Unit

Sandstone lakeshore cliff, Pictured Rocks National Lakeshore, Alger County

S1 GRANITE LAKESHORE CLIFF

Granite lakeshore cliff consists of sparsely vegetated vertical or near-vertical exposures of granitic bedrock that occur along Lake Superior in west-central Upper Michigan. The cliffs range in height from 2 to 10 meters (6 to 30 ft). Soil development is limited to organic deposits that form from decaying roots and other plant material and accumulate in cracks, crevices, and depressions in the bedrock, primarily along the cliff summit. The thin soils are acidic. Although the community experiences high levels of moisture due to its proximity to Lake Superior, plant growth and establishment are limited by the lack of suitable substrate, desiccation, constant erosion, and direct exposure to waves, wind, and ice. The community supports less than 25% vascular plant cover, although lichens, mosses, and liverworts are abundant on some rock surfaces. Characteristic species include pines (*Pinus* spp.), quaking aspen (*Populus tremuloides*), paper birch (*Betula papyrifera*), serviceberries (*Amelanchier* spp.), low sweet blueberry (*Vaccinium angustifolium*), bearberry

(*Arctostaphylos uva-ursi*), common juniper (*Juniperus communis*), bush honeysuckle (*Diervilla lonicera*), hair grass (*Deschampsia cespitosa*), poverty grass (*Danthonia spicata*), three-toothed cinquefoil (*Sibbaldiopsis tridentata*), grass-leaved goldenrod (*Euthamia graminifolia*), and large-leaved aster (*Eurybia macrophylla*). Lichens, mosses, and liverworts can be common on the cliff face.

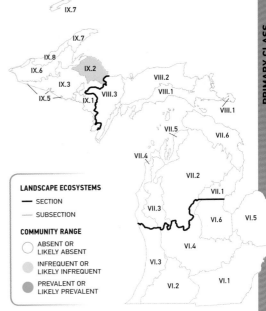

LANDSCAPE ECOSYSTEMS
— SECTION
— SUBSECTION

COMMUNITY RANGE
○ ABSENT OR LIKELY ABSENT
◐ INFREQUENT OR LIKELY INFREQUENT
● PREVALENT OR LIKELY PREVALENT

CHARACTERISTIC PLANTS

GRAMINOIDS
- poverty grass (*Danthonia spicata*)
- tufted hair grass (*Deschampsia cespitosa*)

FORBS
- harebell (*Campanula rotundifolia*)
- large-leaved aster (*Eurybia macrophylla*)
- grass-leaved goldenrod (*Euthamia graminifolia*)
- three-toothed cinquefoil (*Sibbaldiopsis tridentata*)

SHRUBS
- serviceberries (*Amelanchier* spp.)
- bearberry (*Arctostaphylos uva-ursi*)
- bush honeysuckle (*Diervilla lonicera*)
- common juniper (*Juniperus communis*)
- low sweet blueberry (*Vaccinium angustifolium*)

TREES
- serviceberries (*Amelanchier* spp.)
- paper birch (*Betula papyrifera*)
- jack pine (*Pinus banksiana*)
- red pine (*Pinus resinosa*)
- white pine (*Pinus strobus*)
- quaking aspen (*Populus tremuloides*)
- northern white-cedar (*Thuja occidentalis*)

PLACES TO VISIT
- MARQUETTE: Little Presque Isle, Gwinn State Forest Management Unit

JOSHUA G. COHEN

Granite lakeshore cliff, Little Presque Isle, Gwinn State Forest Management Unit, Marquette County

VOLCANIC LAKESHORE CLIFF

Volcanic lakeshore cliff consists of sparsely vegetated vertical or near-vertical exposures of volcanic bedrock on Lake Superior primarily along the Keweenaw Bay shoreline of the Keweenaw Peninsula, the southern shoreline of Manitou Island, and the northern shoreline of Isle Royale. The cliffs range in height from 3 to 80 meters (10 to 260 ft). There is little soil development on the steep rock face of the cliffs; some organic soil accumulation occurs in crevices in the rock face and on the upper lip of the cliffs. Although the community experiences high levels of moisture due to its proximity to Lake Superior, plant growth and establishment are limited by the lack of suitable substrate,

desiccation, constant erosion, and direct exposure to waves, wind, and ice. The community supports less than 25% vascular plant cover, although lichens, mosses, and liverworts are abundant on some rock surfaces. Common herbaceous plants include downy oat-grass (*Trisetum spicatum*), harebell (*Campanula rotundifolia*), common polypody (*Polypodium virginianum*), balsam ragwort (*Packera paupercula*), yarrow (*Achillea millefolium*), hair grass (*Deschampsia cespitosa*), and goldenrods (*Solidago* spp.). Scattered woody species are concentrated along the lip of the cliff and include white spruce (*Picea glauca*), northern white-cedar (*Thuja occidentalis*), paper birch (*Betula*

papyrifera), mountain ash (*Sorbus decora*), balsam fir (*Abies balsamea*), mountain alder (*Alnus viridis*), soapberry (*Shepherdia canadensis*), serviceberries (*Amelanchier* spp.), and wild rose (*Rosa acicularis*).

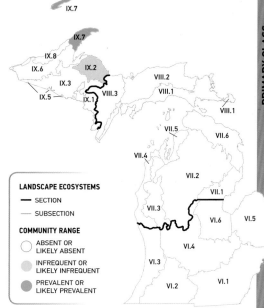

LANDSCAPE ECOSYSTEMS

— SECTION

— SUBSECTION

COMMUNITY RANGE

○ ABSENT OR LIKELY ABSENT

◑ INFREQUENT OR LIKELY INFREQUENT

● PREVALENT OR LIKELY PREVALENT

CHARACTERISTIC PLANTS

GRAMINOIDS

- poverty grass (*Danthonia spicata*)
- tufted hair grass (*Deschampsia cespitosa*)
- downy oat-grass (*Trisetum spicatum*)*

FORBS

- yarrow (*Achillea millefolium*)
- harebell (*Campanula rotundifolia*)
- wild strawberry (*Fragaria virginiana*)
- balsam ragwort (*Packera paupercula*)
- three-toothed cinquefoil (*Sibbaldiopsis tridentata*)
- upland white goldenrod (*Solidago ptarmicoides*)
- Gillman's goldenrod (*Solidago simplex*)

FERNS

- common polypody (*Polypodium virginianum*)

SHRUBS

- mountain alder (*Alnus viridis*)
- serviceberries (*Amelanchier* spp.)
- wild rose (*Rosa acicularis*)
- soapberry (*Shepherdia canadensis*)

TREES

- balsam fir (*Abies balsamea*)
- serviceberries (*Amelanchier* spp.)
- paper birch (*Betula papyrifera*)
- white spruce (*Picea glauca*)
- white pine (*Pinus strobus*)
- mountain-ash (*Sorbus decora*)
- northern white-cedar (*Thuja occidentalis*)

PLACES TO VISIT

- KEWEENAW: Bare Bluff, Michigan Nature Association (Grinnell Memorial Nature Sanctuary at Bare Bluff)
- KEWEENAW: Bete Grise, Michigan Nature Association (Grinnell Memorial Nature Sanctuary at Bare Bluff)
- KEWEENAW: Isle Royale National Park
- KEWEENAW: Manitou Island, Baraga State Forest Management Unit

MICHAEL A. KOST

Volcanic lakeshore cliff, Manitou Island, Baraga State Forest Management Unit, Keweenaw County

INLAND CLIFF GROUP

Inland Cliffs are sparsely vegetated communities on vertical or near-vertical inland exposures of bedrock occurring primarily in northern Michigan but also locally in the southern Lower Peninsula. Bedrock types that support Inland Cliffs include limestone, sandstone, granite, and volcanics. There is almost no soil development on the cliffs except where shallow mineral and organic deposits accumulate along the narrow cliff summit and ledges, in crevices in the cliff face, and at the base of the cliff. Plant growth and establishment are limited by the lack of suitable substrate, constant erosion, and exposure to wind, ice, and desiccating conditions.

Four natural community types fall within the Inland Cliff group, including limestone cliff, sandstone cliff, granite cliff, and volcanic cliff. Classification of these Inland Cliff types is based on differences in bedrock composition, although species composition and community structure also vary by substrate.

Granite cliff, Gwinn State Forest Management Unit, Marquette County
JOSHUA G. COHEN

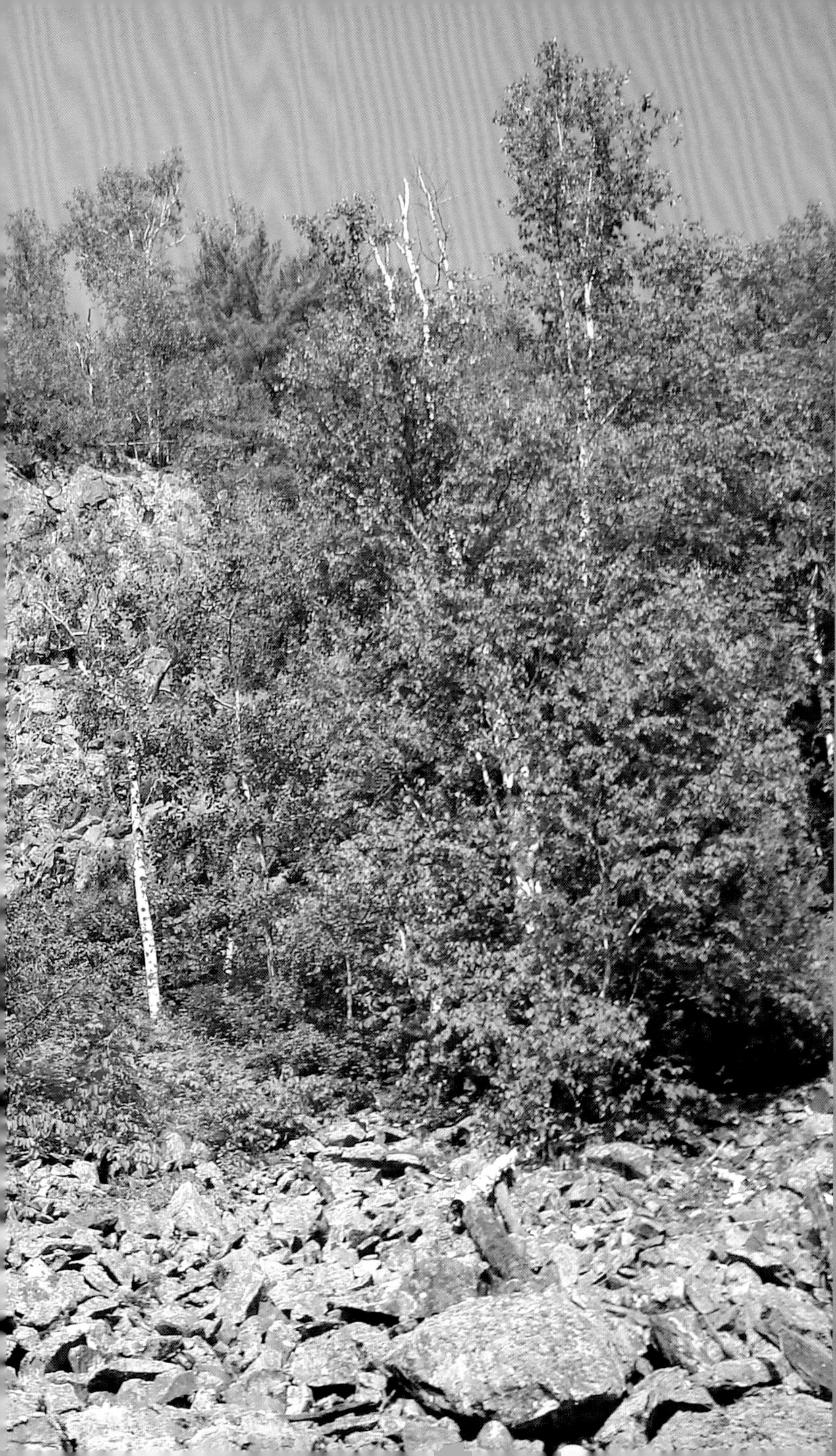

LIMESTONE CLIFF

Limestone cliff consists of vertical or near-vertical exposures of limestone bedrock and occurs primarily in the Upper Peninsula and infrequently in the northern Lower Peninsula. Documented limestone cliffs range in height from 1.5 to 30 meters (5 to 100 ft). Soil development is primarily limited to

thin, mildly alkaline organic soils that form from decaying roots and other plant materials along the top of the cliff escarpment and ledges, in cracks

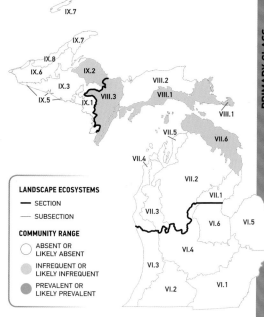

LANDSCAPE ECOSYSTEMS
— SECTION
— SUBSECTION

COMMUNITY RANGE
○ ABSENT OR LIKELY ABSENT
◔ INFREQUENT OR LIKELY INFREQUENT
● PREVALENT OR LIKELY PREVALENT

BRADFORD S. SLAUGHTER

and crevices in the bedrock, and at the base of the cliff. Plant growth and establishment are limited by the lack of suitable substrate, constant erosion, and exposure to wind, ice, and desiccating conditions. Although vegetation cover is sparse, abundant cracks and crevices combined with calcareous conditions result in greater plant diversity and coverage than on other inland cliff types. The community typically supports less than 25% vascular plant cover, although some rock surfaces can be densely covered with lichens, mosses, and liverworts. Common herbaceous plants include common polypody (*Polypodium virginianum*), large-leaved aster (*Eurybia macrophylla*), wild sarsaparilla (*Aralia nudicaulis*), Canada mayflower (*Maianthemum canadense*), maidenhair spleenwort (*Asplenium trichomanes*), fragile fern (*Cystopteris fragilis*), smooth cliff brake (*Pellaea glabella*), bracken fern (*Pteridium aquilinum*), Oregon woodsia (*Woodsia oregana*), grass-leaved goldenrod (*Euthamia graminifolia*), herb

317

Limestone cliff, Delta County

Robert (*Geranium robertianum*), and wild columbine (*Aquilegia canadensis*). Scattered woody species include bush honeysuckle (*Diervilla lonicera*), soapberry (*Shepherdia canadensis*), mountain maple (*Acer spicatum*), choke cherry (*Prunus virginiana*), red elderberry (*Sambucus racemosa*), paper birch (*Betula papyrifera*), balsam fir (*Abies balsamea*), and northern white-cedar (*Thuja occidentalis*).

CHARACTERISTIC PLANTS

GRAMINOIDS
- poverty grass (*Danthonia spicata*)

FORBS
- wild sarsaparilla (*Aralia nudicaulis*)
- harebell (*Campanula rotundifolia*)
- large-leaved aster (*Eurybia macrophylla*)
- grass-leaved goldenrod (*Euthamia graminifolia*)
- wild strawberry (*Fragaria virginiana*)

- herb Robert (*Geranium robertianum*)
- Canada mayflower (*Maianthemum canadense*)
- starflower (*Trientalis borealis*)

FERNS
- wall-rue (*Asplenium ruta-muraria*)*
- maidenhair spleenwort (*Asplenium trichomanes*)
- slender rock-brake (*Cryptogramma stelleri*)
- bulblet fern (*Cystopteris bulbifera*)
- fragile fern (*Cystopteris fragilis*)
- oak fern (*Gymnocarpium dryopteris*)
- smooth cliff-brake (*Pellaea glabella*)
- common polypody (*Polypodium virginianum*)
- bracken fern (*Pteridium aquilinum*)
- Oregon woodsia (*Woodsia oregana*)

FERN ALLIES
- dwarf scouring rush (*Equisetum scirpoides*)

WOODY VINES
- poison-ivy (*Toxicodendron radicans*)

SHRUBS
- round-leaved dogwood (*Cornus rugosa*)
- bush honeysuckle (*Diervilla lonicera*)
- Canadian fly honeysuckle (*Lonicera canadensis*)
- choke cherry (*Prunus virginiana*)
- thimbleberry (*Rubus parviflorus*)
- wild red raspberry (*Rubus strigosus*)
- red elderberry (*Sambucus racemosa*)
- soapberry (*Shepherdia canadensis*)
- Canada yew (*Taxus canadensis*)

TREES
- balsam fir (*Abies balsamea*)
- sugar maple (*Acer saccharum*)
- mountain maple (*Acer spicatum*)
- paper birch (*Betula papyrifera*)
- northern white-cedar (*Thuja occidentalis*)

PLACES TO VISIT
- ALGER: Rock River Canyon, Hiawatha National Forest
- CHIPPEWA: Marblehead (Drummond Island), Sault Sainte Marie State Forest Management Unit

SANDSTONE CLIFF

Sandstone cliff consists of sparsely vegetated vertical or near-vertical exposures of sandstone bedrock in the central and western Upper Peninsula and locally in the southern Lower Peninsula. Documented limestone cliffs range in height from 1.5 to 20 meters (5 to 65 ft). There is almost no

soil development on the cliffs except where shallow, organic deposits and sand particles accumulate along the narrow cliff summit and ledges, in

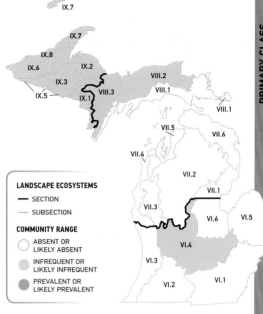

LANDSCAPE ECOSYSTEMS

—— SECTION

—— SUBSECTION

COMMUNITY RANGE

○ ABSENT OR LIKELY ABSENT

◯ INFREQUENT OR LIKELY INFREQUENT

● PREVALENT OR LIKELY PREVALENT

JOSHUA G. COHEN

crevices in the cliff face, and at the base of the cliff. Plant growth and establishment are limited by the lack of suitable substrate, constant erosion, and exposure to wind, ice, and desiccating conditions. Characteristic ground cover species include harebell (*Campanula rotundifolia*), fireweed (*Chamerion angustifolium*), grass-leaved goldenrod (*Euthamia graminifolia*), yarrow (*Achillea millefolium*), dwarf raspberry (*Rubus pubescens*), fragile fern (*Cystopteris fragilis*), common polypody (*Polypodium virginianum*), northern beech fern (*Phegopteris connectilis*), lady fern (*Athyrium filix-femina*), and spinulose woodfern (*Dryopteris carthusiana*). Scattered woody species include bush honeysuckle (*Diervilla lonicera*), ninebark (*Physocarpus opulifolius*), mountain alder (*Alnus viridis*), serviceberries (*Amelanchier* spp.), witch-hazel (*Hamamelis virginiana*), sugar maple (*Acer saccharum*), paper birch (*Betula papyrifera*), and northern white-cedar

Sandstone cliff, Laughing Whitefish Falls State Park, Alger County

(*Thuja occidentalis*). Lichens, mosses, and liverworts occur primarily in moist areas associated with seepages.

CHARACTERISTIC PLANTS

GRAMINOIDS
- tufted hair grass (*Deschampsia cespitosa*)

FORBS
- yarrow (*Achillea millefolium*)
- wild columbine (*Aquilegia canadensis*)
- wild sarsaparilla (*Aralia nudicaulis*)
- harebell (*Campanula rotundifolia*)
- fireweed (*Chamerion angustifolium*)
- bluebead lily (*Clintonia borealis*)

- large-leaved aster (*Eurybia macrophylla*)
- grass-leaved goldenrod (*Euthamia graminifolia*)
- wild strawberry (*Fragaria virginiana*)
- hairy hawkweed (*Hieracium gronovii*)
- downy Solomon seal (*Polygonatum pubescens*)
- marsh violet (*Viola cucullata*)

FERNS
- maidenhair spleenwort (*Asplenium trichomanes*)
- lady fern (*Athyrium filix-femina*)
- slender rock-brake (*Cryptogramma stelleri*)
- fragile fern (*Cystopteris fragilis*)
- spinulose woodfern (*Dryopteris carthusiana*)

- northern beech fern (*Phegopteris connectilis*)
- common polypody (*Polypodium virginianum*)
- rusty woodsia (*Woodsia ilvensis*)

FERN ALLIES
- common horsetail (*Equisetum arvense*)

WOODY VINES
- poison-ivy (*Toxicodendron radicans*)

SHRUBS
- bush honeysuckle (*Diervilla lonicera*)
- witch-hazel (*Hamamelis virginiana*)
- Canadian fly honeysuckle (*Lonicera canadensis*)
- ninebark (*Physocarpus opulifolius*)
- choke cherry (*Prunus virginiana*)
- thimbleberry (*Rubus parviflorus*)
- dwarf raspberry (*Rubus pubescens*)
- wild red raspberry (*Rubus strigosus*)
- red elderberry (*Sambucus racemosa*)

TREES
- sugar maple (*Acer saccharum*)
- mountain maple (*Acer spicatum*)

- yellow birch (*Betula alleghaniensis*)
- paper birch (*Betula papyrifera*)
- white spruce (*Picea glauca*)
- white pine (*Pinus strobus*)
- balsam poplar (*Populus balsamifera*)
- northern white-cedar (*Thuja occidentalis*)
- hemlock (*Tsuga canadensis*)

PLACES TO VISIT
- ALGER: Laughing Whitefish Falls, Laughing Whitefish Falls State Park
- ALGER: Miners Falls Cliffs, Pictured Rocks National Lakeshore
- ALGER: Mosquito River Gorge, Pictured Rocks National Lakeshore
- EATON: Fitzgerald Park, Eaton County Parks Department
- GOGEBIC: Big Carp River and Presque Isle River, Porcupine Mountains Wilderness State Park
- GOGEBIC: Black River Gorge, Ottawa National Forest
- LUCE: Tahquamenon Falls, Tahquamenon Falls State Park

Sandstone cliff along the Big Carp River, Porcupine Mountains Wilderness State Park, Gogebic County

S2 GRANITE CLIFF

Granite cliff consists of sparsely vegetated vertical or near-vertical exposures of granitic bedrock in the western Upper Peninsula. Documented granite cliffs range in height from 3 to 50 meters (10 to 165 ft). Soil development is limited to shallow, organic deposits that form from decaying roots and

other plant material that accumulates in cracks, crevices, ledges, and flat areas or depressions in the bedrock. The thin soils are acidic to slightly alkaline.

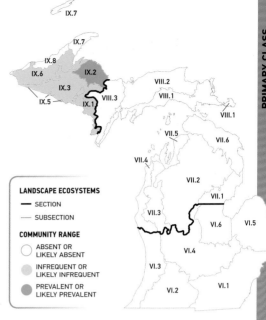

LANDSCAPE ECOSYSTEMS
— SECTION
— SUBSECTION

COMMUNITY RANGE
○ ABSENT OR LIKELY ABSENT
◐ INFREQUENT OR LIKELY INFREQUENT
● PREVALENT OR LIKELY PREVALENT

JOSHUA G. COHEN

Plant growth and establishment are limited by the lack of suitable substrate, constant erosion, and exposure to wind, ice, and desiccating conditions. The community is characterized by sparse cover of vascular plants, lichens, mosses, and liverworts. Characteristic herbaceous species include wild columbine (*Aquilegia canadensis*), hair grass (*Deschampsia cespitosa*), poverty grass (*Danthonia spicata*), three-toothed cinquefoil (*Sibbaldiopsis tridentata*), large-leaved aster (*Eurybia macrophylla*), common polypody (*Polypodium virginianum*), maidenhair spleenwort (*Asplenium trichomanes*), and rusty woodsia (*Woodsia ilvensis*). Scattered woody species include pines (*Pinus* spp.), red oak (*Quercus rubra*), paper birch (*Betula papyrifera*), northern white-cedar (*Thuja occidentalis*), big-toothed aspen (*Populus grandidentata*), serviceberries (*Amelanchier* spp.), choke cherry (*Prunus virginiana*), low sweet blueberry (*Vaccinium angustifolium*), bearberry (*Arctostaphylos uva-ursi*), common

▶

325

Granite cliff, Crystal Falls State Forest Management Unit, Dickinson County

juniper (*Juniperus communis*), and bush honeysuckle (*Diervilla lonicera*).

CHARACTERISTIC PLANTS

GRAMINOIDS
- poverty grass (*Danthonia spicata*)
- tufted hair grass (*Deschampsia cespitosa*)

FORBS
- small-leaved pussytoes (*Antennaria neglecta*)
- wild columbine (*Aquilegia canadensis*)
- wild sarsaparilla (*Aralia nudicaulis*)
- bluebead lily (*Clintonia borealis*)
- rock whitlow-grass (*Draba arabisans*)*
- large-leaved aster (*Eurybia macrophylla*)
- wild strawberry (*Fragaria virginiana*)
- Canada mayflower (*Maianthemum canadense*)
- downy Solomon seal (*Polygonatum pubescens*)
- three-toothed cinquefoil (*Sibbaldiopsis tridentata*)
- twisted-stalks (*Streptopus* spp.)

FERNS
- maidenhair spleenwort (*Asplenium trichomanes*)
- fragrant woodfern (*Dryopteris fragrans*)*
- marginal woodfern (*Dryopteris marginalis*)
- oak fern (*Gymnocarpium dryopteris*)
- smooth cliff-brake (*Pellaea glabella*)
- common polypody (*Polypodium virginianum*)
- bracken fern (*Pteridium aquilinum*)
- rusty woodsia (*Woodsia ilvensis*)

WOODY VINES
- red honeysuckle (*Lonicera dioica*)

poison-ivy (*Toxicodendron radicans*)

SHRUBS

serviceberries (*Amelanchier* spp.)
bearberry (*Arctostaphylos uva-ursi*)
bunchberry (*Cornus canadensis*)
bush honeysuckle (*Diervilla lonicera*)
wintergreen (*Gaultheria procumbens*)
common juniper (*Juniperus communis*)
Canadian fly honeysuckle (*Lonicera canadensis*)
choke cherry (*Prunus virginiana*)
thimbleberry (*Rubus parviflorus*)
dwarf raspberry (*Rubus pubescens*)
wild red raspberry (*Rubus strigosus*)
low sweet blueberry (*Vaccinium angustifolium*)

TREES

balsam fir (*Abies balsamea*)
sugar maple (*Acer saccharum*)

- mountain maple (*Acer spicatum*)
- serviceberries (*Amelanchier* spp.)
- paper birch (*Betula papyrifera*)
- white spruce (*Picea glauca*)
- jack pine (*Pinus banksiana*)
- red pine (*Pinus resinosa*)
- white pine (*Pinus strobus*)
- big-toothed aspen (*Populus grandidentata*)
- quaking aspen (*Populus tremuloides*)
- red oak (*Quercus rubra*)
- northern white-cedar (*Thuja occidentalis*)

PLACES TO VISIT

- DICKINSON: Lost Lake Outcrops, Crystal Falls State Forest Management Unit
- MARQUETTE: Mulligan Cliffs, Gwinn State Forest Management Unit
- MARQUETTE: Van Riper Cliffs, Van Riper State Park

Mulligan Cliffs, Gwinn State Forest Management Unit, Marquette County

S2 VOLCANIC CLIFF

Volcanic cliff consists of sparsely vegetated vertical or near-vertical exposures of volcanic bedrock. Volcanic cliff occurs on inland exposures of the resistant Middle Keweenawan volcanic rock, which runs from the north tip of the Keweenaw Peninsula south into Wisconsin and also along the entire

length of Isle Royale. The cliffs can be as high as 80 meters (260 ft). There is little soil development on the steep rock face of the cliffs. Thin, slightly acidic to

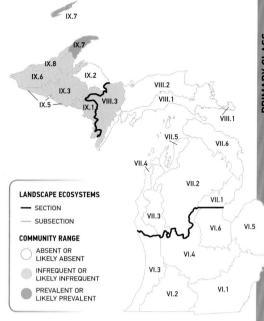

LANDSCAPE ECOSYSTEMS

— SECTION

— SUBSECTION

COMMUNITY RANGE

○ ABSENT OR LIKELY ABSENT

◐ INFREQUENT OR LIKELY INFREQUENT

● PREVALENT OR LIKELY PREVALENT

JOSHUA G. COHEN

circumneutral organic soil accumulation occurs in crevices in the rock face, on the upper lip of the cliffs, on ledges, and at the base of the cliff face. Plant growth and establishment are limited by the lack of suitable substrate, constant erosion, and exposure to wind, ice, and desiccating conditions. The community typically supports less than 25% vascular plant cover, although lichens, mosses, and liverworts are abundant on some rock surfaces. Characteristic herbaceous species include harebell (*Campanula rotundifolia*), balsam ragwort (*Packera paupercula*), wild strawberry (*Fragaria virginiana*), yarrow (*Achillea millefolium*), hair grass (*Deschampsia cespitosa*), and common polypody (*Polypodium virginianum*). Scattered woody species include soapberry (*Shepherdia canadensis*), serviceberries (*Amelanchier* spp.), wild rose (*Rosa acicularis*), red oak (*Quercus rubra*), paper birch (*Betula papyrifera*), and northern white-cedar (*Thuja occidentalis*).

▶

329

JOSHUA G. COHEN

Northern white-cedar (*Thuja occidentalis*) clinging to a crevice in volcanic cliff

CHARACTERISTIC PLANTS

GRAMINOIDS
- poverty grass (*Danthonia spicata*)
- tufted hair grass (*Deschampsia cespitosa*)

FORBS
- yarrow (*Achillea millefolium*)
- wild columbine (*Aquilegia canadensis*)
- wild sarsaparilla (*Aralia nudicaulis*)
- wormwood (*Artemisia campestris*)
- low bindweed (*Calystegia spithamea*)
- harebell (*Campanula rotundifolia*)
- fireweed (*Chamerion angustifolium*)
- bluebead lily (*Clintonia borealis*)
- small blue-eyed Mary (*Collinsia parviflora*)*
- large-leaved aster (*Eurybia macrophylla*)
- wild strawberry (*Fragaria virginiana*)
- early saxifrage (*Micranthes virginiensis*)
- balsam ragwort (*Packera paupercula*)
- downy Solomon seal (*Polygonatum pubescens*)

FERNS
- maidenhair spleenwort (*Asplenium trichomanes*)
- common polypody (*Polypodium virginianum*)
- rusty woodsia (*Woodsia ilvensis*)

WOODY VINES
- poison-ivy (*Toxicodendron radicans*)
- riverbank grape (*Vitis riparia*)

SHRUBS
- serviceberries (*Amelanchier* spp.)
- bearberry (*Arctostaphylos uva-ursi*)
- redstem ceanothus (*Ceanothus sanguineus*)*
- bush honeysuckle (*Diervilla lonicera*)
- common juniper (*Juniperus communis*)
- ninebark (*Physocarpus opulifolius*)
- choke cherry (*Prunus virginiana*)
- staghorn sumac (*Rhus typhina*)
- wild rose (*Rosa acicularis*)
- red elderberry (*Sambucus racemosa*)
- soapberry (*Shepherdia canadensis*)
- snowberry (*Symphoricarpos albus*)

TREES
- balsam fir (*Abies balsamea*)
- sugar maple (*Acer saccharum*)
- mountain maple (*Acer spicatum*)
- serviceberries (*Amelanchier* spp.)
- yellow birch (*Betula alleghaniensis*)
- paper birch (*Betula papyrifera*)
- ironwood (*Ostrya virginiana*)

Volcanic cliff, Grinnell Memorial Nature Sanctuary at Bare Bluff, Keweenaw County

- white pine (*Pinus strobus*)
- red oak (*Quercus rubra*)
- northern white-cedar (*Thuja occidentalis*)
- basswood (*Tilia americana*)

PLACES TO VISIT

- GOGEBIC & ONTONAGON: Escarpment Trail Cliffs, Porcupine Mountains Wilderness State Park
- KEWEENAW: Bare Bluff Cliffs, Michigan Nature Association (Grinnell Memorial Nature Sanctuary at Bare Bluff)
- KEWEENAW: Isle Royale National Park
- ONTONAGON: Traps Hills Escarpment, Ottawa National Forest

JOSHUA G. COHEN

Volcanic cliff, Porcupine Mountains Wilderness State Park, Ontonagon County

Sinkhole, Rockport State Recreation Area,
Presque Isle County
JOSHUA G. COHEN

Subterranean/
Sink Class

KARST GROUP

The Subterranean/Sink class includes natural communities that occur in karst landscapes below the general land surface. These karst features form from the underground dissolution of limestone, dolomite, or gypsum. The Subterranean/Sink class includes one ecological group, Karst. This ecological group includes two natural community types, cave and sinkhole, which are distinguished based on their distinct landscape settings. A cave is a cavity that has formed beneath the earth's surface, and a sinkhole is a subsidence or depression in the earth's surface caused by the dissolution of the surficial bedrock.

Sinkhole, Atlanta State Forest Management Unit, Presque Isle County

JOSHUA G. COHEN

S1 CAVE

Cave is a naturally occurring cavity beneath the earth's surface, often with an opening to the surface. The community is characterized by little or no light, no primary producers, and biotic communities of one or two trophic levels that import energy from outside the system. In Michigan,

naturally occurring caves are karst features found in the eastern Upper Peninsula and, historically, in the southeast Lower Peninsula. Caves are subterranean depressions in the landscape that form following the dissolution and collapse of subsurface limestone, dolomite, or gypsum.

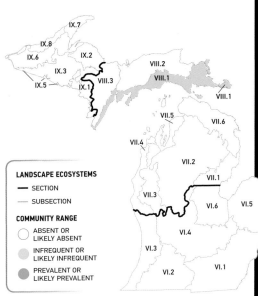

LANDSCAPE ECOSYSTEMS
— SECTION
— SUBSECTION

COMMUNITY RANGE
○ ABSENT OR LIKELY ABSENT
◐ INFREQUENT OR LIKELY INFREQUENT
● PREVALENT OR LIKELY PREVALENT

CHARACTERISTIC PLANTS

- It is assumed that there is no vegetation within Michigan's caves.

PLACES TO VISIT [15]

- MACKINAC: Hendrie River Water Cave, Sault Sainte Marie State Forest Management Unit and Michigan Karst Conservancy

- MACKINAC: Kochab Cave, Sault Sainte Marie State Forest Management Unit and Michigan Karst Conservancy
- MACKINAC: Quarry Cave, Michigan Karst Conservancy

Hendrie River Water Cave, Mackinac County

Sinkhole is a depression in the landscape caused by the dissolution and collapse of subsurface limestone, dolomite, or gypsum. Sinkholes are karst features found predominantly in the northeastern Lower Peninsula and eastern Upper Peninsula. Some sinkholes are perennially dry while others seasonally or permanently hold water. Vegetation typically resembles that of the surrounding landscape, but moister and cooler conditions within a sinkhole can provide habitat for additional ferns, mosses, lichens, and wetland plants.

CHARACTERISTIC PLANTS

GRAMINOIDS

- big bluestem (*Andropogon gerardii*)
- blue-joint (*Calamagrostis canadensis*)
- sedges (*Carex aurea, C. eburnea, C. flava, C. pensylvanica, C. viridula,* and others)
- twig-rush (*Cladium mariscoides*)
- poverty grass (*Danthonia spicata*)
- common spike-rush (*Eleocharis palustris*)
- fowl manna grass (*Glyceria striata*)
- Canadian rush (*Juncus canadensis*)
- little bluestem (*Schizachyrium scoparium*)
- hardstem bulrush (*Schoenoplectus acutus*)
- green bulrush (*Scirpus atrovirens*)
- cordgrass (*Spartina pectinata*)

FORBS

- wild sarsaparilla (*Aralia nudicaulis*)
- jack-in-the-pulpit (*Arisaema triphyllum*)
- wormwood (*Artemisia campestris*)
- harebell (*Campanula rotundifolia*)
- marsh cinquefoil (*Comarum palustre*)
- large-leaved aster (*Eurybia macrophylla*)
- wild strawberry (*Fragaria virginiana*)

- wild blue flag (*Iris versicolor*)
- cardinal flower (*Lobelia cardinalis*)
- Kalm's lobelia (*Lobelia kalmii*)
- common water horehound (*Lycopus americanus*)
- northern bugle weed (*Lycopus uniflorus*)
- Canada mayflower (*Maianthemum canadense*)
- false spikenard (*Maianthemum racemosum*)
- water smartweed (*Persicaria amphibia*)
- downy Solomon seal (*Polygonatum pubescens*)
- mad-dog skullcap (*Scutellaria lateriflora*)

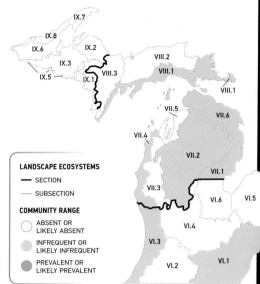

LANDSCAPE ECOSYSTEMS
— SECTION
— SUBSECTION

COMMUNITY RANGE
○ ABSENT OR LIKELY ABSENT
◔ INFREQUENT OR LIKELY INFREQUENT
● PREVALENT OR LIKELY PREVALENT

FERNS

- lady fern (*Athyrium filix-femina*)
- rattlesnake fern (*Botrypus virginianus*)
- bulblet fern (*Cystopteris bulbifera*)
- oak fern (*Gymnocarpium dryopteris*)
- sensitive fern (*Onoclea sensibilis*)
- royal fern (*Osmunda regalis*)
- bracken fern (*Pteridium aquilinum*)
- marsh fern (*Thelypteris palustris*)

WOODY VINES

- poison-ivy (*Toxicodendron radicans*)

SHRUBS

- bearberry (*Arctostaphylos uva-ursi*)
- sweetfern (*Comptonia peregrina*)
- bunchberry (*Cornus canadensis*)
- gray dogwood (*Cornus foemina*)
- round-leaved dogwood (*Cornus rugosa*)
- American hazelnut (*Corylus americana*)
- alder-leaved buckthorn (*Rhamnus alnifolia*)
- soapberry (*Shepherdia canadensis*)
- blueberries (*Vaccinium angustifolium* and *V. myrtilloides*)

TREES

- balsam fir (*Abies balsamea*)
- sugar maple (*Acer saccharum*)
- paper birch (*Betula papyrifera*)
- American beech (*Fagus grandifolia*)
- white ash (*Fraxinus americana*)
- pines (*Pinus banksiana*, *P. resinosa*, and *P. strobus*)
- big-toothed aspen (*Populus grandidentata*)
- quaking aspen (*Populus tremuloides*)
- northern pin oak (*Quercus ellipsoidalis*)
- red oak (*Quercus rubra*)
- northern white-cedar (*Thuja occidentalis*)
- basswood (*Tilia americana*)
- hemlock (*Tsuga canadensis*)

PLACES TO VISIT

- MACKINAC: Fiborn Karst, Sault Sainte Marie State Forest Management Unit and Michigan Karst Conservancy
- PRESQUE ISLE: Rockport Karst, Rockport State Recreation Area
- PRESQUE ISLE: Tomahawk Sinkholes, Sinkholes Pathway, Atlanta State Forest Management Unit

Notes

1. Communities for which these range maps are primarily historical include the following: dry sand prairie, dry-mesic prairie, hillside prairie, inland salt marsh, lakeplain oak openings, lakeplain wet prairie, lakeplain wet-mesic prairie, mesic prairie, mesic sand prairie, oak barrens, oak openings, oak-pine barrens, pine barrens, wet prairie, wet-mesic flatwoods, wet-mesic prairie, and wet-mesic sand prairie. Bur oak plains has been extirpated from Michigan, so its range map is entirely historical.

2. Asterisks throughout the text indicate rare plants.

3. Patterned fen is also referred to as patterned bog, patterned peatland, strangmoor, aapa mire, string bog, and string fen.

4. Inundated shrub swamp is also referred to as buttonbush depression.

5. Rich conifer swamp is also referred to as cedar swamp.

6. Rich tamarack swamp was referred to as relict conifer swamp in early versions of the Michigan natural community classification.

7. Dry-mesic prairie was referred to as woodland prairie in early versions of the Michigan natural community classification.

8. Canopy beech has been locally decimated by beech bark disease.

9. Portions of this complex include ravines supporting mesic northern forest.

10. Limestone bedrock lakeshore is also referred to as alvar pavement or limestone pavement lakeshore.

11. Granite bedrock lakeshore includes bedrock types such as granite, gneiss, schist, and quartzite.

12. Volcanic bedrock lakeshore includes all types of volcanic bedrock, including basalt, rhyolite, and conglomerate composed of volcanic rock.

13. Limestone bedrock glade is also referred to as alvar glade.

14. Northern bald is also referred to as krummholz ridgetop.

15. Michigan Karst Conservancy preserves are open to the public. However, written permission and appropriate equipment are required for entry into the caves.

Glossary

abrasion: The process of wearing away by friction. This mechanical weathering can be caused by ice, mineral soil (e.g., sand), and snow.

acidic: Soil or water having a pH < 7.0, often indicating moderate to low nutrient availability.

aerated: Refers to soil that is aerobic, having free molecular oxygen present and available.

aerobic: A condition characterized by the presence and availability of free molecular oxygen.

alkaline: Soil or water having a pH > 7.0. Equivalent to basic.

anaerobic: A condition characterized by the absence of free molecular oxygen.

annual: A plant that completes its life cycle in a single growing season. A winter annual germinates in fall, overwinters, and sets seed and dies the following growing season.

aquatic plant: A plant that completes its life cycle in water.

aquifer: A subterranean formation that contains sufficient saturated permeable material to yield significant quantities of water. Some aquifers release water at the surface in the form of seepages.

backswamp: Low-lying wet areas on floodplains, located away from the active channel, and where organic soils accumulate.

barrens: In Michigan, a general term sometimes applied to dry savannas, often occurring on extremely acidic sands with low nutrient content and low water-holding capacity.

barrier-beach lagoon: A shallow pond or lagoon sheltered from a large lake's wave energy by a sand or gravel bar that has been deposited by storm waves or nearshore currents.

basalt: Volcanic bedrock deposited as lava flows during the Late Precambrian Era. Characterized by heavy, dark, finely crystalline rock rich in iron-bearing minerals. Basalt is treated as a type of volcanic bedrock in this book.

bedrock: The solid rock that is exposed at the surface or underlies soil and other unconsolidated material. Within Michigan, there are four major categories of bedrock: limestone, sandstone, granite, and volcanic, although there are also areas of siltstone and shale.

beech bark disease: Beech bark disease is a disease complex that was introduced to North America around 1900 and was first detected in Michigan in 2001. The disease results when the bark of beech trees is attacked by the beech scale (*Cryptococcus fagisuga*) and subsequently invaded and killed by fungi, primarily *Nectria coccinea* var. *faginata*, and sometimes *N. galligena*.

billabong: Australian term for a riparian wetland that is periodically flooded by the adjacent stream or river.

biodiversity (biological diversity): The complexity of life at all its levels of organization, including genetic variability within species, species and species interactions, ecological and evolutionary processes, and the distribution across the landscape of species and the natural communities in which they occur.

bluff: A high, steep bank.

bog: An acidic, nutrient-poor, peat-accumulating wetland that is isolated from mineral-rich water sources by deep peat accumulation and therefore receives most of its water and nutrients from precipitation. See **ombrotrophic**.

boreal: Applied to a climate zone with short, cool to mild summers and snowy winters. Also can refer to northern species that occur in this climate.

bottom: Low, poorly drained swamp located in a floodplain and formed by the present drainage system and subject to frequent over-the-bank flooding; soil texture is typically finer than that of the levee.

bottomland: Low-lying land along a watercourse.

brine: Water saturated with salt.

brown moss: A moss species of the family Amblystegiaceae, typically growing in calcium-rich wetlands.

bryophyte: A division of plants including mosses, liverworts, and hornworts; these are nonflowering and nonvascular plants.

buried river mouth (drowned river mouth): A bay formed when high Great Lakes water levels flood the lower stretches of a tributary river.

calcareous: Composed of or containing calcium carbonate, a mineral with a high pH. Often used to describe alkaline soil, groundwater, or surface water that has been in contact with limestone, dolomite, calcium-rich glacial deposits, or lacustrine sands.

calciphile (calcicole): A plant that is adapted to grow in calcium-rich soils or water, or on calcium-rich rock (e.g., limestone and dolomite). Examples of calciphiles include the sedge *Carex viridula* and limestone calamint (*Clinopodium arkansanum*).

calcium carbonate: A chemical compound ($CaCO_3$) found in rocks (particularly limestone), the shells of marine organisms and snails, plant ashes, bones, and eggshells. It occurs in different crystal forms in the minerals calcite and aragonite, which largely constitute limestone.

canopy: The tallest vegetative layer in a natural community.

canopy gap: Openings in the canopy created by the death of a large branch or one or more trees.

carbonate: A salt characterized by the presence of the carbonate ion (CO_3^{2-}). Can refer to minerals and rock that are dominated by the carbonate ion.

catastrophic fire: Infrequent stand-killing crown fire.

characteristic species: A species strongly associated with a particular natural community type, either as a dominant, a ubiquitous nondominant component, or as an indicator of that community type.

circumneutral: Having a pH around neutral, or 7.0 (in the range of 6.6 to 7.3).

clay: A fine-grained and slow-draining mineral soil containing more than 40% clay particles, less than 45% sand particles, and less than 40% silt particles; a soil particle smaller than 0.002 mm in diameter.

cliff: An exposed, very steep to perpendicular or overhanging face of rock.

climatic tension zone: A narrow zone where many species reach the limits of their range due to climatic factors. In Michigan, the climatic tension zone occurs as a band passing through the central portion of the Lower Peninsula.

coarse-textured: Soil or landform characterized by large particle size, often sands or gravels.

cobble: A naturally rounded or smoothed stone larger than a pebble and smaller than a boulder.

community structure (physiognomy): The spatial arrangement of vegetation within a natural community.

conglomerate: A sedimentary rock formed by the cementation of rock fragments varying in size from small pebbles to large boulders. Conglomerates often form in abandoned lake or stream beds.

conifer: A gymnosperm of the order Coniferales; any of a large group of cone-bearing trees and shrubs, mostly evergreens.

connecting river (connecting channel): A major river channel linking the Great Lakes (e.g., St. Marys, Detroit, and St. Clair Rivers).

cove: A small sheltered inlet or bay.

cover: The percentage of area (or "the ground") that would be covered by a vertical projection of a given vegetation layer, group of plants, or plant species.

deciduous: Pertaining to plants that shed their herbaceous tissues after a season's growth.

delta: Fan-shaped areas where stream sediments deposited at the mouth of a river accumulate and create multiple shallow channels, low islands, and abandoned meanders that allow for extensive wetland development.

deposition: The process of soil particles and organic matter (sediment) being deposited by wind or water.

depression: Any relatively sunken part of the earth's surface surrounded by high ground. Depressions often support wetlands.

desiccation: Becoming dried up, typically in reference to soil.

disjunct: A plant that is notably distant from its primary distribution or normal growing range. For example, coastal plain marshes in Michigan support numerous plants that are disjunct from the Atlantic and Gulf coastal plains.

dissolution: The process that occurs when water passing through soluble bedrock (e.g., limestone or dolomite) produces underground cavities. These cavities reduce support to the ground above and can cause localized collapse of the overlying bedrock.

distribution: The geographical extent of a natural community.

dolomite (dolostone): A resistant sedimentary rock with a high content of magnesium-calcium carbonate. Produces calcium- and magnesium-rich soils with high pH and nutrient availability. Dolomite is treated as a type of limestone bedrock in this book.

dominant: A species with the greatest abundance, percent cover, or influence in a natural community or vegetative layer.

drainage: Refers to depth, frequency, and duration of periods of water saturation in a soil. Drainage classes range from excessively well-drained for xeric soils and very poorly drained for flooded soils. Soil drainage is affected by soil texture, landscape position, and groundwater fluctuations.

drought: A prolonged period of dryness.

dry: A soil moisture class. Dry soils are excessively to somewhat excessively drained.

dry-mesic: A soil moisture class. Dry-mesic soils are well-drained; water is removed from the soil readily but not rapidly.

dune: Landform composed of wind-deposited sands. Most of Michigan's dunes were formed along the Great Lakes postglacially, but there are also inland dunes formed during glaciations both in the eastern Upper Peninsula and northern Lower Peninsula.

dune field: An area covered by extensive sand dunes.

Dutch elm disease: A disease of elms caused by an introduced fungus (*Ceratocystis ulmi*) and characterized by yellowing of the foliage, defoliation, and death. Following an epidemic in the 1960s, the disease has virtually eliminated American elm as a dominant overstory tree of swamps throughout Michigan.

ecoregion: A large area defined by its environmental conditions, especially climate, landform, and soil characteristics, where natural community types recur in predictable patterns.

ecotone: A transitional zone where characteristics of immediately adjacent ecosystems and natural communities intermingle or intergrade.

emerald ash borer: Emerald ash borer (*Agrilus planipenis*) is a species of invasive beetle that was introduced to southeastern Lower Michigan around 1990. This species infests and kills all species of ash. Emerald ash borer has decimated mature ash trees in southern hardwood swamps, floodplain forests, and upland forests across southern Lower Michigan.

emergent plant: A wetland plant whose leaves grow mainly above the water, not floating or submerged. May be temporarily to permanently flooded at the base, while the upper portions of the plant grow erect above the water surface. Broad-leaved cat-tail, bulrushes, and spike-rushes are common emergent plants.

end moraine (terminal moraine): A ridge-like accumulation of unsorted glacial till deposited along the margin of an active glacier. A moraine built at the edge of a glacier.

ericaceous: Pertaining to plants of the heath family (Ericaceae).

erosion: The process of wearing away by the action of water, wind, or ice.

escarpment: A relatively continuous cliff or exposure of bedrock produced by erosion or faulting, breaking the general continuity of more gently sloping land surfaces and usually extending a long distance linearly across the landscape.

esker: A long, narrow, often winding ridge of mixed sand and gravel deposited by a glacial meltwater stream flowing through crevasses, holes, and tunnels in a stagnant ice sheet.

evergreen: Pertaining to plants having foliage that does not fall at the end of the growing season.

exfoliation: A weathering process of bedrock where layers of exposed bedrock fall off.

extirpation: Disappearing from a locality or region without becoming extinct; local extinction.

fen: A minerotrophic, peat-accumulating wetland that receives water that has been in contact with mineral soils or bedrock. Fens can range from weakly minerotrophic peatlands that are acidic to strongly minerotrophic peatlands that are alkaline.

fern: Any of a large class of flowerless, spore-producing vascular plants with roots, stems, and leaflike fronds.

fern ally: A seedless vascular plant that is not a true fern, but like a fern, disperses by shedding spores. Clubmosses and horsetails are common fern allies.

fine-textured: Soil or landform characterized by small particle size (e.g., silts and clays).

fire-dependent community: Natural community that depends on fire for maintenance of its species composition and community structure.

fire regime: The frequency, intensity, and type of fires that occur in a particular natural community or ecosystem.

first-order stream: A stream that does not have any other stream feeding into it. Equivalent to a headwater stream.

flagged: A condition in which freezing winds kill branches on the windward side of a tree and the upper branches grow mainly from the leeward side of the tree, like a flag blowing from a flagpole.

flark: Elongated and wet depression in patterned peatlands. The long axis of the flark is oriented perpendicular to the direction of topographic contours and water flow.

floating plant: A wetland plant with leaves on the surface of the water. Floating leaves neither rise above the surface nor live entirely under the surface. Sweet-scented waterlily is a floating plant.

flooding: The hydrologic process whereby the water surface rises above the wetland substrate.

floodplain: Nearly level to gently sloping land adjacent to a stream or river channel, shaped by periodic flooding and long-term lateral migration of the stream.

fluvial landform: Landforms that are derived from fluvial (stream) processes and occur within floodplains.

forb: A generic term for broad-leaved flowering herbaceous plants. A forb is a nonwoody plant that is not a graminoid (grass-like) or a fern.

foredune: In a coastal sand dune system, the dune closest to the Great Lakes that is strongly influenced by wind and wave action.

forest: A tree-dominated upland having at least 60% canopy closure.

frost heave: An upthrust of ground caused by freezing of moist soil.

gabbro: A coarsely crystalline basic igneous rock within the granite bedrock group. Gabbro is treated as a type of granitic bedrock in this book.

gap-phase dynamics: The natural process whereby frequent, small canopy gaps allow for the regeneration of shade-tolerant canopy trees in forested natural communities.

glacial drift: Any material (e.g., clay, silt, sand, gravel, stones, and boulders) transported and deposited by glacial ice or meltwater.

glacial lakebed (proglacial lakebed): The bed of a lake formed between a high land feature and a glacier. Thin clay layers (varves) were deposited annually during the winter on the lake bottom, and often formed thick, flat deposits. Sand was deposited in meltwater streams in the lakebed, typically forming channels. Sand deposits were reworked by waves into beach ridges.

glacial till: Unstratified materials carried and deposited directly by a glacier (till does not come from meltwater).

glacier: A large body of ice moving slowly on a land surface. Over 10,000 years ago, Michigan was covered by glaciers that shaped many of our current landforms and soils.

glade: A savanna or open woodland community that occurs on exposed bedrock and thin soils over bedrock.

gneiss: A metamorphic foliated bedrock formed from either igneous or sedimentary rocks. Gneiss is treated as a type of granitic bedrock in this book.

graminoid: A collective term for grasses and grass-like plants including sedges, bulrushes, spike-rushes, and rushes that are narrow-leaved and herbaceous.

granite: A resistant igneous rock that is composed predominantly of feldspar and quartz and weathers slowly to produce acidic, nutrient-poor soils. The term *granite* is often loosely used to include metamorphic rock types such as gneiss.

grassland: An open-canopy, grass-dominated natural community, including prairies, wet prairies, and alvar.

gravel: A soil type composed primarily of small rock fragments between 2 mm and 7.6 cm in diameter.

ground moraine: Gently sloping, rolling topography formed from material deposited under an active glacier.

groundwater: Water occurring below the earth's surface in openings in bedrock and soils.

groundwater seepage: The movement of water from underground to the surface.

growing season: The period of year when plants grow. Approximately, the period between the last frost of spring and the first frost of autumn. The average growing season is longest in southeastern Lower Michigan and shortest in the interior western Upper Peninsula and locally in the interior northern Lower Peninsula.

growing-season frost: Ice formed during the growing season when moisture condensing at ground level freezes.

gypsum: A sedimentary rock primarily composed of hydrous calcium sulfate [calcium sulfate with water: $CaSO_4-2(H_2O)$].

halite: Rock salt deposits.

halophyte: A terrestrial plant that is adapted to grow in salt-rich conditions.

hardwood: A general term used to indicate a broad-leaved, flowering, deciduous tree.

headwater: The source of a stream or river. A headwater stream is a first-order stream.

herb: A nonwoody vascular plant that has no living parts that persist above the ground after the growing season. Includes forbs, ferns, and graminoids.

hollow: A generally small, variably sized topographic depression found in peatlands, swamps, or upland forests. Hollows or pits are separated from each other by hummocks or mounds and may form as a result of windthrow in swamps and upland forests and differential decomposition and accumulation of peat in peatlands.

hummock: A mound in a peatland or upland community that is separated from other hummocks by hollows or pits. Hummock and hollow microtopography forms as a result of windthrow in swamps and upland forests and differential decomposition and accumulation of peat in peatlands.

hydric: A soil moisture class. Hydric soils are very poorly drained and are saturated or inundated long enough during the growing season to develop anaerobic conditions.

hydrogeomorphic process: Process involving the formation of land or soil structures by water activity.

hydrology: The study of the movement, distribution, and effects of water on the earth's surface and in the soil.

hydrophytic: Adapted to growing in wet conditions.

ice-contact topography: Irregular, steep topography found when a glacier stagnates and then retreats. Typical features are kettle lakes, kames, and eskers. Also called kettle-kame or ice-disintegration topography.

igneous rock: Rock formed by the cooling and solidification of molten material. In Michigan, igneous rock formed during the Precambrian period. Igneous rock is treated as a type of granitic bedrock in this book.

impermeable: Describes soil that does not allow the movement of water.

indicator: A plant species that has a high affinity for a specific natural community or environmental condition.

inland: The interior part of Michigan, away from the Great Lakes shoreline.

interlobate region: A region of southern Lower Michigan with a diverse assemblage of landforms deposited at the boundaries between large lobes of glacial ice. This area is comprised of coarse-textured end moraines and ice-contact features (eskers and kames) that are bordered by glacial outwash.

inundated: Flooded or covered by water, often on a seasonal or periodic basis.

invasive species: A species that does not naturally occur in a specific area, and whose introduction negatively affects native species and degrades natural communities.

kame: A rounded, steep-sided, and often isolated hill composed of water-laid sand and gravel deposited by blocks of stagnant ice.

karst: Topography that is formed in limestone, dolomite, or gypsum by dissolution and that is characterized by sinkholes, caves, and underground drainage.

kettle: A steep-sided depression formed from the delayed melting of a stagnant ice block stranded in glacial outwash. A kettle may or may not be filled with water.

kettle-kame topography: See **ice-contact topography**.

knob: A prominent and often rounded isolated hill with steep sides. In Michigan, knobs are often composed of granitic and volcanic bedrock.

krummholz: Tree growth form

characterized by stunted and twisted condition and common to tops of escarpments and subarctic or subalpine tree lines. Trees are distorted into a krummholz growth form by branch breakage resulting from heavy snow, thick ice, and extreme winds. In Michigan, krummholz is most common on Isle Royale and the Keweenaw Peninsula.

lacustrine soils: Fine sediments (i.e., sands, silts, and clays) deposited in lakes.

lakeplain (glacial lakeplain): A glacial landform formed by large bodies of water, such as the precursors to the Great Lakes, and comprised of low, flat areas formed by the settling of lacustrine sediments on the bottom of the former lakes, and higher, sandy ridges formed by ancient beaches.

landform: A terrain feature that has a definable shape and composition. In Michigan, landforms are often of glacial origin, including moraines, outwash channels, outwash plains, kames, and lakeplains. Other land-forms of more recent origin include floodplains, and along the Great Lakes shoreline, dune complexes, beaches, and eroding bluffs.

landscape setting: The characteristics of the area surrounding a natural community, including topography, natural disturbance factors, and land cover.

landslide: The downward movement of a large mass of earth or rocks from a steep slope or cliff.

lateral flow: The hydrologic process of water moving through saturated organic soils in peatlands.

lens: A banding of soil particles occurring in a soil profile (e.g., clay lens).

levee: A relatively high feature located parallel to the margin of a river channel, where coarse sediment is deposited by fast-moving floodwaters. In contrast to other parts of the floodplain, levees have coarser soil texture and are further above the water table, resulting in better soil drainage and aeration.

lichens: A group of nonvascular plants consisting of a symbiotic association of algae and fungi. Occurs in three growth forms: fruticose (upright), foliose (leafy), and crustose (thin crusts).

limestone: A sedimentary calcareous rock composed primarily of calcium carbonate or calcite. Produces calcium-rich soils with high pH and nutrient availability.

liverworts: Small nonvascular spore-producing plants in the class Hepaticae. (Related to mosses, but differing from them in certain structural and reproductive characteristics.)

loam: A soil consisting of a mixture of varying proportions of sand, silt, and clay. Loam soils contain 23 to 52% sand, 28 to 50% silt, and 7 to 27% clay. Loams are typically fine- to medium-textured (with moderate water-holding capacity and moderate to high nutrient availability).

lowland: Wetland.

low shrub: A shrub that is typically less than one meter (39 in) in height.

magnesium carbonate: A carbonate of magnesium; $MgCO_3$.

marl: A calcium-carbonate precipitate that forms through the metabolic activity of algae growing in water rich in calcium and magnesium carbonates. Marl is usually a fine, wet, silky- textured soil, white to light gray in color, which may also contain clay, silt, and sand.

marsh: A wetland dominated by herbaceous, often graminoid vegetation and characterized by inundated to saturated soils.

matrix system: A natural community type that is dominant in the landscape and often plays the dominant role in landscape processes. Characterized by broad ecological amplitude, occurring across a wide range of soil and bedrock types, slopes, slope aspects, and landscape positions. Covering hundreds to thousands of acres.

meander-scar swamp: Swamp located where a section of stream channel has been abandoned as the stream meanders. Abandoned meanders are characterized by groundwater seepage that saturates the organic soils.

medium-textured: Soil or landform characterized by intermediate particle size.

mesic (moist): A soil moisture class. Mesic soils are well drained and moderately well drained. Mesic soil conditions are characterized by adequate moisture availability for plants throughout the growing season.

metamorphic rock: Rock that has been changed by pressure or heat. In Michigan, metamorphic rock formed from igneous and sedimentary rock during the Precambrian period. Metamorphic rock is treated broadly as part of granitic bedrock in this book.

mineral nutrient: A chemical element essential to a plant's growth and survival that occurs in the soil and is absorbed through the plant's roots. Primary mineral nutrients are nitrogen (N), phosphorus (P), and potassium (K). See **nutrient.**

mineral-rich: Characterized by high mineral availability for plants.

mineral soil: Soil consisting primarily of, and having its properties determined by, mineral particles.

minerotrophic: A term describing wetlands (typically peatlands) that receive minerals and nutrients through contact with either surface water or groundwater sources that have been in contact with mineral soils or bedrock. Compare to **ombrotrophic.**

moat: Area of shallow water surrounding a natural community, especially a bog.

moraine: A glacial landform either deposited at the stagnating terminal margin of ice, producing a large hill (end moraine), or deposited from a broad ice sheet that melts in place, forming a rolling plain (ground moraine). Moraines are characterized by an unsorted mixture of sand, silt, and clay soil particles, the proportion being determined by the sediments that the glacier was carrying at the time of deposition.

moss: A small, nonvascular, chlorophyll-containing, spore-producing plant in the class Musci. Mosses include the "true" or "brown" mosses, as well as the peat mosses or sphagnum mosses.

muck: A dark-colored, unconsolidated organic soil consisting of highly decomposed plant remains where the decomposition has progressed to a point where the contributing plant species are not recognizable. Also called sapric peat.

native: A species that occurs naturally in a specific area and is usually adapted to local or regional ecological conditions. Indigenous.

natural community: An assemblage of interacting plants, animals, and other organisms that repeatedly occurs under similar environmental conditions across the landscape and is predominantly structured by natural processes rather than modern anthropogenic disturbances.

natural processes: Dynamic factors that influence the species composition, structure, and successional pathways of natural communities (e.g., fire, flooding, groundwater seepage, and windthrow).

neutral: Having a pH of 7.0.

Niagaran Cuesta: Gently sloping bedrock plain of resistant marine carbonate rocks limestone and dolomite from the Ordovician and Silurian Periods that occurs near the shorelines of northern Lakes Huron and Michigan adjacent to the Niagaran Escarpment and is characterized by local exposures of bedrock.

Niagaran Escarpment: Exposed resistant marine carbonate rocks limestone and dolomite from the Ordovician and Silurian Periods that occurs along and above the shorelines of northern Lakes Huron and Michigan and locally occurs as a steep ridge.

non-mineral nutrient: A chemical element essential to a plant's growth and survival that occurs in the air and the water. The non-mineral nutrients are hydrogen (H), oxygen (O), and carbon (C). See **nutrient**.

northern: Occurring north of the climatic tension zone.

northern hardwoods: A general term used to indicate several broad-leaved, deciduous tree species prevalent in northern Michigan, especially beech, sugar maple, yellow birch, and basswood.

nutrient: A chemical element essential to a plant's growth and survival.

nutrient-poor: Low nutrient availability for plants.

nutrient-rich: High nutrient availability for plants.

old-growth: A late-successional stage in forest development exhibiting characteristic structural features, species assemblages, and ecological processes.

ombrotrophic: A term describing wetlands (peatlands) that receive all or most of their water and nutrients from precipitation. Compare to **minerotrophic**.

open embayment: Curving sections of Great Lakes shoreline open to strong lake winds and currents, but that offer enough protection that emergent plants can often establish and survive.

organic soils: Soil composed of primarily organic matter rather than mineral materials.

outwash: Glacial drift composed of sand and gravel that has been transported, reworked, sorted, and stratified by glacial meltwater flowing off the glacier.

outwash channel: A glacial landform characterized as a relatively narrow, flat plain deposited by a glacial river. Soils are usually well-sorted sands, sometimes now overlain by accumulated peat in wetland environments.

outwash plain: A glacial landform characterized as a broad, flat to slightly rolling plain deposited by large volumes of glacial meltwater. Soils are usually well-sorted sands.

over-the-bank flooding: Flooding regime characteristic of floodplains where floodwater seasonally inundates the land adjacent to the river or stream.

oxbow: An abandoned river channel that has been cut off from the river by lateral channel migration across the floodplain. Oxbows often develop into swamp or marsh inclusions within the floodplain.

palustrine: Wetlands; ecosystems that are saturated or inundated with water for varying periods during the growing season and characterized by hydrophytic vegetation, soils, and natural communities that have developed under these conditions.

peat: An organic soil composed of partially decomposed organic material that is formed under saturated and anaerobic conditions. Common peat-forming plants are Sphagnum mosses and wetland grasses and sedges (graminoids).

peatland: A wetland that develops where drainage is poor, precipitation is retained, decomposition of organic matter is slow, and peat accumulates.

pH: A measure of acidity or basicity, ranging from 0 (strongly acidic) to 14 (strongly basic or alkaline) on a logarithmic scale, with 7.0 being neutral.

physiognomy: Botanically defined as life form (e.g., tree, shrub, and herb). Ecologically defined as the structural characteristics and spatial arrangement of vegetation within a natural community.

physiography: Physical geography, a subfield of geography that studies patterns and processes of the environment.

pit: See **hollow.**

pitted outwash plain: An outwash plain characterized by numerous kettle depressions.

postglacial uplift (postglacial rebound or isostatic rebound): Gradual rise in land surface that results from the removal of the weight of glacial ice.

prairie: Native grassland dominated by warm-season grasses and herbs with no or few trees.

primary: Occurring on bedrock, cobble, or exposed mineral soils and characterized by little to no soil development.

primary nutrient: A major, limiting nutrient used in large amounts for a plant's growth and survival. These are nitrogen (N), phosphorus (P), and potassium (K). Primary nutrients often occur at very low concentrations in anaerobic habitats such as peatlands (e.g., bogs and fens). See **nutrient.**

primary producer: Organism in an ecosystem that produces biomass from inorganic compounds. In almost all cases these are photosynthetically active organisms (i.e., plants, cyanobacteria, and a number of other unicellular organisms).

protected embayment: Deep shoreline indentations cut into resistant upland shoreline that provide significant protection from wind and wave energy.

quartzite: A compact granular metamorphic rock composed of quartz and derived from sandstone. Quartzite is treated as a type of granitic bedrock in this book.

regeneration: Tree saplings occurring in the understory layer of forested natural communities.

resistant: Describing bedrock that weathers or erodes very slowly.

rhyolite: Fine-grained, light-colored (reddish) volcanic bedrock low in iron and magnesium-bearing minerals. Highly resistant to erosion and more acidic than other volcanic bedrock in Michigan.

rich: Describes environments where nutrients are abundant and/or communities with high species diversity.

ridge: A raised area of land, often linear.

ruderal species: Weedy species, including both native and non-native plants.

saline soil: A soil containing sufficient dissolved salts to influence vegetation.

sand: A soil particle between 0.05 and 2.0 mm in diameter, the largest size class of particles that make up soil. Sand soil contains at least 85% sand particles and is gritty to the touch, with individual grains visible to the naked eye.

sand burial: The nearshore process in which vegetation is buried by wind-blown sands.

sandplain: A flat area of glacial lakeplain or outwash dominated by sandy soils.

sand spit: A small point or narrow embankment of land, formed from sand deposited by longshore drifting, and having one end connected to the mainland and the other terminating in open water.

sand-spit embayment: Shallow embayments formed behind sand spits that occur along gently sloping and curving sections of shoreline where sand transport parallels the shore. The spits are exposed to both wave activity and overwash, but provide good protection from wind and waves on the landward side where extensive wetlands often develop.

sandstone: A sedimentary rock composed of grains of sand deposited by water or wind and bound together by a cement of silica, carbonate, or other minerals. In Michigan, exposed sandstone bedrock features are formed from the Copper Harbor Conglomerate, Jacobsville Sandstone, Nonesuch Shale and Freda Formations, Munising Sandstone, Marshall Sandstone, and Eaton Sandstone.

sapric peat: See muck.

saturated: Constantly filled with water, referring to poorly drained soils that are perennially wet.

savanna: Savannas are grasslands interspersed with open-grown scattered or grouped trees forming a partial canopy between 5 and 60%.

schist: A metamorphic crystalline rock that has closely foliated structure and can be split along approximately parallel planes. Schist is treated as a type of granitic bedrock in this book.

scour: The powerful and concentrated clearing and digging action of flowing air, water, or ice.

secondary nutrient: A chemical element essential to a plant's growth and survival that is used by plants in lesser quantity than a primary nutrient and is typically not limiting. Examples are calcium (Ca), magnesium (Mg), and sulfur (S). Secondary nutrients may be present at high concentrations in habitats such as fens that support low concentrations of primary nutrients. See **nutrient** and **primary nutrient**.

second-order stream: A stream that is formed when two first-order streams come together.

sedge: A grass-like herbaceous plant with narrow leaves of the family Cyperaceae, especially of the genus *Carex*.

sediment: Material deposited by water, wind, or glaciers.

sedimentary rocks: Rocks formed by consolidation of sediments deposited by wind or water. In Michigan, sedimentary rocks were formed during the Paleozoic period and include sandstone, shale, limestone, and dolomite.

seep: A small area of groundwater discharge in a diffuse flow.

seepage: The movement of water through the soil, especially the diffuse, slow oozing out of groundwater onto the earth's surface. Seepage transports nutrients to and through wetlands from soil and bedrock source areas.

shade-tolerant: A species tolerant of shade conditions (e.g., sugar maple, beech, and hemlock).

shale: Sedimentary rock formed by the hardening of clay, silty clay, or silty clay loam deposits and having the tendency to split into thin layers.

shrub: A woody perennial plant that differs from a tree in its short stature and typically multi-stem growth form. A shrub is typically less than 5 meters (approximately 16 ft) tall and branches several times at or near its base.

silt: A fine-grained mineral soil intermediate in size between sand and clay. Silt particles range between 0.05 and 0.002 mm. Silt is smooth and slippery when wet and is typically carried in or deposited by moving water.

sinkhole: A depression in the landscape caused by the dissolution and collapse of subsurface bedrock.

slope: The inclination of the land surface from horizontal.

sloughing: Erosion of bedrock due to weathering, or large areas of mineral soils due to groundwater seepage.

softwater: Water that lacks dissolved minerals, especially calcium.

soil: A dynamic natural body on the surface of the earth in which plants grow, composed of mineral and organic materials and organisms.

soil chemistry: The chemical property of soil, measured by evaluating pH and ranging from acidic to basic. See table 3 for soil pH ranges.

soil development: The process of physical and chemical alteration of parent material into mineral soil under the influence of climate, hydrology, organisms, and time. Refers specifically to development of mineral soils.

soil moisture class: The descriptive terms applied to natural communities to distinguish soil moisture based on frequency and duration of hydrologic conditions, and to describe relative soil moisture availability. The classes are based on runoff, permeability, and internal drainage characteristics. The classes are xeric, dry, dry-mesic, mesic, wet-mesic, and hydric.

soil texture: The relative proportions of

the various soil particles (sand, silt, and clay) in a soil. Three broadly defined categories include coarse-textured, medium-textured, and fine-textured.

southern: Occurring south of the climatic tension zone.

sp.: Species singular.

sphagnum moss: A member of the moss genus *Sphagnum*, also known as peat moss.

spp.: Species plural.

spring thaw: The period when ice and snow melt in the spring.

state rank: The status or rarity of the natural community type in Michigan. State ranks are based on the estimated number of high-quality occurrences of the natural community type, estimated area, geographic range, estimated number of adequately protected examples, and threats to the natural community type.

storm wave: High energy wave from the Great Lakes that influences shoreline processes.

string: Elevated, narrow, and often linear peat ridge in patterned peatlands. The long axis of the string is oriented perpendicular to the direction of contours and water flow.

submergent plant: A wetland or aquatic plant that grows completely beneath the water surface. Coontail is a submergent plant.

subsection: An ecoregional unit within Michigan's hierarchical landscape classification system (Albert 1995) with similar subregional climate, surficial geology, lithology, geomorphic processes, soils groups, and potential natural community types.

subsp.: Subspecies.

substrate: The surface on which vegetation grows and natural communities develop (i.e., mineral soil, organic soil, and bedrock).

subterranean: Occurring beneath the surface of the earth.

succession: The natural and directional changes in species composition within a community over time.

surface fire: Low-intensity fire that burns the litter and understory layers.

surface water: Water occurring on the surface of the earth.

swale: An area of land lower than its surroundings, typically elongate and often lower than the water table, thus retaining water at least seasonally.

swamp: A forested or shrub wetland area whose soil, typically organic, is permanently or periodically saturated or inundated or seasonally inundated.

tall shrub: A shrub that is typically greater than one meter (39 in) in height.

terrace: Elevated portions of fluvial sediments in floodplains. Low terraces may occasionally be flooded while high terraces remain above the flood zone.

terrestrial: Upland ecosystem that has xeric to mesic soils with plants adapted to these growing conditions.

third–order river: River or stream that is formed when two second-order streams come together and is characterized by periodic over-the-bank flooding and cycles of erosion and deposition.

tombolo: Tombolos form when bedrock islands are connected to the mainland by current-deposited sands. The embayment created on the leeward side of the tombolo provides protection from Great Lakes wave action where wetlands can develop.

topography: The configuration of a surface including the position and elevation of its natural features.

tree: A woody perennial plant, usually having one principal stem (typically unbranched at the base) and exceeding 5 meters (approximately 16 ft) high.

trophic level: One of the hierarchical strata of a food web of organisms.

upland: An ecosystem that has xeric to mesic soils and/or exposed bedrock and supports plants adapted to these growing conditions.

vascular plant: A plant with a vascular system; includes trees, shrubs, and herbs, but not bryophytes, lichens, or algae. Vascular plants have a structural system of tissue (xylem and phloem) that conducts water and soluble nutrients.

vernal pool: Ephemeral pools that hold water, typically in the spring, after which they dry up; such pools often have a unique flora and fauna and are especially important for amphibians.

vesicle: Small cavities in volcanic bedrock formed when surface lava flowed quickly, cooled, and bubbles of enclosed gas were entrapped.

vine: A plant that climbs or sprawls by means of twining or tendrils; also a plant that trails or creeps extensively along the ground. Vines can be woody or herbaceous.

volcanic bedrock: Late Precambrian bedrock formed following periods of extensive surface volcanic activity and from vast sheets of flowing lava, interbedded with thin layers of conglomerate, which consisted of both pebbles and cobbles. Volcanic bedrocks in Michigan include basalt, rhyolite, and volcanic conglomerate.

volcanic conglomerate: Rift-filling sedimentary rocks deposited by water during a period of reduced volcanic activity. Composed of rounded fragments varying from small pebbles to large boulders in a cement deposited from the margins of the basin by streams eroding earlier lava flows. Typically containing more than 50% volcanic material. Volcanic conglomerate is treated as a type of volcanic bedrock in this book.

water-holding capacity (water-retaining capacity): The capacity of soil to hold moisture.

water table: The upper surface or limit of groundwater, or that level below which the soil is saturated with water. The water table can fluctuate from season to season and year to year with climatic variations. Most uplands have a water table well below the ground surface, whereas in wetlands the water table is often at or above the ground surface.

water track: Area in peatland characterized by directional flow of minerotrophic water and often marked by distinct string and flark patterning.

weathering: The physical and chemical process of breaking down the original complex molecules of primary minerals in parent material (e.g., bedrock, till) and soil.

wet: A soil moisture class. Wet soils are very poorly drained; water is removed from the soil so slowly that the water table is at or above the surface most of the time.

wetland: An ecosystem that is saturated

or inundated with water for varying periods during the growing season and characterized by hydrophytic vegetation and soils and natural communities that have developed under saturated or inundated conditions.

wet-mesic: A soil moisture class. Wet-mesic soils are somewhat poorly drained to poorly drained. The soils are wet at shallow depths for significant periods during the growing season.

wet prairie: Herbaceous wetland dominated by grasses, sedges, and forbs occurring on saturated to seasonally inundated mineral soils with variable organic content.

windthrow: The uprooting or breakage of trees caused by wind and generating canopy gaps in forested systems. Also called blowdown.

woodland: A woodland is a natural community that is intermediate between a savanna and a forest, usually having a canopy between 50 and 80%.

xeric: A soil moisture class. Xeric soils are excessively drained and characterized by a lack of moisture. Water is removed from the soil very rapidly and extremely dry conditions prevail.

References

Albert, D.A. 1995. Regional landscape ecosystems of Michigan, Minnesota, and Wisconsin: A working map and classification. Gen. Tech. Rep. NC-178. St. Paul, MN: U.S. Department of Agriculture, Forest Service, North Central Forest Experiment Station. Jamestown, ND: Northern Prairie Wildlife Research Center Online. Available at http://www.npwrc.usgs.gov/resource/habitat/rlandscp/index.htm (Version 03JUN1998).

Albert, D.A. 2004. Between Land and Lake: Michigan's Great Lakes Coastal Wetlands. Extension bulletin E-2902. Michigan Natural Features Inventory, Michigan State University Extension, East Lansing, MI. 96 pp.

Albert, D.A. 2006. Borne of the Wind: An Introduction to the Ecology of Michigan Sand Dunes. University of Michigan Press, Ann Arbor, MI. 63 pp.

Albert, D.A., J.G. Cohen, M.A. Kost, B.S. Slaughter, and H.D. Enander. 2008. Distribution Maps of Michigan's Natural Communities. Michigan Natural Features Inventory, Report No. 2008-01, Lansing, MI. 166 pp. Available at http://mnfi.anr.msu.edu/reports/2008-01-Distribution_Maps_of_Michigan's_Natural_Communities.pdf.

Albert, D.A., S.R. Denton, and B.V. Barnes. 1986. Regional landscape ecosystems of Michigan. University of Michigan, School of Natural Resources, Ann Arbor, MI. 32 pp. + map.

Barnes, B.V., and W.H. Wagner, Jr. 1981. Michigan Trees: A Guide to the Trees of Michigan and the Great Lakes Region. University of Michigan Press, Ann Arbor, MI. 383 pp.

Blevins, D., and M.P. Schafale. 2011. Wild North Carolina: Discovering the Wonder of Our State's Natural Communities. University of North Carolina Press, Chapel Hill, NC. 176 pp.

Chapman, K.A. 1986. Michigan Natural Community Types. Michigan Natural Features Inventory, Lansing, MI. 24 pp.

Comer, P.J., and D.A. Albert. 1998. Vegetation of Michigan circa 1800: An Interpretation of the General Land Office Surveys. Michigan Natural Features Inventory, Lansing, MI. 2 Maps: 1: 500,000.

Comer, P.J., D.A. Albert, H.A. Wells, B.L. Hart, J.B. Raab, D.L. Price, D.M. Kashian, R.A. Corner, and D.W. Schuen. 1995. Michigan's Presettlement Vegetation, as Interpreted from the General Land Office Surveys 1816–1856. Michigan Natural Features Inventory, Lansing, MI. Digital Map.

Comer, P., D. Faber-Langendoen, R. Evans, S. Gawler, C. Josse, G. Kittel, S. Menard, M. Pyne, M. Reid, K. Schulz, K. Snow, and J. Teague. 2003. Ecological Systems of the United States: A Working Classification of U.S. Terrestrial Systems. NatureServe, Arlington, VA. 75 pp.

Comer, P., and K. Schulz. 2007. Standardized ecological classification for mesoscale mapping in the southwestern United States. Rangeland Ecology and Management 60: 324–35.

Curtis, J.T. 1959. Vegetation of Wisconsin: An Ordination of Plant Communities. University of Wisconsin Press, Madison, WI. 657 pp.

Dorr, J.A., Jr., and D.F. Eschman. 1970. Geology of Michigan. University of Michigan Press, Ann Arbor, MI. 470 pp.

Edwards, L., J. Ambrose, L. Katherine Kirkman, H.O. Nourse, and C. Nourse. 2013. The Natural Communities of Georgia. University of Georgia Press, Athens, GA. 675 pp.

Eggers, S.D., and D.M. Reed. 1997. Wetland Plants and Plant Communities of Minnesota and Wisconsin. U.S. Army Corps of Engineers, St. Paul, MN. 263 pp.

Faber-Langendoen, D., ed. 2001. Plant Communities of the Midwest: Classification in an Ecological Context. Association for Biodiversity Information, Arlington, VA. 61 pp. + appendix (705 pp.).

Faber-Langendoen, D., T. Keeler-Wolf, D. Meidinger, C. Josse, A. Weakley, D. Tart, G. Navarro, B. Hoagland, S. Ponomarenko, J.-P. Saucier, G. Fults, and E. Helmer. 2012. Classification and description of world formation types. Part 1 (Introduction) and Part 2 (Description of formation types). Hierarchy Revisions Working Group, Federal Geographic Data Committee, FGDC Secretariat. U.S. Geological Survey, Reston, VA, and NatureServe, Arlington, VA.

Farrand, W.R., and D.L. Bell. 1982. Quaternary geology of Michigan. Michigan Department of Natural Resources Geological Survey. Map: 1: 500,000.

Fike, J. 1999. Terrestrial and palustrine plant communities of Pennsylvania. Pennsylvania Natural Diversity Inventory, Pennsylvania Department of Conservation and Natural Resources, Harrisburg, PA. 86 pp.

Gawler, S., and A. Cutko. 2010. Natural Landscapes of Maine: A Guide to Natural Communities and Ecosystems. Maine Natural Areas Program, Maine Department of Conservation, Augusta, ME. 348 pp.

Grossman, D.H., D. Faber-Langendoen, A.S. Weakley, M. Anderson, P. Bourgeron, R. Crawford, K. Goodin, S. Landaal, K. Metzler, K.D. Patterson, M. Pyne, M. Reid, and L. Sneddon. 1998. International Classification of Ecological Communities: Terrestrial Vegetation of the United States. Volume 1, The National Vegetation Classification System: Development, Status, and Applications. The Nature Conservancy, Arlington, VA.

Herman, K.D., L.A. Masters, M.R. Penskar, A.A. Reznicek, G.S. Wilhelm, W.W. Brodowicz, and K.P. Gardiner. 2001. Floristic quality assessment with wetland categories and computer application programs for the state of Michigan. Michigan Department of Natural Resources, Wildlife Division, Natural Heritage Program, Lansing, MI.

Hoffman, R.M. 2002. Wisconsin's Natural Communities: How to Recognize Them, Where to Find Them. University of Wisconsin Press, Madison, WI. 375 pp.

Janssens, J.A. 2005. Bryophytes of the Hiawatha National Forest, Upper

Peninsula, Michigan: Inventory, assessment, and recommendations for conservation. Available from Lambda-Max Ecological Research, janss008@tc.umn.edu.

Kost, M.A., D.A. Albert, J.G. Cohen, B.S. Slaughter, R.K. Schillo, C.R. Weber, and K.A. Chapman. 2007. Natural Communities of Michigan: Classification and Description. Michigan Natural Features Inventory, Report No. 2007–21, Lansing, MI. 314 pp. Available at http://mnfi.anr.msu.edu/communities/index.cfm.

Kost, M.A., and D.A. Hyde. 2009. Exploring the Prairie Fen Wetlands of Michigan. Extension Bulletin E-3045. Michigan Natural Features Inventory, Michigan State University Extension, East Lansing, MI. 106 pp.

Kost, M.A., J.G. Cohen, B.S. Slaughter, and D.A. Albert. 2010. A Field Guide to the Natural Communities of Michigan. Michigan Natural Features Inventory, Lansing, MI. 189 pp.

Michigan Natural Features Inventory (MNFI). 2006. Michigan County Mosaics of the 1998 series USGS Digital Orthophoto Quadrangles. Image acquisition scale: 1:40,000.

Michigan Natural Features Inventory (MNFI). 2014. Biotics Database. Michigan Natural Features Inventory, Lansing, MI.

Mitsch, W.J., and J.G. Gosselink. 2000. Wetlands. John Wiley & Sons, New York, NY. 920 pp.

National Wetland Working Group. 1988. Wetlands of Canada. Ecological Land Classification Series, No. 24. Sustainable Development Branch, Environment Canada, Ottawa, ON, and Polyscience Publications Inc., Montreal, QC. 452 pp.

NatureServe. 2013. NatureServe Explorer: An Online Encyclopedia of Life. Version 7.1. NatureServe, Arlington, VA. Available at http://www.natureserve.org/explorer.

Nelson, P.W. 2010. The Terrestrial Natural Communities of Missouri. Missouri Department of Natural Resources. Jefferson City, MO. 550 pp.

Noss, R.F., and A.Y. Cooperrider. 1994. Saving Nature's Legacy: Protecting and Restoring Biodiversity. Island Press, Washington, DC. 416 pp.

O'Connor, R.P., M.A. Kost, and J.G. Cohen. 2009. Prairies and Savannas in Michigan: Rediscovering Our Natural Heritage. Michigan State University Press, East Lansing, MI. 139 pp.

Reed, R.C., and J. Daniels. 1987. Bedrock geology of northern Michigan. State of Michigan Department of Natural Resources. Map: 1:500,000.

Reznicek, A.A., E.G. Voss, and B.S. Walters. 2011. Michigan Flora Online. University of Michigan, Ann Arbor, MI. Available at: http://michiganflora.net/home.aspx.

Ricketts, T.H., E. Dinerstein, D.M. Olson, C.J. Loucks, W. Eichbaum, D. DellaSala, K. Kavanagh, P. Hedao, P.T. Hurley, K.M. Carney, R. Abell, and S. Walters. 1999. Terrestrial Ecoregions of North America: A Conservation Assessment. Island Press, Washington, DC. 485 pp.

Sperduto, D.D., and B. Kimball. 2011. The Nature of New Hampshire: Natural Communities of the Granite State. University of New Hampshire Press, Durham, NH. 341 pp.

Swink, F., and G. Wilhelm. 1994. Plants of the Chicago Region. Indiana Academy of Science, Indianapolis, IN. 921 pp.

Thompson, E.H., and E.R. Sorenson. 2005. Wetland, Woodland, Wildland: A Guide to the Natural Communities of Vermont. Vermont Department of Fish and Wildlife and The Nature Conservancy. University Press of New England, Lebanon, NH. 456 pp.

United States Department of Agriculture (USDA). 2013. Natural Resources Conservation Service, Plants Database. Available at http://plants.usda.gov/java/.

Veatch, J.O. 1953. Soils and Land of Michigan. Michigan State College Press, East Lansing, MI. 241 pp.

Voss, E.G. 1972. Michigan Flora. Part I: Gymnosperms and Monocots. Bulletin of the Cranbrook Institute of Science 55 and University of Michigan Herbarium, Bloomfield Hills, MI. 488 pp.

Voss, E.G. 1985. Michigan Flora. Part II: Dicots (Saururaceae–Cornaceae). Bulletin of the Cranbrook Institute of Science 59 and University of Michigan Herbarium, Ann Arbor, MI. 724 pp.

Voss, E.G. 1996. Michigan Flora. Part III: Dicots (Pyrolaceae–Compositae). Bulletin of the Cranbrook Institute of Science 61 and University of Michigan Herbarium. Ann Arbor, MI. 622 pp.

Voss, E.G., and A.A. Reznicek. 2012. Field Manual of Michigan Flora. University of Michigan Press, Ann Arbor, MI. 990 pp.

The culmination of three decades of work by Michigan Natural Features Inventory ecologists, this essential guidebook to the natural communities of Michigan introduces the diverse terrain of a unique state. Small enough to carry in a backpack, this field guide provides a system for dividing the complex natural landscape of Michigan into easily understood and describable components called natural communities. Providing a new way to explore Michigan's many environments, this book details natural communities ranging from patterned fen to volcanic bedrock glade and beyond. The descriptions are supplemented with distribution maps, vibrant photographs, and comprehensive lists of characteristic plant species. The authors suggest places to visit to further study each type of natural community and provide a comprehensive glossary of ecological terms, as well as a dichotomous key for aiding field identification. An invaluable resource, this book is meant to serve as a tool for those seeking to understand, describe, document, conserve, and restore the diversity of natural communities native to Michigan.

Michigan Natural Features Inventory's natural community classification has been the basis for ecosystem-level conservation in Michigan for well over a decade. Our state has an incredibly diverse landscape of forests, prairies, wetlands, sand dunes, bedrock, and Great Lakes shoreline. This field guide is an essential reference for anyone wanting to understand the natural communities of Michigan.
—GLENN PALMGREN, Ecologist, Michigan Department of Natural Resources

This is a fantastic and exhaustive inventory and description of the native vegetation types in Michigan. Gone are the days, thankfully, of oversimplified Clementsian community classifications that pigeon-hole the remarkable diversity of our state into stale, arbitrary categories that either are difficult to identify in the field or are too idealized to be of use. Complete with type descriptions, distribution maps, and detailed plant lists and organized in a hierarchical way, *A Field Guide to the Natural Communities of Michigan* provides something comprehensive and useful for both academic and recreational use that will be a wonderful complement to studying and understanding whole ecosystems on Michigan's landscape.
—DAN KASHIAN, Associate Professor of Biological Sciences, Wayne State University

A Field Guide to the Natural Communities of Michigan is an excellent resource for ecologists, botanists, conservationists, and naturalists, as well as anyone learning about the vast diversity of ecosystems in our state. The authors' cumulative field experience is unsurpassed, and they have wisely built and expanded upon the work of previous ecologists, using the past as a guide and providing a solid ecological framework for understanding changes in community structure and composition in the future.
—DOUG PEARSALL, Senior Conservation Scientist, The Nature Conservancy

Joshua G. Cohen is the Lead Ecologist with Michigan Natural Features Inventory, Michigan's natural heritage program. **Michael A. Kost** was the Lead Ecologist for Michigan Natural Features Inventory from 2004 to 2012 and is the Native Plants Specialist with the Matthaei Botanical Gardens and Nichols Arboretum of the University of Michigan. **Bradford S. Slaughter** is Michigan Natural Features Inventory's Lead Botanist. **Dennis A. Albert** was the Lead Ecologist for Michigan Natural Features Inventory from 1987 through 2004, and he is research faculty in the Department of Horticulture at Oregon State University.

MICHIGAN STATE
UNIVERSITY PRESS
MSUPRESS.ORG

Printed and bound in China.

978-1-61186-134-1 | $34.95

53495
9 781611 861341